PART 3

Paper 3.2

Advanced Taxation
(Finance Act 2006)

EXAM KIT

Approved Publisher

KAPLAN

PUBLISHING

FOULKS LYNCH

British Library Cataloguing-in-Publication Data

A catalogue record for this book is available from the British Library.

Published by:
Kaplan Publishing Foulks Lynch
Unit 2 The Business Centre
Molly Millar's Lane
Wokingham
Berkshire
RG41 2QZ

ISBN 978 1 84390 898 2

© FTC Kaplan Limited, December 2006

Printed and bound in Great Britain by William Clowes Ltd, Beccles, Suffolk

Acknowledgements

The past ACCA exam questions are the copyright of the Association of Chartered Certified Accountants. The original answers to the questions from June 1994 onwards were produced by the examiners themselves and have been adapted by Kaplan Publishing Foulks Lynch.

We are grateful to the Chartered Institute of Management Accountants and the Institute of Chartered Accountants in England and Wales for permission to reproduce past exam questions. The answers have been prepared by Kaplan Publishing Foulks Lynch.

CONTENTS

Section

INDEX TO QUESTIONS AND ANSWERS

Taxation of individuals

Taxation of corporate businesses

SYLLABUS AND EXAM FORMAT

Format of the exam

	Number of marks
Section A: 2 compulsory scenario-based questions	50
Section B: Choice of 2 from 4 (25 marks each)	50
	100

Total time allowed: 3 hours

Aim

To ensure candidates can apply judgement and technique in the provision of a range of taxation services. In particular to equip candidates with the ability to resolve problems involving the computation of tax liabilities, basic tax and financial planning and which draw upon the interaction of a wide range of taxes. The primary focus of the paper will be based around taxation issues.

Objectives

On completion of this paper candidates should be able to:

- prepare computations for and advise clients on issues relating to the tax liabilities of individuals arising from income receipts, capital disposals and transfers of value

- prepare computations for and advise clients on issues relating to the tax liabilities of corporations arising from income generation and capital disposals

- provide advice on minimising or deferring tax liabilities for individuals or corporations by using exemptions and/or reliefs

- evaluate a corporation's and individual's financial position with particular regard to the importance of taxation in decision making and to recommend appropriate personal financial plans and

- demonstrate the skills expected in Part 3.

Position of the paper in the overall syllabus

This is the final tax paper and builds upon the knowledge acquired in Paper 2.3 Business Taxation concerning the taxation of businesses and employees. A thorough understanding of the Paper 2.3 syllabus is therefore considered requisite for Paper 3.2. Candidates also need to understand formats of accounts used for sole traders, partnerships and companies from Paper 1.1 and also the need to have an understanding of some of the financial reporting standards from Paper 2.5. There is no substantial integration with other papers in Part 3.

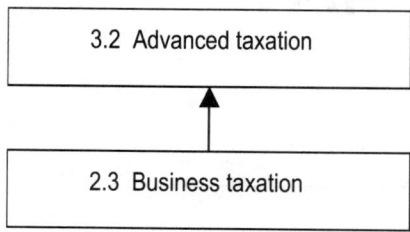

Syllabus content

1 Taxation of individuals

(a) Principles of income tax

(b) Income tax on income from land and buildings

(c) Income tax on income from investment

(d) Income tax on income from employment

(e) Income tax on income from self-employment

(f) Capital gains tax

(g) Trusts

(h) Administration of income tax and CGT

(i) Inheritance tax

(j) Overseas aspects of income tax, capital gains tax, inheritance tax and value added tax

(k) Value added tax

(l) National insurance contributions

(m) Stamp duty and stamp duty reserve tax.

2 Taxation of corporate businesses

(a) Corporation tax on income and chargeable gains of single companies and groups of companies and consortia trading in the UK and overseas

(b) Value added tax

(c) National insurance contributions

(d) Stamp duty and stamp duty reserve tax.

3 Financial planning

(a) Sources of Finance

(b) Personal Financial Planning

(c) Financial Services Products

(d) The Regulatory Framework.

Excluded topics

1 Taxation of individuals

(c) Income tax on income from investments

– detailed knowledge of anti-avoidance procedures

(d) Income tax on income from employment

– PAYE system

– an employee share ownership plan (ESOP) will not be examined in its own right

(e) Income tax on income from self-employment

– averaging of farmers profits

– averaging of profits for authors and creative artists

– the allocation of notional profits and losses for a partnership

– research and development expenditure

- capital allowances for agricultural buildings, patents, flats above shops, scientific research and know-how

- in respect of industrial buildings allowance: enterprise zones, initial allowances and the sale of an industrial building at less than original cost following a period of non-industrial use (note that sales for more than original cost are examinable)

- detailed anti-avoidance legislation

(f) Capital gains tax

- assets held at 31 March 1982

- the grant of a lease or sub-lease out of either a freehold, long lease or short lease

- a detailed knowledge of the statements of practice on partnership capital gains

- retirement relief

- relief for losses on loans made to traders

(h) Trusts

- overseas aspects

(j) Inheritance Tax

- double grossing up on death

- pre 18 March 1986 lifetime transfers

- woodlands relief

- conditional exemption for heritage property

- relief on relevant business property and agricultural property given as exempt legacies

- valuation of an annuity or an interest in possession where the trust interest is subject to an annuity

- detailed knowledge of the double charges legislation

- an accumulation and maintenance trust ceasing to qualify

- double taxation relief calculation involving the formula $\dfrac{A}{A + B} \times C$

- IHT aspects of discretionary trusts prior to 27 March 1974

(k) Value added tax

- capital goods scheme

- in respect of property and land leases and do it yourself builders

- flat rate scheme for farmers

- special schemes for retailers

(l) National insurance contributions

- detailed calculation of director's NIC on a month by month basis a knowledge of the annual earnings period rules (including where a person becomes a director part way through a tax year is, however, required)

- offset of trading losses against non-trading income (for Class 4 purposes).

2 Taxation of corporate businesses

(a) Corporation tax on income and chargeable gains of single companies and groups of companies and consortia trading in the UK and overseas

- a detailed knowledge of anti-avoidance provisions (with the exception of those detailed in the Study Guide)

- corporation tax rates on companies in the process of winding up

- 51% groups and group income elections

- quarterly accounting for income tax

- anti-avoidance provisions where arrangements exist for a company to leave a group

- detailed knowledge of double taxation agreements

- migration of a UK resident company

- mixer companies

- expense relief in respect of overseas tax

- detailed computational questions on the carry back and carry forward of unrelieved foreign tax

- an awareness of these provisions is required

- detailed computational questions on the 'onshore pooling' provisions again an awareness of these provisions is all that is required

(b)   Value added tax

    –   as for individuals

(c)   National insurance contributions

    –   detailed calculations of director's NIC on a month by month basis a knowledge of the annual earnings period rules (including where a person becomes a director part way through a tax year is, however, required).

3   Financial planning

(a)   Sources of finance

    –   the mortgage code

(c)   Financial services products

    –   detailed knowledge of the conditions which must be met to obtain HMRC approval for an occupational pension scheme

    –   personal pension rules applicable prior to 6 April 2001

    –   knowledge of the different maximum benefit regimes in occupational schemes

    –   calculation of maximum or actual benefits available on early or late retirement

    –   calculation of a pension cash equivalent transfer value.

Approach to examining the syllabus

The examination is a three-hour paper divided into two sections.

Section A: Two compulsory scenario based questions worth a total of 50 marks set in the following areas:

- Non-business income tax (although including employment income)

- Capital gains tax

- Inheritance tax

- Overseas aspects of income tax, inheritance tax and capital gains tax

The detailed syllabus areas that will feature are those set out in italics within the Study Guide. It is to be noted that these are primarily the syllabus areas new to 3.2.

Section B: Four 25-mark scenario based questions from which candidates will be required to select and answer two. One of these questions, at least, will focus upon business taxation. One of the questions in Section B will have as its main focus personal financial planning. The other questions will be set on other areas of the syllabus.

The following further guidance should be noted:

Section A

- To assist in the transition from Paper 2.3 to Paper 3.2 the compulsory questions, whilst being set within a scenario involving some elements of planning and tax interaction, will focus on computation (as an approximate guide around 50%). A mainly discursive question is therefore unlikely in Section A.

- As a general guide Section A questions will primarily focus upon non-business income tax, Inheritance tax and capital gains tax (both business and non-business aspects).

- Questions involving mainly financial planning will not feature in Section A. Note, however, that questions may involve the taxation elements of, for example, investment or pension products (for example calculating an individual's maximum permissible pension contributions).

- Whilst no detailed questions will be set involving income tax aspects of businesses this will not preclude the inclusion within questions of, for example, a trading profit figure (or possibly even series of figures). Candidates will, however, not be required to calculate those figures as part of Section A questions.

- A question will not be set that exclusively examines the taxation of trusts or overseas taxation aspects although these may feature as part of a question.

Section B

- The 25-mark format adopted in Section B will allow more developed optional questions.

- Questions can be set in any area of the syllabus but within the broad overall guidelines mentioned above.

- The question focusing upon financial planning is likely to be scenario based, including some taxation elements, with candidates required to analyse a particular set of circumstances and make sensible financial planning recommendations going forward. As a guide it is likely that the pure financial planning elements of this question will not exceed 60–70%.

- As a general rule it is likely that Section B questions will examine letter or report-writing skills to a greater extent than Section A. Two marks will always be allocated within one of the Section B questions covering these skills.

The 3.2 examiner has provided the following advice in connection with the style of future examination questions:

- **Interaction of taxes**

  Rarely do real-life transactions involve considering only one tax at a time. Most transactions require tax advisors to be able to advise on the overall tax consequences of a particular course of action. In past examinations, some questions have already taken this approach. However, I intend questions involving the interaction of taxes to be more prevalent and frequent in future papers.

- **Decision-making**

  In reality, the tax consequences of actions may also influence the decisions an individual or a business may take. Questions will continue to emphasise decision-making, based on the facts of a particular situation. This type of question emphasises the application of tax knowledge to 'real-life' situations.

- **Layered marking**

  Questions will, where possible, be layered, with marks awarded in proportion to the effort required to answer the different layers of the question. There will be some easy marks for routine tasks, some harder sections where more application and understanding is required, and a few marks will be reserved to reward those who have really learnt and understood the subject.

- **Real life transactions**

  Tax should really be regarded as relevant to real-life transactions. I intend my exams to make the study of advanced tax more relevant, by relating questions to the real world and to show students that tax can be relevant, interesting and enjoyable.

Additional information

ACCA adopts a six-month rule in that questions requiring an understanding of new legislation will not be set until at least six calendar months after the last day of the month in which the legislation received Royal Assent. The same rule applies to the effective date of the provisions of an Act introduced by Statutory Instrument. It would however be considered inappropriate to examine legislation it is proposed to repeal or substantially alter.

Knowledge of section numbers will not be needed to understand questions in this paper, nor will students be expected to use them in their answers. If students wish to refer to section numbers they may do so and will not be penalised if old, or even incorrect, section numbers are used.

Names of cases or a detailed knowledge of judgements are not required but knowledge of the principles decided in leading cases is required.

The Study Guide provides more detailed guidance on the syllabus.

Wider reading is also desirable, especially regular study of relevant articles in ACCA's *Student Accountant.*

ANALYSIS OF PAST PAPERS

June 2004

1   IT computation including age allowance and MCA; IHT and CGT implications of lifetime gift vs bequeathed in will

2   CGT, principal private residence; property business income, furnished holiday accommodation

3   Close company; company cars and loans made available to employee and participator; company purchase of own shares

4   Employed vs self-employed; personal services company

5   Corporation tax – company residence, group losses, transfer pricing

6   Personal pension schemes; occupational pension schemes

December 2004

1   Income tax, Capital gains tax and IHT computations for non-UK domiciled individual. Deferral of capital gains. IHT gift with reservation.

2   Property business income computation including furnished holiday accommodation. Capital gains computations including exempt assets and chattels. CGT and IHT implications of lifetime gifts, including BPR and gift relief.

3   VAT issues for a new business. Comparison of cost of employee/shareholder owning car versus transferring ownership of car to company.

4   Group companies, group relief, consortium relief, capital gains reliefs. Tax implications (CT, VAT, stamp duty/stamp duty land tax) of selling the shares of a company versus selling the trade and assets.

5   Tax implications of sole trader employing wife compared with forming a partnership. Self assessment administration. Most beneficial use of personal income tax losses.

6   Comparison of operating as a sole trader versus incorporating the business. Equity versus loan finance. Pension contributions; personal pensions and occupational schemes.

June 2005

1   IHT on lifetime transfers and death estate, including gift with reservation and related property rules. IHT administration. IHT planning involving lifetime gifts, skipping a generation, shares qualifying for 100% BPR.

2   IT computation for UK resident, non-UK domiciled individual with foreign assets generating income. Employment income benefits; car, fuel, living accommodation. CGT implications of a corporate takeover. Conditions to be satisfied for a 'share for share exchange'. Implications if consideration received in shares, cash or qualifying corporate bonds QCB). Definition of a QCB.

3   Corporation tax (CT) computation, including adjustments to taxable trading profits. CT admin; payment date rules for large companies, filing dates, interest and penalties. VAT default surcharge rules and VAT bad debt relief.

4   Sole trader starting in business. Letter re badges of trade. IT and capital gains computations for first four years of the business. Explanation of loss reliefs available and recommendation of most tax efficient use of trading losses. CGT negligible value claim and S574 ICTA88 loss relief.

5   Corporation tax computation for group of companies, including capital gain and rollover relief, group relief when company joins the group in the year and most tax efficient use of trading losses. Substantial shareholding provisions. VAT groups.

6   Employee; IT, NIC and CGT treatment of gift of shares and share options under an unapproved share incentive scheme. Detailed rules of Enterprise Management Incentive schemes. Personal financial planning protection products. Employee tax position if protection products provided by employer.

December 2005

1   CGT disposal including principal private residence reliefs. IHT on death computation. BPR rules for different types of shares. Lifetime IHT planning recommendations.

2   CGT disposal of shares involving FA 1985 pool, rights issue and reorganisation of share capital. CGT and IHT implications of gifting shares. CGT and IT implications of selling UK holiday home and replacing with overseas property.

3   Group structure and use of trading loses. Recommendation of unproved corporate structure. CT computation with and without group reorganisation. CT and VAT implications of expanding overseas.

4   Residency position of individual coming to UK. VAT registration and recovery of pre-registration VAT. Sole trader; IT computation for early years of business, NIC liabilities and NIC & IT payment values.

5   Comparison of IT, NIC and CT liabilities of operating as a sole trader or a company, including calculation of disposable income. Corporation tax computation including non-corporate dividends. Capital gains computation. Use of trading losses by sole trader in early years of trading.

6   Comparison of extraction of profits from a company through a dividend or by liquidating the company. Tax implications and financial risks associated with different types of property. IHT and CGT implications of partner acquiring asset used by partnership. Loans to participator rules.

June 2006

1   Income tax in year of death, IHT on lifetime gifts due to death and on the death estate, including QSR. CGT and IHT implications of three possible lifetime gifts – a part disposal, cash and shares.

2   Incorporation relief for CGT, the disadvantages of incorporation relief and discussion of alternative reliefs on incorporation. Consequences of exercising unapproved share options and later disposing of shares. CGT and income tax issues in setting up a discretionary trust or an accumulation and maintenance trust.

3   Taxation consequences of low emission cars for the employee and the employer. Overseas issues of determining the status of an individual and the income tax consequences. CGT consequences of a share for share exchange. Advice to minimise the group corporation tax liability by charging management charges. VAT and stamp duty issues in changing the group structure.

4   Tax efficient extraction of funds via a dividend or bonus. Tax advice concerning the sale of shares and the importance of timing the disposal. Tax consequences of a company repurchasing its own shares.

5   Allowances available for intellectual property. Corporation tax loss computation with group relief. Restriction of carry forward of losses with a change in the nature of trade. Sale of building with pre-entry capital loss. Corporation tax issues in acquiring a foreign subsidiary by purchasing the shares or purchasing the assets. Submission of an incorrect VAT return leading to default surcharges, interest and misdeclaration penalties.

6   Chargeable gain on the assignment of a lease. Disposal of gilt-edged securities and the accrued income scheme. EIS income tax and CGT reliefs and conditions. Issues relating to equity versus loan finance. Characteristics of a defined benefit and defined contribution pension scheme.

REVISION GUIDANCE

Planning your revision

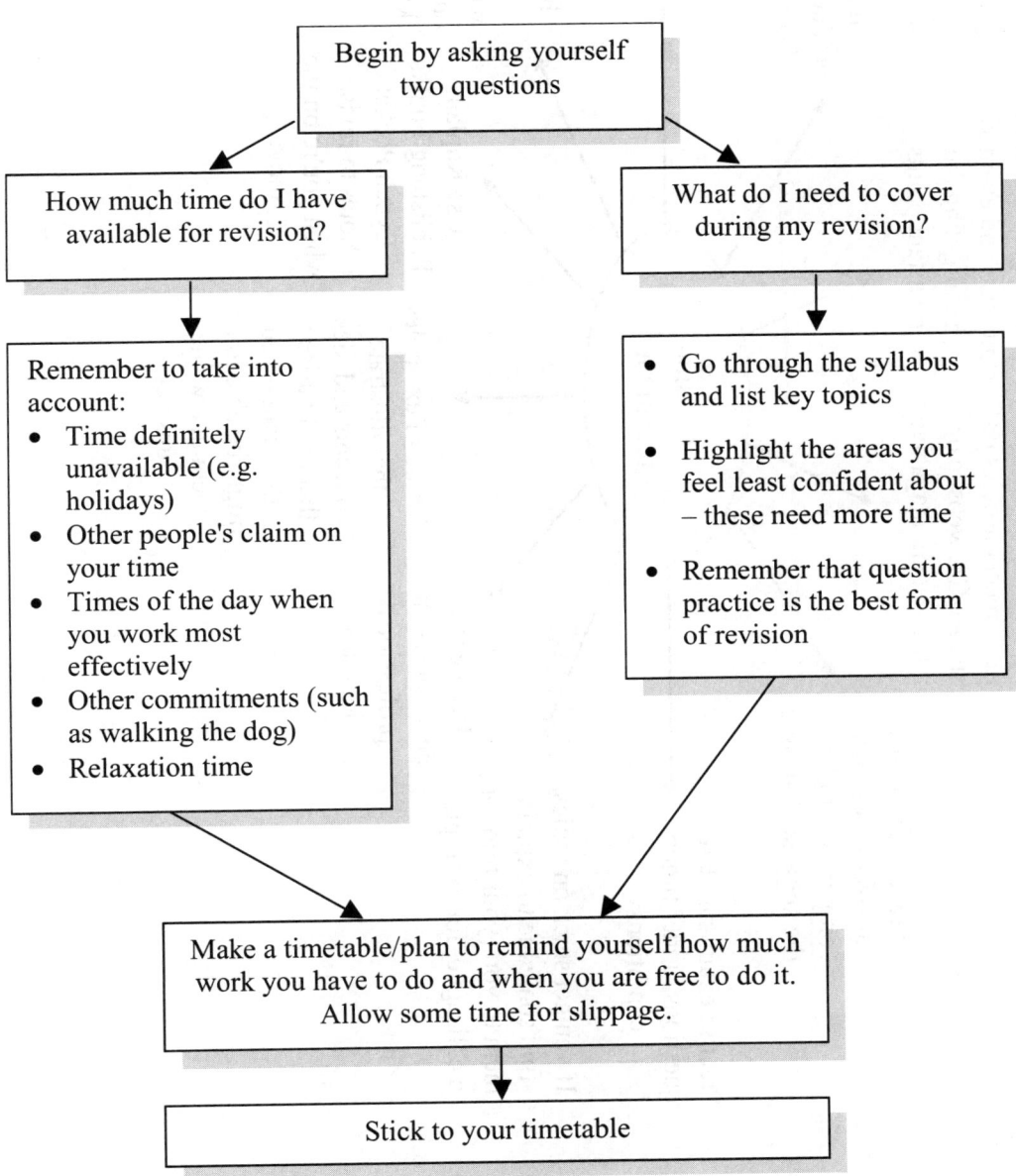

Begin by asking yourself two questions

How much time do I have available for revision?

What do I need to cover during my revision?

Remember to take into account:
- Time definitely unavailable (e.g. holidays)
- Other people's claim on your time
- Times of the day when you work most effectively
- Other commitments (such as walking the dog)
- Relaxation time

- Go through the syllabus and list key topics
- Highlight the areas you feel least confident about – these need more time
- Remember that question practice is the best form of revision

Make a timetable/plan to remind yourself how much work you have to do and when you are free to do it. Allow some time for slippage.

Stick to your timetable

Revision techniques

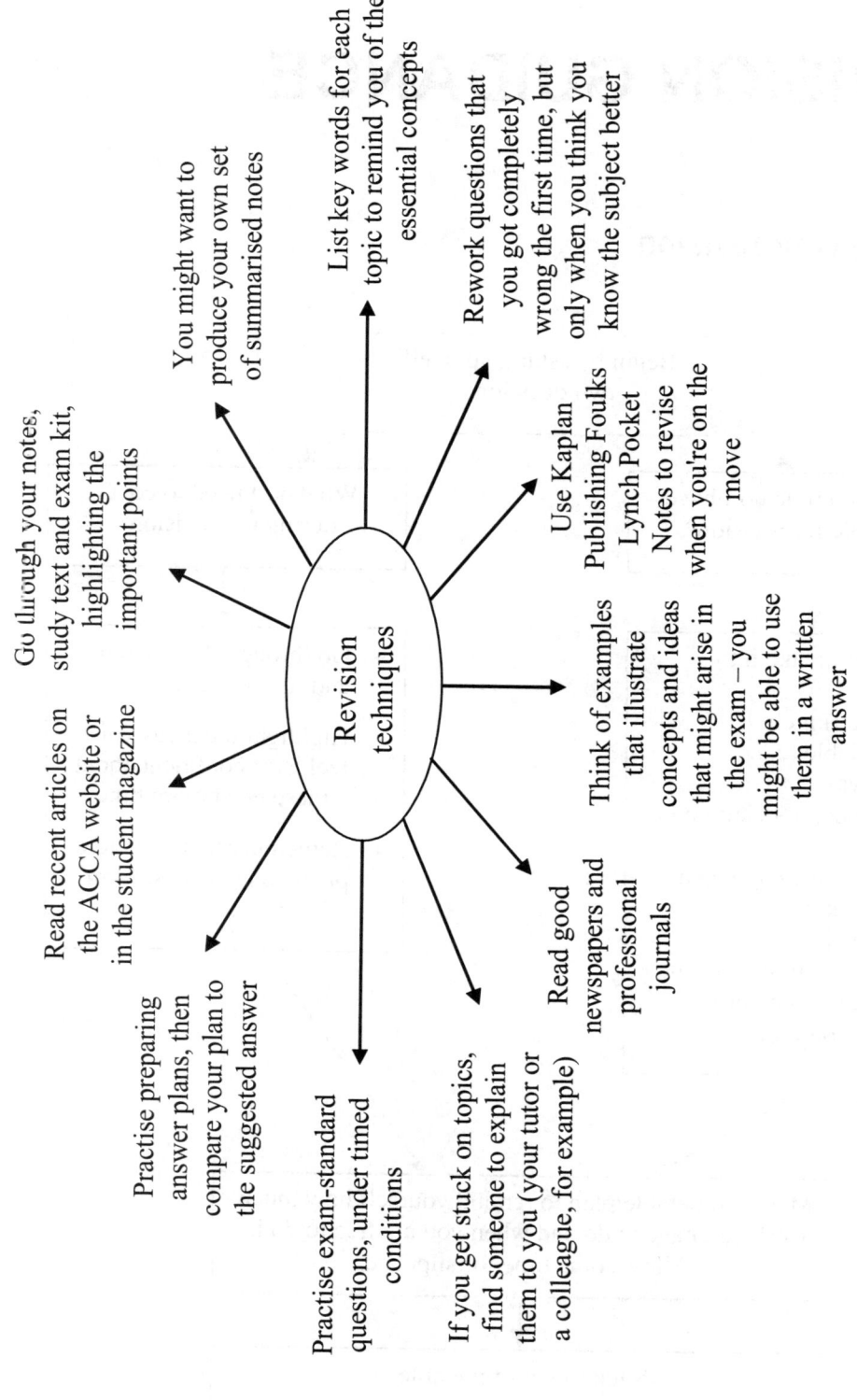

EXAM TECHNIQUES

- You might want to spend the first few minutes of the exam **reading the paper**.

- Where you have a **choice of question**, decide which questions you will do.

- Unless you know exactly how to answer the question, spend some time **planning** your answer.

- **Divide the time** you spend on questions in proportion to the marks on offer. One suggestion is to allocate 1½ minutes to each mark available, so a 10 mark question should be completed in 15 minutes.

- Spend the last **five minutes** reading through your answers and **making any additions or corrections**.

- If you **get completely stuck** with a question, leave space in your answer book and **return to it later.**

- Stick to the question and **tailor your answer** to what you are asked. Pay particular attention to the verbs in the question.

- If you do not understand what a question is asking, **state your assumptions**. Even if you do not answer in precisely the way the examiner hoped, you should be given some credit, if your assumptions are reasonable.

- You should do everything you can to make things easy for the marker. The marker will find it easier to identify the points you have made if your **answers are legible**.

- **Essay questions**: Your essay should have a clear structure. It should contain a brief introduction, a main section and a conclusion. Be concise. It is better to write a little about a lot of different points than a great deal about one or two points.

- **Computations**: It is essential to include all your workings in your answers. Many computational questions require the use of a standard format: company profit and loss account, balance sheet and cash flow statement for example. Be sure you know these formats thoroughly before the exam and use the layouts that you see in the answers given in this book and in model answers.

- **Case studies**: To write a good case study, first identify the area in which there is a problem, outline the main principles/theories you are going to use to answer the question, and then apply the principles/theories to the case.

- **Reports, memos and other documents**: Some questions ask you to present your answer in the form of a report or a memo or other document. So use the correct format - there could be easy marks to gain here.

RATES AND ALLOWANCES TABLES

Tax rates and allowances

Some tax rates and allowances will be reproduced in the examination paper for Paper 3.2. In addition, other specific information necessary for candidates to answer individual questions will be given as part of the question.

Income Tax

		%
Starting rate	£1 – £2,150	10
Basic rate	£2,151 – £33,300	22
Higher rate	£33,301 and above	40

Personal Allowances and Tax Reducers

		£
Personal allowance		5,035
	65–74	7,280
	75 and over	7,420
Married couples age allowance	71 – 74 (born before 6 April 1935)	6,065
	75 and over	6,135
Minimum married couples age allowance where income exceeds the limit		2,350
Income limit for age related allowances		20,100
Blind person's allowance		1,660

Car Benefit Percentage

The base level of CO_2 emissions is 140 grams per kilometre.

Car Fuel Benefit

The base figure for calculating the car fuel benefit is £14,400.

Personal Pension Contribution Limits

The maximum contribution that can be made without being supported by earned income is £3,600.

Annual allowance £215,000

eg. if someone contributes 265000 then 50 000 is taxed @ 40%.

Authorised Mileage Allowance

All cars:

Up to 10,000 miles	40p
Over 10,000 miles	25p

Capital Allowances

Plant and machinery

	%
Writing-down allowance	25
First-year allowance	
– Plant and machinery (see below)	40
– Low emission motor cars (CO_2 emissions of less than 120 grams per kilometre) (17 April 2002 to 31 March 2008)	100

For the periods from 1 April 2004 to 31 March 2005 and 1 April 2006 to 31 March 2007 (6 April 2004 to 5 April 2005 and 6 April 2006 to 5 April 2007 for unincorporated businesses) the rate of plant and machinery first-year allowance is increased to 50% for small businesses.

Long life assets

	%
Writing-down allowance	6

Industrial buildings

Writing-down allowance	4

Corporation Tax

Financial year	2004	2005	2006
Starting rate	Nil	Nil	N/A
Small companies rate	19%	19%	19%
Full rate	30%	30%	30%
	£	£	£
Starting rate lower limit	10,000	10,000	N/A
Starting rate upper limit	50,000	50,000	N/A
Small companies rate lower limit	300,000	300,000	300,000
Small companies rate upper limit	1,500,000	1,500,000	1,500,000
Marginal relief fraction			
Starting rate	19/400	19/400	N/A
Small companies rate	11/400	11/400	11/400

Marginal Relief

$(M - P) \times I/P \times$ Marginal relief fraction

Value Added Tax

	£
Registration limit	61000
Deregistration limit	59000

Inheritance Tax

	%
£1 – £285,000	Nil
Excess	40

Rates of Interest

Official rate of interest:	5.0%
Rate of interest on underpaid tax:	6.5% (assumed)
Rate of interest on overpaid tax:	2.25% (assumed)

Capital Gains Tax: Annual Exemption

	£
Individuals	8,800
Trusts (divided by number of qualifying settlements created by the same settlor on the same day to a minimum of one-fifth)	4,400

Capital Gains Tax: Taper Relief

Complete years after 5 April 1998 for which asset held	Gains on business assets	Gains on non-business assets
1	50%	100%
2	25%	100%
3	25%	95%
4	25%	90%
5	25%	85%
6	25%	80%
7	25%	75%
8	25%	70%
9	25%	65%
10	25%	60%

National Insurance Contributions

(Not contracted out rates)

		%
Class 1 Employee	£1 – £5,035 per year	Nil
	£5,036 – £33,540 per year	11.0
	£33,541 and above per year	1.0
Class 1 Employer	£1 – £5,035 per year	Nil
	£5,036 and above per year	12.8
Class 2	£2.10 per week	
Class 4	£1 – £5,035 per year	Nil
	£5,036 – £33,540 per year	8.0
	£33,541 and above per year	1.0
Class 1A		12.8

Stamp Duty Land Tax

Ad Valorem Duty	*Rate*
Property (other than shares)	
£125,000 or less	Nil
£125,001 – £250,000	1%
£250,001 – £500,000	3%
£500,001 or more	4%

Stamp Duty

Shares	0.5%
Fixed duty	£5

Retail prices index

Figures for the retail prices index will be provided to you in the examination where necessary.

	1982	1983	1984	1985	1986	1987	1988	1989	1990
January	–	82.61	86.84	91.20	96.25	100.0	103.3	111.0	119.5
February	–	82.97	87.20	91.94	96.60	100.4	103.7	111.8	120.2
March	79.44	83.12	87.48	92.80	96.73	100.6	104.1	112.3	121.4
April	81.04	84.28	88.64	94.78	97.67	101.8	105.8	114.3	125.1
May	81.62	84.64	88.97	95.21	97.85	101.9	106.2	115.0	126.2
June	81.85	84.84	89.20	95.41	97.79	101.9	106.6	115.4	126.7
July	81.88	85.30	89.10	95.23	97.52	101.8	106.7	115.5	126.8
August	81.90	85.68	89.94	95.49	97.82	102.1	107.9	115.8	128.1
September	81.85	86.06	90.11	95.44	98.30	102.4	108.4	116.6	129.3
October	82.26	86.36	90.67	95.59	98.45	102.9	109.5	117.5	130.3
November	82.66	86.67	90.95	95.92	99.29	103.4	110.0	118.5	130.0
December	82.51	86.89	90.87	96.05	99.62	103.3	110.3	118.8	129.9

	1991	1992	1993	1994	1995	1996	1997	1998	1999
January	130.2	135.6	137.9	141.3	146.0	150.2	154.4	159.5	163.4
February	130.9	136.3	138.8	142.1	146.9	150.9	155.0	160.3	163.7
March	131.4	136.7	139.3	142.5	147.5	151.5	155.4	160.8	164.1
April	133.1	138.8	140.6	144.2	149.0	152.6	156.3	162.6	165.2
May	133.5	139.3	141.1	144.7	149.6	152.9	156.9	163.5	165.6
June	134.1	139.3	141.0	144.7	149.8	153.0	157.5	163.4	165.6
July	133.8	138.8	140.7	144.0	149.1	152.4	157.5	163.0	165.1
August	134.1	138.9	141.3	144.7	149.9	153.1	158.5	163.7	165.5
September	134.6	139.4	141.9	145.0	150.6	153.8	159.3	164.4	166.2
October	135.1	139.9	141.8	145.2	149.8	153.8	159.5	164.5	166.5
November	135.6	139.7	141.6	145.3	149.8	153.9	159.6	164.4	166.7
December	135.7	139.2	141.9	146.0	150.7	154.4	160.0	164.4	167.3

	2000	2001	2002	2003	2004	2005	2006	2007
January	166.6	171.1	173.3	178.4	183.1	188.9	193.4	199.6e
February	167.5	172.0	173.8	179.3	183.8	189.6	194.2	200.0e
March	168.4	172.2	174.5	179.9	184.6	190.5	195.0	200.4e
April	170.1	173.1	175.7	181.2	185.7	191.6	196.0e	200.8e
May	170.7	174.2	176.2	181.5	186.5	192.0	196.4e	
June	171.1	174.4	176.2	181.3	186.8	192.2	196.8e	
July	170.5	173.3	175.9	181.3	186.8	192.2	197.2e	
August	170.5	174.0	176.4	181.6	187.4	192.6	197.6e	
September	171.7	174.6	177.6	182.5	188.1	193.1	198.0e	
October	171.6	174.3	177.9	182.6	188.6	193.3	198.4e	
November	172.1	173.6	178.2	182.7	189.0	193.6	198.8e	
December	172.2	173.4	178.5	183.5	189.9	194.1	199.2e	

e – estimated

Leases – Wasting asset table

Years	%	Years	%	Years	%
50 or more	100	33	90.280	16	64.116
49	99.657	32	89.354	15	61.617
48	99.289	31	88.371	14	58.971
47	98.902	30	87.330	13	56.167
46	98.490	29	86.226	12	53.191
45	98.059	28	85.053	11	50.038
44	97.595	27	83.816	10	46.695
43	97.107	26	82.496	9	43.154
42	96.593	25	81.100	8	39.399
41	96.041	24	79.622	7	35.414
40	95.457	23	78.055	6	31.195
39	94.842	22	76.399	5	26.722
38	94.189	21	74.635	4	21.983
37	93.497	20	72.770	3	16.959
36	92.761	19	70.791	2	11.629
35	91.981	18	68.697	1	5.983
34	91.156	17	66.470	0	0

Section 1

PRACTICE QUESTIONS

TAXATION OF INDIVIDUALS

INCOME TAX ON INCOME FROM INVESTMENTS

1   MURIEL GRAND

On 31 December 2006 Muriel Grand, aged 52, made a gift of a house in London to her brother Bertie, aged 53. Muriel had bought the house on 1 April 1986 for £60,000. Surplus land adjoining the house was sold for £24,000 to a neighbour in June 1987, at which date the market value of the property retained was £72,000. The market value at 31 December 2006 has been agreed by HMRC as £320,000.

Muriel occupied the house as her main residence until 30 September 1993, and then moved in to another house that she owned in Glasgow. Muriel elected for the house in Glasgow to be treated as her main residence from 1 January 1995 onwards. From 1 January 1988 to 30 September 1993 Muriel used 20% of the house exclusively for business purposes.

Bertie is to rent out the house in London, either unfurnished or as furnished holiday accommodation. In either case, the roof of the house must be repaired at a cost of £24,000 before it will be possible to let the house. The roof was badly damaged by a gale on 5 December 2006.

If the house is let unfurnished, then Bertie will have to decorate it at a cost of £3,600. The forecast rental income is £28,000 pa.

If the house is let as furnished holiday accommodation, then the house will be converted into two separate units at a cost of £41,000. The total cost of furnishing the two units will be £9,000. This expenditure will be financed by a £50,000 bank loan at an interest rate of 8% pa. The total forecast rental income is £45,000 pa, although 22.5% of this will be deducted by the letting agency. Other running costs, such as cleaning, will amount to £3,500 pa in total.

Bertie plans to sell the house when he retires aged 60, and anticipates making a substantial capital gain. Both Muriel and Bertie are 40% taxpayers. Muriel has a portfolio of investments valued in excess of £1 million, and has already utilised her CGT annual exemption for 2006/07.

The relevant retail price index figures are:

April 1986	97.67
April 1998	162.6
December 2006	199.2

Required:

(a)   Calculate the CGT liability that will arise from Muriel's gift of the house in London to Bertie.   **(4 marks)**

(b)   Advise Muriel as to how it would be possible to defer the gain on the house in London by making an investment in unquoted trading companies.

Your answer should cover the Enterprise Investment Scheme and Venture Capital Trusts, and you should describe the other tax implications of making such investments.

(8 marks)

(c)   Advise Bertie of the tax implications of letting out the house in London either (i) unfurnished, or (ii) as furnished holiday accommodation.

Your answer should include details of the tax advantages of letting the house as furnished holiday accommodation.   **(13 marks)**

(Total: 25 marks)

2   TRIXIE DAVENPORT

Over the years Trixie Davenport, who is 60, has built up a substantial and varied portfolio of residential and commercial investment properties. Trixie lets all of her investment properties unfurnished. She derives all of her income from this source. Her rental income accounts which require no adjustment for tax purposes are as shown below.

Trixie Davenport
Rental Income Accounts for the year ended 5 April 2006

	£	£
Rents receivable		1,089,040
Insurance	100,140	
Ground rent	18,300	
Repairs	214,350	
Accountancy	9,600	
Advertising	4,020	
Gardening	11,400	
Water rates	18,000	
Agents commission	124,860	
Interest	273,000	(773,670)
		315,370

On 3 August 2006 Trixie made a gift of one of her investment properties, Wroxley Lodge, to her niece Stella on the occasion of her marriage. The property had cost Trixie £50,000 in March 1983 and at the date of the gift was valued at £711,000. Stella and Trixie have agreed that Stella will be responsible for any inheritance tax liabilities that may result from the gift. Trixie has made no other gifts in the previous seven years.

Stella is a rising star in the fashion industry and has recently set up her own company Sunshine Fashions Limited. The company has recently won a contract to supply a major high street clothes retailer whose image is in need of modernisation. In order to fulfil the contract Sunshine Fashions needs a capital injection of £450,000. Accordingly the company has applied for finance through the Enterprise Investment Scheme.

Trixie is eager to reduce her tax liabilities as much as possible. Her attitude to risk may be described as adventurous. She has £500,000 to invest. Sunshine Fashions is the only Enterprise Investment Scheme prospectus open at this time. Trixie is however aware of other venture capital investment opportunities.

Assume that the indexation factor from March 1983:

to April 1998 is   0.956, and
to August 2006 is   1.377

Required:

(a)   Compute Trixie's income tax liability for the 2006/07 tax year on the assumption that she invests £450,000 into EIS investments and the balance of the £500,000 into VCTs.

(3 marks)

(b)   Compute Trixie's capital gains tax liability for the 2006/07 tax year on the assumption that she invests the full £500,000 at her disposal into EIS investments and VCTs as in part (a).   **(10 marks)**

(c)   Advise Stella of the amount of any capital taxes' liabilities to which she may be exposed as a result of Trixie's gift and how she may protect herself against them.

Explain carefully how the protection you have recommended would work in practice.

(7 marks)

(Total: 20 marks)

3   FAGUS

You should assume that today's date is 15 April 2007.

You have recently been approached by Fagus, who married Ulmus on 31 January 2007. Fagus was born on 28 December 1934 whilst Ulmus was born on 15 November 1951. The following information is relevant for the couple.

Fagus

He owns a cottage which was originally purchased for his own holiday use. Since the summer of 1996, however, the cottage, which is furnished, has been let to the public for holiday use. From this point in time, Fagus ceased using it privately. The cottage was let on a commercial basis for 26 weeks in 2006/07 with each individual letting not expected to exceed 2 weeks in duration. The letting generated total rental income of £8,250. Advertising, maintenance and loan interest costs of £1,300, £5,300 and £2,200 respectively were incurred in this tax year. The maintenance costs relate to roof repairs following gale damage.

Fagus also owns 2,000 ordinary shares in Quercus Limited, a trading company set up by him many years ago. His holding represents 10% of the issued share capital with the remaining shares held by his son. Net dividends of £23,625 were paid to Fagus in 2006/07. He also received, in 2006/07, £2,000 gross interest on a loan of £25,000 made to Quercus Limited many years ago which was used to acquire some plant and machinery for use in its trade. The money loaned to Quercus Limited was borrowed from his bank. Annual interest charges payable to the bank and relating to this loan amounted to £2,500 in 2006/07.

The only other income that Fagus received in 2006/07 was net building society interest amounting to £7,400 and state retirement pension amounting to £4,250.

Ulmus

The only income Ulmus received in 2006/07 was net building society interest amounting to £1,450 and gross employment income of £12,500 (related PAYE tax credit is £1,384).

Fagus has heard that it may be beneficial from an income tax perspective to gift some of his income bearing assets to Ulmus. He is also under the impression that gifts between spouses in and after the year of marriage are free of any capital taxes.

Required:

(a)   Explain the likely tax treatment of Fagus's cottage for the 2006/07 tax year and any implications arising from this treatment.

Your answer should include a calculation of Fagus's net assessable property business income for this tax year.   **(4 marks)**

(b)   Calculate Fagus's and Ulmus's income tax payable or repayable for 2006/07.

Your answer should include an explanation of the treatment of the loan interest paid by Fagus and of the allowances and tax reducing allowances to which Fagus and/or Ulmus are entitled.   **(17 marks)**

(c)   Prepare notes for a meeting with Fagus:

(i)   Explaining whether Fagus is correct in believing that gifts between spouses are free of any capital taxes in and after the year of marriage.

(ii) Assuming the couple do not replace any of their existing assets evaluate the possible ways in which the couple could reduce their income tax liabilities.

For this question part you are not required to prepare amended detailed income tax computations for Fagus and Ulmus.

You should assume that the tax rates and allowances for 2006/07 apply throughout this part of the question.   **(9 marks)**

(Total: 30 marks)

INCOME TAX ON INCOME FROM EMPLOYMENT

4   TARIKI PUTIN

Tariki Putin is married with four young children. Both he and his wife, Juliette, are resident, ordinarily resident and domiciled in the United Kingdom. Their only asset is the jointly owned family house, which is worth £185,000, on which there is a mortgage of £165,000. Tariki's wife is fully occupied looking after the house and the children and has no income.

He is employed by A V Ltd as a sales manager and earns a salary of £29,500 out of which he contributes 2% into the company's occupational pension scheme. He would like to contribute more into the scheme but has never felt able to afford to. A V Ltd contributes a further 8% into the scheme.

Tariki owns a Ford car with a 1.6 litre petrol engine. In 2006/07 he drove 15,400 miles of which 5,700 related to his employment duties. A V Ltd paid him 35 pence per mile in respect of the business miles. The authorised mileage rates are 40p per mile for the first 10,000 miles and 25p per mile thereafter.

On 1 July 2004 A V Ltd purchased a video camera for £3,000 for a project carried out by Tariki. The company allowed Tariki to borrow the camera on 1 January 2005 once the project had been completed at which time it was worth £2,200. On 1 October 2006 Tariki was allowed to purchase the camera for £250, its market value at that time.

Vladimir Putin, Tariki's uncle, died on 10 April 2007. He did not make any gifts in his lifetime and left the whole of the following estate to Tariki.

	Probate value
	£
House in Bristol	270,000
House in Padua	50,000
United Kingdom quoted shares	135,000
United Kingdom shares in ISAs	32,200
Cash in a United Kingdom bank account	7,600
Chattels	19,000
Car	17,800

Vladimir's personal representatives incurred administration costs in Padua in respect of the house of £4,100. A further £2,700 was spent on Vladimir's funeral. There was no inheritance tax in Padua on the property.

Vladimir was born in Padua in 1940 and moved to the United Kingdom in 1996, following the death of his sister, to be near his only living relative, Tariki's father. Tariki visited him every week to listen to him complain about England and talk of his determination to return to Padua.

The car, chattels and some of the quoted shares will be sold to pay the inheritance tax due. Tariki will rent out the house in Padua for £300 per month, net of expenses. He understands that 15% tax will be levied on the net income in Padua. The Bristol house will also be rented out, unfurnished, for £950 per month, net of expenses. He will keep the remainder of the shares and has been told that they will generate dividends of £5,940 per annum. He also expects to receive bank interest of £880 per annum (net).

Tariki has not had to think about tax planning until now and has asked you to suggest ways in which he can reduce his income tax liability. He has indicated that he would be happy to transfer investments to Juliette in order to save tax.

Required:

Using the rates and allowance for 2006/07 throughout:

(a)   Compute the 2006/07 income tax liability of Tariki.   **(5 marks)**

(b)   (i)   Compute the inheritance tax liability arising on the death of Vladimir, highlighting any contentious issues.   **(5 marks)**

        (ii)   State how much of the tax can be paid by instalments and outline the rules governing instalment payments. State when the remainder of the liability is due.

(2 marks)

(c)   Explain how Tariki's investment income will be taxed and compute the extra tax that he will have to pay on the investment income over a full year.   **(8 marks)**

(d)   (i)   Advise Tariki, without producing detailed computations, of the income tax, capital gains tax and inheritance tax implications of transferring investments to Juliette.   **(6 marks)**

        (ii)   Advise Tariki of the maximum investment he can make into an ISA and explain the tax advantages available.   **(2 marks)**

(Total: 28 marks)

5   LANDSCAPE LTD

Landscape Ltd is an unquoted trading company that operates a nation-wide chain of retail shops. Landscape Ltd is a close company.

(a)   Landscape Ltd employed Peter Plain as a computer programmer until 31 December 2006. On that date he resigned from the company, and set up as a self-employed computer programmer. Peter has continued to work for Landscape Ltd, and during the period 1 January to 5 April 2007 has invoiced them for work done based on an hourly rate of pay. Peter works five days each week at the offices of Landscape Ltd, uses their computer equipment, and does not have any other clients. The computer function is an integral part of Landscape Ltd's business operations. Peter now considers himself to be self-employed but Landscape Ltd's accountant is not sure if this is the correct interpretation.

(b)   Landscape Ltd operates an approved company share incentive plan whereby employees receive fully paid up ordinary shares in the company free of charge. On 1 January 2004 Richard Rosland, the personnel manager, received the maximum entitlement of shares allowed under the scheme. At that date the shares were worth £1.50 each. He sold half of these shares on 31 January 2007 for £2,800. No employees are offered partnership shares under the scheme.

(c)   On 15 March 2007 Landscape Ltd dismissed Simon Savannah, the manager of their shop in Manchester, and gave him a lump sum redundancy payment of £55,000. This amount included statutory redundancy pay of £2,400, holiday pay of £1,500, and £5,000 for agreeing not to work for a rival company. The balance of the payment was compensation for loss of office, and £10,000 of this was not paid until 31 May 2007.

(d)   Trevor Tundra is one of Landscape Ltd's shareholders, but is neither a director nor employee of the company. On 6 April 2006 Landscape Ltd provided Trevor with a new motor car with a list price of £13,500 and carbon dioxide emissions of 221 g/km. No private petrol was provided, and Trevor did not drive any business mileage during 2006/07. On 1 July 2006 Landscape Ltd made a loan of £40,000 to Trevor. He repaid £26,500 of the loan on 31 August 2006, and the balance of the loan was written off on 31 March 2007.

(e)   On 1 October 2006 Landscape Ltd opened a new shop in Cambridge, and assigned three employees from the London shop to work there on a temporary basis.

   (1)   Ursula Upland is to work in Cambridge for a period of 18 months. Her ordinary commuting is a daily total of 90 miles, and her daily total from home to Cambridge is 40 miles. She uses her private motor car for business mileage.

   (2)   Violet Veld was initially due to work in Cambridge for a period of 30 months, but this was reduced to a period of 20 months on 1 January 2007. In London, Violet walks to work whereas the cost of her train fare from home to Cambridge is £30 per day. This is paid by Landscape Ltd.

   (3)   Wilma Wood is to work in Cambridge for a period of six months. Her ordinary commuting is a daily total of 30 miles, and her daily total from home to Cambridge is 150 miles. Wilma passes the London shop on her daily journey to Cambridge. She uses her private motor car for business mileage.

All three employees worked at Cambridge for 120 days during 2006/07. Landscape Ltd pays a mileage allowance of 36 pence per mile for business use. The authorised mileage allowance payment (AMAP) rates are 40 pence per mile for the first 10,000 miles, and 25 pence per mile thereafter.

Required:

Explain the income tax implications, for the recipients, arising from the payments and benefits that have been made or provided by Landscape Ltd to (a) Peter, (b) Richard, (c) Simon, (d) Trevor and (e) Ursula, Violet and Wilma.

Your answer should be confined to the implications for 2006/07.

Marks for this question will be allocated on the basis of:

(6 marks to (a))
(4 marks to (b))
(4 marks to (c))
(4 marks to (d))
(7 marks to (e))
(Total: 25 marks)

6 WORKOUT PLC

Workout plc runs a nation-wide chain of health clubs, with each club being run by a manager who is paid an annual salary of £42,500. The company has a flexible remuneration policy in that it allows managers to enhance their salary by choosing from a package of benefits.

Gareth Step is to be appointed as a manager of Workout plc on 6 April 2006 and he has asked for your advice regarding the tax implications arising from each aspect of the benefits package.

The package is as follows:

Motor car

Option 1:

Workout plc will provide a new 2198cc petrol powered motorcar with a list price of £19,200 and carbon dioxide emissions of 182 g/km, and will pay for all running costs, including private fuel. Gareth will make a capital contribution of £3,000 towards the cost of the motor car, and will also be required to contribute a further £50 per month towards its private use. He will drive a total of 1,750 miles per month, of which 60% will be in respect of journeys in the performance of his duties for Workout plc.

Option 2:

Alternatively, Workout plc will pay Gareth additional salary of £500 per month, and he will lease a private motorcar. Workout plc will then pay an allowance of 30 pence per mile for business mileage. The statutory rates allowed are 40 pence per mile for the first 10,000 miles, and 25 pence per mile thereafter.

Accommodation

Option 1:

Gareth currently lives 140 miles from where he is to be employed by Workout plc. The company will pay £7,500 towards the cost of relocation, and will also provide an interest free loan of £90,000 in order for Gareth to purchase a property. The loan will be repaid in monthly instalments of £1,000 commencing on 15 April 2006.

Option 2:

Alternatively, Workout plc will provide living accommodation for Gareth. This will be in a house that the company purchased in 1994 for £86,500. The house has a rateable value of £7,700 and is currently valued at £135,000. The furniture in the house cost £12,400. Workout plc will pay for the annual running costs of £3,900.

Telephone

Option 1:

Workout plc will provide Gareth with a mobile telephone costing £500, and will pay for all business and private telephone calls.

Option 2:

Alternatively, Workout plc will pay Gareth £75 per month towards the cost of his fixed telephone at home. The total annual cost will be £1,400, of which £300 is for line rental, £650 for business telephone calls and £450 for private telephone calls.

Club membership

Option 1:

Free membership to Workout plc's health clubs is provided to each manager. The normal cost of membership is £650 pa, with this figure being made up of direct costs of £40, variable overhead cost of £100, fixed overhead cost of £260 and profit of £250. Although the budgeted membership has been exceeded, each of the health clubs currently has surplus capacity.

Option 2:

Alternatively, Workout plc will pay for Gareth's golf club membership of £800 pa.

Incentive scheme

Option 1:

Workout plc operates an approved share incentive plan whereby employees receive fully paid up shares in the company free of charge. Gareth will receive the maximum possible entitlement of shares allowed under the scheme. The company's shares are currently valued at £3, and are forecast to be worth £6.75 in five years time. No employees are offered partnership shares under the scheme.

Option 2:

Alternatively, Gareth will be granted options to purchase 10,000 ordinary shares in Workout plc. The options will be provided free, and will be exercisable in five years time at a discount of 40% to the current value of the shares of £3. The options will not be granted under a HMRC approved scheme.

Required:

Explain the tax implications for Gareth arising from each aspect of the benefits package. You should assume that benefits are provided on 6 April 2006.

NIC, VAT and the tax implications for Workout plc should be ignored.   **(25 marks)**

7   **ALFIE**

You should assume today's date is 1 March 2006.

Alfie is planning to start a computer repair and sale business on 6 April 2006. A limited company has been formed for this purpose. Alfie anticipates that he will drive 22,000 miles in the 2006/07 tax year of which 20,000 will be for business purposes.

He is considering:

1   Whether the vehicle should be acquired by himself personally or by the limited company.

2   Whether the vehicle should be a car or a van.

All running costs, including fuel will be paid for by the limited company in the event that it acquires the vehicle and by Alfie personally if he acquires the vehicle.

The vehicle that Alfie is considering buying is either a petrol engined 1,500cc car with a list price of £15,000 including VAT and CO_2 emission of 160 g/kilometre or a petrol engined 1,500cc van with the same list price and CO_2 emission level.

Irrespective of who buys the vehicle it will be acquired under a 0% finance hire purchase contract with the cost being £3,000 per year.

The running costs per year for each of the vehicles will be:

	£
Insurance	500
Repairs/servicing	500
Road fund licence	100
Fuel	3 per 40 miles

All figures include VAT where appropriate.

HMRC Authorised Mileage Allowances Payments (AMAPs) for 2006/07 for both vans and cars are 40p per mile for the first 10,000 miles and 25p per mile for additional miles.

Alfie will be a higher rate tax payer in 2006/07 by virtue of the salary that he will draw from the business. The company, which will be registered for VAT from 6 April 2006, will pay corporation tax at the rate of 19%.

Required:

(a)   Assuming the vehicle acquired is a car advise Alfie of the income tax, corporation tax, VAT and national insurance implications for both the limited company and himself of acquiring the vehicle, either:

(i)   personally; or

(ii)   by the limited company.

Detailed calculations are not required for this question part.   **(11 marks)**

(b)   Advise Alfie how your answer to (a) would be different if the vehicle acquired was a van.   **(3 marks)**

(c)   Assuming that the vehicle acquired is a car and that the mileage allowances are paid at the authorised rates for *business* mileage only, advise which of the two alternatives (acquisition by Alfie personally or by the limited company) would be the most tax efficient.

For both alternatives your answer should take account of the *aggregate* tax position for both Alfie personally *and* the limited company.

For this part of the question you can ignore the effect of VAT.   **(11 marks)**

(Total: 25 marks)

8   ADVANCED TECHNOLOGIES LTD

(a)   Assume today's date is 1 January 2007.

Advanced Technologies Limited ('ATL') is involved in the development of computer software. The company prepares its accounts to 31 March each year and is a small company for Companies Act purposes. ATL pays corporation tax at a marginal rate of 19%.

ATL is considering engaging Bill either on an employed or self-employed basis to undertake work of a one-off nature for a specific development project for one of their clients. The engagement which will begin on 6 April 2007 will run for one year.

If Bill is employed:

– He will travel in his own car and charge ATL 60p per mile for travelling to ATL and their client. The total mileage expected is as follows:

	miles
Travelling to ATL client's premises	4,160
Travelling to ATL's premises	1,560

– His salary will be £39,000.

– In addition ATL will pay Bill £10 per month for the additional costs incurred in working from home.

– ATL will purchase computer equipment costing £5,000 required for Bill's exclusive use on the project.

If Bill is self-employed

– He will charge a fixed all-inclusive price to ATL of £48,000 for the services performed.

– He will again use his own vehicle for travelling. Bill's car, which does not qualify as a low-emission vehicle, will have a value of £12,000 on 6 April 2007. Bill's total mileage in the year to 5 April 2008 is expected to be 11,440 miles. Total vehicle expenses over the year are expected to be £2,500.

– Bill will purchase the required computer equipment costing £5,000 himself and it will be used 100% for the assignment.

– Other allowable business expenses of £500 are anticipated.

– Providing the project is completed within one year Bill can organise his work schedule as he pleases and, if he wishes, use his own staff to perform the work.

Bill has no other income or outgoings and does not have any children.

Required:

(i) Advise Bill and Advanced Technologies Limited of the corporation tax, income tax and national insurance contribution implications of engaging Bill on either an employed or self-employed basis.

Detailed calculations are not required for this question part. **(10 marks)**

(ii) Calculate from Advanced Technologies Limited's perspective whether it is more beneficial for Bill to be treated as self-employed.

You should assume that the rates and allowances for the Financial Year 2006 and 2006/07 apply throughout. **(5 marks)**

(b) Advanced Technologies Limited has heard that whilst there may be saving and administrative convenience in engaging Bill on a self-employed basis this may be imprudent without first obtaining HMRC's approval. They have also heard that if Bill were to trade through a limited company rather than on a self-employed basis any potential problems from their perspective may be avoided.

Required:

(i)   Discuss, in the context of Bill's engagement, the factors that will be considered in determining whether he will be regarded by HMRC as employed by Advanced Technologies Limited. **(5 marks)**

(ii) Advise Bill of any potential tax savings that he could make if he were to perform the services for Advanced Technologies Limited through a limited company rather than on a self-employed basis, and explain to Bill any tax legislation of which he needs to be aware.

Detailed calculations are not required for this question part.   **(5 marks)**

(Total: 25 marks)

9   OLIVER

Assume today's date is 15 February 2007.

Oliver is single, aged 38, and currently works in London as a business consultant with Hardlife Limited. Although he receives a reasonable salary and benefits, Oliver wants to work in the countryside, where his main residence is. He has therefore been looking for a job which will give him a similar salary, but which will allow him to leave London.

Oliver currently earns £62,000 per year. There are no bonus arrangements. He has use of a Jaguar company car. The company paid £24,640 for the car in January 2006, which included £3,450 of extras. The list price (without extras) at that time was £22,870. The car is a diesel and emits 237g/km of carbon dioxide. Free fuel is also provided.

Oliver is provided with accommodation in the form of a one bedroom apartment near the office, which he uses during the week while working in London. The apartment cost £170,000, has an annual rateable value of £7,200, and would command a market rent of £950 per month. Oliver pays the utility bills, but his employer pays the council tax, which was £1,400 in the year ended 5 April 2007. Oliver has furnished the property himself with the exception of a television (worth £1,200) which has been provided by the company since February 2005.

Oliver is also provided with free work-place parking at a cost to Hardlife Ltd of £2,150 per year.

Oliver has recently been offered consultancy work with Easylife Limited, a company based 30 miles from his country home - the same distance he currently travels, but in the opposite direction. The contract would pay £3,750 per month for 12 months, with the possibility of extending the contract for a further period. Easylife Ltd does not provide any benefits, and pays a mileage car allowance of 35p per mile for the business use of his own car. Oliver estimates that he will drive 23,000 miles during the year of which 13,000 would be business miles on Easylife Ltd business. He estimates that buying an equivalent car to the current one will cost £6,000 per year, plus £3,000 in running expenses.

Hardlife Ltd does not provide any pension arrangements, but Oliver pays £3,120 per annum net of tax into his own personal pension scheme. He intends to maintain this level of payments for the foreseeable future.

The new role with Easylife Ltd would allow Oliver to work from his study at home for up to 3 days per week. For the remainder of his time, he would either work at Easylife's office or visit clients, often directly from home. Oliver estimates that he could earn an additional £10,000 per year by consulting for clients other than Easylife Ltd. He is unsure what effect this would have on his personal tax situation, but a friend has told him that he is likely to be treated as self-employed.

Oliver is unsure whether or not to accept the offer from Easylife Ltd, as he does not know if he will be better off or not in cash terms. If he does accept the offer, his consultancy role would start on 6 April 2007.

Oliver has no savings or investment income.

Required:

(a) List the characteristics that are used to determine self-employment status, and comment on their application to Oliver's situation where relevant. **(6 marks)**

(b) Advise Oliver on whether or not he should accept Easylife's contract and commence a new role as a consultant.

Support your advice with calculations of Oliver's cash income for 2007/08 after income tax (IT) and national insurance contributions (NIC) for both alternatives.

Assume that Oliver will be treated as self-employed if he accepts the new role .

(13 marks)

(c) State the income tax (IT) and capital gains tax (CGT) implications of Oliver working from home. **(3 marks)**

(d) Assuming that Oliver accepts the contract with Easylife Limited and commences a new role as a consultant, calculate the maximum personal pension contributions that he could make for the year 2007/08, based on the taxable income figures that you have calculated in part (b). **(3 marks)**

For this question you should assume that the rates and allowances for 2006/07 apply throughout. **(Total: 25 marks)**

10 JAN

Assume that today's date is 1 July 2007.

Jan is aged 45 and single. He is of Danish domicile but has been working in the United Kingdom since 1 May 2006 and intends to remain in the UK for the medium to long term. Although Jan worked briefly in the UK in 1988, he has forgotten how UK taxation works and needs some assistance before preparing his UK income tax return.

Jan's salary from 1 May 2006 was £74,760 per annum. Jan also has a company car – a Jaguar XJ8 with a list price of £42,550 including extras, and CO_2 emissions of 237g/km. The car was available to him from 1 July 2006. Free petrol is provided by the company. Jan has other taxable benefits amounting to £3,965.

Jan's other 2006/07 income comprises:

	£
Dividend income from UK companies (cash received)	3,240
Interest received on an ISA account	230
Interest received on a UK bank account	740
Interest remitted from an offshore account (net of 15% withholding tax)	5,100
Income remitted from a villa in Portugal (net of 45% withholding tax)	4,598

The total interest arising on the offshore account was £9,000 (gross). In addition, Jan has not remitted other Portuguese rental income arising in the year, totalling a further £1,500 (gross).

Jan informs you that his employer is thinking of providing him with rented accommodation while he looks for a house to buy. The accommodation would be a two bedroom flat, valued at £155,000 with an annual value of £6,000. It would be made available from 6 August 2007.

The company will pay the rent of £600 per month for the first six months. All other bills will be paid by Jan.

Jan also informs you that he has 25,000 ordinary shares in Gilet Ltd ('Gilet'), an unquoted UK trading company. He has held these shares since August 1986 when he bought 2,500 shares at £4.07 per share. In January 1994, a bonus issue gave each shareholder nine shares for each ordinary share held. In the last week all Gilet's shareholders have received an offer from Jumper plc ('Jumper') who wishes to acquire the shares. Jumper has offered the following:

- 3 shares in Jumper (currently trading at £3.55 per share) for every 5 shares in Gilet, and

- 25p cash per share

Required:

(a) Calculate Jan's income tax (IT) payable for 2006/07. **(11 marks)**

(b) Calculate the taxable benefit in 2007/08 if Jan were to use the accommodation offered by his employer. You may assume that the rules for calculating benefits are the same as in 2006/07. **(3 marks)**

(c) (i) Explain the capital gains tax (CGT) implications of a takeover where the consideration is in the form of shares (a 'paper for paper' transaction) stating any conditions that need to be satisfied. **(4 marks)**

    (ii) Calculate the chargeable gain arising as a consequence of Jan accepting Jumper's offer. Assume that the shares are a business asset for taper relief purposes throughout the period of ownership. **(4 marks)**

    (iii) Define a qualifying corporate bond for the purposes of capital gains tax (CGT) and explain the effect on the chargeable gain calculated in (ii) if the cash element in the offer were replaced with a qualifying corporate bond. **(3 marks)**

Relevant retail price index figures are:

August	1986	97.82
January	1994	141.3
April	1998	162.6
June	2007	200.4

(Total: 25 marks)

11 JOANNE

Assume today's date is 5 February 2007.

Joanne is 37, she was born and has lived all her life in Germany until 2005. She recently married Fraser, aged 38, who is a UK resident, but who worked briefly in Germany. They have no children.

The couple moved to the UK to live permanently on 9 October 2006. Joanne was employed by an American company in Germany, and she continued to work for them in the UK until the end of November 2006. Her earnings from the American company were £5,000 per month. Joanne has not remitted any of the income she earned in Germany prior to her arrival in the UK.

Joanne resigned from her job at the end of November 2006. The company did not hold her to the three months notice stipulated in her contract, but still paid her for that period. In total, Joanne paid £4,000 in UK income tax under PAYE for the tax year 2006/07.

Joanne wishes to sell the shares she holds in a German listed company. The shareholding cost the equivalent of £3,500 in September 1986, and its current value is £21,500. She intends to sell the shares in March 2007 and to invest the proceeds from the sale in the UK. Joanne has made no other capital disposals in the year.

Prior to her leaving employment, Joanne investigated the possibility of starting her own business providing a German translation service for UK companies, and took some advice on the matter. She paid consultancy fees of £5,000 (excluding value added tax (VAT)) and bought a computer for £2,000 (excluding VAT), both on 23 October 2006. Joanne started trading on 1 December 2006. She made sales of £2,000 in December, and estimates that her sales will rise by £1,000 every month to a maximum of £7,000 per month. Joanne believes that her monthly expenses of £400 (excluding VAT) will remain constant. Her year end will be 31 March, and the first accounts will be drawn up to 31 March 2007.

Although Joanne has registered her business for tax purposes with HMRC, she has not registered for VAT and is unsure what is required of her in this respect.

Required:

(a)   State, giving reasons, whether Joanne will be treated as resident or non-resident in the UK for the year of assessment 2006/07, together with the basis on which her income and gains of that year will be subject to UK taxation.   **(3 marks)**

(b)   Write a letter to Joanne setting out the value added tax (VAT) registration requirements and advising on whether or not she should or could register for VAT. In addition, if registered advise whether she could recover the VAT suffered on the consultancy fees and computer purchased in October 2006.   **(7 marks)**

(c)   Assuming that Joanne registers for value added tax (VAT) with effect from 1 April 2007:

(i)   Calculate her income tax (IT) and capital gains tax (CGT) payable for the year of assessment 2006/07.

You are not required to calculate any national insurance liabilities in this sub-part.   **(6 marks)**

(ii)   Calculate her income tax (IT) and national insurance (NIC) payable for the year of assessment 2007/08.   **(4 marks)**

(iii)   Prepare a schedule of the payments (tax and national insurance) she will be required to make directly to HMRC in respect of the years of assessment 2006/07 and 2007/08, clearly identifying for each payment listed, the amount, the nature of the liability/liabilities, and the due date.   **(5 marks)**

Assume that the tax rates and allowances for 2006/07 apply throughout this question.

Relevant retail price index figures are:

September	1986	98.3
April	1998	162.6

          (Total: 25 marks)

12   ALASDAIR

Alasdair, aged 42, is single. He is considering investing in property, as he has heard that this represents a good investment. In order to raise the funds to buy the property, he wants to extract cash from his personal company, Beezer Limited, whose year end is 31 December.

Beezer Limited was formed on 1 May 1999 with £1,000 of capital issued as 1,000 £1 ordinary shares, and traded until 1 January 2007 when Alasdair sold the trade and related assets. The company's only asset is cash of £120,000. Alasdair wants to extract this cash from the company with the minimum amount of tax payable. He is considering either, paying himself a dividend of £120,000, on 31 March 2008, after which the company would have no assets and be wound up or, leaving the cash in the company and then liquidating the company. Costs of liquidation of £5,000 would then be incurred.

Since Beezer Limited ceased trading, Alasdair has been taken on as a partner at a marketing firm, Gallus & Co. He estimates his profit share for the year of assessment 2007/08 will be £30,000. He has not made any capital disposals in the current tax year.

Alasdair wishes to reinvest the cash extracted from Beezer Limited in property but is not sure whether he should invest directly in residential or commercial property, or do so via some form of collective investment. He is aware that Gallus & Co are looking to rent a new warehouse which could be bought for £200,000. Alasdair thinks that he may be able to buy the warehouse himself and lease it to his firm, but only if he can borrow the additional money to buy the property.

Alasdair has a 25% shareholding in another company, Glaikit Limited, whose year end is 31 March. The remaining shares in this company are held by his friend, Gill. Alasdair is considering borrowing £15,000 from Glaikit Limited on 1 January 2008. He does not intend to pay any interest on the loan, which is likely to be written off some time in 2009. Alasdair does not have any connection with Glaikit Limited other than his shareholding.

Required:

(a)   Advise Alasdair whether or not a dividend payment will result in a higher after-tax cash sum than the liquidation of Beezer Limited. Assume that either the dividend would be paid on 31 March 2008 or the liquidation would take place on 31 March 2008.   **(9 marks)**

Assume that Beezer Limited has always paid corporation tax at or above the small companies rate of 19% and that the tax rates and allowances for 2006/07 apply throughout this part.

(b)   (i)   Advise Alasdair of the tax implications and relative financial risks attached to the following property investments:

(1)   buy to let residential property;

(2)   commercial property;

(3)   shares in Real Estate Investment Trust (REIT); and

(3)   shares in a property investment company/unit trust.   **(9 marks)**

(ii)   State, giving reasons, the tax reliefs in relation to inheritance tax (IHT) and capital gains tax (CGT) which would be available to Alasdair if he acquires the warehouse and leases it to Gallus & Co, rather than to an unconnected tenant.   **(4 marks)**

(c)   State the tax consequences for both Glaikit Limited and Alasdair if he borrows money from the company, as proposed, on 1 January 2008.   **(3 marks)**

(Total: 25 marks)

INCOME TAX ON INCOME FROM SELF-EMPLOYMENT

13   THE BARTON PARTNERSHIP

The Barton Partnership had been trading for many years until the partners decided to transfer the business to BPK Ltd on 30 November 2006. Details of the partners at that date, their overlap profits and their profit sharing arrangements are set out below.

Name	Age	Date joined partnership	Unrelieved overlap profits £	Salary £	Share of profits / gains
Eric	58	1 June 1989	12,000		50%
Fred	54	1 February 1996	8,000	8,000	25%
George	46	1 May 2004	14,000		25%

The business was worth £840,000 on 30 November 2006. It was transferred to BPK Ltd in exchange for 537,600 shares worth £1.25 each with the balance left on loan account. Half of the consideration was paid to Eric with the other half split equally between Fred and George. The transfer of the business gave rise to capital gains after indexation of £375,000.

The recent taxable trading profits of the partnership are as follows:

	£
Year to 31 May 2005	43,500
Year to 31 May 2006	41,200
Period to 30 November 2006	12,800

Eric retired on 30 November 2006 and now lives on his investment income. He has made personal pension contributions for a number of years and will draw a pension when he is 62. Fred and George are both working full time for BPK Ltd. All three of them are 40% taxpayers who have used the 2006/07 annual exemption against their other gains.

Required:

(a)   Compute the profits assessable on each partner for 2006/07 and state briefly the alternative reliefs available in respect of any losses.   **(8 marks)**

(b)   (i)   Compute the capital gains tax payable by each of the partners as a result of the sale of the business ignoring any possible relief for losses and state the base cost of the shares held.   **(5 marks)**

(ii)   Eric is considering selling his shares before 5 April 2007 for £500,000. What advice would you give him and show the tax saving he would make if he follows your advice. State the date that any relevant elections must be submitted by.   **(6 marks)**

(c)   State the VAT implications of the sale of the business.   **(2 marks)**

(Total: 21 marks)

14   ALPHABET ENGINEERING

(a)   You are the tax advisor to Alphabet Engineering, a three person partnership running an engineering business that commenced trading on 1 January 2005. Until 30 June 2006 the partnership consisted of Alfred, Bertie and Claude, with profits being shared in the ratio 5:3:2. On 30 June 2006 Claude resigned as a partner, and was replaced on 1 July 2006 by Daniel. The basis of profit sharing remained unchanged, with Daniel taking over Claude's profit share.

The partnership's tax adjusted trading profit for the year ended 31 December 2005 was £122,000 (after capital allowances).

The partnership's profit and loss account for the year ended 31 December 2006 is forecast to be as follows:

		£	£
Gross profit			420,000
Less:	Administration expenses (all allowable)	253,600	
	Depreciation	5,400	
	Amortisation of lease	2,500	
			(261,500)
Net profit for the year			158,500

The partnership paid a premium of £25,000 for the grant of a 10 year lease on a workshop on 1 January 2005. The tax written-down value of plant and machinery at 31 December 2005 was as follows:

	£
Pooled assets	22,000
Partners' motor cars (owned by the partnership):	
Alfred – 40% private use	14,500
Bertie – 80% private use	8,000
Claude – 80% private use	15,000

Claude retained his motor car when he resigned from the partnership on 30 June 2006, at which date it was valued at £13,500. On 1 July 2006 Daniel introduced his private motor car into the partnership at a value of £10,000. The private use of this motor car is 70%.

The partnership's estimated tax adjusted trading profit for the year ended 31 December 2007 is £190,000 (after capital allowances).

Required:

Advise the partners of the partnership profits that will be assessed on each of them for 2006/07. Your calculations should be made on a monthly basis. **(12 marks)**

(b) On 31 December 2007 Alphabet Engineering is to sell the lease on its leasehold workshop (see part (a)) for £45,000, and will purchase the freehold of a new workshop for £65,000.

Required:

Advise the partners of Alphabet Engineering of the tax implications arising from the disposal of the leasehold workshop and the acquisition of the freehold workshop. Use the following lease percentages:

7 years   35.414
10 years   46.695
                                                                    (4 marks)

                                                          (Total: 16 marks)

15   MING AND NINA

(a)   Ming Khan and Nina Lee are in partnership running a music recording studio. The partnership commenced trading on 1 May 2006, and their first accounts for the 15 month period to 31 July 2007 show a tax adjusted trading loss (*before* capital allowances) of £51,000.

On 1 May 2006 the partnership purchased a freehold building and converted it into a recording studio at a cost of £207,720, made up as follows:

	£
Land and building	69,500
Recording equipment	48,700
Installation of electrical system for the recording equipment	19,400
Sound insulation	34,800
Replacement doors and windows	2,500
Heating system	5,100
VAT	27,720
	207,720

Profits and losses are shared 60% to Ming and 40% to Nina. The partnership is registered for VAT, and all of its supplies are standard rated.

Required:

(i)   Show how the partnership's tax adjusted trading loss for the 15 month period to 31 July 2007 will be allocated between Ming and Nina for 2006/07 and 2007/08. Your calculations should be made on a monthly basis.   **(4 marks)**

(ii)   State the possible ways of relieving the trading loss.   **(3 marks)**

(b)   Ming was previously employed by a music company at an annual salary of £42,000. She was made redundant on 28 February 2006, and received an *ex gratia* redundancy payment of £60,000.

Nina was previously a student. She had inherited investments on the death of her parents, and sold these for £125,000 on 31 March 2006 in order to finance her partnership capital. The disposal resulted in a chargeable gain of £40,700 (no taper relief is available). Until 31 March 2006 Nina received dividend income of £6,520 (gross) pa.

Both Ming and Nina are single, and have no other income or outgoings. They forecast that the partnership will make a tax adjusted trading profit (*after* capital allowances) of approximately £40,000 for the year ended 31 July 2008.

Required:

(i)   Advise Ming and Nina as to which loss relief claims would be the most beneficial for them.   **(4 marks)**

(ii)   Calculate the tax refunds that will be due to Ming and Nina. You should ignore the possibility of any repayment supplement being due.

You should use the tax rates and allowances for 2006/07 throughout.   **(7 marks)**

(c)   Ming and Nina are concerned about the partnership's financial position. They have asked for your advice on the following matters:

(i)   One of the partnership's clients owes the partnership £23,500, and this amount is now four months overdue. Ming and Nina want to know how relief for irrecoverable debts can be obtained.

(ii)   The partnership needs to purchase new generation digital recording equipment costing £61,100, but does not have sufficient funds to do so outright. The equipment can either be leased for three years at a cost of £28,200 pa or can be bought on hire purchase for an initial payment of £11,100 (including VAT of £9,100), followed by 35 monthly payments of £2,000.

The digital recording equipment will be replaced after three years use, at which time it will be worthless. Ming and Nina want to know the tax implications of each alternative method of financing the equipment.

All figures are inclusive of VAT where appropriate.

Required:

Advise Ming and Nina in respect of the matters that they have raised. Your answer should cover both the income tax and the VAT implications. You should ignore the implications of SSAP 21: Accounting for Leases and Hire Purchase Contracts.

(7 marks)

(Total: 25 marks)

16   BASIL AND SYBIL PERFECT

Basil Perfect commenced self-employment on 1 July 2004, and is involved in the provision of educational services. His wife Sybil commenced self-employment on 1 June 2006, and is also involved in the provision of educational services.

You should assume that today's date is 20 March 2007, and that the tax rates and allowances for 2006/07 apply throughout.

(a)   Basil and Sybil are planning to combine their two businesses into a partnership on 1 April 2007. Basil's tax adjusted trading profits are as follows:

	£
Year ended 30 June 2005	38,640
Year ended 30 June 2006	49,920
Period ended 31 March 2007 (forecast)	47,700

Sybil's forecast tax adjusted profits for the ten month period to 31 March 2007 are £11,100. The partnership is planning to have an accounting date of 31 March. Its forecast profits for the year ended 31 March 2008 are £80,000, and these are to be shared 75% to Basil and 25% to Sybil.

Required:

(i)   Calculate Basil and Sybil's trading income assessments for 2006/07 and 2007/08.   **(5 marks)**

(ii)   Advise Basil and Sybil of the advantages and disadvantages of having an accounting date of 31 March as compared to an accounting date of 30 June.   **(3 marks)**

(b)   Basil is registered for VAT. Sybil is not registered because she is below the VAT registration turnover limit and her supplies are all to the general public in a competitive market. Basil and Sybil are concerned that they will have to pay additional VAT as a result of forming a partnership on 1 April 2007, compared to operating as sole-traders. Their individual sales and expenses for the year ended 31 March 2008 are forecast to be as follows:

		Basil	*Sybil*
		£	£
Sales:	Standard rated	170,000	47,000
	Exempt	115,000	–
Expenses:	Standard rated	160,000	26,000

25% of Basil's expenses directly relate to standard rated sales, 30% directly relate to exempt sales, with the balance not directly attributable. Basil's standard rated sales include a supply of £15,000 to Sybil. There are no expenses related to this supply. All of the above figures are *exclusive* of VAT where applicable.

Required:

(i)   Advise Basil and Sybil of the additional amount of VAT that will be payable for the year ended 31 March 2008 if they form the partnership on 1 April 2007, as compared to the position if they had remained as sole traders.   **(8 marks)**

(ii)   Basil and Sybil understand that even if a partnership is not formed, they could still be required to account for VAT as a single taxable person if HMRC make a direction under the disaggregation rules. Explain the circumstances in which such a direction will be made.   **(3 marks)**

(c)   Although they are planning to share the forecast partnership profits of £80,000 for the year ended 31 March 2008 on the basis of 75% to Basil and 25% to Sybil, the couple want to know if it would be beneficial to instead share profits 60% to Basil and 40% to Sybil. Basil is aged 52, and will make a payment of £15,210 into a personal pension scheme. Neither Basil nor Sybil has any other income or outgoings.

Required:

Advise Basil and Sybil of the income tax and NIC implications of the two alternative profit sharing arrangements.   **(6 marks)**

(Total: 25 marks)

17   NURTURE AND OVERSEE

(a)   You are the tax advisor to the partnership of Nurture and Oversee, a firm of management consultants that commenced trading on 1 January 2004.

Until 30 September 2006 the partnership consisted of Michael Manage, Nigel Nurture and Onika Oversee, with profits being shared equally. On 30 September 2006 Michael resigned as a partner, and was replaced on 1 October 2006 by Petra Plan. Profits continued to be shared equally.

The partnership's tax adjusted trading profits since 1 January 2004 are as follows:

	£
Year ended 31 December 2004	354,000
Year ended 31 December 2005	396,000
Year ended 31 December 2006 (forecast)	420,000
Year ended 31 December 2007 (forecast)	450,000

Required:

Calculate each partner's trading income assessment for 2006/07. **(5 marks)**

(b) The partners are considering the incorporation of the partnership's business with effect from 31 December 2006. Upon incorporation the partnership's business will be transferred to a new company, NOP Ltd. Nigel, Onika and Petra will all become directors of NOP Ltd, and will each receive director's remuneration of £100,000 pa. They each have sufficient investment income to utilise their personal allowances and basic rate income tax bands.

NOP Ltd's tax adjusted trading profit for the year ended 31 December 2007 is forecast to be £450,000. This figure is *before* taking account of director's remuneration. No dividends will be paid by NOP Ltd.

Required:

Advise the partners as to whether it would be beneficial for the partnership's business to be incorporated. Your answer should be based on a calculation of:

(i)   The income tax and NIC liability of the partners for 2007/08 if the partnership is not incorporated.

(ii) The corporation tax liability of NOP Ltd for the year ended 31 December 2007, and the income tax and NIC liability of the directors for 2007/08 if the partnership is incorporated on 31 December 2006.

You should include a comparison of the respective due dates of the tax liabilities under each alternative. The tax rates for 2006/07 should be used throughout.

(11 marks)

(c) As an alternative to incorporating the partnership's business, the partners are considering the change of the partnership's accounting date from 31 December to 31 March. This will be achieved by preparing accounts for the period 1 January 2008 to 31 March 2008. The forecast tax adjusted trading profit for this period is £120,000.

(i)   State the qualifying conditions that must be met for a change of accounting date to be valid, and calculate each partner's trading income assessment for 2007/08 if the partnership changes its accounting date from 31 December to 31 March.

(6 marks)

(ii) Advise the partners of the advantages and the disadvantages for tax purposes of the partnership changing its accounting date from 31 December to 31 March.

(3 marks)

(Total: 25 marks)

18   DAVID AND PATRICIA

(a) Assume that today's date is 1 December 2006.

David is 35 years old and married to Patricia who is 32 years old. The couple have one child who is six years old.

David has been employed since 1998 earning £3,500 per month (monthly PAYE deducted £770). He will have other income in the tax year 2006/07. From 6 April 2007 he will have a source of property business income of £40,000 per year.

David intends to cease his current employment on 31 December 2006, and start trading as a self-employed businessman on 1 January 2007 preparing accounts to 31 March each year. His business plan shows profits in the region of £54,500 per year, before any payment to his wife, Patricia.

Patricia has been employed as a bookkeeper since 2000, earning £1,000 per month (monthly PAYE deducted £116). She will also cease her current employment on 31 December 2006 and will keep the books and prepare the accounts for David's business from 1 January 2007. She will continue to work the same number of hours per week as she does in her current employment.

David would like some advice on the taxation implications of involving his wife, Patricia, in his business either as an employee, or, alternatively, by taking her into partnership.

David has never previously had dealings with HMRC, so would also like details as to when he should notify HMRC about his new business for income tax purposes; when his 2006/07 self assessment income tax tax return is due; and how he should pay the income tax due on the profits made by the business in both the first and subsequent years.

Required:

(i)   Evaluate the taxation implications for David of:

(1)   David employing his wife Patricia, and

(2)   taking her into partnership.

Support your answer with calculations of the income tax (IT) and National Insurance Contributions (NIC) payable, based on the expected trading results of the first full year of operation and the tax rates and allowances for 2006/07.

(11 marks)

(ii)   State the information David requires concerning tax administration.   **(4 marks)**

(b)   Assume that today's date is 1 May 2007.

David decided to form a partnership with his wife, Patricia, sharing profits and losses equally, and to adopt a 31 March year end for accounting purposes.

The business in fact showed a loss of £40,000 in the three month period to 31 March 2007, but profits of £54,500 per annum are still anticipated for future years.

Required:

Identify the loss reliefs available to David and explain which of the available reliefs would be most beneficial for him to claim. Support your answer with calculations of the income tax (IT) saving achieved in each case.   **(10 marks)**

Assume that the tax rates and allowances for 2006/07 apply throughout this question.

(Total: 25 marks)

19   LINDA

Assume today's date is 15 June 2007.

Linda is 46, single, and has a property investment business that she has built up over several years. Her current investments are all commercial properties, mostly offices. Her business has a 31 March year end. Linda is a higher rate taxpayer.

Linda is considering the acquisition of a factory in a nearby town. The purchase date is to be 1 July 2007. The proposed purchase price is £260,000 of which £235,000 relates to the building and £25,000 to the fixtures. The building was first occupied on 1 October 2001. Linda has obtained the following information regarding the factory and its previous owner.

Year End:	31 December annually
Costs of construction	£
Land	75,000
Land preparation	25,000
Building	165,000
Fixtures	35,000
Use	
Industrial use	1 October 2001 – 31 January 2004
Temporarily unoccupied	1 February 2004 – 31 March 2004
Industrial use	1 April 2004 – 31 January 2005
Non-industrial use	1 February 2005 – 31 March 2006
Industrial use	1 April 2006 – 31 January 2007
Unoccupied	1 February 2007 – date

Linda has two prospective tenants for the factory, both of whom would occupy the building for 5 years. The first tenant, Murcia, is a law firm looking to store old documents in the factory premises. They would be prepared to pay £20,000 per year in rent. The second tenant, Navarra, is a manufacturing company, who would use the factory for manufacturing purposes. They would be prepared to pay £17,000 per year in rent. Linda expects to keep the property for another 20 years.

In May 1999 Linda had taken out a 45 year lease on a Birmingham property, paying a premium of £100,000. She had used this property as her business office until May 2006, when she assigned her interest in the lease for £115,000 in order to raise funds for other projects.

Linda also informs you of the following additional facts relating to the year ended 5 April 2007.

- Her rental income from properties amounted to £251,000.

- She paid interest costs of £115,425 on loans to buy properties.

- Other costs totalled £43,540, including a £6,400 bank fee for mortgage arrangements, a £940 survey fee, £750 professional fees relating to the purchase of a new short lease, and £400 for amending an existing short lease. All other costs related to the repair, maintenance or management of the properties and were allowable deductions against property income.

- The tax written down value of her capital allowance pool at 6 April 2006 was £85,424

- She has property business losses brought forward of £7,500 at 6 April 2006.

- Linda also had chargeable gains of £6,800 (after deductions for indextion allowance and taper relief) from the sale of capital assets. These gains do not include any gain arising on the assignment of the Birmingham lease.

Linda has been advised to put some property into a self invested personal pension scheme (SIPP). She is currently considering either buying a new factory or using another property she already owns, which is unused and has high capital growth potential for this purpose, but she does not know which to choose.

Required:

(a)   Assuming that Linda buys the factory on 1 July 2007, advise her on which of the two tenants she should choose. Support your answer with relevant calculations, including the effect of capital allowances.

(8 marks)

(b)   Calculate the chargeable gain arising on the assignment of the lease on the Birmingham property in May 2006. **(4 marks)**

(c)   Calculate the income tax (IT), national insurance contributions (NIC) and capital gains tax (CGT) payable by Linda for the tax year 2006/07, giving reasons for your treatment of each of the 'other cost' items listed. **(9 marks)**

(d)   Briefly outline the key features of a self invested personal pension scheme (SIPP) and advise Linda on the suitability of the two properties she is thinking of using for this purpose. **(4 marks)**

You may find the following information useful in answering this question:

Extract from the leasehold depreciation table:

38 years   94.189

45 years   98.059

(Total: 25 marks)

20   BOB

Assume today's date is 15 May 2007.

In March 2001, Bob was made redundant from his job as a furniture salesman. He decided to travel round the world, and did so, returning to the UK in May 2003. Bob then decided to set up his own business selling furniture. He started trading on 1 October 2003. After some initial success, the business made losses as Bob tried to win more customers. However, he was eventually successful, and the business subsequently made profits.

The results for Bob's business were as follows:

Period	Tax Trading Profits/(losses) £
1 October 2003 – 30 April 2004	3,500
1 May 2004 – 30 April 2005	(18,000)
1 May 2005 – 30 April 2006	28,000

In 2006/07, Bob required additional funds for his business, so he raised money in three ways:

(1)   Bob is a keen cricket fan, and in the 1990s, he collected many books on cricket players. To raise money, Bob started selling books from his collection. These had risen considerably in value and sold for between £150 and £300 per book. None of the books form part of a set. Bob created an internet website to advertise the books.

Bob has not declared this income, as he believes that the proceeds from selling the books are non-taxable.

(2)   He disposed of two paintings and an antique silver coffee set at auction, realising chargeable gains totalling £23,720.

(3)   Bob took a part time job in a furniture store on 1 January 2005. His annual salary has remained at £12,600 per year since he started this employment.

Bob has 5,000 shares in Willis Ltd, an unquoted trading company based in the UK. He subscribed for these shares in August 2002, paying £3 per share. On 1 December 2006, Bob received a letter informing him that the company had gone into receivership. As a result, his shares were almost worthless. The receivers dealing with the company estimated that on the liquidation of the company, he would receive no more than 10p per share for his shareholding. He has not yet received any money.

Required:

(a) Write a letter to Bob advising him on whether or not he is correct in believing that his book sales are non-taxable.

Your advice should include reference to the badges of trade and their application to this case. **(9 marks)**

(b) Assuming that the income from the sale of the books is not treated as trading income, calculate Bob's taxable income and gains for all relevant tax years, using any loss reliefs in the most tax-efficient manner.

Your answer should include an explanation of the loss reliefs available and your reasons for using (or not using) them. **(12 marks)**

Assume that the rates and allowances for 2006/07 apply throughout this part of the question.

(c) State any reliefs Bob could claim regarding the fall in value of his shares in Willis Ltd, and describe how the operation of any such reliefs could reduce Bob's taxable income. **(4 marks)**

Relevant retail price index figures are:

September	1990	129.3
April	1998	162.6
December	2006	199.2

(Total: 25 marks)

21 DONALD

(a) For this part, assume today's date is 15 August 2006.

Donald is aged 22, single, and about to finish his university education. He has plans to start up a business selling computer games, and intends to start trading on 1 April 2007, preparing accounts to 31 March annually.

He believes that his business will generate cash (equal to taxable profits) of £47,500 in the first year. He originally intended to operate as a sole trader, but he has recently discovered that as an alternative, he could operate through a company. He has been advised that if this is the case, he can take a maximum gross salary of £42,681 out of the company.

Required:

(i) Advise Donald on the income tax (IT), National Insurance (NIC) and corporation tax (CT) liabilities he will incur for the year ended 31 March 2008 trading under each of the two alternative business structures (sole trade/company).

Your advice should be supported by calculations of disposable income for both alternatives assuming that in the company case, he draws the maximum salary stated. **(8 marks)**

(ii) Assuming that Donald operates through a company, advise Donald on the corporation tax (CT) that would be payable for the year ended 31 March 2008 if he pays himself a gross salary of £31,000, plus a net dividend of £10,000, instead of a gross salary of £42,681. **(2 marks)**

(iii) Calculate the cash remaining in the company as a result of the salary and dividend payments made in (ii) above. **(2 marks)**

(b)   Donald actually decided to operate as a sole trader. The first year's results of his business were not as he had hoped, and he made a trading loss of £8,000 in the year to 31 March 2008. However, trading is now improving, and Donald has sufficient orders to ensure that the business will make profits of at least £30,000 in the year to 31 March 2009.

In order to raise funds to support his business over the last 15 months, Donald has sold a painting which was given to him on the death of his grandmother in January 1998. The probate value of the painting was £3,200, and Donald sold it for £8,084 (after deduction of 6% commission costs) in November 2007.

He also sold other assets in the year of assessment 2007/08, realising further chargeable gains of £8,775 (after indexation of £249 and taper relief of £975).

Required:

(i)   Calculate the chargeable gain on the disposal of the painting in November 2007.

(4 marks)

(ii) Write a letter to Donald advising him on the most tax efficient manner in which he can relieve the loss incurred in the year to 31 March 2008.

Your letter should briefly outline the types of loss relief available and explain their relative merits in Donald's situation.

Assume that Donald will have no source of income other than the business in the year of assessment 2007/08 and that any income he earned on a part-time basis while at university was always less than his annual personal allowance.

(9 marks)

Assume that the corporation tax rates and allowances for the Financial Year 2006 and the income tax rates and allowances for 2006/07 apply throughout this question.

Relevant retail price index figures are:

January	1998	159.5
April	1998	162.6

(Total: 25 marks)

CAPITAL GAINS TAX

22   TAHOA

Tahoa was born on 20 May 1951 and is resident and ordinarily resident in the United Kingdom. He is a 40% taxpayer and will pay any tax due in respect of the disposals set out below.

On 10 October 2006 he sold an overseas apartment in Lilliput for £128,000. He had used the apartment for regular holidays since acquiring it on 4 February 1983 for £27,000 and the indexation factor to April 1998 is 0.960. The Lilliputian tax authorities have issued a tax demand for £12,300 in respect of the gain.

During 2006/07, Tahoa made the following gifts.

1   On 22 December 2006 Tahoa gave his son, Tirua, 80,000 shares in BTP Plc. The shares were quoted at £2.70–£2.78, with recorded bargains of £2.68, £2.71, £2.72 and £2.78. The intention is that Tirua will sell the shares in 2011 when he leaves school.

Tahoa purchased 60,000 shares in BTP Plc in January 1990 for £68,000 (including indexation allowance to April 1998). He purchased a further 30,000 shares on 11 January 2005 for £56,000. BTP Plc is a trading company with an issued share capital of 12 million ordinary shares. Tahoa is not employed by the company.

2   On 18 November 2006 Tahoa gave his daughter a necklace on her wedding day. The necklace was worth £7,400 and had been inherited by Tahoa in May 1997 from his mother. Tahoa's mother purchased the necklace for £2,300 in June 1984. It was worth £4,200 when she died. The indexation factor to April 1998 is 0.036.

3   On 4 March 2007 Tahoa gave all of his 40,000 shares in AJB Ltd to a discretionary trust which he established for the benefit of his three nephews. AJB Ltd is an investment company owned in six equal shares by Tahoa, his two brothers, and their three wives. Tahoa acquired the shares in 1988 for £60,000 (including indexation allowance to April 1998) and has never worked for the company.

The relevant values of a share in AJB Ltd on 4 March 2007 were as follows:

Shareholding	Value per share £
Up to 24%	14.40
25% to 49%	18.60
50% to 70%	24.10
More than 70%	29.50

Required:

(a)   (i)   State, together with supporting calculations, the capital gains tax implications of the sale of the apartment and the three gifts and explain any available reliefs. You should ignore the annual exemption.

(ii)   Explain whether or not Tahoa can pay any of the tax due in instalments.

(14 marks)

(b)   State, together with supporting calculations, the inheritance tax implications of the three gifts. You should ignore the annual exemption.
(5 marks)

(c)   State the income tax implications of the gifts of shares.
(3 marks)

(Total: 22 marks)

23   DELIA JONES

Delia Jones, aged 42, has been running a successful restaurant business as a sole trader since 1 September 1996. She has recently accepted an offer from Fastfood Ltd, an unconnected company quoted on the Alternative Investment Market, to purchase her business. Fastfood Ltd would like to complete the purchase on 31 March 2007, but are prepared to delay until 30 April 2007 should this be beneficial for Delia. The purchase consideration will consist of either cash or ordinary shares in Fastfood Ltd. The following information is available:

(1)   Delia's tax adjusted trading profits are as follows:

	£
Year ended 31 August 2005	65,400
Year ended 31 August 2006	77,200
Period ended 31 March 2007 (forecast)	58,500
April 2007 (forecast)	9,000

The figures for the years ended 31 August 2005 and 2006 are adjusted for capital allowances, whilst those for the period ended 31 March 2007 and for April 2007 are before taking account of capital allowances. Delia has overlap profits brought forward of £24,200.

(2) The forecast market values of Delia's business assets at both 31 March 2007 and
30 April 2007 are as follows:

	£
Goodwill	125,000
Freehold property (A)	462,000
Freehold property (B)	118,000
Fixtures and fittings	240,000
Net current liabilities	(95,000)
	850,000

Freehold property (A) cost £230,000 in 1995 (indexed to April 1998). Freehold
property (B) was purchased during June 2006 for £94,000. The goodwill has a nil cost.

(3) The tax written down value of the fixtures and fittings at 31 August 2006 was
£114,000. Fixtures and fittings costing £31,000 were purchased on 15 December 2006.
All of Delia's fixtures and fittings qualify as plant and machinery for capital
allowances purposes, and are being sold for less than original cost.

(4) Delia has unused capital losses of £12,400 brought forward from 2005/06.

(5) Delia currently has no other income or outgoings. Her investment income will exceed
£40,000 pa for 2007/08 onwards, regardless of whether the consideration is taken as
cash or shares.

(6) Delia will not become an employee or director of Fastfood Ltd. If the consideration is
in the form of shares in Fastfood Ltd, then Delia's holding will represent 7.5% of the
company's share capital. Delia will sell the shares at regular intervals over the next ten
years.

(7) Both Delia and Fastfood Ltd are registered for VAT.

Required:

(a) Assuming that the business is sold on 31 March 2007 with the consideration being
wholly in the form of cash:

  (i)   Calculate Delia's trading income assessment for 2006/07.   **(5 marks)**

  (ii) Calculate Delia's CGT liability for 2006/07.   **(6 marks)**

  (iii) Advise Delia of the VAT implications arising from the sale.   **(2 marks)**

(b) Advise Delia as to the income tax, CGT and NIC implications of:

  (i)   Delaying the sale of the business until 30 April 2007.   **(7 marks)**

  (ii) Taking the consideration wholly in the form of ordinary shares in Fastfood Ltd,
        rather than as cash.   **(5 marks)**

You should assume that the tax rates and allowances for 2006/07 apply throughout.

(Total: 25 marks)

24   ARMADA ENTERPRISES

Basil is planning to incorporate his sole trader business, Armada Enterprises, on 31 January 2008 and wants some advice regarding the capital taxes position.

You ascertain the following:

In December 1993 Basil's wife had transferred 10,000 shares in Moonbeam plc, a quoted UK trading company, into joint ownership with Basil. At that date the shares were quoted at 1004 – 1008. The total shares issued by Moonbeam plc are 10 million. Basil's wife acquired these shares in April 1986 for £50,000. She died in a car accident in September 1997 when the shares were quoted at 988 – 996. Under the terms of her will these shares were transferred solely into Basil's ownership.

Basil acquired an additional 2,000 Moonbeam plc shares in May 2002 for £10,500 before selling all of the shares in June 2003 for £78,000.

The proceeds from the share sale and some additional personal funds were used to acquire Armada Enterprises in July 2003. The assets acquired together with the price paid for them in July 2003 and their current market values are as follows:

	Price paid in July 2003	Current value
	£	£
Freehold land & buildings	50,000	80,000
Goodwill	25,000	40,000
Stock	5,000	5,000
Plant & machinery	10,000	8,000*
Trade debtors	–	10,000
	90,000	143,000

* No individual item of plant & machinery has a value in excess of its cost.

Required:

(a)   Calculate the capital gain or loss arising on the disposal of Basil's shareholding in Moonbeam plc in June 2003. Your answer should include an explanation of the Capital Gains Tax base costs used.   **(8 marks)**

Retail Price Indices	April 1986	97.87
	December 1993	141.9
	September 1997	159.3
	April 1998	162.6
	May 2002	176.2
	June 2003	181.3

(b)   Assuming that the total consideration of £143,000 for the transfer of Armada Enterprises to the limited company will be a mixture of ordinary shares and cash:

   (i)   State the principal conditions that need to be satisfied for the incorporation of Armada Enterprises to qualify for the form of Capital Gains Tax rollover relief available upon a transfer of an unincorporated business to a limited company.

   (ii)   Calculate the amount of cash consideration that Basil can receive before he becomes liable to Capital Gains Tax.

   (iii)   Briefly explain any potential tax related disadvantages of receiving this form of rollover relief.   **(13 marks)**

Assume that the tax rates and allowances for 2006/07 apply throughout.

(Total: 21 marks)

25 PAUL AND SUSAN

Assume that today's date is 1 April 2007.

Paul is 40 years old and his wife, Susan, is 35 years old. The couple have two children, a son aged six and a daughter aged nine.

Susan is employed and earns a salary of £15,000 per year.

Paul is also employed and earns a salary of £40,000 per year. He owns two properties, Property A and Property B, which he rents out. Both of the properties are furnished and Property A qualifies as furnished holiday accommodation.

Income and expenses for the two properties for 2006/07 are as follows:

	£
Property A	
Rental income	2,000
Management expenses	1,500
Capital allowances	1,200
Interest on a loan to purchase the property	1,000
Property B	
Rental income	4,000
Management expenses	700

Paul had a property business loss brought forward of £3,000, at 6 April 2006.

Paul received dividends of £6,000 from his shareholding in Alpha plc and £9,750 from his shareholding in Beta Ltd, during the 2006/07 tax year (see further below).

Paul had no other sources of taxable income in the 2006/07 tax year.

Paul disposed of the following assets in January 2007:

		Date purchased	Purchase cost £	Disposal proceeds £
(1)	Vintage car	1 June 1998	20,000	47,500
(2)	Racehorse	1 August 2001	35,000	55,000
(3)	Painting	1 May 2000	4,800	5,750
(4)	Antique vase	1 November 1996	7,250	5,200
(5)	Diamond ring	1 January 1999	5,400	6,600

Paul owns the following shareholdings:

(1) A 4% holding in Alpha plc, a quoted trading company. These shares were bought in August 1991 for £65,000 and have a current market value of £100,000.

(2) 30% of the £1 ordinary shares in Beta Ltd, an unquoted trading company. Paul had originally acquired this 30% holding in Beta Ltd in March 2005 for £100,000.

The remaining shares in Beta Ltd are held as follows:

Paul's wife – Susan	55%
Paul's father	10%
Unconnected persons	5%

The current (April 2007) values of the Beta Ltd shares have been agreed by HMRC as follows:

% holding	£
95%	925,000
85%	765,000
80%	645,000
70%	490,000
15%	100,000

Paul intends to gift either his entire holding in Alpha plc or one half of his holding in Beta Ltd to his son on 3 April 2007.

In March 2006 Paul transferred £400,000 into a discretionary trust for his daughter. Other than this, Paul has made no previous lifetime transfers for the purposes of inheritance tax. His wife, Susan has never made any gifts of capital assets.

Required:

(a) (i) State the conditions necessary for a property to qualify as furnished holiday accommodation. **(2 marks)**

(ii) Calculate Paul's taxable income for 2006/07, assuming that any beneficial elections are made and that the amount of discretionary trust income chargeable on Paul, as settlor, is zero. **(3 marks)**

(b) (i) Calculate Paul's capital gains tax (CGT) liability, if any, on the disposals of assets made by him in January 2007, assuming that the April 2007 disposals do not take place. **(4 marks)**

(ii) Explain the taxation implications of gifting either the shareholding in Alpha plc or the shareholding in Beta Ltd on 3 April 2007. Support your answer with relevant capital gains tax (CGT) and inheritance tax (IHT) calculations.

(10 marks)

(iii) Assuming that Paul decides to gift the quoted shares in Alpha plc, advise him of any courses of action relating to the disposal of these shares, which could reduce or eliminate the tax liabilities identified in (ii) above. **(6 marks)**

Relevant retail price index figures are:

August 1991	134.1
November 1996	153.9
April 1998	162.6

(Total: 25 marks)

26   DYLAN

Assume today's date is 8 January 2007.

Dylan, aged 45, is married to Ermintrude, aged 40. The couple do not have any children. Both Dylan and Ermintrude have lived in the United Kingdom all of their lives. Dylan and Ermintrude have come to you with some tax issues on which they would like advice. They are both higher rate taxpayers.

Dylan has 5,000 shares in Puligny plc a UK resident, trading company. This shareholding represents less than 5% of the issued share capital of the company. These shares cost £2.50 each in November 1996. He sold the entire shareholding on 6 April 2006 for £4.25 per share. Dylan was an employee of Puligny plc from 1 May 1996 until 6 April 2002.

Dylan owns a sole trader business, a shop selling fine art, which he started in 1994. In the next month or so, he wants to incorporate this business, with himself as the sole shareholder. The business has built up a good reputation. He estimates that he will have a capital gain of £65,000 after indexation but prior to taper relief.

The assets and estimated capital gains on incorporation are as follows:

Asset	Cost	Market value	Estimated capital gains (after indexation allowance, but before taper relief)
	£	£	£
Stock	30,000	30,000	Nil
Goodwill	Nil	50,000	50,000
Property	60,000	80,000	15,000

The consideration for the shares in the company will be the assets of the business.

Dylan understands that there are two ways in which capital gains tax relief can be obtained when incorporating a business, and he would like advice on the relative benefits of these reliefs in this case.

In May 1991, Dylan inherited some land on the death of his uncle.

- The probate value of the land, in May 1991, was £100,000.

- Dylan gifted the land to Ermintrude in July 1996 when the land was worth £400,000.

- In November 2003 Ermintrude sold a third of the land, for sale proceeds of £200,000, when the portion of land sold was really worth £250,000, to her sister, Florence. At the date of sale, the remaining two thirds of the land was valued at £600,000.

- In May 2006 Ermintrude gifted the remaining two thirds of the land to an unconnected third party, Zebedee, when the market value of the two thirds of the land was £800,000.

- The land has never been used for business purposes.

Required:

(a) Calculate Dylan's chargeable gain (after taper relief) on the sale of his shares in Puligny plc. Assume the current definition of business assets applied throughout the whole period of ownership. **(4 marks)**

(b) Identify the two capital gains tax (CGT) deferral reliefs available to Dylan on the incorporation of his business, stating the conditions necessary for each relief to be given, including the time limit for any claims to be made.

You are not required to consider the use of either an Enterprise Investment Scheme (EIS) or a Venture Capital Trust (VCT). **(7 marks)**

(c) Assuming that Dylan has decided to retain the business property as a personal asset, rather than transferring it to the company, and to charge rent to the company for the use of the property.

  (i) State the effect, if any, of retaining the property, on the availability of the capital gains tax (CGT) deferral reliefs identified in (b) above. **(1 mark)**

  (ii) Calculate the maximum amount of cash sale proceeds Dylan could receive for the sale of the goodwill to the new company, without incurring a capital gains tax (CGT) liability. **(2 marks)**

  (iii) Advise Dylan and the new company of the tax consequences, if any, of Dylan retaining the property and charging rent to the company. **(2 marks)**

(d) Explain both the capital gains tax (CGT) and inheritance tax (IHT) implications of each of the following transactions:

    (i) the gift of the land by Dylan to Ermintrude in July 1996

    (ii) the sale of one third of the land by Ermintrude to Florence in November 2003

    (iii) the gift of the remaining two thirds of the land by Ermintrude to Zebedee in May 2006.

Support your explanations with calculations, where appropriate.　　　　**(7 marks)**

Relevant retail price index figures are:

May 1991	133.5
July 1996	152.4
November 1996	153.9
April 1998	162.6

(Total: 23 marks)

27　GRAEME

Graeme, aged 57, is married to Catherine, aged 58. They work as medical consultants, and both are higher rate taxpayers. Barry, their son, is aged 32. Graeme, Catherine and Barry are all UK resident, ordinarily resident and domiciled. Graeme has come to you for some tax advice.

Graeme has invested in shares for some time, in particular shares in Thistle Dubh Limited. He informs you of the following transactions in Thistle Dubh Limited shares:

(i) In December 1986, on the death of his grandmother, he inherited 10,000 £1 ordinary shares in Thistle Dubh Limited, an unquoted UK trading company providing food supplies for sporting events. The probate value of the shares was 360p per share.

(ii) In March 1992, he took up a rights issue, buying one share for every two held. The price paid for the rights shares was £10 per share.

(iii) In October 1999, the company underwent a reorganisation, and the ordinary shares were split into two new classes of ordinary share – 'T' shares and 'D' shares, each with differing rights. Graeme received two 'T' and three 'D' shares for each original Thistle Dubh Limited share held. The market values for the 'T' shares and the 'D' shares on the date of reorganisation were 135p and 405p per share respectively.

(iv) On 1 May 2006, Graeme sold 12,000 'T' shares. The market values for the 'T' shares and the 'D' shares on that day were 300p and 600p per share respectively.

(v) In October 2006, Graeme sold all of his 'D' shares for £85,000.

(vi) The current market value of 'T' shares is 384p per share. The shares remain unquoted.

Graeme and Catherine have owned a holiday cottage in a remote part of the UK for many years. In recent years, they have used the property infrequently, as they have taken their holidays abroad and the cottage has been let out as furnished holiday accommodation.

Graeme and Catherine are now considering selling the UK country cottage and purchasing a holiday villa abroad. Initially they plan to let this villa out on a furnished basis, but following their anticipated retirement, would expect to occupy the property for a significant part of the year themselves, possibly moving to live in the villa permanently.

Required:

(a) Calculate the total chargeable gains arising on Graeme's disposals of 'T' and 'D' ordinary shares in May and October 2006 respectively.　　　**(7 marks)**

(b) Explain the capital gains tax (CGT) and inheritance tax (IHT) implications of Graeme gifting his remaining 'T' ordinary shares at their current value either:

(i) to his wife, Catherine; or

(ii) to his son, Barry.

Your answer should be supported by relevant calculations and clearly identify the availability and effect of any reliefs (other than the CGT annual exemption) that might be used to reduce or defer any tax liabilities arising. **(9 marks)**

(c) Advise Graeme of the potential CGT and income tax (IT) implications of selling the UK country cottage and replacing it with a holiday villa abroad as proposed.

You are not required to discuss the income tax treatment of the UK country cottage. **(9 marks)**

Relevant retail price index figures are:

December	1986	99.6
March	1992	136.7
April	1998	162.6

(Total: 25 marks)

RESIDENCE ISSUES

28 DANIELLA DRAKE

Daniella Drake is a key employee of Drew Jenner Whisky, the UK subsidiary of multi-national distillers Bourbon Inc. On 1 December 2006 she was seconded to work for the group's Swiss subsidiary on an 18 month assignment. During the secondment Daniella's salary will continue to be paid by Drew Jenner Whisky. Until 30 November 2006 she had always been resident and ordinarily resident in the UK. Daniella has no intention of changing her domicile.

(1) Daniella is paid a salary at the UK equivalent rate of £34,500 per annum. In addition she has use of an Audi Quattro 2.2 litre that had a list price of £24,000 when made available to her in 2003. The company provide her with petrol for both business and private use. In the eight months to 30 November 2006 Daniella had travelled 12,500 miles in the car on business. The car will not be available to her once she leaves the UK. Its carbon dioxide emissions are 180 g/km.

(2) The company contributes to a personal pension scheme on Daniella's behalf with Saxa plc at the rate of 9% of her salary. The company also pays premiums into a group permanent health insurance policy in respect of its employees and has taken out key person insurance on Daniella's life for the sum of £156,000.

(3) In 1997 Daniella bought 10,000 shares in Bourbon Inc. when she became an employee of the group. The cost of the shares indexed to April 1998 is £46,400. On 3 April 2007 she sold 5,000 shares for £54,000. The shares in Bourbon Inc. only count as business assets for taper relief purposes from 6 April 2000.

(4) Bourbon Inc paid dividends in September 2006 and March 2007 of £4,500 and £2,340 both net of 10% withholding tax.

(5) Daniella invested £580 per month into a 2003/04 UK equity fund ISA managed by Venus Investments and £580 per month into a 2004/05 Global Technology ISA with the same company.

(6) From 1 December 2006 Daniella has arranged to let her main residence, a flat in Woodside Place in Glasgow at £1,175 per month.

Required:

(a) Explain why Daniella will be treated as not resident or ordinarily resident in the UK during the eighteen month period working overseas commencing on 1 December 2006. **(3 marks)**

(b) (i) Calculate the UK income tax liability by Daniella for 2006/07. **(8 marks)**

(ii) Advise Daniella of her UK CGT liability for 2006/07. **(3 marks)**

(iii) Explain why it would have been beneficial for Daniella to have delayed the disposal of the shares in Bourbon Inc. on 3 April 2007 until 6 April 2007. **(2 marks)**

(c) (i) Explain how Drew Jenner Whisky might continue making approved pension contributions following Daniella's departure from the UK. **(1 mark)**

(ii) Explain how the payment of Daniella's salary and the premiums for group permanent health insurance and key person insurance will be treated in Drew Jenner Whisky's corporation tax computation following Daniella's departure from the UK. **(1 mark)**

(iii) Explain how Daniella's investment in ISAs will be affected following her departure from the UK. **(2 marks)**

(Total: 20 marks)

29 BUXUS

You have recently received a letter from a new personal client, Buxus. Extracts from this letter read as follows:

'As you know on 31 October 2006 I resigned as a director of Buxus Limited and on 1 November 2006 I went to work as a full time director of our newly formed overseas subsidiary Abies Inc, a company operating in the country of Abelia.

My contract of employment with Abies Inc is for an initial two year period and states that all of my duties will be performed in Abelia, with Abies Inc paying all of my overseas salary.

My earnings in the 2006/07 tax year are as follows:

Buxus Limited £14,625 (PAYE deducted – £2,134)

Abies Inc £12,000 (Abelian income tax deducted £2,500)

In addition I received gross dividend income from Buxus Limited of £22,000 on 28 February 2007.

For the 2006/07 tax year I paid for all of my travelling expenses between the UK and Abelia personally but it is proposed that either Buxus Limited or Abies Inc will start reimbursing these in the current 2007/08 tax year.

On 1 March 2007 I gifted 75% of a property, used by Buxus Limited, to my son Acer. I bought this property on 6 October 1996 for £75,000 with incidental acquisition costs amounting to £2,500. On 7 November 1998 a further £38,000 was spent on improving this property. Since 6 October 1996 only 60% of this property has been used in the trade of Buxus Limited. The remainder has been let to third parties for an annual rent of £3,600. The value of the entire property as at 1 March 2007 was £250,000.'

You ascertain the following additional information:

1 Buxus was born on 30 September 1965.

2 Buxus Limited is a UK resident trading company. Buxus owns 20% of the issued ordinary share capital of this company.

3   There is no double tax treaty between the UK and Abelia.

4   RPI factors are as follows:

October 1996   153.8
April 1998   162.6
November 1998   164.4
March 2007   200.4

Required:

Make notes in order to respond to Buxus which includes:

(a)   A calculation of his UK Income Tax payable for the 2006/07 tax year.

Your letter should explain to Buxus the rules governing the extent to which his income is liable to UK income tax for this tax year.

(b)   A brief explanation of whether the travelling expenses should be reimbursed from Buxus Limited or Abies Inc.

(c)   An explanation of the Capital Gains Tax implications arising from the gift of the interest in the property to his son.

Your letter should include a calculation of any Capital Gains Tax payable assuming that any beneficial claims or elections are made and also explain to him whether it might have been better if he had waited until after 5 April 2007 before making this gift.

Marks are allocated on the following basis:	Presentation	**(2 marks)**
	(a)	**(7 marks)**
	(b)	**(3 marks)**
	(c)	**(8 marks)**
		(Total: 20 marks)

ADMINISTRATION

30   BARRY BLOCK

You should assume that today's date is 15 March 2007.

Barry Block has been a self-employed builder since 1985. His income for 2006/07 is forecast to be as follows:

(1)   Tax adjusted trading profits of £28,500 for the year ended 5 April 2007.

(2)   On 1 April 2007 Barry is planning to let out an unfurnished property. On that date he will receive a premium of £5,000 for the grant of a ten year lease, and rent of £450 for the month of April 2007.

(3)   Building society interest of £360 (net) and dividends of £9,540 (net).

(4)   On 25 March 2007 Barry is planning to sell an antique painting for £18,500. The painting was bought during 1983, and has an indexed cost of £3,130.

Barry is a widower with a daughter aged 19, and has no other income and outgoings. He will make payments on account of his 2006/07 tax liability totalling £2,640.

Barry is concerned that he will have a high tax liability to pay on 31 January 2008, and therefore wants your advice regarding the following actions that could be undertaken during April 2007:

(1)   The trading profit of £28,500 is calculated after taking account of a weekly wage of £60 that Barry pays to his 19 year old daughter for acting as his secretary. This is significantly less than Barry would have to pay if he employed a secretary, and so he is considering the payment of a bonus of £2,500 to his daughter on 5 April 2007. The daughter has no other income or outgoings.

(2)   The tenant of the unfurnished property that is to be let on 1 April 2007 is prepared to delay the tenancy agreement until 6 April 2007.

(3)   The purchaser of the antique painting that is to be sold on 25 March 2007 for £17,500 is prepared to postpone the transaction until 6 April 2007.

Required:

(a)   Calculate Barry's liability to income tax, Class 4 NIC and CGT for 2006/07, and the amount of tax that he will have to pay on 31 January 2008.

Your answer should be *before* taking accounting of any of the actions that Barry could undertake during April 2007.   **(11 marks)**

(b)   (i)   Advise Barry of the implications if the tax due on 31 January 2008 is paid late.
                                                                                        (2 marks)

        (ii)   Advise Barry of the circumstances in which he will be able to make a claim to reduce his payments on account for 2007/08, and the implications if such a claim proves to be excessive.   **(3 marks)**

(c)   Explain the tax implications of each of the actions that Barry could undertake during April 2007. Your answer should be supported by appropriate calculations.

You should assume that in all circumstances Barry will be a basic rate taxpayer in 2007/08, and that the tax rates and allowances for 2006/07 apply throughout.
                                                                                        (9 marks)

                                                                        (Total: 25 marks)

31   CECILE GRAND

(a)   Cecile Grand has been a self-employed antiques dealer since 1988. Her income for 2005/06 was as follows:

	£
Adjusted trading profit	34,900
Dividends (net)	4,860
Property business profit	800
Chargeable gain	7,800

The chargeable gain was in respect of a let property that was sold on 30 June 2005. The property business profit is for the period 6 April 2005 to 30 June 2005. Cecile has been a widow for five years, and she has a 20 year old daughter.

Her forecast income for 2006/07 is as follows:

	£
Adjusted trading profit	21,750
Dividends (net)	4,320
Chargeable gain	20,850

The chargeable gain is in respect of quoted shares sold on 30 July 2006. Due to the fall in profits, Cecile will not pay a personal pension contribution during 2005/06.

Required:

(i) Calculate Cecile's payments on account and balancing payment or repayment for 2006/07. You should assume that Cecile *does not* make a claim to reduce her payments on accounts, and that the rates and allowances for 2006/07 apply throughout. **(10 marks)**

(ii) Based on the above figures, advise Cecile of the amount of the maximum claim that she could make to reduce her payments on account for 2006/07 . **(2 marks)**

(b) Cecile's adjusted trading profit for 2006/07 is an estimated figure based on her provisional accounts for the year ended 31 March 2007. The actual figures will not be available until 31 August 2007, because of the difficulty that Cecile has in separating antiques acquired for business purposes, from those acquired for private purposes.

Required:

(i) Assuming that Cecile makes the maximum claim to reduce the payments on account for 2006/07, explain the tax implications if her actual taxable income for 2006/07 is higher than the estimated figure. **(2 marks)**

(ii) Advise Cecile of the powers that HMRC have with regard to enquiring into her tax return for 2006/07. **(2 marks)**

(iii) Briefly advise Cecile of the tax implications if HMRC enquire into her tax return for 2006/07, and decide that the trading profits for the year ended 31 March 2007 are understated. **(2 marks)**

(c) Cecile is planning to change her accounting date from 31 March to 30 September by preparing her next accounts for the six month period to 30 September 2007. The forecast profit for this period is £18,000.

Required:

(:) State the qualifying conditions that must be met for Cecile's change of accounting date to be valid. **(2 marks)**

(ii) Explain the tax implications of Cecile changing her accounting date from 31 March to 30 September.

Your answer should include a calculation of Cecile's trading income assessment for 2007/08. **(2 marks)**

(iii) Briefly advise Cecile of the advantages and disadvantages for tax purposes, of changing her accounting date from 31 March to 30 September. **(3 marks)**

(Total: 25 marks)

32   MIN CHEW

(a) Min Chew has been running a management consultancy business as a sole trader since 1 January 1996. He has always produced accounts to 5 April. Min is concerned that he will have a high tax liability to pay on 31 January 2008 as a result of the successful year that he has had to 5 April 2007.

(1) Min's tax adjusted trading profit for the year ended 5 April 2007 is £72,800. This figure is before taking account of capital allowances. He has no other income for 2006/07.

(2)   The tax written down values for capital allowances purposes as at 6 April 2006 are as follows:

	£
General pool	26,400
Expensive motor car	16,400
Computer (short-life asset)	2,600

The following transactions took place during the year ended 5 April 2007:

10 April 2006	Purchased office furniture for £16,750
5 July 2006	Purchased a motor car for £9,800. This was for the use of an employee.
28 August 2006	Sold the expensive motor car for £18,300 (the original cost was £22,400) and purchased a new motor car for £25,700. These motor cars were used by Min with 30% of the mileage being for private purposes. Neither of the cars were low emission cars.
7 March 2007	Scrapped the current computer subject to a short-life asset claim, and purchased new computer equipment for £7,200.

(3)   For 2005/06 Min had an income tax liability of £3,870, a Class 4 NIC liability of £860 and a CGT liability of £1,340.

Required:

Calculate Min's liability to income tax and Class 4 NIC for 2006/07 , and the amount of tax that he will have to pay on 31 January 2008.

Your answer should show the written down values of capital allowances carried forward at 5 April 2007.   **(10 marks)**

(b)   Min has received an offer to sell his business to an unrelated third party for £750,000, with the purchase consideration being paid in cash. If the offer is accepted, the sale will take place on 30 June 2007. The purchase consideration is made up as follows:

	£
Goodwill	440,000
Freehold property	265,000
Fixtures and fittings	30,000
Motor car	8,000
Computer equipment	7,000
	750,000

The goodwill has a nil cost. The freehold property was purchased in 1994 and has an indexed cost up to April 1998 of £110,000. The fixtures and fittings all qualify as plant and machinery for capital allowances purposes, and are being sold for less than original cost. The figures for the motorcar and computer equipment relate to the purchases on 5 July 2006 and 7 March 2007 respectively. On 30 June 2007 Min will personally retain the motor car purchased on 28 August 2006. Its value on that date will be £20,000.

Min's tax adjusted trading profit for the period 6 April to 30 June 2007 will be £28,000. This figure is before taking account of capital allowances. He will receive building society interest of £2,800 (net) and dividends of £4,500 (net) during 2007/08.

Required:

Assuming that the business is sold on 30 June 2007 and that the tax rates, allowances and reliefs for 2006/07 apply throughout.

(i)   Advise Min of the amount of the maximum claim that he could make to reduce his payments on account for 2007/08.   **(9 marks)**

(ii)   Advise Min of his CGT liability for 2007/08.   **(6 marks)**

(Total: 25 marks)

INHERITANCE TAX

33   DOROTHY LAKE

You are the tax advisor to Dorothy Lake, aged 75. Under the terms of her will, Dorothy has left her entire estate to her daughter Alice, since Dorothy's husband is wealthy in his own right. Dorothy does not expect to live past her eightieth birthday which is on 31 December 2011, and she therefore wants to know whether or not it would be beneficial for tax purposes to make a lifetime gift of assets to Alice.

The gift will be made on 30 June 2007, and will consist of the following assets:

(1)   50,000 £1 ordinary shares in Windermere Ltd, an unquoted trading company. Dorothy owns a total of 100,000 shares in Windermere Ltd, and her husband also owns 100,000 shares in the company. Windermere Ltd has an issued share capital of 400,000 £1 ordinary shares. At present, the relevant values of Windermere Ltd's shares are as follows:

Shareholding	Value per share
	£
50%	4.50
37.5%	3.55
25%	2.95
12.5%	2.50

By 31 December 2011, these values are likely to have increased by 40%. Windermere Ltd owns investments in quoted shares that represent 12% of the value of its total assets.

Dorothy originally acquired 50,000 £1 ordinary shares in Coniston Ltd in March 1988 for £96,000. Coniston Ltd was taken over by Windermere Ltd on 15 October 1997, at which time Dorothy received two £1 ordinary shares in Windermere Ltd and £0.80 in cash for each share held in Coniston Ltd. On 15 October 1997 a 25% holding of Windermere Ltd's ordinary shares was worth £1.20 per share. Dorothy has never been a director of either Coniston Ltd or Windermere Ltd.

Alice is a risk averse investor, and would therefore sell the shares in Windermere Ltd soon after receiving them.

(2)   An antique painting worth £8,500. This was acquired in June 1988 for £1,400. The painting is not likely to change in value before 31 December 2011.

(3)   A holiday cottage worth £165,000. Dorothy inherited the cottage on the death of her sister in May 1997 when it was worth £188,000. Because the cottage is situated on cliffs that are being eroded, it is only likely to be worth £105,000 on 31 December 2011. The cottage does not qualify to be treated as a furnished holiday letting.

Dorothy has other assets worth £350,000, has not made any previous lifetime transfers of assets, has not disposed of any assets during 2007/08, and is a 40% taxpayer. Apart from the shares in Windermere Ltd, it is likely that the assets gifted to Alice will still be owned by her at the date of Dorothy's death. Alice is also a 40% taxpayer.

Required:

Advise Dorothy of whether or not it would be beneficial for tax purposes to make the gift of assets to Alice on 30 June 2007.

Your answer should include a calculation of the inheritance tax and capital gains tax liabilities that would arise if Dorothy:

(a)   *Makes* the gift to Alice on 30 June 2007.

(b)   Does *not make* the gift to Alice on 30 June 2007.

You should assume that Dorothy dies on 31 December 2011, that wherever possible, elections or claims are made to postpone tax liabilities, and that the tax rates and allowances for 2006/07 apply throughout.

Your answer should show the due date of any IHT liabilities, and the amount of IHT that can be paid under the instalment option. You should include any tax planning advice that you consider to be relevant.

(25 marks)

34   JANE MACBETH

(a)   Jane Macbeth, aged 61, died on 20 November 2006. At the date of her death Jane owned the following assets:

(1)   A main residence valued at £235,000. This has an outstanding repayment mortgage of £40,000.

(2)   Building society deposits of £87,000.

(3)   10,000 £1 ordinary shares in Banquo plc. On 20 November 2006 the shares were quoted at 945–957, with bargains on that day of 937, 961 and 939.

Jane inherited the shares as a specific gift on the death of her sister on 10 August 2004 when they were valued at £68,000. The sister's executors paid IHT of £54,000 on an estate valued at £360,000.

(4)   A life assurance policy on her own life. Immediately prior to the date of Jane's death, the policy had an open market value of £86,000. Proceeds of £104,000 were received following her death.

(5)   Agricultural land valued at £168,000, but with an agricultural value of £110,000. The land was purchased during 1991, and it has always been let to tenant farmers. The most recent tenancy commenced on 1 January 2003.

Jane made the following gifts during her lifetime (any IHT arising was paid by Jane):

(1)   On 28 November 1998 she made a cash gift of £92,000 into a discretionary trust.

(2)   On 15 April 2002 she made a gift of 50,000 shares in Shakespeare Ltd, an unquoted trading company, to her son as a wedding gift. The shares were valued at £155,000, and were originally acquired by Jane in 1991. Her son still owned the shares on 20 November 2006. Shakespeare Ltd has 20% of the value of its total assets invested in quoted shares.

(3)   On 10 March 2003 she made a cash gift of £268,000 into a discretionary trust.

Jane's husband Duncan is wealthy in his own right. Under the terms of her will Jane has therefore left a specific gift of £100,000 to her brother, with the residue of the estate being left to her children.

Required:

(i)   Calculate the IHT that will be payable as a result of Jane's death. Assume that the tax rates and allowances for 2006/07 apply throughout. **(15 marks)**

(ii)   State who is primarily liable for the tax, the due dates of the IHT liabilities, the amount of IHT that can be paid under the instalment option, and the amount of inheritance that will be received by Jane's children. **(4 marks)**

(b)   Jane's husband Duncan is aged 58. He is in good health, and expects to live for at least ten more years.

The Macbeth family appreciate that Jane's estate may not have been distributed in a tax efficient manner. They have therefore agreed that the terms of her will are to be varied so that the entire estate is left to Duncan.

Duncan will then make gifts totalling £500,000 to the children and Jane's brother during 2007 and 2008.

Required:

(i)   State the conditions that must be met in order that the variation of the terms of Jane's will is valid for IHT purposes. **(2 marks)**

(ii)   Advise the Macbeth family of the IHT implications of the proposed plan. You are not expected to calculate the revised IHT liability or to consider anti-avoidance legislation. **(4 marks)**

(Total: 25 marks)

35   MING WONG

Ming Wong, aged 63, was born in the country of Yanga, but has lived in the UK since 6 April 1992. Ming is resident and ordinarily resident in the UK, but is not domiciled in the UK. Following her marriage to a UK citizen, Ming is planning to become UK domiciled.

Ming is employed by the Yangan National Bank in London, and was paid a salary of £34,220 during 2006/07 . At 5 April 2007 Ming owned the following assets:

(1)   A main residence valued at £245,000. This is situated in the UK, and has an outstanding endowment mortgage of £80,000.

(2)   A house in Yanga worth £60,000, from which rental income of £7,500 (gross) was received during 2006/07 . Yangan tax at the rate of 35% was paid on the rental income.

(3)   40,000 shares in Ganyan Inc., a company quoted on the Yangan Stock Exchange at 308 – 316. Dividends of £5,950 (net) were received during 2006/07, after the deduction of Yangan tax at the rate of 15%.

(4)   Antiques worth £61,500. These were bought in Yanga, but are now situated in Ming's UK residence.

(5)   Bank deposits of £58,000 with the Yangan National Bank, of which £38,000 is held at the London branch and £20,000 at the main branch in Yanga. During 2006/07 interest of £1,680 (net) was credited to the account in London, and £1,530 (net of Yangan tax at the rate of 15%) was credited to the account in Yanga.

(6)   An interest-free loan of £15,000 to Ming's brother who is resident in Yanga. The loan was used to purchase property situated in the UK.

None of the income arising in Yanga has been remitted to the UK.

Ming has made no lifetime gifts.

Under the terms of her will, Ming has left all of her assets to her three children. If she were to die, Yangan death duty of £13,600 would be payable in respect of the house situated in Yanga and £34,400 in respect of the 40,000 shares in Ganyan Inc., irrespective of her domicile. No foreign death duty is payable in respect of the Yanga bank account.

There is no double taxation agreement between the UK and Yanga. All of the above figures are in pounds sterling.

You are required to:

(a)   Advise Ming of

      (i)   when she will be treated as domiciled in the UK for the purposes of IHT, and

      (ii)   how she could acquire domicile in the UK under general law.   **(4 marks)**

(b)   Advise Ming as to the potential increase in her liability to UK IHT if she were to become domiciled in the UK.

      Your answer should include an explanation of why Ming's assets are or are not subject to UK IHT.   **(12 marks)**

(c)   (i)   Calculate the UK income tax payable by Ming for 2006/07.

      (ii)   Calculate the additional UK income tax that would have been payable by Ming for 2006/07 if she had been domiciled in the UK as from 6 April 2006.

                                                               (9 marks)

                                                             (Total: 25 marks)

36   JOAN ARK

Joan Ark, aged 76, has asked for your advice regarding the following gifts that she has made during 2006/07:

(a)   On 30 May 2006 Joan made a gift of 250,000 ordinary shares in Orleans plc, a quoted company into a discretionary trust for the benefit of her granddaughters. On that day the shares were quoted at 146 – 150, with recorded bargains of 140, 144, 149 and 155. Joan originally purchased 200,000 shares in Orleans plc during 1993 at a cost of £149,000 (indexed to April 1998). Joan also bought 75,000 shares on 15 August 2005 for £69,375 and has subsequently bought 10,000 shares on 21 July 2006 for £14,800. Orleans plc has an issued share capital of 10 million ordinary shares and Joan has never been a director or employee of the company.

(b)   On 15 June 2006 Joan gave 20,000 of her 40,000 ordinary shares in Rouen Ltd, an unquoted trading company, to her son Michael. Rouen Ltd has an issued share capital of 100,000 ordinary shares. Joan's husband also owns 40,000 ordinary shares in the company. On 15 June 2006 the relevant values of Rouen Ltd's shares were as follows:

Shareholding	Value per share £
100%	22.30
80%	17.10
60%	14.50
40%	9.20
20%	7.90

Joan purchased her 40,000 shares in Rouen Ltd during 1987 for £96,400 (indexed to April 1998).

(c)　On 4 November 2006 Joan gave her grandson an antique vase worth £8,500 as a wedding present. Joan purchased the vase during 1985 for £4,150 (indexed to April 1998).

(d)　On 15 January 2007 Joan gave agricultural land with an agricultural value of £175,000 to her son Charles. Joan had purchased the land during 1988 for £92,000 (indexed to April 1998), and it has always been let out to tenant farmers. The most recent tenancy agreement which stated in June 1997 will soon come to an end, and Joan has obtained planning permission to build residential accommodation on the land. The value of the land with planning permission is £300,000. Charles owns adjoining agricultural land, and the value of this land will increase from £210,000 to £250,000 as a result of the gift.

(e)　On 31 March 2007 Joan made a gift of her main residence valued at £265,000 to her daughter Catherine. However, as a condition of the gift, Joan has continued to live in the house rent free. The house was purchased on 1 July 1986 for £67,000 (indexed to April 1998), and Joan occupied it as her main residence until 31 December 1990. The house was unoccupied between 1 January 1991 and 31 December 1994, and was rented out as furnished accommodation between 1 January 1995 and 31 December 2004. Since 1 January 2005 Joan has again occupied the house as her main residence.

Joan is a 40% taxpayer, and has not previously made any lifetime transfers of assets. She is to pay any IHT and CGT liabilities arising from the above gifts.

Required:

Advise Joan of the IHT and CGT implications arising from the gifts made during 2006/07.

Your answer should be supported by appropriate calculations, and should include an explanation of any reliefs that are available. You should ignore the instalment option and the effect of annual exemptions both for IHT and CGT.

Marks for this question will be allocated on the basis of:

(6 marks to (a))
(5 marks to (b))
(3 marks to (c))
(4 marks to (d))
(7 marks to (e))
(Total: 25 marks)

37　JIMMY GENEROUS

You should assume that today's date is 4 June 2007.

Jimmy Generous is a wealthy individual aged 57, in good health and married to Jane, aged 54 and also in good health. The couple have two children, Jack, aged 34 and Jill, aged 37, who both have children of their own.

Jimmy currently owns 60% of the issued share capital of JG Limited, a UK resident trading company, which he set up in 1983. The remaining shares are held, 20% by his daughter Jill and 20% by unconnected third parties. The company has been very successful in recent years. He works as a part-time director for JG Limited receiving a gross salary of £25,000 per year.

The following additional information relating to Jimmy is relevant for 2006/07.

(1)　He contributed 10% of his salary to a registered charity under an approved payroll deduction scheme run by JG Limited.

(2)　He contributed £3,750 to JG Limited's approved occupational pension scheme.

(3)　He made a series of cash gifts totalling £3,120 to a registered charity.

(4)   He received the following net investment income:

    (a)   £45,000 dividend income from JG Limited.

    (b)   £8,000 building society interest.

(5)   He has no other income or outgoings in 2006/07.

In addition to the gifts to registered charities referred to above Jimmy has made the following gifts during his lifetime. Jimmy agreed that he would pay any Inheritance Tax arising on these gifts.

4 June 1999	£291,000 cash gift to a discretionary trust.
4 March 2001	£10,000 cash as a wedding gift to his son Jack.
4 March 2001	20% of the shares in JG Limited to his daughter Jill. At this time the JG Limited shares were valued as follows.

Shareholding	Value £
20%	100,000
60%	450,000
80%	600,000
100%	800,000

4 June 2005	A further £100,000 cash gift to the discretionary trust created on 4 June 1999. Jimmy is also considering gifting some further shares in JG Limited to his children.

Required:

(a)   Explain what action Jimmy should take to obtain tax relief under the Gift Aid scheme for the cash gifts totalling £3,120 made in 2006/07.

Your answer should include an explanation of how tax relief is effected from both Jimmy's and the charities' perspectives.   **(4 marks)**

(b)   Assuming that he takes the necessary action to obtain the tax relief for the Gift Aid payments in 2006/07 calculate Jimmy's income tax and national insurance contribution liabilities for 2006/07.   **(7 marks)**

(c)   Explain the Inheritance Tax implications arising from the gifts made between 4 June 1999 and 4 June 2005.

Your answer should include a calculation of any Inheritance Tax payable and an explanation of any exemptions or reliefs available. You are not required to consider the implications for the trustees of the discretionary trust.

You should assume that the rates and allowances for 2006/07 apply throughout this part of the question.   **(10 marks)**

(d)   Explain:

    (i)   The main advantages in lifetime giving for IHT purposes.

    (ii)   The main factors that need to be considered in deciding which assets to gift.

    (iii)   Whether or not you would advise Jimmy to make further lifetime gifts of his holding in JG Limited shares.   **(7 marks)**

(Total: 28 marks)

38   HENRY

Henry, aged 77, died on 5 October 2006 survived by his wife, Sally, also aged 77, and two children, Cecil and Ida. Sally is herself in a frail condition and not expected to live for much longer. Both Cecil and Ida have children of their own and are relatively wealthy in their own right.

Henry owned the following assets:

(1)   100,000 £1 ordinary shares in Peel plc a quoted company with an issued share capital of 10,000,000 £1 ordinary shares. On 5 October 2006 the price for these shares was quoted at 200–208 per share with marked bargains on that day of 201, 204 and 207. A dividend of 9p per share had been paid on 30 September 2006.

(2)   £20,000 10% Government Stock quoted at 95–97 ex interest. Interest is payable half yearly on 30 April and 31 October.

(3)   The following capital deposits both of which have been held for several years:

–   £25,000 deposited with a building society.

–   £18,000 invested in an ISA account.

The following interest was received during 2006/07.
Building Society   £320 on 30 June 2006 with a further £304 on 31 December 2006.
ISA   £360 on 30 June 2006 with a further £360 on 31 December 2006.

All interest figures relate to the actual amount received.

(4)   A house valued on 5 October 2006 at £450,000. This property was his and Sally's family home but was owned outright by Henry.

Under the terms of his will Henry has left £20,000 each to Cecil and Ida with the remainder of his estate left to his wife. Sally's will currently leaves her estate equally to their two children.

The only gifts made by Henry during his lifetime were cash gifts of £168,000 on 1 January 1999 and £137,000 on 1 January 2002 respectively. Both gifts were made to a discretionary trust. Henry had agreed to pay any inheritance tax arising on these lifetime gifts.

The only other taxable income Henry received during the period 6 April 2006 to 5 October 2006 was a State Retirement Pension of £4,380 and gross annuity income of £5,100. Lower rate income tax at the rate of 20% was deducted from the annuity income. The annuity did not have any capital value on Henry's death.

Required:

(a)   Explain how Henry's income will be taxed in 2006/07, the tax year of his death, and calculate his Income Tax payable for this tax year.   **(7 marks)**

(b)   Calculate the Inheritance Tax liabilities arising:

(i)   from the lifetime gifts of cash to the discretionary trust; and

(ii)   arising as a consequence of Henry's death on 5 October 2006.   **(10 marks)**

(c)   Explain any action that could be taken following Henry's death to reduce or defer any Inheritance Tax liability that may become payable upon the future death of his wife, Sally.

Your answer should state any qualifying conditions that need to be satisfied and, where the information permits, include a calculation of any potential tax savings.

(8 marks)

You should assume that the rates and allowances for 2006/07 apply throughout parts (b) and (c).   **(Total: 25 marks)**

39   ETHEL SMITH

Assume today's date is 30 June 2007.

Ethel Smith is aged 78 years. She is married to George, who is independently wealthy in this own right. The couple have one child, Simone. Ethel has unfortunately recently become terminally ill and is expected to live for only another four years. She owns the following assets:

(1)   10,000 ordinary £1 shares in Bluebird plc, a quoted UK resident trading company with an issued share capital of 1 million ordinary shares. The company makes up its accounts to 31 March each year. The shares are currently quoted at 1460-1468. Ethel acquired 5,000 of her shares in June 1996 for £25,000 with the remainder being acquired by way of a rights issue in June 2002 for a further £50,000.

Ethel was a director of this company for many years until she had to retire for health reasons on 31 May 2006. During 2006/07 she earned £8,800 in director's fees from Bluebird plc. The company has paid the following dividends in recent years:

Company year ended	Dividend	Payment date
31 March 2006	25 pence per share	30 April 2006
31 March 2007	30 pence per share	30 April 2007

(2)   A 25% beneficial interest in £100,000 10% loan stock in Chaffinch plc, a quoted UK resident trading company. This loan stock is currently quoted at 102-106 and is held jointly with George who has always owned the remaining 75% beneficial interest in it. This loan stock was acquired in June 2002 for £90,000. The couple have not made a declaration of beneficial interest to HMRC in respect of this asset. This loan stock is a qualifying corporate bond.

(3)   Main residence valued at £500,000.

(4)   Three antique plates which are part of a set of six. Ethel bought her three plates in June 2002 for £2,500. On the same day George bought two of the plates for £1,500 whilst Simone bought the remaining plate for £750.

The value of the plates is currently as follows:

	£
1 plate	1,000
2 plates	2,200
3 plates	3,800
4 plates	6,000
5 plates	10,000
6 plates	20,000

(5)   Cash deposits amount to £145,000, which generated net interest receipts in 2006/07 of £4,200.

(6)   Sundry personal chattels collectively worth £20,000 with no individual asset worth more than £5,000.

Under the terms of Ethel's will, all of her assets are to be left to Simone with the exception of the house and her sundry personal chattels which are bequeathed to George. Due to her failing health, Ethel and her family are currently considering whether she should either:

(i)   gift all of her assets, with the exception of the house and her sundry personal chattels, to Simone upon her death in four years time, or

(ii)   make these gifts to Simone now.

In four years time her assets are expected to be valued at the following amounts for inheritance tax purposes:

	£
Bluebird plc shareholding	200,000
100% of the Chaffinch plc loan stock	100,000
Residence	600,000
Antique plates	10,000
Cash deposits	160,000
Sundry personal chattels	20,000
	1,090,000

For 2006/07 Ethel has made a joint election with George to transfer the maximum permissible married couples allowance to her.

The only previous gift made by Ethel was a cash gift, net of annual exemptions, of £320,000 made to Simone in September 2005.

Required:

(a)   Calculate Ethel's 2006/07 income tax liability.   **(5 marks)**

(b)   Advise Ethel and George whether it would be beneficial to make a declaration of beneficial interest to HMRC in respect of the loan stock held in Chaffinch plc.

Detailed calculations are not required for this question part.   **(3 marks)**

(c)   Advise Ethel whether she should

(i)   make the transfers of the selected assets to Simone upon her death in four years time, or

(ii)   make the transfers now.

Your answer should consider the likely inheritance tax and capital gains tax implications and should include a calculation of any capital taxes likely to arise under each option.

Stamp duty and stamp duty land tax should be ignored.

For this question part you should assume that the rates and allowances for 2006/07 apply throughout and that the current definition of business assets for taper relief purposes applies throughout the whole period.

Retail price index factors are as follows:

June 1996	153.0
April 1998	162.6
June 2002	176.2
June 2007	201.2

(18 marks)

(Total: 26 marks)

40   AMY

Assume that today's date is 1 May 2007.

Amy is 43 years old. She is single and does not have any children. For tax purposes, Amy is classed as resident and ordinarily resident in the UK but domiciled overseas. Amy received the following income in the year to 5 April 2007.

(1)   A salary of £19,200 (PAYE deducted of £5,085). In addition her employer also provided her with a diesel company car with a list price of £15,000. This car has an emission rate of 175 grams per km. Her employer also paid for diesel fuel for both her private and business use. Amy has paid £4,910 into her personal pension scheme.

(2)   Interest of £180 (amount received) from a National Savings Bank EASA.

(3)   Interest of £400 (amount received) from a UK bank deposit account.

(4)   A dividend of £1,800 (amount received) from 50,000 £1 ordinary shares in Red plc, a UK quoted company.

(5)   A dividend of £1,300 (amount received) from Black Inc, a company quoted overseas. Withholding tax of 35% had been deducted at source. Only £650 of this net dividend was remitted to the UK.

(6)   Rent of £850 per month (amount received) from a property overseas, which had been let for many years. Withholding tax of 15% had been deducted at source. All of this net rent was remitted to the UK. This property was gifted to her brother Michael, on 6 November 2006 (see below).

(7)   Rent of £1,200 per month (net of expenses), from a UK property which had been let since July 2001. This property was not her main residence and has never been used as a business asset. The expenses included interest of £140 per month on a loan taken out to purchase the property. This property was gifted to her brother Michael on 6 January 2007 (see below).

During the year to 5 April 2007 Amy gifted the following assets to her brother, Michael.

(1)   50,000 £1 ordinary shares in Red plc on 1 June 2006. Amy had inherited these shares in April 2004 (probate value £20,000) from her aunt, who had bought them in March 2000 for £17,200. On 1 June 2006 the shares were quoted at 221–229p, with bargains on that day of 219p, 220p and 225p. Amy has never been an employee or officer of Red plc and holds less than 5% of the company's shares.

(2)   The overseas property on 6 November 2006 when its market value was £245,000. Amy had bought this property in August 2002 for £220,000.

(3)   The UK property on 6 January 2007 when its market value was £125,000. Amy had bought it in June 1994 for £67,000.

Amy has not previously made any lifetime transfers of assets.

Amy is concerned about her future inheritance tax liabilities. She intends to gift her main residence to her niece, Erica, on 1 June 2007. The house which is currently worth in the region of £400,000 was bought in January 2002 for £235,000. The house has always been Amy's main residence and she intends to continue to live in this house after the gift, regardless of the inheritance tax implications.

Required:

(a)   (i)   State the basis on which Amy will be charged to income tax (IT), capital gains tax (CGT) and inheritance tax (IHT) given her UK residence and ordinary residence and non-UK domicile status.   **(3 marks)**

(ii) Calculate Amy's IT, CGT and IHT payable for 2006/07, clearly identifying any actions she can take to defer the chargeable gains that have arisen. **(15 marks)**

Relevant retail price index figures are:

June 1994   144.7
April 1998   162.6

(b) (i) Explain the inheritance tax (IHT) implications of Amy making the gift of her main residence to her niece, and calculate the IHT arising if Amy should die on 1 September 2011.

Assume that the value of the property will still be £400,000, that Amy retains her non-UK domicile for the purpose of inheritance tax and that the tax rates and allowances for 2006/07 apply throughout. **(6 marks)**

(ii) Suggest a way by which the IHT liability calculated in (i) above could be reduced and indicate any other tax implications arising from this advice.

(1 mark)

(Total: 25 marks)

41 DEE LIMITED

Today's date is 8 June 2007.

David and Debbie were an elderly couple who had worked hard and over a number of years they built up a successful family company, Dee Limited. Their success allowed them to accumulate a series of investments. David died in May 2007. Debbie is 66 and still in good health.

The couple had two children, Andrew and Allison. Andrew, aged 37, is single but is shortly to be married. He is the managing director of the family trading company, Dee Limited, which was set up 30 years ago by David and Debbie. Both Andrew and Allison are shareholders in the company, although Allison does not work for the company. She is 32, and lives abroad with her husband and two children (aged 2 and 4) in a villa gifted to her by Debbie in June 2005. The villa was worth £192,000 at that time, but the current value has fallen to £110,000 as a result of exchange rate movements.

Dee Limited is currently worth £1,260,000 in total, and the value is unlikely to change in the foreseeable future.

The shareholdings in the company at the date of David's death (May 2007) were held as follows:

Shareholders	Shares	%
David	3,000	60
Debbie	500	10
Andrew	1,000	20
Allison	500	10

In addition, David and Debbie had the following other assets as at the date of David's death in May 2007:

Asset	David £	Debbie £
Family home (jointly owned)	275,000	275,000
Cash deposits	60,000	40,000
Paintings	12,000	6,300
Death in Service policy	200,000	–
Quoted shares in Don plc	125,000	25,000

(Representing a 6% holding for David and a 1% holding for Debbie)

Additional information

The wills of David and Debbie currently leave all assets to the surviving spouse. On the death of the second spouse, all assets pass to the children in equal proportions.

David gifted a holiday cottage worth £70,000 to Andrew in February 2000. The gift was on the condition that David was allowed to occupy the cottage for two months per year, which he did up to the date of his death. The value of the cottage is now £150,000.

David gifted £293,000 into a discretionary trust in June 2001. He paid the tax due himself. In addition, David also gifted shares in Dee Limited to both his children in February 2002. Andrew received 20% of the shares, and Allison received 10%. The values of holdings in Dee Limited on the relevant dates were as follows:

	On gift (Feb 2002) £	At death (May 2007) £
100% holding	900,000	1,260,000
90% holding	730,000	1,022,000
70% holding	475,000	665,000
60% holding	405,000	567,000
30% holding	175,000	245,000
20% holding	110,000	154,000
10% holding	50,000	70,000

Required:

(a) Calculate the inheritance tax (IHT) that will be payable as a result of David's death.

Your answer should include calculations of the tax arising on any lifetime transfers and give reasons for any reliefs given. **(12 marks)**

(b) (i) Calculate the inheritance tax (IHT) that will be payable if Debbie were to die today (8 June 2007).

Assume that no tax planning measures are taken and that there has been no change in the value of any of the assets since David's death. **(4 marks)**

(ii) State when the inheritance tax (IHT) calculated in (i) would be payable and by whom. **(2 marks)**

(c) Assuming that she will survive until July 2011, advise on the lifetime inheritance tax (IHT) planning measures that could be undertaken by Debbie, quantifying the savings that can be made. **(7 marks)**

For this question you should assume that the rates and allowances for 2006/07 apply throughout. **(Total: 25 marks)**

42 ALEX

Assume today's date is 20 February 2007.

Alex, a widower, died on 5 February 2007, aged 85 years. His will leaves his assets split in equal shares to his son, Brian and his daughter, Beatrice. The assets comprised in Alex's estate were as follows:

	Market Value 5 February 2007 £
Residence	475,000
Building society account	15,000
National savings bank EASA account	55,000
National savings certificates	180,000
Various chattels	40,000
Shares in Touriga Ltd	Note 1
Shares in Nacional plc	Note 2
Other quoted investments	115,000

Notes

(1)   Touriga Ltd is an unquoted trading company. Alex bought his 2,450 ordinary shares (representing 35% of the issued shares) in September 2004 for £8.50 per share. The shares were worth £11.00 per share at the time of his death.

(2)   Nacional plc is a quoted company in which Alex held 20,000 shares (representing less than 1% of the issued shares) at the time of his death. On 5 February 2007, the shares were listed ex div at 624p - 632p with marked bargains at 625p, 629p and 630p. A dividend of 18 pence per share was declared on 5 December 2006, and was received on 11 February 2007 by the executors.

Alex had made two lifetime gifts. The first was a villa in Spain. This was given to Brian in July 2001. The value at that time was £293,000. In addition, Alex settled an equal amount on a discretionary trust in March 2002. Alex agreed to pay any tax due on the gifts.

Prior to his death, Alex had the following income in 2006/07:

	£
Pension (gross – PAYE deducted at source £1,230)	9,000
Building society interest received	1,280
National savings bank EASA interest received	370
Dividends received (other than from Nacional plc (note 2 above))	8,100

Brian, Alex's son, is aged 58, is in poor health, and is not expected to live more than a few years. His wife died ten years ago, since when he has lived alone. He owns a house, currently worth £400,000 with an £80,000 mortgage outstanding and has other assets in the form of cash investments worth £80,000, and personal belongings worth £50,000. Consequently, Brian has no need of his inheritance from Alex and so intends to gift his share of his father's estate to his two children, Colin and Charlotte, in equal shares.

Colin, who is 18, is in his first year at university, but Brian is worried that his son will spend all of the money at once. Charlotte, who is 15, is still at school but is likely to go to university in the near future. Again, Brian worries about the money being spent unwisely, and therefore wishes to use some form of trust to control the capital sums gifted to both his children. Brian has made no lifetime gifts to date.

Required:

(a) Calculate the income tax (IT) payable/repayable for Alex for the income tax year 2006/07. **(5 marks)**

(b) Calculate the inheritance tax (IHT) liabilities (including any additional tax due on his lifetime gifts) arising on the death of Alex, and quantify the inheritance (after tax) due to Brian and Beatrice.

Assume that the current inheritance tax rates and allowances apply throughout. **(10 marks)**

(c) (i) Explain how Brian could use a discretionary trust to maintain control of the capital he intends to gift to Colin and Charlotte following Alex's death and the inheritance tax (IHT) treatment of the trust. **(4 marks)**

(ii) State, giving reasons, what other inheritance tax (IHT) planning advice you would offer Brian with regard to setting up a discretionary trust for Colin and Charlotte with the assets he has inherited. **(3 marks)**

(Total: 22 marks)

43 STUART

Stuart is a self-employed business consultant aged 58. He is married to Rebecca, aged 55. They have one child, Sam, who is aged 24 and single.

In November 2006 Stuart sold a house in Plymouth for £422,100. Stuart had inherited the house on the death of his mother on 1 May 1994 when it had a probate value of £185,000. The subsequent pattern of occupation was as follows:

1 May 1994 to 28 February 1995	occupied by Stuart and Rebecca as main residence
1 March 1995 to 31 December 1998	unoccupied
1 January 1999 to 31 March 2001	let out (unfurnished)
1 April 2001 to 30 November 2001	occupied by Stuart and Rebecca
1 December 2001 to 30 November 2006	used occasionally as second home

Both Stuart and Rebecca had lived in London from March 1995 onwards. On 1 March 2001 Stuart and Rebecca bought a house in London in their joint names. On 1 January 2002 they elected for their London house to be their principal private residence with effect from that date, up until that point the Plymouth property had been their principal private residence.

No other capital disposals were made by Stuart in the tax year 2006/07. He has £29,500 of capital losses brought forward from previous years.

Stuart intends to invest the gross sale proceeds from the sale of the Plymouth house, and is considering two investment options, both of which he believes will provide equal risk and returns. These are as follows:

(1) acquiring shares in Omikron plc; or

(2) acquiring further shares in Omega plc.

Notes:

1 Omikron plc is a listed UK trading company, with 50,250,000 shares in issue. Its shares currently trade at 42p per share.

2   Stuart and Rebecca helped start up the company, which was then Omega Ltd. The company was formed on 1 June 1990, when they each bought 24,000 shares for £1 per share. The company became listed on 1 May 1997. On this date their holding was subdivided, with each of them receiving 100 shares in Omega plc for each share held in Omega Ltd. The issued share capital of Omega plc is currently 10,000,000 shares. The share price is quoted at 208p – 216p with marked bargains at 207p, 211p, and 215p.

Stuart and Rebecca's assets (following the sale of the Plymouth house but before any investment of the proceeds) are as follows:

Assets	Stuart £	Rebecca £
Family house in London	450,000	450,000
Cash from property sale	422,100	–
Cash deposits	65,000	65,000
Portfolio of quoted investments	–	250,000
Shares in Omega plc	see above	see above
Life insurance policy		

Note: The life insurance policy will pay out a sum of £200,000 on the death of the first spouse to die.

Stuart has recently been diagnosed with a serious illness. He is expected to live for another two or three years only. He is concerned about the possible inheritance tax that will arise on his death. Both he and Rebecca have wills whose terms transfer all assets to the surviving spouse. Rebecca is in good health.

Neither Stuart nor Rebecca has made any previous chargeable lifetime transfers for the purposes of inheritance tax.

Required:

(a)   Calculate the taxable capital gain on the sale of the Plymouth house in November 2006.
(9 marks)

(b)   Given his recent diagnosis, advise Stuart as to which of the two proposed investments (Omikron plc/Omega plc) would be the more tax efficient alternative. Give reasons for your choice.
(3 marks)

(c)   Assuming that Stuart:

(i)   purchased 201,000 shares in Omega plc on 3 December 2006; and

(ii)   dies on 20 December 2008,

calculate the potential inheritance tax (IHT) liability which would arise if Rebecca were to die on 1 March 2009, and no further tax planning measures were taken.

Assume that all asset values remain unchanged and that the current rates of inheritance tax continue to apply.
(6 marks)

(d)   Advise on any lifetime inheritance tax (IHT) planning that could be undertaken in respect of both Stuart and Rebecca to help reduce the potential inheritance tax (IHT) liability calculated in (c) above.
(7 marks)

Relevant retail price index figures are:

May	1994	144.7
April	1998	162.6

(Total: 25 marks)

VAT

44   GEWGAW LTD

Gewgaw Ltd commenced trading as a manufacturer of children's toys on 1 April 2006, and will make up its accounts to 31 March 2007.

VAT return

Gewgaw Ltd is in the process of completing its VAT return for the quarter ended 31 March 2007. The following information is available:

(1)   Standard rated sales amounted to £62,500, with £54,200 being received from customers. Gewgaw Ltd offers its customers a 2.5% discount for payment within 30 days, and this is taken by 70% of them.

(2)   Standard rated purchases amounted to £21,000, with £19,400 being paid to suppliers.

(3)   On 31 March 2007 the company wrote off irrecoverable debts of £2,000 and £840 in respect of invoices due for payment on 10 August and 5 November 2006 respectively.

(4)   On 1 January 2007 the company purchased a new 1600 cc motorcar costing £17,300 for the use of its managing director. This figure includes a sunroof costing £800 that was fitted prior to the delivery of the motorcar. Both these figures are *inclusive* of VAT.

(5)   Standard rated expenses amounted to £14,640. This includes £480 for entertaining suppliers, £1,200 for repairs to the managing director's motorcar, and the cost of petrol for this motorcar of £900. The figure for petrol includes both business and private mileage. The relevant quarterly scale charge is £311 *(inclusive of VAT)*.

Unless stated otherwise all of the above figures are *exclusive* of VAT.

Gewgaw Ltd does not operate the cash accounting scheme. The company's first three VAT returns were submitted on 20 August 2006, 26 October 2006 and 25 January 2007 respectively. The VAT payable in respect of the second and third returns was not paid until 11 November 2006 and 5 March 2007 respectively.

Bookkeeping

Gewgaw Ltd's bookkeeping is currently maintained by a bookkeeping agency at a cost of £525 per month net of VAT (this is included within the standard rated expenses of £14,640). An employee of Gewgaw Ltd with the relevant financial experience has offered to do the bookkeeping by working one extra day per week. The employee is currently paid a salary of £15,000 pa, and wants £100 per week, net of all taxes, for the extra day's work. He has no other income.

Required:

(a)   (i)   Calculate the amount of VAT payable by Gewgaw Ltd for the quarter ended 31 March 2007, and explain the implications if this VAT payable is not paid until 20 May 2007.   **(8 marks)**

        (ii)   State the conditions that Gewgaw Ltd needs to satisfy before it will be permitted to use the cash accounting and annual accounting schemes, and advise the company of whether it will be beneficial for it to use either scheme.   **(6 marks)**

(b)   Advise Gewgaw Ltd as to whether it would be beneficial to accept the employee's offer to maintain the company's bookkeeping.   **(3 marks)**

(Total: 17 marks)

45   CONFUSED LTD

You should assume that today's date is 15 January 2007.

Charles Clear has recently been appointed as managing director of Confused Ltd, a manufacturer of furniture that prepares its accounts to 31 March. The company's sales are all standard rated for VAT purposes, and it does not operate the cash accounting scheme.

VAT return

Confused Ltd is in the process of completing its VAT return for the quarter ended 31 December 2006. The managing director has undertaken a review of the company's previous VAT returns, and has discovered the following:

(1)   On 20 September 2006 Confused Ltd wrote off £18,000 due from a customer as a irrecoverable debt. The debt was in respect of three invoices, each of £6,000, which had been issued on 5 April, 24 May and 22 June 2006 respectively. Confused Ltd requires its customers to pay within 30 days, and offers them a 5% discount for payment within this period.

(2)   Confused Ltd has not been claiming for the input VAT on £100 that is paid each month for the rental of the company's coffee machines. The same monthly amount has been paid since 1 April 1998.

(3)   On 10 April 2006 Confused Ltd acquired three computers from VAT registered company in a country that is a member of the European Union, and imported two computers from a country that is outside the European Union. The computers cost £2,400 each. No entries have so far been made on any VAT returns in respect of these computers.

(4)   On 23 December 2006 Confused Ltd completed a contract to manufacture furniture for a customer. The total value of the contract is £15,000, and an invoice for this amount was raised on 3 January 2007. The customer paid Confused Ltd a deposit of £4,000 on 31 August 2006. No entry has been made on any VAT returns in respect of this deposit.

All of the above figures are *exclusive* of VAT where appropriate.

Aeroplane

Confused Ltd uses an aeroplane for business purposes. A new aeroplane costing £650,000 *(exclusive* of VAT) is to be acquired on 1 April 2007. The new aeroplane will have an expected working life of 30 years.

Confused Ltd was planning to purchase the aeroplane on hire purchase, with the company making 20 quarterly payments of £36,500 commencing on 1 April 2007. VAT will be paid with the first instalment. However, the managing director has now decided that the new aeroplane should instead be leased for a period of five years at a cost of £83,000 *(inclusive* of VAT) pa payable annually in advance on 1 April each year.

Aeroplane pilot

Confused Ltd uses a 'self-employed' pilot to fly the company aeroplane. The contract between Confused Ltd and the pilot is for a twelve-month period, and it provides that the pilot must work exclusively for Confused Ltd. The pilot is paid a monthly fee of £2,400, and he invoices Confused Ltd for this amount each month. The managing director considers the pilot to be employed rather than self-employed. He appreciates that classifying the pilot as an employee will result in an additional NIC liability, and so as an employee the pilot is to be paid a monthly salary of £2,550. The pilot is single and has no other income.

Required:

(a) Advise the managing director how the items that he has discovered should be treated when preparing Confused Ltd's VAT return for the quarter ended 31 December 2006.

(12 marks)

(b) Explain the corporation tax and VAT implications for the year ended 31 March 2008 if Confused Ltd:

(i) Purchases the new aeroplane on hire purchase.

(ii) Leases the new aeroplane.

You should assume that the tax rates and allowances for 2006/07 apply throughout.

(5 marks)

(c) (i) Explain why the managing director is probably correct in considering the pilot to be employed rather than self-employed. **(3 marks)**

(ii) Calculate whether it will be beneficial from the pilot's point of view for him to be paid a monthly salary of £2,550 as an employee, compared to a monthly fee of £2,400 as a self-employed person. **(5 marks)**

(Total: 25 marks)

46 JIMMY CHAN

Jimmy Chan has passed the Financial Planning Certificate examinations and is also a qualified accountant. He practises as a financial advisor to small businesses and private clients, providing both financial services advice, for which he receives commissions from product providers and accounting services, for which he is paid fees by his clients. He operates the annual accounting scheme for VAT and prepares his accounts annually to 30 April.

Jimmy's business runs two cars, one for his use, the other for his personal assistant. The tax written down value of these and the other fixed assets of the business at 1 May 2005 were as follows:

Employee's car (originally cost over £12,000)	£7,995
Proprietor's car – 25% private use	£4,471
General pool	£1,447

During the year ended 30 April 2006 Jimmy made the following acquisitions and disposals of cars and equipment.

16 November 2005 upgraded his 1.6 Toyota for a new model of the same car. He received a part exchange allowance of £7,000 against the VAT inclusive cost of £14,813 for the new one.

12 December 2005 part exchanged the Mitsubishi Spacewagon used by the personal assistant which has an engine capacity of 1,998cc for £7,650 against a Volkswagen Polo which has an engine capacity of 1,390cc and VAT inclusive cost £11,446. Jimmy pays for all the fuel costs of his personal assistant.

31 March 2006 bought three new filing cabinets for £548 net of VAT.

20 April 2006 bought a new lap top computer for £2,800 net of VAT.

Jimmy's Profit and Loss Account for the year ended 30 April 2006 is as set out below. The figures are stated exclusive of VAT.

Jimmy's output tax in the year was £9,728. His recoverable input tax, none of which was directly attributable, was £2,940. Both of these calculations are before any adjustments that may be necessary for the use of fuel for non business use or as a result of partial exemption. Jimmy has made nine monthly payments on account of VAT of £505.

Jimmy Chan

Profit & Loss Account
Year ended 30 April 2006

	Notes	£	£	£
Fees			57,191	
Commissions			28,596	85,787
Salaries		12,659		
Telephone		1,287		
Printing, postage and stationery		1,375		
Software rental and maintenance		3,692		
Advertising		3,510		
Entertainment	1	255		
Motor expenses	2	4,259		
Travel and subsistence		1,075		
Cleaning		877		
Rent		4,500		
Rates and water		1,520		
Light and Heat		422		
Professional fees		1,490		
Books and journals		1,504		
Insurance		536		
Repairs		3,641		
Legal fees	3	228		
Sundries	4	874		
Bank Interest and charges		1,316		
Depreciation		8,241		
Profit on disposal of fixed assets		(4,908)		(48,353)
Net profit				37,434

Notes

1   Entertainment is made up as follows:

	£
Entertaining staff	100
Entertaining customers	155
	255

2   Motor expenses are made up as follows:

	£
Proprietor's car	2,872
Employee's car	1,387
	4,259

3   Legal fees were incurred in recovering a doubtful debt

4   Sundry expenses are all allowable trading expenses

Required:

(a)   Calculate Jimmy's tax adjusted trading profit for the year ended 30 April 2006.

(10 marks)

(b)   Calculate any partial exemption adjustment that may be necessary for the purposes of VAT.   **(4 marks)**

(c)   (i)   Calculate the balance owed by Jimmy to HMRC or vice versa in respect of VAT for the annual accounting period ended 30 April 2006.

(4 marks)

(ii)   State the due date for payment/(refund) of the VAT balance calculated in (i) above.   **(1 mark)**

(iii)   Calculate the likely VAT payments on account for the annual accounting period ending on 30 April 2007.

The annual fuel scale figures (VAT inclusive) are £1,095 for 1400cc or less and £1,385 for 1401cc – 2000cc.   **(1 mark)**

(Total: 20 marks)

47   P LTD

Assume that today's date is 1 June 2006.

(a)   You are the tax advisor to a new company, P Ltd, which is in the process of being set up by Peter. P Ltd intends to start trading on 1 July 2006, and expects the following:

Sales:

Monthly turnover of £13,000, remaining steady for about two years, then increasing. 80% of sales will be standard rated for value added tax (VAT), the rest will be exempt. Sales will be mostly to VAT registered customers.

Usually invoices will be prepared within seven days of the goods being collected, and payment due within 30 days of the invoice date. Occasionally, the customer will be invoiced before the goods are collected. P Ltd expects some customers to pay late, and some irrecoverable debts.

Purchases:

Purchases (all standard rated) will be in the region of £6,000 per month (excluding VAT), 80% relating to the standard rated sales, and 20% relating to the exempt sales. P Ltd will be given 14 days' credit.

Other information:

(1)   Assets and stock for use in the business have already been purchased over the last 12 months.

(2)   The flat rate scheme percentage for P Ltd's trade is 11%.

Required:

Explain the value added tax (VAT) issues facing P Ltd. You are not required to give details of the procedures for VAT accounting and invoicing.   **(20 marks)**

(b)   Peter is a 35 year old single man with no children. He will own the entire share capital of P Ltd and work full time for the company. Peter wants some advice on where the ownership of his car should be located once the company is formed.

Peter expects to drive 15,000 miles on business each year. His private mileage is 5,000 miles each year. The car which he currently owns personally has a market value of £18,000. The list price of the vehicle when new was £24,000 and the emission rate is 212 grams per kilometre.

The annual running costs of the car are £2,000, plus an additional £2,800 for petrol.

HMRC Authorised Mileage Allowance Payments (AMAPs) are 40p per mile for the first 10,000 miles, and 25p per mile thereafter.

Peter is unsure whether he should retain ownership of the car, and charge P Ltd the AMAP, or if he should transfer the car to P Ltd. P Ltd would pay Peter market value (£18,000) for the car and would be responsible for the annual running costs of the vehicle plus all petrol costs. You may assume that the annual running costs for the company are the same as for Peter, that is, £2,000, plus an additional £2,800 for petrol.

Required:

Identify whether it would be more tax efficient for Peter to retain ownership of his car, or to transfer it to P Ltd.

Support your answer by means of calculations based on the assumption that P Ltd pays tax at 19% and Peter at 22% and that all other rates and allowances are as for 2006/07.

Ignore the effects of VAT for this part of the question.　　　　　　　　**(5 marks)**

(Total: 25 marks)

TAXATION OF CORPORATE BUSINESSES

SINGLE COMPANIES

48　JAMES & MELVIN

Assume today's date is 1 January 2007.

Your have recently held a meeting with James and Melvin who are both UK resident. They each own 50% of the issued ordinary share capital of JM Limited, an unquoted trading company which prepares its accounts to 31 March each year. JM Limited is a close company and was formed on 1 May 2002 with 1,000 £1 ordinary shares being issued at par value　Melvin is both a director of and employed by JM Limited whereas James is neither employed nor a director of this company. Both James and Melvin are higher rate taxpayers.

JM Limited has been reasonably successful and James now wishes to partially realise some of his investment in the company either by a direct sale to Melvin or via a company purchase of its own shares. He is, however, currently undecided as to how many of his ordinary shares he will sell although this will be no less than 100 and no more than 350. Each JM Limited share currently has a market value of £500 which will be the price paid for each share in any sale. It is anticipated that the share sale will occur on 31 March 2007 but it could be deferred until 31 May 2007.

Your further ascertain the following

(1)　Throughout 2006/07 both James and Melvin were provided with new cars by JM Limited. Both cars use petrol and have a CO_2 emission level of 157 grams per kilometre and a list price of £18,000. In addition both James and Melvin are provided with fuel for private purposes.

(2) On 6 July 2006 JM Limited paid some personal bills for James amounting to £20,000. It is probable that this amount will be written off by JM Limited at some point in the future.

Required:

Write a letter to James and Melvin which is supported by relevant calculations:

(a) Advising them of the tax and national insurance implications for both themselves individually and for JM Limited arising from the provision of cars to James and Melvin and the settling of some of James' personal bills by the company. **(11 marks)**

(b) Advising them of the tax implications arising from the proposed sale of shares by James either directly to Melvin or via a company purchase of own shares. **(14 marks)**

Marks will be awarded for presentation, structure and format. **(Total: 25 marks)**

49 FLOP LIMITED

Assume that today's date is 10 May 2007.

You have recently been approached by Fred Flop. Fred is the managing director and 100% shareholder of Flop Limited, a UK trading company with one wholly owned subsidiary. Both companies have a 31 March year end.

Fred informs you that he is experiencing problems in dealing with aspects of his company tax returns. The company accountant has been unable to keep up to date with matters, and Fred also believes that mistakes have been made in the past. Fred needs assistance and tells you the following:

Year ended 31 March 2005

The corporation tax return for this period was not submitted until 2 November 2006, and corporation tax of £123,500 was paid at the same time. Profits chargeable to corporation tax were stated as £704,300.

A formal notice (CT203) requiring the company to file a self-assessment corporation tax return (dated 1 February 2006) had been received by the company on 4 February 2006.

A detailed examination of the accounts and tax computation has revealed the following.

- Computer equipment totalling £50,000 had been expensed in the accounts. No adjustment has been made in the tax computation.

- A provision of £10,000 was made for repairs, but there is no evidence of supporting information.

- Legal and professional fees totalling £46,500 were allowed in full without any explanation. Fred has subsequently produced the following analysis:

Analysis of legal & professional fees

	£
Legal fees on a failed attempt to secure a trading loan	5,000
Debt collection agency fees	12,800
Obtaining planning consent for building extension	5,700
Accountant's fees for preparing accounts	14,000
Legal fees relating to a trade dispute	9,000

- No enquiry has yet been raised by HMRC.

- Flop Ltd was a large company in terms of the Companies Act definition for the year in question.

- Flop Ltd had taxable profits of £595,000 in the previous year.

Year ended 31 March 2006

The corporation tax return has not yet been submitted for this year. The accounts are late and nearing completion, with only one change still to be made. A notice requiring the company to file a self-assessment corporation tax return (CT203) dated 27 July 2006 was received on 1 August 2006. No corporation tax has yet been paid.

- The computation currently shows profits chargeable to corporation tax of £815,000 before accounting adjustments, and any adjustments for prior years.

- A company owing Flop Ltd £50,000 (excluding VAT) has gone into liquidation, and it is unlikely that any of this money will be paid. The money has been outstanding since 3 September 2005, and the irrecoverable debt will need to be included in the accounts.

Fred also believes there are problems in relation to the company's VAT administration. The VAT return for the quarter ended 31 March 2007 was submitted on 5 May 2007, and VAT of £24,000 was paid at the same time. The previous return to 31 December 2006 was also submitted late. In addition, no account has been made for the VAT on the irrecoverable debt. The VAT return for 30 June 2007 may also be late. Fred estimates the VAT liability for that quarter to be £8,250.

Required:

(a)   (i)   Calculate the revised corporation tax (CT) payable for the accounting periods ending 31 March 2005 and 2006 respectively.

             Your answer should include an explanation of the adjustments made as a result of the information which has now come to light.   **(7 marks)**

      (ii)   State, giving reasons, the due payment date of the corporation tax (CT) and the filing date of the corporation tax return for each period, and identify any interest and penalties which may have arisen to date.   **(8 marks)**

             Assume that the rates and allowances for the Financial Year 2006 apply throughout this part.

(b)   Explain the consequences of filing the VAT returns late and advise Fred how he should deal with the underpayment and irrecoverable debt for VAT purposes.

           Your explanation should be supported by relevant calculations.   **(10 marks)**

                                          (Total: 25 marks)

GROUPS AND CONSORTIA

50   PACIFIC GROUP

The structure of the Pacific Group of companies, which has not changed for a number of years, is set out below. All of the companies prepare accounts to 31 March and are resident in the United Kingdon with the exception of Caspian Inc, which is resident in Mordor.

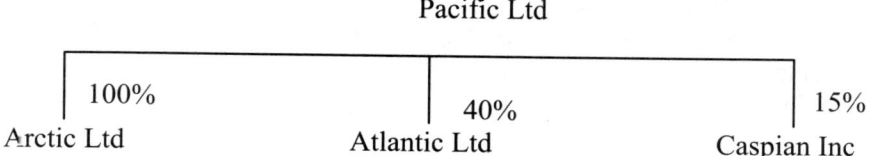

Pacific Ltd

100% Arctic Ltd   40% Atlantic Ltd   15% Caspian Inc

Pacific Ltd has the following results for the year to 31 March 2007.

	£
Tax adjusted trading profit	930,000
Bank interest receivable on a non-trading account	14,000
Dividend received from Caspian Inc	16,356
Dividends received (net) from UK resident companies	3,780
Profit on disposal of industrial unit	645,000
Gift Aid payments	3,400

Pacific Ltd purchased the industrial unit on 1 May 1985 for £260,000. It was sold on 1 July 2006 for £820,000. Pacific Ltd is renting a replacement unit and has no intention to acquire any buildings in the foreseeable future. The indexation factor from May 1985 to July 2006 is 1.071.

Arctic Ltd has profits chargeable to corporation tax for the year to 31 March 2007 of £80,000. The company has recently identified a supplier of freezers in Eisland, Icebox Inc, and intends to start importing them shortly. It acquired a new storage facility on 14 October 2006 for £790,000 and sent two of its employees to Eisland for meetings with Icebox Inc.

Arctic Ltd paid for the employees' flights and hotel bills while they were in Eisland. It also reimbursed them £18 per night each in respect of incidental expenses and provided them with medical cover for the trip at a cost of £140 each.

It is intended that Arctic Ltd will acquire Icebox Inc in due course. It is a profitable company with a worldwide customer base. It pays tax in Eisland at 14%, rather than the normal rate of 26% due to the existence of regional incentives for Eislandic companies. There is no double tax treaty between the United Kingdom and Eisland.

Atlantic Ltd made a trading loss in the year to 31 March 2007 of £76,000. Tasman Gmbh, a company resident in Germany, owns its remaining share capital.

The dividend received from Caspian Inc is after the deduction of 6% withholding tax in Mordor where the rate of corporation tax is 20%. Caspian Inc had the following results for the year ended 31 March 2007, out of which the dividend was paid to Pacific Ltd.

	£
Profit before tax	650,000
Tax charge	(149,500)
Profit after tax	500,500
Tax actually paid to the Mordor tax authorities	110,500

Pacific Ltd has appointed a new Finance Director who has had very little tax experience. He has asked you to summarise the rules concerning the dates on which Pacific Ltd and Arctic Ltd should file their tax returns and the penalties for late filing. He has also requested details of the dates on which the companies should pay their corporation tax liabilities in respect of the two years to 31 March 2008.

Required:

(a) Compute the corporation tax liability of Pacific Ltd for the year ended 31 March 2007 on the assumption that all claims and elections that will reduce the company's liability are made.

Provide supporting notes for the proposed claims and elections. **(11 marks)**

(b) Describe the VAT implications of the proposed imports of Arctic Ltd. **(3 marks)**

(c)   State the tax implications for the two employees of the payments they received in respect of the trip to Eisland.   **(3 marks)**

(d)   State the corporation tax implications of Arctic Ltd acquiring the trade and assets of Icebox Inc compared with acquiring the share capital of the company.   **(5 marks)**

(e)   Provide the Finance Director with the information requested.   **(3 marks)**

(Total: 25 marks)

Note: Ignore National Insurance contributions.

51   APPLE LTD

You should assume that today's date is 30 November 2007.

Apple Ltd has owned 80% of the ordinary share capital of Bramley Ltd and 85% of the ordinary share capital of Cox Ltd since these two companies were incorporated on 1 April 2005. Cox Ltd acquired 80% of the ordinary share capital of Delicious Ltd on 1 April 2006, the date of its incorporation.

The tax adjusted trading profits/(losses) of each company for the years ended 31 March 2006, 2007 and 2008 are as follows:

	Year ended 31 March 2006	Year ended 31 March 2007	Year ended 31 March 2008 (forecast)
	£	£	£
Apple Ltd	620,000	250,000	585,000
Bramley Ltd	(64,000)	52,000	70,000
Cox Ltd	83,000	(58,000)	40,000
Delicious Ltd	n/a	90,000	(15,000)

The following information is also available:

(1)   Apple Ltd sold a freehold office building on 10 March 2007 for £380,000, and this resulted in a capital gain of £120,000.

(2)   Apple Ltd sold a freehold warehouse on 5 October 2007 for £365,000, and this resulted in a capital gain of £80,000.

(3)   Cox Ltd purchased a freehold factory on 20 September 2007 for £360,000.

(4)   Delicious Ltd is planning to sell a leasehold factory building on 15 February 2008 for £180,000, and this will result in a capital loss of £44,000.

As each of the subsidiary companies has minority shareholders, the managing director of Apple Ltd has proposed that:

(1)   Trading tax losses should initially be carried back and relieved against profits of the loss making company, with any unrelieved amount then being carried forward.

(2)   Chargeable assets should not be transferred between group companies, and rollover relief should only be claimed where reinvestment is made by the company that incurred the chargeable gain. Similarly any other opportunities for 'grouping' gains and losses should be ignored.

Required:

(a) (i) Explain the group relationship that must exist for trading losses to be surrendered between group companies.

Distinguish this from the relationship that must exist for chargeable assets to be transferred between two companies in a group without incurring a chargeable gain or an allowable loss. **(4 marks)**

(ii) Explain the factors that should be taken into account by the Apple Ltd group when deciding to which group companies the trading losses should be surrendered. **(3 marks)**

(iii) Explain how groups can minimise corporation tax on capital gains. **(2 marks)**

(b) (i) Assuming that the managing director's proposals are followed, calculate the profits chargeable to corporation tax for each of the companies in the Apple Ltd group for the years ended 31 March 2006, 2007 and 2008 respectively.

(5 marks)

(ii) Advise the Apple Ltd group of the amount of corporation tax that could be saved for the years ended 31 March 2006, 2007 and 2008 if reliefs were instead claimed in the most beneficial manner.

You should assume that the corporation tax rates for the Financial Year 2006 will continue to apply. **(11 marks)**

(Total: 25 marks)

52 JUGLANS LTD AND LARIX LTD

Bob has owned all of the issued share capital of two UK resident companies, Juglans Limited and Larix Limited, for a number of years. Both companies qualify as small or medium sized enterprises.

(a) Juglans Limited has always had an accounting date of 31 December. Its most recent accounts have been prepared to 31 December 2006. The company is, however, now planning to prepare its accounts to 31 March and is considering whether it should prepare two sets of accounts, one to 31 March 2007 and the other to 31 March 2008 or whether it should prepare a single set of accounts for the fifteen month period ended 31 March 2008.

The following information is relevant:

1 Taxable trading profits *(before* capital allowances) are expected to accrue as follows:

£25,000 per calendar month for the 12 months to 31 December 2007

£35,000 per calendar month for the 3 months to 31 March 2008.

2 The tax written down value of Juglans Limited's capital allowance pool as at 31 December 2006 is £72,000. Juglans Limited bought some additional equipment on 30 April 2007 costing £90,000.

3 Juglans Limited sold two properties, one on 15 February 2007 realising a chargeable gain (after indexation) of £92,000 and the other on 30 June 2007 realising a capital loss of £32,000.

Required:

Advise Juglans Limited whether it would be beneficial to:

(i)   prepare two sets of accounts, one to 31 March 2007 and the other to 31 March 2008; or

(ii)   one set of accounts for the fifteen month period to 31 March 2008.

Your answer should explain how the various items are allocated where there is a long period of account and also include a calculation of the corporation tax liabilities payable under both options.

You should assume that the tax rates applicable to the Financial Year 2006 apply throughout.

(12 marks)

(b)   Larix Limited is expected to make a tax adjusted loss of £45,000 and a capital loss of £30,000 for its twelve month accounting period ended 31 March 2008.

In addition, whilst Juglans Limited makes only taxable supplies for the purposes of VAT, 90% of the supplies made by Larix Limited are exempt for VAT purposes. The following information is relevant for the 12 month period ended 31 March 2008.

		£
Juglans Limited	Total supplies (excluding VAT)	1,100,000
	Input tax	125,000
Larix Limited	Total supplies (excluding VAT)	1,550,000
	Input tax	
	Relating to exempt supplies	134,000
	Relating to taxable supplies	12,000
	Unattributed	20,000

There is no trading between Juglans Limited and Larix Limited. £123,000 of the total input tax for Juglans Limited is directly attributed to making its taxable supplies.

Bob has heard that there are various 'reliefs' for groups of companies that may be of benefit to Juglans Limited and Larix Limited and has asked you for advice in this regard.

Required:

(i)   Having specific regard to the trading and capital losses made by Larix Limited in its accounting period ended 31 March 2008 advise Bob of the reliefs available to groups of companies and explain whether Juglans Limited is able to benefit from these reliefs.

(4 marks)

(ii)   Advise Bob whether Juglans Limited and Larix Limited can be group registered for VAT purposes and explain whether a group VAT registration is likely to be beneficial.

(4 marks)

(Total: 20 marks)

53   ROMEO LTD

You should assume the date is 4 June 2007.

(a)   Romeo Limited is a UK resident company which prepares its accounts to 30 June each year. The company will be paying corporation tax at the full rate for the first time on its profits for the accounting period ended 30 June 2007.

Tony, the finance director of Romeo Limited, is concerned that the company will need to make quarterly corporation tax payments for its accounting period ending 30 June 2008 which is likely to put a strain on the company's forthcoming cash-flow. He has therefore asked you to assist with the preparation of forecast corporation tax computations for the period ending 30 June 2008.

You have been provided with the following information for the accounting period ending 30 June 2008:

(i)   Tax adjusted trading profits (before capital allowances) are expected to be £840,000.

(ii)   The following fixed asset transactions are forecast:

Acquisitions

1   2 cars costing £18,000 each – one of these will be a low CO_2 emission vehicle.

2   2 commercial vehicles costing £25,000 each.

3   Computer equipment costing £100,000.

4   Other equipment costing £60,000 which will include £20,000 on energy saving plant and machinery.

Disposals

1   A car originally costing £16,667 in October 2003 will be sold for £8,000 in October 2007.

2   Machinery originally costing £62,500 in December 2003 will be sold for £10,000 in December 2007.

3   An item of moveable specialised plant originally costing £25,000 in March 1997 will be sold for £33,000 in July 2007.

4   An office building originally costing £125,000 in March 1997 will be sold for £509,000 in July 2007.

(iii)   The expected tax written down values as at 1 July 2007 are:

	£
Plant	420,000
Expensive car	6,000
Short Life Asset	15,820

The asset in the short life asset pool is the machinery originally costing £62,500 which will be disposed of in December 2007.

(iv)   Romeo Limited has one associated company Alpha Limited which is a wholly owned subsidiary.

(v)   The Romeo group falls within the limits for a medium sized company for Companies Act purposes.

(vi)   Relevant Retail Price Index factors are as follows:

   March 1997   155.4
   April 1998   162.6
   July 2007   202.0

Required:

Advise Tony whether Romeo Limited will need to make quarterly corporation tax payments for its accounting period ending 30 June 2008.

Your answer should include a calculation of the forecast corporation tax liability for this period together with a note of when any payments will be due.

You should assume that the rates and allowances for the Financial Year 2006 apply throughout this part of the question.   **(13 marks)**

(b)   To guard against the possibility of quarterly corporation tax payments Tony has informed you that Romeo Limited has the opportunity to purchase all of the issued share capital of Leylander Limited, a UK resident trading company, for £50,000 on 30 June 2007. Leylander Limited also prepares its accounts to 30 June each year.

Tony informs you that this company operates in a similar trade area to Romeo Limited. Whilst Leylander Limited was once profitable the company's trading activities have now become negligible and there are trading losses brought forward amounting to £300,000. Tony believes that the Romeo Limited group of companies will be able to make use of these losses either under the group relief provisions or by placing profitable contracts from Romeo Limited into Leylander Limited post acquisition.

During the course of your review you ascertain that Romeo Limited's existing subsidiary, Alpha Limited is planning to acquire a factory in its accounting period ended 30 June 2008 which will cost £400,000 and will be immediately brought into use in Alpha Limited's trade.

Required:

Advise Tony

(i)   whether it will be possible to obtain relief for the brought forward Leylander Limited trading losses in the manner he believes; and   **(7 marks)**

(ii)   of any other action that may be taken by the Romeo Limited group to avoid Romeo Limited having to make quarterly corporation tax payments.   **(5 marks)**

                                                                    (Total: 25 marks)

54   ARABELLO

Assume today's date is 1 January 2007.

Arabello has recently approached you for advice regarding his group of companies. You ascertain the following:

Arabello is the managing director of Bastello Limited, a large unquoted trading company incorporated in the UK, and he owns all of the ordinary shares of this company. Arabello lives in the UK.

Bastello Limited has the following shareholdings in other unquoted companies.

1   75% of the ordinary shares of Castillo Limited a trading company also incorporated in the UK.

2   100% of the ordinary shares in Doimio Inc a non-UK resident trading company

3   10% of the ordinary shares in Estio Inc a non-UK resident trading company.

All the above companies prepare their accounts to 31 March each year. To date all of the companies have been reasonably profitable and this is expected to continue, with the exception of Doimio Inc, which has recently lost an important contract.

For the year ending 31 March 2008 the following results are anticipated:

	Tax adjusted trading profit/(loss) £	Chargeable gain profit/(loss) £
Bastello Limited	680,000	100,000
Castillo Limited	350,000	125,000
Doimio Inc	(300,000)	(75,000)
Estio Inc	600,000	–

The £75,000 capital loss of Doimio Inc is the expected loss than will be realised upon the disposal of a property by this company in the year ended 31 March 2008. £25,000 of this loss accrues on a time apportioned basis to the period before 1 April 2007.

Bastello Limited will make a gift aid donation of £5,000 in the year ending 31 March 2008. In this year Estio Inc is expected to pay a dividend of £40,500 to Bastello Limited. This is after deducting withholding taxes of 10%. It is anticipated that Estio Inc will pay £120,000 of overseas tax on its profits for this year.

Arabello believes that the trading and capital losses expected by Doimio Inc can automatically be relieved against the profits of Bastello Limited and Castillo Limited in the year ended 31 March 2008. As an alternative he believes that it will be possible to 'shift' profits to Doimio Inc by allowing this company to purchase products at below market value from Bastello Limited.

Required:

(a)   State the circumstances in which a company is regarded as UK resident for the purposes of corporation tax and explain, in the context of a group of companies, the significance of being so regarded.   **(5 marks)**

(b)   Explain to Arabello, giving reasons, whether he is correct in believing that:

(i)   Doimio Inc's losses can be automatically offset; and/or

(ii)   profits may be shifted to Doimio Inc

in the manner he has suggested in the year ending 31 March 2008.   **(7 marks)**

(c)   Advise Arabello of the actions that could be taken to allow relief for Doimio Inc's losses within the Bastello group of companies for the year ending 31 March 2008.
                    (3 marks)

(d)   Assuming that the trading and capital losses of Doimio Inc can now be relieved and will be used either by Bastello Limited or Castillo Limited, calculate the forecast corporation tax liabilities of Bastello Limited and Castillo Limited for the year ending 31 March 2008.

Your answer should explain the allocation of any reliefs within and between the two companies.

You should assume that the rates and allowances for the Financial Year 2006 apply throughout this part of the question.   **(10 marks)**

                    (Total: 25 marks)

55   A, B, C AND D

The following diagram illustrates a group of companies:

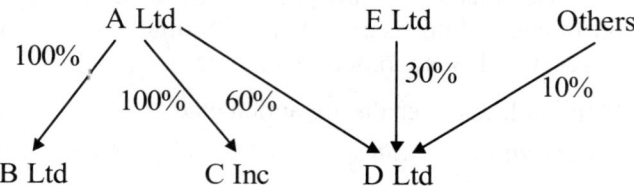

Additional information:

1.   All the companies are trading companies and all are resident in the UK with the exception of C Inc, which is resident overseas.

2.   All the companies prepare their accounts to 31 March with the exception of B Ltd, which prepares its accounts to 31 December.

3.   The group structure and related shareholdings have been unchanged for several years.

The most recent results of the four group companies, A Ltd, B Ltd, C Inc and D Ltd are as follows:

	A Ltd Year ended 31.3.2007 £	B Ltd Year ended 31.12.2006 £	C Inc Year ended 31.3.2007 £	D Ltd Year ended 31.3.2007 £
Trading profit/(loss)	205,000	(202,000)	100,000	(120,000)
Property income		50,000		
Chargeable gain	50,000			20,000
Tax provision			28,000	
Dividends paid	40,000		35,000	

The dividend paid by C Inc is stated before the deduction of 15% withholding tax. The corporation tax actually paid by C Inc was £800 more than provided for.

A Ltd's and D Ltd's chargeable gains arose from disposals made in June and November 2006 respectively.

B Ltd had a capital loss brought forward of £20,000 as at 1 January 2006.

Required:

(a)   Calculate the corporation tax (CT) payable by A Ltd, B Ltd and D Ltd, clearly identifying the beneficial reliefs that should be claimed/elections to be made.

Assume that all three companies wish to take relief for losses as early as possible.

(9 marks)

(b)   The managing director of A Ltd intends to sell the trade of B Ltd, as the company has been loss making for several years.

Advise him of the corporation tax (CT) (including capital gains), value added tax (VAT) and stamp duty/stamp duty land tax (SD/SDLT) consequences resulting from:

(1)   selling all of the shares in B Ltd to a third party; or

(2)   selling the assets of B Ltd to a third party, but retaining the shares in B Ltd.

Assume that any sale will take place in December 2007 and that B Ltd is not part of a VAT group.   **(16 marks)**

(Total: 25 marks)

56   THE GOLF GROUP

Assume today's date is 25 May 2007.

The Golf Group of companies is based in the UK and produces various types of storage vessels. The year end for all companies is 31 March. There are 5 companies in the group.

Golf plc (Golf) is the holding company. Hotel GmbH (Hotel) is a German subsidiary, all the other group companies are UK resident. Golf owns 100% of the issued share capital of each of the subsidiary companies, Hotel GmbH, India Ltd (India) and Juliet Ltd (Juliet). Juliet owns 100% of the issued share capital of Kilo Ltd (Kilo).

The group structure is as follows:

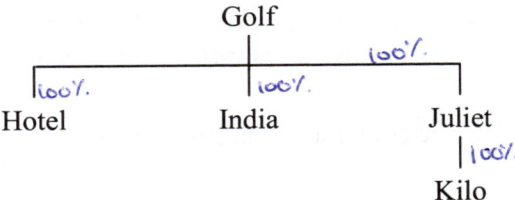

The results for the UK subsidiary companies for 2006 and 2007 are as follows:

Year ended 31 March 2006

Company	India	Juliet	Kilo
	£	£	£
Trading profit	335,000	(40,000)	35,000
Property business income	0	0	30,000
Interest income	0	5,000	2,500
Overseas property income (Note 1)	15,000	0	0
Chargeable gains / losses	25,000	0	0
Charges on income paid – Gift Aid	15,000	0	0

Note 1: This figure is shown gross of £6,000 withholding tax.

Year ended 31 March 2007 (draft figures)

	£	£	£
Trading profit	215,000	(120,000)	30,000
Property business income	0	0	25,000
Interest income	0	2,000	2,500
Chargeable gains / losses	(40,000)	20,000	0
Charges on income paid – Gift Aid	10,000	0	0

Additional information:

- Golf plc has investment income of approximately £1,000 per year in both years, in addition to dividends received from its subsidiaries.

- India paid corporation tax at the full rate of 30% in the year ended 31 March 2005. It was the only group company to do so.

- India has capital losses brought forward of £45,000 as at 1 April 2005. It is currently considering acquiring a new factory costing £470,000.

- In February 1996, India bought a property for £300,000. This property was transferred to Kilo for the same amount in March 2002. Its market value at that time was £510,000. This property has always been used for trading purposes.

- In April 2007, the group received an offer from a third party to acquire all of the shares of Kilo for a price of £1,200,000. Kilo's biggest asset is the property which was transferred from India in March 2002, which has been valued at £1,000,000. The terms of the purchase offer are that the Golf Group will pay all taxes arising directly from the disposal of Kilo. The proposed date of sale is June 2007, but the corporation tax liability of Kilo for the year ended 31 March 2008 will be paid by the purchasers.

- Kilo was originally incorporated in May 1998 and the base cost of its shares for capital gains tax was £25,000.

Required:

(a) (i) Calculate the UK corporation tax (CT) payable by the subsidiary companies for both accounting periods, making full use of any available reliefs in the most tax-efficient manner and clearly identifying any losses carried forward at 1 April 2007.

You are not required to calculate the corporation tax payable by Golf plc.

(13 marks)

(ii) State the tax payment dates for each of the UK group companies for the year ended 31 March 2006.
(3 marks)

(b) Quantify the potential corporation tax (CT) liabilities arising on the sale of Kilo Ltd in June 2007.

Clearly identify any reliefs available to reduce or defer the tax liabilities arising and explain their effect.
(7 marks)

(c) India Ltd, Juliet Ltd and Kilo Ltd form a registered group for VAT purposes, state giving reasons what action should be taken in respect of this group VAT registration on the sale of Kilo Ltd.
(2 marks)

You should assume that the rates and allowances for the Financial Year 2006 apply throughout.

Relevant retail price index figures are:

February 1996	150.9
May 1998	163.5
March 2002	174.5
June 2007	201.6 (estimated)

(Total: 25 marks)

57   ALANTECH LTD

Assume today's date is 1 May 2007.

On 1 April 2000, Alan set up his own company, Alantech Ltd to design and produce technology components in mobile phones. He personally owns 100% of the share capital. Accounts are drawn up to 31 December each year.

The company was successful, and the profits made allowed Alantech Ltd to buy 7.5% of the ordinary shares in another technology company, Mobile Ltd, on 1 July 2002. The price paid for the shares was £75,000. At this time, the remaining ordinary shares in Mobile Ltd were held by Boron Ltd (7.5%), Carbon plc (40%) and Diamond Ltd (45%).

Technology companies faced difficult trading during this time, and although Alantech Ltd continued to make profits, other companies suffered. This allowed Alantech Ltd to buy 100% of the shares of Boron Ltd (together with its 100% subsidiary, Bubble Ltd) at a low price as both companies were performing poorly. The acquisition took place on 1 July 2006, and was funded by the sale of a building used in Alantech Ltd's trade. The building had cost £150,000 on 1 September 2000, and was sold for £250,000 on 1 May 2006.

The results for the companies are as follows:

Company Period end	Alantech Ltd 31.12.2006 £	Boron Ltd 31.12.2006 £	Bubble Ltd 31.12.2006 £
Tax adjusted trading profits (losses)	160,000	(120,000)	75,000
Chargeable gain	See above	40,000	
Interest receivable	10,000		

Additional information:

- Boron Ltd's chargeable gain arose prior to its acquisition by Alantech Ltd.

- Bubble Ltd has brought forward trading losses of £25,000 as at 1 January 2006.

- It is anticipated that Boron Ltd will make a small tax adjusted trading loss in 2007.

- Mobile Ltd is profit making.

Alan believes that to improve the Boron Ltd business, the company needs to invest in new high-tech fixed machinery within the next year. The projected cost of the fixed machinery is £200,000. In order to raise funds, Alantech Ltd and Boron Ltd will have to sell the shares in Mobile Ltd. From an examination of Boron Ltd's accounting records, Alan understands that Boron Ltd's holding of shares in Mobile Ltd was bought on 1 November 2001 for £55,000.

Alan has identified a possible sale of the group's entire shareholdings (15%) in Mobile Ltd for £300,000 to Carbon plc, as this will give Carbon plc a controlling shareholding in Mobile Ltd. He plans to sell the shares at the beginning of June 2007. Alan has heard that there is a form of tax relief available to companies selling shares and would like advice on whether or not it applies to his situation.

In addition, Alan has struggled to deal with the VAT returns for each company in the group, in particular the intra-group transactions, and wonders if there is any way in which the VAT accounting for the group can be simplified.

Required:

(a) Calculate the chargeable gain arising on Alantech Ltd's disposal of the building in May 2006. State clearly any reliefs available, and the conditions to be satisfied to obtain such reliefs. **(6 marks)**

(b) Calculate the corporation tax (CT) liabilities for Alantech Ltd, Boron Ltd and Bubble Ltd for the year ending 31 December 2006 on the assumption that loss reliefs are taken as early as possible. **(9 marks)**

Assume that the Financial Year 2006 rates and allowances apply throughout the whole period.

(c) Advise Alan on the proposed disposal of the shares in Mobile Ltd.

Your answer should include calculations of the potential capital gain, and explain any options available to Alan to reduce this tax liability. **(7 marks)**

(d) Briefly describe how the VAT position for the group can be simplified. **(3 marks)**

Assume that the relevant retail price index figures are:

September 2000	171.7
November 2001	173.6
July 2002	175.9
May 2006	196.4
June 2007	201.6

(Total: 25 marks)

58   AQUA LIMITED

Assume today's date is 1 May 2007.

Irroy is aged 45, and owns 75% of the ordinary share capital of two companies, Aqua Limited and Aria Limited. Her brother, Irwin, owns the remaining 25% of the shares in both companies.

Aqua Limited makes water tanks for aquariums, and has been trading for five years. Aria Limited makes loudspeakers, and is a new company, having started trading on 1 April 2006. Both companies have a 31 March year end.

The tax adjusted profits/(losses) for the two companies are as follows:

Year ended 31 March:	2007	2008 (estimated)	2009 (estimated)
	£	£	£
Aqua Limited	140,000	175,000	200,000
Aria Limited	(30,000)	(60,000)	(20,000)

Irroy would like to obtain tax relief for Aria Limited's trading losses as soon as possible.

Irroy wishes to expand the Aqua business, and is thinking of incorporating a subsidiary, Green Limited, in the Republic of Ireland in April 2008. Green Limited will sell water tanks supplied by Aqua Limited from the UK. Irroy estimates that the combined taxable profits of Aqua Limited and its Irish subsidiary, Green Limited, would increase from £200,000 to £275,000 for the year ended 31 March 2009.

The group currently qualifies as a small and medium sized enterprise (SME) under European Union (EU) definitions, and Irroy believes that this will continue to be the case after incorporating Green Limited.

In the Republic of Ireland, the standard rate of corporation tax (CT) is 12.5%, and the standard rate of value added tax (VAT) is 21%. A double tax treaty exists between the UK and the Republic of Ireland, based on the OECD model. Both countries are part of the EU.

Required:

(a)   (i)   Explain why the current corporate structure prevents the early relief of Aria Limited's losses.

Advise Irroy of two alternative ways in which the current structure can be amended so as to obtain such early relief.   **(6 marks)**

(ii)   Illustrate the benefit of revising the corporate structure by calculating the corporation tax (CT) payable for the year ended 31 March 2008, on the assumptions that:

(1)   no action is taken; and

(2)   an amended structure as recommended in (i) above is implemented from 1 June 2007.   **(3 marks)**

Assume that the corporation tax rates for the Financial Year 2006 apply throughout.

(b)   Explain the corporation tax (CT) and value added tax (VAT) issues that Irroy should be aware of, if she proceeds with her proposal for the Irish subsidiary, Green Limited.

Your answer should clearly identify those factors which will determine whether or not Green Limited is considered UK resident or Irish resident and the tax implications of each alternative situation.

You need not repeat points that are common to each situation.   **(16 marks)**

(Total: 25 marks)

TAXATION OF CORPORATE BUSINESSES – OTHER ASPECTS

59   RIMU LTD

Rimu Ltd has been a client of your firm since it was incorporated in the UK on 1 July 1992. The company imports exotic wood from managed plantations in Australia, which it uses to manufacture furniture.

The number of £1 ordinary shares owned by each shareholder on 1 November 2006 (today's date) is as follows.

George Napier	10,000
Clare Hastings	6,000
Zed Stone	9,000
Ben Steel	15,000

Ben Steel also owns 60% of Office Design Ltd, a UK unquoted trading company, which specialises in designing and furnishing executive offices and boardrooms. The companies are managed and operated independently but Office Design Ltd buys furniture from Rimu Ltd at 90% of that company's normal selling price.

George Napier, one of the original shareholders and the company's sales director, has come to you for advice following a falling out between him and his daughter, Clare, on the one side and Zed Stone and Ben Steel on the other.

George gave Clare the 6,000 shares on 1 November 1995, her 20th birthday. George was 47 at the time of the gift. They elected to hold over the gain which arose. Zed and Ben were the other original shareholders with George. The shares were originally subscribed for at par. It can be assumed that indexation allowance of £1.50 per share is available.

George and Clare want to sell all of their shares to the company as they feel that it is not possible to reconcile the two factions. Zed and Ben have agreed to the company purchasing its own shares in principle but have made it clear that there is only £180,000 available. This is to be used to purchase all of George's shares and as many of Clare's shares as possible. The purchase will take place on 31 December 2006 when a share is expected to be worth £15.70.

George and Clare both have taxable income in excess of £50,000. Clare owns a portfolio of shares, inherited from her mother, and regularly makes gains of £12,000 per annum.

Required:

(a)   State the conditions which must be satisfied by George, Clare and Rimu Ltd, for the purchase of own shares not to be treated as a distribution by the company.

Ignore the exemption available where the proceeds are used to pay an inheritance tax liability.   **(4 marks)**

(b)   On the assumption that all of the other conditions are satisfied, compute the number of shares which must be purchased from Clare in order for her to be subject to capital gains tax on the amount received.   **(3 marks)**

(c)   Explain, by reference to the amount of tax per share sold, why it is beneficial for Clare to be subject to capital gains tax on the amount received rather than income tax.

Assume that the share price is £14.00 and that the shares qualified as business assets for taper relief purposes throughout.   **(6 marks)**

(d)   (i)   Compute the price per share which George and Clare must accept if Clare is to obtain the beneficial treatment.   **(1 mark)**

(ii)   Compute the net cash, after deduction of tax, that George and Clare will have after the purchase of own shares.   **(6 marks)**

(e)   Advise Ben of any VAT and transfer pricing implications arising from his ownership of Rimu Ltd and Office Design Ltd, assuming that the two companies are classified as large for the transfer pricing legislation.   **(5 marks)**

(Total: 25 marks)

60   BLUETONE LTD

Bluetone Ltd is an unquoted trading company that manufactures compact discs. The company has four full-time working directors, each of whom owns 25% of its share capital of 200,000 £1 ordinary shares. These are currently valued as follows:

Shareholding	Value per share £
15%	9.00
25%	11.00
35%	12.50
50%	15.00

Melody Brown

Melody has recently been appointed a director after inheriting her father's 50,000 shares in Bluetone Ltd. Melody's father purchased the shareholding on 12 November 2006, but died on 15 February 2007. At the date of his death he also owned the following assets:

(1)   42,000 50p ordinary shares in Expanse plc quoted at 312 – 320, with bargains on that day of 282, 288, 306 and 324.

(2)   26,000 units in World-Growth, a unit trust. The bid price was 80 and the offer price was 84.

(3)   Building society deposits of £32,000 of which £11,000 were in an ISA.

(4)   His main residence valued at £125,000 with an outstanding repayment mortgage of £42,000.

(5)   A life insurance policy on his own life with an open market value of £53,000. Proceeds of £61,000 were received on 4 March 2007.

On 15 February 2007, Melody's father had an income tax liability of £6,600 and gambling debts of £1,200. Funeral expenses came to £3,460.

Under the terms of his will, Melody was left the shares in Bluetone Ltd. The shares are to bear their own IHT. Melody wants to retain the full 25% holding, so she is to personally account for the IHT liability. The residue of the estate was left to Melody's brother.

Melody's father made the following lifetime gifts:

(1)   On 10 February 2003 he made a wedding gift of £50,000 to Melody.

(2)   On 4 June 2003 he made a gift of £179,000 into a discretionary trust.

Liam and Opal White

Liam and Opal, a married couple aged 47 and 48 respectively, have been directors and shareholders of Bluetone Ltd since its incorporation on 1 October 1992 when they acquired their shares at par.

On 20 March 2007 Liam is to sell 30,000 of his shares in Bluetone Ltd to their son for £75,000. Liam is a 40% taxpayer, and has not previously made any lifetime gifts of assets.

Noel Green

Noel is aged 48 and has been a director and shareholder of Bluetone Ltd since its incorporation on 1 October 1992. For the past two years he has disagreed with the other directors of Bluetone Ltd over the company's business policies. He is therefore to resign as a director on 31 March 2007, and it has been agreed that Bluetone Ltd will purchase his shareholding for £550,000.

HMRC has given advance clearance that the purchase qualifies for the special treatment applying to a company's purchase of its own shares, and can therefore be treated as a capital gain.

Noel acquired the shares at par, and is a 40% taxpayer.

For the year ended 31 March 2007 Bluetone Ltd is forecast to have profits chargeable to corporation tax of £1,100,000 and to pay dividends of £250,000 during the year. The company has no chargeable non-business assets.

Required:

(a) Calculate Melody's IHT liability and state when this will be due. **(10 marks)**

(b) Advise Liam of the CGT and IHT implications of selling the 30,000 shares in Bluetone Ltd to his son.

You should assume that reliefs are claimed in the most favourable manner. **(8 marks)**

(c) Advise Noel of whether it will be beneficial to have the purchase of his 25% shareholding treated as a capital gain under the special treatment, rather than as a distribution by Bluetone Ltd. **(7 marks)**

(Total: 25 marks)

Assume the rates and allowances for 2006/07 apply throughout.

61 INSECT LTD

Insect Ltd is an unquoted trading company that is under the control of four brothers, John, Paul, Richard and George Bug. Insect Ltd is a close company, and its share capital consists of 200,000 £1 ordinary shares, of which John, Paul, Richard and George each own 50,000 shares. John, Paul and Richard are full-time working directors of Insect Ltd, but George is neither a director nor an employee.

John is aged 47 and has been a full-time working director and shareholder of Insect Ltd since its incorporation on 1 October 1994, when he subscribed for his shares at their par value. In recent years, John has disagreed with his brothers over the company's business policies. He therefore resigned as a director on 31 March 2007, on which date Insect Ltd purchased his 50,000 £1 ordinary shares for £680,000.

On 6 April 2006 Insect Ltd provided Paul, Richard and George with new 2200cc motor cars with a list price of £27,000 and carbon dioxide emissions of 187 g/km each. During 2006/07 the brothers' business mileage was Paul 8,800 miles, Richard 22,400 miles and George nil miles. Paul made a capital contribution of £6,000 towards the cost of his motor car. No private petrol was provided during 2006/07 to any of the brothers.

On 6 July 2006 Insect Ltd made interest free loans of £75,000 each to Paul, Richard and George. Paul used the loan to finance the purchase of his main residence, and Richard and George used their loans to purchase holiday apartments in the USA. Insect Ltd wrote off £25,000 of George's loan on 31 March 2007.

John, Paul, Richard and George are all 40% taxpayers, and are resident and ordinarily resident in the UK. Insect Ltd makes up its accounts to 31 March each year, pays the small company rate of corporation tax, and has no chargeable non-business assets.

Required:

(a)   (i)   Explain briefly why Insect Ltd's purchase of John's 50,000 £1 ordinary shares will qualify to be treated as a capital gain under the special treatment, rather than as a distribution by Insect Ltd.

                                                          (4 marks)

       (ii)   Advise both Insect Ltd and John as to whether it is beneficial for the purchase of John's 50,000 £1 ordinary shares to be treated as a capital gain rather than as a distribution.

                The relevant indexation indices are 145.2 for October 1994 and 162.6 for April 1998.

                                                          (9 marks)

(b)   Advise both Insect Ltd and Paul, Richard and George of the corporation tax and income tax implications arising from:

       (i)   The provision of the three company motors cars.

       (ii)   The provision of the interest free loans of £75,000.

       Your answer should be confined to the implications for 2006/07, and should include calculations of any tax liabilities except NIC and VAT which should be ignored.

                                                          (12 marks)

                                                     (Total: 25 marks)

RESIDENCE ISSUES

62   GLOBAL PLC

Global plc is a large UK resident manufacturing company whose taxable trading profits for the year ended 30 September 2007 are forecast to be £2,250,000. The company has asked for your advice regarding transactions taking place during the year ended 30 September 2007.

You should assume that today's date is 15 March 2007.

(1)   On 1 November 2006 Global plc purchased a 90% shareholding in Nouveau Inc., a manufacturing company resident in and controlled from the country of Northia. Its forecast profits for the year ended 31 March 2007 are £700,000, and these will be subject to corporation tax at the rate of 25% in Northia. On 15 April 2007 Nouveau Inc. is planning to pay a dividend of £300,000, and this will be subject to withholding tax at the rate of 5%.

(2)   During May 2007 Global plc is planning to sell 10,000 units of a product to Nouveau Inc. at a price of £12.75 per unit. This is 25% less than the trade-selling price given to other customers.

(3)   On 1 November 2006 Global plc set up a branch in the country of Eastina. The branch is controlled from Eastina, and its forecast profits for the period to 30 September 2007 are £175,000. These are subject to tax at the rate of 40% in Eastina. 50% of the after tax profits will be remitted to the UK.

(4)   On 31 March 2007 Global plc is planning to sell its 80% shareholding in Surplus Ltd, a company resident in the UK, for £1,750,000. The disposal will result in a gain of £990,000. The indexation allowance is £150,000. However, the sale agreement states that the sale proceeds will be reduced by any corporation tax liability that Surplus Ltd has in respect of intra-group capital transactions taking place prior to the date of sale.

Global plc transferred a factory to Surplus Ltd on 20 June 2001, when the factory was valued at £630,000. The factory originally cost Global plc £260,000 on 17 May 1992. It is still owned by Surplus Ltd, and is currently valued at £720,000. The indexation allowance from May 1992 to June 2001 is £65,520, and from May 1992 to March 2007 it is £114,140. Surplus Ltd prepares its accounts to 30 September and pays corporation tax at the full rate.

(5)   On 1 February 2007 Global plc purchased an 85% shareholding in Wanted Ltd, a UK resident company. The company is forecast to make a tax adjusted trading loss of £240,000 for the year ended 30 September 2007. On 20 December 2006 Wanted Ltd sold investments for £425,000, resulting in a capital loss of £170,000.

In all cases, the overseas forecast profits are the same for accounting and taxation purposes. The double taxation treaties between the UK and Northia and Eastina provide that overseas taxes are relieved as a tax credit against UK corporation tax. Nouveau Inc is not a controlled foreign company.

Required:

(a)   Advise Global plc of the corporation tax implications of each of the transactions during the year ended 30 September 2007.   **(18 marks)**

(b)   Explain how Global plc will be affected by the requirement to make quarterly instalment payments in respect of its corporation tax liability for the year ended 30 September 2007.   **(4 marks)**

You are *not expected* to calculate Global plc's corporation tax liability for the year ended 30 September 2007.

(Total: 22 marks)

63   HORIZON LTD

(a)   Horizon Ltd is a UK resident company that manufactures electrical components. The following information relates to the year ended 31 March 2007:

(1)   Horizon Ltd's tax adjusted trading profit for the year was £44,000.

(2)   Horizon Ltd has shareholdings of ordinary share capital in three UK resident companies. For the year ended 31 March 2007 each company made a tax adjusted trading loss and paid total dividends as follows:

Company	Percentage shareholding	Trading loss £	Dividends paid £
Arc Ltd	80%	81,000	27,000
Bend Ltd	60%	41,000	13,500
Curve Ltd	20%	44,000	54,000

The remaining ordinary share capital of each company is held by Zero Ltd, an unconnected company

(3)   Horizon Ltd has shareholdings of ordinary share capital in two companies that are resident in, and controlled from, the country of Slozobia. The results of each company for the year ended 31 March 2007 are as follows:

Company	Percentage shareholding	Pre-tax Profits £	Dividends paid £
Deep Inc	60%	480,000	237,120
Even Inc	5%	810,000	400,140

Profits are subject to corporation tax at the rate of 35% in Slozobia, and are the same for both accounting and taxation purposes. All dividends paid are net of withholding tax at the rate of 5%. The double taxation treaty between the UK and Slozobia provides that overseas taxes are relieved as a tax credit against UK corporation tax.

Deep Inc is not a controlled foreign company.

(4) On 15 June 2006 Horizon Ltd sold a freehold office building for £242,000, and this resulted in a capital gain of £52,000. During April 2007 Arc Ltd and Bend Ltd purchased freehold factories for £210,000 and £235,000 respectively.

Required:

Calculate Horizon Ltd's corporation tax liability for the year ended 31 March 2007.

You should assume that any available reliefs are claimed in the most favourable manner. **(17 marks)**

(b) Horizon Ltd undertook the following transactions during June 2007:

(1) An interest free loan of £500,000 was made to Deep Inc on 1 June 2007. The subsidiary would pay an interest rate of 8% if it had borrowed directly from a bank.

(2) Electrical components manufactured by Horizon Ltd were sold to Deep Inc for £120,000. This is 20% more than the trade-selling price given to other customers.

Required:

Advise Horizon Ltd of the UK corporation tax 'transfer pricing' implications of the transactions undertaken during June 2006.

Assume that Horizon Ltd is a large company for the purpose of the transfer pricing legislation. **(4 marks)**

(c) A sales manager employed by Deep Inc is to be assigned to work for Horizon Ltd in the UK for a period of thirty months. The manager, who is currently resident and domiciled in Slozobia, will continue to be employed by Deep Inc, and will perform duties both in the UK and in Slozobia. The manager has rental income from a property situated in Slozobia.

Required:

Briefly state the circumstances in which the manager will be liable to UK income tax in respect of:

(i) Earnings for duties performed in Slozobia.

(ii) Earnings for duties performed in the UK.

(iii) The rental income arising in Slozobia. **(4 marks)**

(Total: 25 marks)

64   BERTIE OVERSEAS

You have recently met with Bertie, a UK resident individual, who requires some preliminary advice concerning setting up an overseas operation. You ascertain during the course of the meeting that Bertie owns 30% of the share capital and is the managing director of Bertie Limited a successful UK resident trading company which manufactures lawnmowers in the UK. The remaining shares are held by other third party individuals.

Bertie Limited operates on a wholesale basis and currently only sells products in the UK. Bertie, however, believes the time is right for overseas expansion and is considering setting up a distribution operation in the country of Picea ('Bertie Overseas') which will be wholly owned by Bertie Limited. It is planned that Bertie Overseas will also operate on a wholesale basis and will only buy lawnmowers from Bertie Limited.

The following additional information is available:

1   Bertie Limited currently pays corporation tax at the full rate.

2   The rate of Picean corporation tax is 10%, irrespective of whether the trading entity is a branch or a company incorporated in Picea. Picean tax law only allows the offset of trading losses generated against other profits earned in the same period. Under Picean tax law no withholding tax is deductible on overseas profits remittances. There is no double tax treaty between the UK and Picea.

3   The mark up currently achieved by Bertie Limited, after all selling and distribution costs, on sales to its UK customers is 100%. The mark up on sales to Bertie Overseas will be 80%. Bertie Overseas will be responsible for all of its own selling and distribution costs including meeting carriage costs from the UK. Bertie believes that, in the absence of Bertie Overseas, Bertie Limited would achieve a comparable mark up on sales to Picea of 85%.

4   Setting up the Picean operation will involve the acquisition of some freehold premises as well as necessary vehicles and equipment.

5   Local Picean management will be appointed to run the day to day operations of Bertie Overseas. Bertie is considering retaining a high level of ultimate control over Bertie Overseas.

6   Bertie Limited is planning to charge Bertie Overseas interest on any loan finance provided at the rate of 4% per year. If Bertie Overseas were to arrange its own loan finance via an independent bank it would have been charged 6% per year.

7   The business plans produced indicate that Bertie Overseas is likely to make a loss for its first trading period and will then produce progressively stronger profits. Once profits are being generated it is planned to remit 25% of these to Bertie Limited.

Bertie has asked that you write to him setting out the principal business tax issues that need to be considered in advance of a future meeting where these issues will be discussed in more detail.

Required:

Write a letter to Bertie identifying the principal business tax issues that can be identified from the above information regarding the setting up of Bertie Overseas. You are not required to discuss any employee or sales tax issues.

The points covered should include *(but not be restricted to)* an analysis of whether Bertie Overseas should be set up as a branch or a limited company, the anti-avoidance legislation that HMRC could use to tax the overseas profits in the UK and whether relief will be available in the UK for any Picean taxes paid.

Marks will be awarded for presentation, structure and format.   **(25 marks)**

TAX PLANNING

65 CARL

It is September 2007 and you have just had a meeting with Carl Egmont.

Carl is employed as a chef by Diamond Hotels Ltd on a salary of £2,480 per month. His only other income is annual bank interest received of £1,040 on a 'nest egg' of £30,000, which he has been saving for a number of years for his old age. He also owns his own house, which is currently worth £150,000 on which there is a mortgage of £100,000.

Carl intends to open a restaurant 'Chez Egmont', on 1 January 2008. On 1 September 2006 he sold an oil painting for £88,000 to provide funds to start the business. He had inherited the painting on 12 October 2004, on the death of his father, when it was worth £66,000. His father acquired the painting in July 1987 for £14,000. Carl had not made a capital gain prior to the disposal of the painting.

He has spent the summer of 2007 researching business opportunities. This has involved Carl and two friends visiting a large number of local hotels and restaurants, at a cost of £2,500, as well as market research by an advertising agency, which cost a further £4,500.

Carl has identified suitable premises which will cost £100,000. This includes the cost of a considerable amount of work which is required before the restaurant can open for business. In particular, Carl wants to install a wooden floor and decorative romantic lighting in the restaurant area.

Carl will continue working for Diamond Hotels until 30 November 2007.

The restaurant will take some time to establish itself. As a result of this it will make an adjusted loss in the year to 31 December 2008, its first trading period, of £27,500. It is expected to be profitable from then on with a profit in the next year of £20,000. The costs incurred by Carl in the summer, together with the cost of the wooden floor and the lighting have been ignored in arriving at these figures.

Carl has come to you for advice on the tax and financial implications of the start up of the business. Carl has retained all of the funds from the sale of the oil painting, less the amount spent in the summer of £7,000, and is planning to fund the balance of the £100,000 funds required by agreeing an overdraft facility of £25,000. He believes that this will provide him with sufficient funds to fund the purchase of the premises plus £6,000 for his working capital requirements for the first year without having to use his 'nest egg'.

Required:

Using the tax rates and allowances for 2006/07 throughout, write a letter to Carl, which both explains and advises on the following issues.

(a)   How much of the funds generated by the sale of the oil painting will be required to settle the capital gains tax liability arising from the sale and why his plans to finance the funds required by the business in the first year are not feasible. Suggest an alternative approach.   **(5 marks)**

(b)   How the loss for the year to 31 December 2008 can be used, the strategy which saves the maximum amount of tax and the amount of tax saved. The cost of the wooden floor and the lighting (together with the costs of finance identified in part (a)) should be ignored for this part of this question.   **(15 marks)**

(c)   The tax treatment of the cost of the wooden floor and the lighting.   **(3 marks)**

Candidates should be aware that marks are specifically awarded for letter writing skills.

(2 marks)

(Total: 25 marks)

66   GARDEN LTD

(a)   Garden Ltd is a medium-sized unquoted company involved in the manufacture of gardening equipment. Due to a rapid expansion of its trade, the company requires an additional factory. Two alternative options have been identified as follows:

    (i)   A new factory can be constructed by a building company. This will take six months to complete, and will cost £470,000 as follows:

	£
Land	80,000
Levelling the land	10,300
Architects and legal fees	24,300
Ventilation and heating systems	12,500
Fire alarm and sprinkler system	6,400
Strengthened concrete floor to support machinery	16,500
General offices	62,500
Factory	187,500
VAT	70,000
	470,000

    (ii)   A suitable factory is available for rent. The owners of the factory are prepared to grant a 40 year lease for a premium of £470,000. The annual rent payable will be £35,250. The owners will exercise their option to tax the grant of the lease, and it will therefore be standard rated. Both figures are inclusive of VAT where applicable.

Whichever alternative is chosen, it will be financed as follows:

    (i)   A loan of £200,000 will be raised by an issue of 12% debentures. If the alternative of building the new factory is chosen, the debenture interest relating to the period of construction will be capitalised.

    (ii)   A warehouse will be sold for £270,000 (including land of £90,000). The warehouse cost £120,000 (including land of £50,000) when it was acquired seven years ago. The warehouse was originally built 10 years ago at a cost of £102,000 (including land of £42,000). It has always been used to store raw materials. The relevant RPI factor in respect of this disposal is 0.360.

Garden Ltd is registered for VAT. None of the above buildings are situated in Enterprise Zones.

Required:

Advise Garden Ltd of the tax implications arising from the two alternatives, and from the financing of whichever alternative is chosen.   **(13 marks)**

(b)   During August 2006 Garden Ltd increased its share capital to 1,000,000 ordinary shares, by issuing 500,000 new ordinary shares at £1 per share. These were subscribed for as follows:

	Shares
Alex Bush	50,000
Carol Daisy	215,000
Edward Fern	185,000
Gary Hedge	50,000
	500,000

Garden Ltd's original share capital of 500,000 ordinary shares has been held by Alex Bush since 1986.

Alex and Gary have been directors of Garden Ltd since 1986, whilst Carol and Edward are going to be appointed as directors during 2007. Carol and Edward have not previously been employed by the company.

Alex is 57 years old, Gary is 51, whilst Carol and Edward are both 40. None of the shareholders are connected to each other. They are all 40% taxpayers.

Carol financed the cost of her shareholding by selling a property for £350,000, which resulted in a chargeable gain of £225,000.

Due to its rapid expansion, Garden Ltd is planning to obtain a Stock Exchange listing within the next two or three years. This will be achieved by the company issuing 500,000 new ordinary shares on the Stock Exchange.

Required:

Advise each of the shareholders of Garden Ltd of the tax implications arising from:

(i)   their subscription for new ordinary share capital in Garden Ltd during August 2006.

(ii)   Garden Ltd's proposed listing on the Stock Exchange in two or three years' time.

(12 marks)

(Total: 25 marks)

67   SCHOONER LTD

Schooner Ltd is an unquoted company that constructs yachts. The company has recently accepted a large contract to supply yachts to Highseas plc. The new contract will commence on 1 January 2007, and will have the following implications for Schooner Ltd:

(a)   Each yacht will take three months to construct, and will be sold for £350,000. Highseas plc will pay a deposit of £50,000 at the beginning of the three-month period, and a further payment on account of £100,000 two months later. An invoice for the total price of £350,000 plus VAT will be raised ten days after completion of each yacht, and the balance due will be paid within 60 days. The three-monthly construction periods will be coterminous with Schooner Ltd's quarterly VAT periods.

(b)   Schooner Ltd will acquire new equipment costing £800,000 on 1 January 2007.

(1)   The company has sufficient funds to purchase £250,000 of the equipment outright, and all of this is to be imported into the UK. Equipment costing £160,000 will be imported from countries that are members of the European Union, with the remainder imported from countries that are outside the European Union.

(2)   Equipment costing £200,000 will be bought on hire purchase, with the company making 16 quarterly payments of £17,250 commencing on 1 January 2007. VAT will be paid with the first quarterly payment.

(3)   Equipment costing £350,000 will be leased at a cost of £145,000 pa. The lease will be treated as a finance lease, and therefore the equipment will be capitalised as a fixed asset by Schooner Ltd.

All figures are exclusive of VAT where appropriate.

(c)   Schooner Ltd will raise additional finance of £650,000 on 1 January 2007 in order to provide working capital.

(1)   The managing director of Schooner Ltd, Alex Barnacle, will borrow £100,000 at an interest rate of 8% using his main residence as security. This amount will be lent interest free to Schooner Ltd. At present, the main residence is not mortgaged. Alex owns 35% of Schooner Ltd's ordinary share capital.

(2)   An issue of 10% debentures will raise a loan of £300,000. The debentures will be issued at a 5% discount to their nominal value, and will be redeemable in five years time. Professional fees of £8,000 will be incurred in respect of the issue.

(3)   An issue of new ordinary £1.00 shares at £1.60 per share will raise £250,000. Chloe Dhow is to subscribe for 100,000 of the new shares. She presently has no connection with Schooner Ltd, but will be appointed a director following the share issue. Professional fees of £12,500 will be incurred in respect of the issue.

Schooner Ltd prepares its accounts to 31 December. It is a close company, currently has an issued share capital of 1,000,000 £1 ordinary shares, and is a small company as defined by the Companies Acts. The company's sales are all standard rated.

Required:

(a)   Advise Schooner Ltd of the VAT rules relating to the time of supply for goods, and explain the output tax entries that will be made in respect of the new contract on its quarterly VAT returns.   **(5 marks)**

(b)   (i)   Advise Schooner Ltd of the effect that the acquisition of the new equipment will have on its tax adjusted trading profits for the year ended 31 December 2007.

(ii)   Advise Schooner Ltd of the VAT implications of acquiring the new equipment.
                                              (9 marks)

(c)   (i)   Advise Schooner Ltd of the effect that raising the additional finance will have on its tax adjusted trading profits for the year ended 31 December 2007.

(ii)   Advise Alex and Chloe of the tax relief that will be available to them in respect of their investment in Schooner Ltd.   **(11 marks)**

                                              (Total: 25 marks)

68   PHOENIX

Assume today's date is 1 December 2007.

Phoenix has been trading as a self-employed mechanic since 1 October 2005 preparing accounts to 31 December. His actual and forecast tax adjusted trading profits for the accounting periods from commencement to 31 December 2007 are as follows:

	Profit/(loss) £
1 October 2005 to 31 December 2006 *(after* capital allowances)	4,500
Forecast for year ended 31 December 2007 *(before* capital allowances)	(5,000)

To date his business has not been that successful. Phoenix has, however, recently been awarded a contract to maintain the company car fleet of a large local company. This contract will commence on 1 January 2008. It is anticipated that tax adjusted trading profits (before capital allowances and the new contract) for the year ended 31 December 2008 will amount to £7,000, whilst the new contract will produce additional tax adjusted profits in the order of £40,000 per year.

The tax written down value for capital allowance purposes of Phoenix's plant and machinery pool as at 31 December 2006 is £6,250. At 31 December 2007 the market value of pooled assets is expected to be £8,000. In all cases the market value for individual assets is less than original cost.

Prior to commencing self-employment Phoenix had been unemployed for several years. His only other taxable income in 2005/06 was income based job seekers allowance amounting to £1,380. He will have no other income for the tax years 2006/07 to 2008/09 inclusive, other than income from his business.

Phoenix has heard that there may be some advantages in transferring his business to a newly formed limited company which would be called Phoenix Limited. If the incorporation proceeds Phoenix will become a director and the company will begin trading on 1 January 2008 and make up its first accounts to 31 December 2008. After seeking advice he proposes that, if he incorporates, his salary for the period 1 January 2008 to 5 April 2008 will be £4,400 and for 2008/09 will be £7,500 (which will be paid evenly through this tax year). In addition he will receive gross dividends from Phoenix Limited of £12,000 on 31 December 2008.

Required:

(a) Explain how the forecast trading loss for the year ended 31 December 2007 can be used, if:

  (i)   Phoenix does not incorporate his business; or

  (ii) Phoenix incorporates on 1 January 2008.

  Advise in each case how the loss may be used in the most tax efficient manner.

  You are not required to perform calculations for this part of the question.   **(7 marks)**

(b) Assuming Phoenix incorporates his business on 1 January 2008 explain the options that are open to him regarding the calculation of his capital allowances for the year ended 31 December 2007. Advise which of these options is preferable.   **(5 marks)**

(c) Advise whether Phoenix should:

  (i)   Continue as a sole trader; or

  (ii) Incorporate his business on 1 January 2008.

  Your answer should be restricted to a consideration of taxation issues only and include detailed calculations of the income tax and Class 1 and Class 4 National Insurance payable for the tax years 2005/06 to 2008/09 inclusive and corporation tax for the year ended 31 December 2008.

You should assume that the tax rates and allowances for 2006/07 apply throughout.

(18 marks)

(Total: 30 marks)

69   ETHEL

Today's date is 3 December 2007.

Ethel, who is aged 47, is the sole shareholder and director of Ethel Endeavours Limited, a trading company preparing its accounts to 31 December each year. Ethel has run this business from her home for several years. After a successful year to date the company's tax adjusted trading profits for the year ended 31 December 2007 have been forecast at £85,000 after a gross salary for Ethel of £26,000. Apart from this salary, Ethel currently has no other income.

Ethel has written to you seeking advice concerning the payment to her of a bonus of £20,000 gross before 31 December 2007. She has suggested that this could either be in the form of an additional lump sum salary payment or a dividend.

As alternatives Ethel would also like to know the tax implications if the payment takes the form of:

(1)   A lump sum premium by Ethel Endeavours Limited to an occupational pension fund for her benefit

(2)   An interest free loan made to herself. Ethel does not currently charge any rent to Ethel Endeavours Limited for the company's use of her property upon which she has a fairly large mortgage.

You have also been discussing with Ethel the possibility of gifting some of her shares in Ethel Endeavours Limited to her daughter who is aged 25.

Required:

Write a letter to Ethel advising her:

(a)   Whether the 'bonus' payment of £20,000 should take the form of additional salary or a dividend payment. Your answer should be supported by relevant calculations.

(4 marks)

(b)   Of the principal Corporation Tax, Income Tax, Capital Gains Tax and National Insurance Contribution implications of:

(i)   the two alternatives (pension payment or interest free loan) she has suggested; and

(ii)   charging a rent to Ethel Endeavours Limited for the company's use of her property. **(14 marks)**

(c)   Of the Capital Gains Tax implications of gifting some of her shares in Ethel Endeavours Limited to her daughter. **(5 marks)**

The tax rates and allowances for 2006/07 and Financial Year 2006 should be used throughout.

Presentation, structure and format of the answer. **(2 marks)**

(Total: 25 marks)

PERSONAL FINANCIAL PLANNING

70 ALICE AND ZARA

You should assume that today's date is 15 February 2007.

Alice and Zara Sibling are two sisters who have recently inherited £75,000 each. They have asked for your advice regarding the following proposals concerning the investment of their inheritance:

(1) Alice and Zara will both invest the maximum amount possible in Individual Savings Accounts (ISAs). Alice wants to invest in the cash component, with the balance in low risk investments within the stocks and shares component. Zara wants to invest solely in the stocks and shares component, with investments being made in ordinary shares.

(2) Alice and Zara will both invest the maximum tax-deductible amount into pension schemes. Alice was born on 15 June 1956, and earns a salary of £55,000 pa. She contributes 6% of her salary into her employer's HMRC registered occupational pension scheme, with the employer contributing a further 6%. Zara was born on 4 November 1968, and is self-employed. She has not previously made any provision for retirement. Zara's taxable trading profits for 2006/07 is expected to be £47,400.

(3) Alice is to invest the balance of her inheritance in an open-ended investment company aimed at capital growth. Zara is to use the balance of her inheritance to subscribe for new ordinary shares in a Venture Capital Trust that invests in unquoted high technology companies.

Alice already has investments worth £140,000, and receives investment income of £10,000 pa.

Her investment criteria are

(1) capital growth is more important than additional income,

(2) she is prepared to take a moderate amount of risk, and

(3) the capital is not needed for at least ten years.

Zara currently has no investments, and does not have any other income.

Her investment criteria are

(1) income is more important than capital growth,

(2) she is prepared to accept a high level of risk, and

(3) the capital will be needed in three years' time when Zara plans to buy a new house.

Required:

(a) For each of the proposed investments:

(i) Explain the potential income tax and CGT implications. Your answer should include details of the maximum amount that can be invested in each case, and be confined to the implications for 2006/07.

(ii) Advise Alice and Zara as to the suitability of each investment in relation to their investment criteria.   **(18 marks)**

(b) (i) Explain briefly whether or not you, as a Chartered Certified Accountant, would need to be authorised to conduct investment business under the Financial Services and Markets Act 2001 in order to provide the financial advice given to Alice and Zara in (a) above.   **(3 marks)**

(ii)   State the implications arising from the carrying on of investment business by a person who is *not authorised* to do so under the Financial Services and Markets Act 2001.   **(2 marks)**

(Total: 23 marks)

71   ABDUL, EMMA AND GEORGE

You should assume that today's date is 15 December 2006.

(a)   Abdul Bright won £12,000 in a competition on 3 April 2006. On 6 April 2006 he invested £3,500 of the winnings in a building society deposit account paying interest of 6% (gross) pa throughout 2006/07. The other £8,500 was used to purchase 8,500 £1 ordinary shares in Fast-Buck plc, a quoted company. Abdul received a dividend of £630 (net) from Fast-Buck plc on 15 September 2006, and sold the shares on 30 November 2006 for £29,750.

He now regrets not holding his investments within an Individual Savings Account (ISA). Abdul wants to know the amount of tax that he would have saved for 2006/07 if his investments had been held within an ISA. Abdul is a 40% taxpayer and has already utilised his CGT annual exemption for 2006/07.

(b)   Emma Flash subscribed for 25,000 £1 ordinary shares at par in Web-Com Ltd, an unquoted trading company on 30 November 1997. She subscribed for a further 150,000 £1 ordinary shares at par in the company on 30 January 2006. Emma claimed the maximum possible relief available under the Enterprise Investment Scheme (EIS) in respect of these subscriptions.

On 5 January 2007 she is going to sell her total holding of 175,000 £1 ordinary shares in Web-Com Ltd to an unrelated third party for £850,000.

Emma wants to know

(i)   the tax implications arising from the disposal of her 175,000 £1 ordinary shares in Web-Com Ltd, and

(ii)   if it will be possible to defer the capital gain arising on the disposal of the shares by reinvesting some or all of the disposal proceeds.

Emma is a 40% taxpayer and has already utilised her CGT annual exemption for 2006/07.

(c)   George Hardy inherited a house in London on 15 August 2006. During October 2006 the roof of the house was damaged by a gale, and was replaced at a cost of £9,700. George spent £6,900 decorating the house during November 2006.

He is planning to let out the house on 1 January 2007 either unfurnished or as furnished holiday accommodation. If the house is let unfurnished, George will receive a premium of £2,500 on 1 January 2007 for the grant of a five-year lease. The rent will be £12,000 pa payable annually in advance. If the house is let as furnished holiday accommodation, then it will be furnished at a cost of £13,500 during December 2006. The forecast rental income is £1,950 per month (accruing evenly throughout the year) based upon 40 weeks' letting each year. The running costs will be £450 per month.

George wants to know the income tax implications for 2006/07 of letting out the house either unfurnished or as furnished holiday accommodation.

Required:

Advise Abdul, Emma and George regarding the queries that they have raised.

You should assume that the tax rates and allowances for 2006/07 apply throughout.

Marks will be allocated on the basis of:

(6 marks to (a))
(6 marks to (b))
(7 marks to (c))
(Total: 19 marks)

72   CYRIL AND MABEL

(a)   You have recently been approached by Cyril (aged 34) and his wife Mabel (aged 36) who commenced in partnership on 1 October 2004 sharing profits and losses equally. The couple, who do not have any children, have not yet filed any tax returns or paid any tax to HMRC.

You ascertain that their taxable trading profits are as follows:

	£
1/10/2004 to 31/01/2005	120,000
Year ended 31/01/2006	24,000
Year ended 31/01/2007	36,000

Cyril also received taxable jobseekers allowance amounting to £2,540 in 2004/05.

Required:

Calculate the couples Income Tax and Class 4 National Insurance liabilities for the tax years 2004/05 to 2006/07 inclusive.

You should assume that the rates and allowances for 2006/07 apply throughout this part of the question.

(6 marks)

(b)   Following negotiations with HMRC it is anticipated that a tax settlement figure of £21,000, which includes interest and penalties, will shortly be agreed.

The couple have indicated that they believe they would have difficulty in meeting a tax settlement of this order in the near future. They have therefore requested that you review their financial affairs in the hope that recommendations can be made.

During your review you ascertain the following:

Business overdraft

The business currently has an unsecured overdraft facility of £15,000. This facility was originally used to acquire a vehicle and much of the equipment now used in the business. Since the beginning of the business the partners have struggled to keep within this limit which has frequently been exceeded for short periods of time leading to fairly substantial bank charges being incurred. Their bank manager has expressed a reluctance to further extend the overdraft facility although he is willing to explore the possibility of a loan.

As their projections indicate that the business has a positive future and will in time become more profitable it is not in the couple's plans to discontinue the business. Currently Cyril and Mabel only draw sufficient from the business to meet the needs of their fairly basic lifestyle.

Personal overdrafts/Credit Cards

Cyril has a personal overdraft facility of £3,000 of which £500 remains free. Mabel has a credit card facility of £2,500 of which £2,000 remains free.

Savings etc.

Cyril and Mabel have savings in the form of building society deposits of approximately £2,500 and £3,000 respectively.

Cyril contributes £100 per month (gross) into a personal pension plan. He also pays £75 per month for £200,000 worth of term assurance covering his wife's and his own lives.

House

The couple own the freehold in their home which is currently worth approximately £250,000. They have a repayment mortgage with approximately £185,000 of capital outstanding.

Required:

(i) Advise Cyril and Mabel whether it was sensible from a financial planning perspective to use the original overdraft facility to purchase the fixed assets used in their business. **(3 marks)**

(ii) Explain the sources of finance that are or may be available to the couple to pay the outstanding tax settlement of £21,000. **(10 marks)**

(iii) Make reasoned recommendations to the couple identifying the most appropriate sources of finance to fund the tax settlement and helping to resolve any other financial problems identified. **(6 marks)**

(Total: 25 marks)

73 FREDERICK FAIRCHILD

(a) Frederick Fairchild has recently approached you for advice. You learn that he is aged 56, married with no children and has been informed that he is being made redundant from Freestone Enterprises Limited in February 2007, where he has worked for many years in a senior managerial capacity. Upon his departure Frederick will become entitled to a redundancy package comprising the following elements:

(1) £25,000 under the terms of his contract of employment.

(2) Statutory redundancy pay of £5,000.

(3) A lump sum payment from the company's registered occupational pension scheme of £30,000 together with a reduced annual pension.

(4) A payment of £10,000 to prevent Frederick from starting up a company in competition against Freestone Enterprises Limited.

(5) £60,000 described as an ex-gratia payment.

Frederick, who is a higher rate taxpayer, is currently undecided whether he will be seeking future employment.

Required:

Advise Frederick of the income tax implications of his redundancy package and why HMRC are likely to be interested in whether or not he will be seeking further employment. **(8 marks)**

(b) Following Frederick's redundancy he approaches you again for some further advice. You learn that he has decided to actively look for another job and that he has approximately £100,000 to invest as a result of the after tax lump sum payments received from his former employer and the pension scheme.

He further informs you that he is considering using these funds to:

(1)   Redeem his outstanding repayment mortgage of £50,000 which has 10 years left to run. He currently pays interest at an annual rate of 8.5%.

(2)   Acquire an equity interest in a limited company called Exciting Escapades Limited run by a friend of his. His investment could be as high as £30,000 for the issue to him of 25,000 new ordinary shares in this company. Currently there are 75,000 ordinary shares in issue and Frederick's wife owns 7,500 of them.

His friend has suggested that Frederick could join this company as an employee earning a salary of £35,000 per year either before or after making the investment.

If Frederick acquires these shares he would be looking to sell them in a few years time when he finally decides to retire.

Frederick believes that whilst this investment may be considered high risk it will attract significant tax advantages and as a result is willing to consider it further.

(3)   Acquire low to medium risk investments offering the potential for tax-free returns where capital growth over the medium to longer term is more important than income generation.

Required:

Advise Frederick of:

(i)   The factors that he needs to consider when deciding whether to use part of his lump sum to redeem his outstanding mortgage.   **(4 marks)**

(ii)   The main issues that he needs to consider in securing the tax advantages to which he refers upon making an investment in the ordinary share capital of Exciting Escapades Limited, together with an explanation of those advantages.
                                                                                   (9 marks)

(iii) Two types of additional investments suitable for the funds remaining after redeeming his mortgage and purchasing some of the share capital of Exciting Escapades Limited.

Your answer should include a brief explanation of why the investments you have chosen are considered suitable.   **(4 marks)**

                                                                          (Total: 25 marks)

74   PHILIP

Assume today's date is 15 February 2007.

Philip is 48, and married to Rachel, 44. He is a higher rate taxpayer, and has recently been told that he is to be made redundant from Stelvin Ltd, the unquoted trading company he works for, with effect from 31 March 2007.

Philip has been offered the following severance package.

	£
Remaining two months notice period	10,000
Ex-gratia payment	40,000
Help with finding new employment, valued at	2,000
Use of a company car for 8 months, valued at	4,400

Philip had 4,500 share options in Stelvin Ltd granted to him in October 2000. The options were granted under an approved company share option plan. He exercised these options in July 2006 at an exercise price of £3.50 per share being the market value of the shares when the options were granted. The market value of the shares at that time was £5.50, and is now £6.20. He is permitted to sell or transfer the shares prior to leaving the company. His intention is to sell the shares next week. Philip has not made any other disposals of capital.

Philip wants to invest the money received from both the severance package and the share sale. He is attracted towards buying shares in new companies which require funds for their development, and for which tax reliefs might be available. However, Rachel is more cautious, and would prefer to invest some of the money in investments with less risk to their capital, but with a reasonable return.

Required:

(a)   Calculate the income tax (IT) payable on Philip's severance package, stating clearly your reasons for the tax treatment of each item.   **(4 marks)**

(b)   Calculate the capital gains tax on the sale of Philip's shares in Stelvin Limited.
                                                                                        (2 marks)

(c)   (i)   Identify two tax incentives which Philip might utilise when buying shares in new and/or developing companies, stating clearly the tax implications of each.
                                                                                        (9 marks)

        (ii)   Identify three types of low risk investment that would meet Rachel's stated investment objectives. In each case state the factors that qualify the investment as low risk together with their tax treatment.   **(5 marks)**

(d)   Briefly describe the operation of business protection (key person) insurance. Your answer should identify the types of insurance most frequently used for this purpose and state how they are treated for tax purposes.   **(5 marks)**

                                                                            (Total: 25 marks)

75   HAPPY HOME LTD

Assume today's date is 16 April 2007.

Henry, aged 48, is the managing director of Happy Home Ltd, an unquoted UK company specialising in interior design. He is wealthy in his own right and is married to Helen, who is 45 years old. They have two children – Stephen, who is 19, and Sally who is 17.

As part of his salary, Henry was given 3,000 shares in Happy Home Ltd with an option to acquire a further 10,000 shares. The options were granted on 15 July 2005, shortly after the company started trading, and were not part of an approved share option scheme. The free shares were given to Henry on the same day.

The exercise price of the share options was set at the then market value of £1.00 per share. The options are not capable of being exercised after 10 years from the date of grant. The company has been successful, and the current value of the shares is now £14.00 per share. Another shareholder has offered to buy the shares at their market value, so Henry exercised his share options on 14 April 2007 and will sell the shares next week, on 20 April 2007.

With the company growing in size, Henry wishes to recruit high quality staff, but the company lacks the funds to pay them in cash. Henry believes that giving new employees the chance to buy shares in the company would help recruit staff, as they could share in the growth in value of Happy Home Ltd. Henry has heard that there is a particular share scheme that is suitable for small, fast growing companies. He would like to obtain further information on how such a scheme would work.

Henry has accumulated substantial assets over the years. The family house is owned jointly with Helen, and is worth £650,000. Henry has a £250,000 mortgage on the house. In addition, Henry has liquid assets worth £340,000 and Helen has shares in quoted companies currently worth £125,000. Henry has no forms of insurance, and believes he should make sure that his wealth and family are protected. He is keen to find out what options he should be considering.

Required:

(a)   (i)   State how the gift of the 3,000 shares in Happy Home Ltd was taxed. **(1 mark)**

        (ii)   Explain the Income tax (IT), National Insurance (NIC) and Capital Gains tax (CGT) implications arising on the grant to and exercise by an employee of an option to buy shares in an unapproved share option scheme and on the subsequent sale of these shares.

            State clearly how these would apply in Henry's case. **(8 marks)**

(b)   Identify the most appropriate approved share option scheme for Happy Home Ltd. Outline the scheme requirements and the tax benefits of using it compared to the current unapproved scheme. **(6 marks)**

(c)   (i)   Provide three examples of personal financial planning protection products that would be of use in Henry's situation.

            Justify your selections by reference to the type of protection provided.**(6 marks)**

        (ii)   Briefly outline the tax consequences for Henry if the types of protection identified in (i) were to be provided for him by Happy Home Ltd compared to providing them for himself.

            You are not required to discuss the corporation tax (CT) consequences for Happy Home Ltd. **(4 marks)**

                                           (Total: 25 marks)

Section 2

ANSWERS TO PRACTICE QUESTIONS

TAXATION OF INDIVIDUALS

INCOME TAX ON INCOME FROM INVESTMENTS

1   MURIEL GRAND

(a)   **Capital gains tax liability on gift of London house**

Deemed proceeds (Market value)
Cost (TN1)

Unindexed gain

Indexation $45,000 \times \dfrac{162.6 - 97.67}{97.67}$ (0.665)

Indexed gain   245,075

Fully chargeable (245,075 × 123/249) (TN 2)   121,061
Partially chargeable (245,075 × 69/249 × 20%)   13,582

Indexed gain after PPR   134,643

As a non-business asset with eight years of ownership (including the bonus year), the gain is 65% chargeable.

Chargeable gain (65%)   87,518

As Muriel's annual exemption has already been utilised, all of the chargeable gain is taxable at 40%.

CGT liability (87,518 × 40%)   35,007

Tutorial notes:

(1)   **Deemed cost of house**

June 1987 – Disposal of surplus land

Deemed cost = $60,000 \times \dfrac{24,000}{24,000 + 72,000}$ = £15,000

Deemed cost of remaining house = (60,000 – 15,000) = £45,000.

KAPLAN PUBLISHING   **95**

Handwritten sticky notes:

Cost of house
= Bought × MV of Remainder
over
MV of Remainder + Part Disposal

Indexation Allowance = Cost × _____

(2) **Principal private residence relief**

Total ownership period = 1 April 1986 to 31 December 2006 = 249 months

Period of non-occupation (excluding final 36 months):

1 October 1993 to 31 December 2003 = 123 months

Period of partial use as main residence:

1 January 1988 to 30 September 1993 = 69 months

Note that provided the property has been the owner's main residence at some time, the last 36 months of ownership are treated as 'occupation' regardless of whether an election has already been made for some other property to be the main residence.

(b) **Deferral of gain on house in London**

Enterprise Investment Scheme (EIS)

Muriel will be entitled to capital gains deferral relief if the 'proceeds' from the disposal of the house are 're-invested' in the ordinary share capital of unquoted trading companies which qualify under the EIS scheme.

Muriel will need to invest £134,643 in order for the entire gain to be deferred. The gain would normally be deferred until the shares are disposed of, although further reinvestment could be made at that time.

The investment must be made in the period beginning on 1 January 2006 and ending on 31 December 2009, and the investment must be in newly issued shares.

In addition to CGT deferral relief Muriel will be entitled to income tax relief of £26,929 (134,643 × 20%) in respect of the EIS investment.

Provided the shares are held for three years, their disposal will be exempt from CGT although the deferred gain on the sale of the house would then become chargeable. The original taper relief of 35% will be available on the crystallising gain.

If a loss is made on the disposal of the EIS shares, then relief will be available against either capital gains or income. The cost of the shares in the capital loss calculation is reduced by any EIS income tax relief obtained and not withdrawn.

Venture Capital Trusts (VCTs)

Capital gains deferral relief will not be available to defer the gain arising on the sale of the house if Muriel reinvests in a VCT.

There are however other tax advantages of investing in VCTs.

Muriel would be entitled to income tax relief at the rate of 30% on amounts subscribed (up to £200,000 p.a.) for new shares in a VCT. Dividend income, which under the EIS scheme remains taxable, is exempt under a VCT scheme.

Capital gains on the disposal of shares in a VCT are exempt, regardless of the period of ownership, but there is no relief for capital losses.

Conclusion

Muriel can only defer the gain which arises on the gift of the house in London by making an investment in eligible unquoted company shares under the EIS scheme.

There are however other capital gains and income tax reliefs available for investments in both EIS shares and VCTs.

(c)   **Tax implications of letting property**

In either case, Bertie will be assessed on the profits of a business of letting property, i.e. as property business income. The assessment will be on a strict actual basis from 6 April to 5 April, and will be calculated in accordance with most of the rules used in calculating assessable trading profits. Rents will be assessable on an accruals basis.

Repairs to roof

The roof was damaged before Muriel transferred the house to Bertie. Since the roof must be repaired before the house can be let, the house would not appear to be usable at the time of the transfer. The cost of repair of £24,000 is therefore likely to be classed as capital expenditure following *Law Shipping Co Ltd v CIR (1923)*. This will increase Bertie's base cost for CGT purposes.

Let as unfurnished accommodation

The cost of decoration would normally be a revenue expense. However, the house has been unoccupied since 1 October 1993, and some of the expenditure may be classed as capital if the house was in a bad state of repair on 31 December 2006. The decoration will presumably be carried out before letting commences, and so will be pre-trading expenditure. This will be allowed as an expense on the first day of business.

Any capital gain arising on the disposal of the house when Bertie retires at 60, will be fully chargeable with only the non-business rate of taper relief available.

Let as furnished holiday accommodation

The cost of converting the house into two separate units will be mainly capital expenditure, and this will increase Bertie's base cost for CGT purposes. The figure of £41,000 may include some revenue expenditure, such as decorating costs, and this will be treated as above. The £9,000 cost of furnishing the two units will be capital expenditure.

Bertie will be able to claim the following deductions from his annual gross rents of £45,000:

1   The loan interest of £4,000 (£50,000 at 8%).

2   A wear and tear deduction in respect of the furniture. This will be based on either 10% of the rent received (which is likely to be £45,000 × 10% = £4,500) or on a renewals basis.

3   The letting agency fees of £10,125 (£45,000 at 22.5%).

4   The other running costs of £3,500.

Expenses will be restricted if Bertie occupies the house for his own use.

Given Bertie's level of rental income the letting is likely to qualify for the special rules applicable to furnished holiday lettings.

This will mean that:

1   Capital allowances will be available on plant and machinery, such as furniture and kitchen equipment. This will almost certainly be more beneficial than the wear and tear allowance.

2   The property business profit will qualify as relevant earnings for personal pension purposes.

3   Loss relief will be available against total income.

Qualification as furnished holiday accommodation will also mean that Bertie will be entitled to the business rate of taper relief when the house is disposed of.

The letting of holiday accommodation is standard rated for VAT purposes. The forecast rental income of £45,000 is below the VAT registration limit of £61,000, but the impact of VAT will have to be considered if Bertie is already registered for VAT, or if there is an increase in rental income.

Conclusion

Letting the house as a furnished holiday letting will produce annual income of approximately £27,375 (45,000 - 4,000 - 10,125 - 3,500), compared to £28,000 (given in the question) if the house is let unfurnished.

It will also be necessary to incur additional expenditure of £46,400 (41,000 + 9,000 - 3,600).

This must be compared against the potential CGT saving upon the disposal of the house arising from the business rate of taper relief available for finished holiday letting which is not available for unfurnished property.

Key answer tips

As is often the case with tax planning, it is necessary to balance a cash flow advantage now (higher rental from unfurnished letting) against a tax saving in the future (lower CGT on furnished holiday accommodation).

---

2   TRIXIE DAVENPORT

(a)   **Income tax liability for the year ended 5 April 2007**

		£
Property business income		315,370
Personal allowance		(5,035)
Taxable income		310,335
2,150 × 10 %		215
31,150 × 22 %		6,853
277,035 × 40 %		110,814
310,335		
		117,882
EIS relief (£400,000 (note) × 20%)		(80,000)
VCT relief (£50,000 × 30%)		(15,000)
Income tax liability		22,882

Note: Income tax relief on the EIS investment of £250,000 will be restricted to £80,000 (£400,000, maximum investment × 20%)

[Handwritten margin note: ENTERPRISE INVESTMENT RELIEF = MAX INV £200 000 × 20%. VENTURE CAPITAL TRUST RELIEF = REMAINDER × 40%]

(b)   **Chargeable Gain on the Disposal of Wroxley Lodge on 3 August 2006**

	Notes		£
Disposal proceeds	1		711,000
Less: Cost			(50,000)
Unindexed gain			661,000
Less: Indexation	2	£50,000 × 0.956	(47,800)
Indexed gain			613,200
Less EIS relief	3		(450,000)
			163,200
Less Taper relief (35%)	4		(57,120)
Chargeable gain (65%)			106,080
Less Annual exemption			(8,800)
Taxable gain			97,280
CGT liability (97,280 × 40%)			38,912

Notes

1   Disposal proceeds are open market value as the disposal is by way of gift. Gift relief is not available because the gift is not a qualifying business asset for gift relief purposes, and there is no immediate charge to inheritance tax.

2   Indexation allowance is given for the period from 31 March 1983 to 5 April 1998 only, as Trixie is an individual.

3   ELS reinvestment relief is available in respect of proceeds reinvested in EIS shares. The amount of the relief is the lower of the indexed gain and the amount of the EIS investment. Capital gains deferral relief is not available for reinvestment in VCTs.

4   The asset is a non-business asset for taper relief purposes. As it has been held for nine qualifying years (including the bonus year), the gain is 65% chargeable.

(c)   **Exposure to the capital taxes**

Inheritance tax

As Stella has agreed with Trixie to be responsible for any inheritance tax liability arising from the gift her exposure to inheritance tax is calculated as follows:

The gift by Trixie is a PET. If Trixie were to die within three years of making the gift Stella would be liable to IHT of £167,600 (see below). If she died after three years but before the start of the eighth year then taper relief applies, the amount of inheritance tax payable decreasing at the rate of 20% per annum.

Lifetime Inheritance Computation

	£	IHT £	Year 4 80 %	Year 5 60 %	Year 6 40 %	Year 7 20 %	Year 8 Exempt
3 August 2006							
Wroxley Lodge	711,000						
Less marriage exemption	(1,000)						
Less 2006/07 AE	(3,000)						
Less 2005/06 AE	(3,000)						
	704,000						
Less nil rate band	(285,000)						
Gross taxable amount	419,000	167,600	134,080	100,560	67,040	33,520	Nil

Stella could protect her exposure to inheritance tax by taking out a gifts inter vivos policy on Trixie's life. The proceeds from this policy would pay out on Trixie's death mirroring the tapering inheritance tax liability. Her insurable interest is her exposure to inheritance tax as a result of Trixie's death.

Capital gains tax

Stella has no exposure to capital gains tax as gift relief is not available.

3 FAGUS

(a) **Treatment of Fagus' cottage**

The investment property is likely to be regarded as furnished holiday letting because it is:

(i) situated in the UK, furnished and let on a commercial basis

(ii) available for letting to the public for not less than 140 days in 2006/07

(iii) so let for at least 70 days in the year

(iv) not let for periods of long term occupation totally in excess of 155 days in the relevant 12 month period.

Long term occupation is a period of more than 31 consecutive days let to the same person.

The net assessable property business income for 2006/07 will be as follows:

	£	£
Income		8,250
Expenditure:		
Advertising	1,300	
Maintenance (*Note*)	5,300	
Loan interest	2,200	
		(8,800)
Loss on property business		(550)

The net assessable income for 2006/07 is therefore nil with a loss of £550 available for relief.

Note: The cost of the roof repairs following the gale being simply the restoration of the cottage to its former state should be allowed as a deductible expense under general principles for trading income purposes.

Consequences

As a result of being classified as a furnished holiday letting, relief for any losses which may arise is enhanced. Rather than simply carrying forward the loss against future property business income the loss can be treated as if it was a trading loss with, for example, the ability to offset it against other income of Fagus in the 2006/07 tax year.

(b) **Income Tax Computations - 2006/07**

	Fagus £	*Ulmus* £
Pension	4,250	
Employment income		12,500
Interest received		
Building Society (£7,400 × 100/80)	9,250	
(£1,450 × 100/80)		1,812
Quercus Limited (Note (1))	2,000	
Dividends (£23,625 × 100/90)	26,250	
	41,750	
Less: Charge on income (Note (2))	(2,500)	
Loss relief (see part (a))	(550)	
Statutory Total Income	38,700	14,312
Less: Personal allowance (Note (3))	(5,035)	(5,035)
Taxable income	33,665	9,277

Analysis of income:
Fagus: Dividends £26,250, Savings £7,415
Ulmus: Savings £1,812, Other income £7,465

Income Tax £		
2,150 × 10% (savings)	215	
5,265 × 20% (savings)	1,053	
25,885 × 10% (dividends)	2,588	
33,300		
365 × 32·5% (dividends)	119	
33,665	3,975	
2,150 × 10% (other income)		215
5,315 × 22% (other income)		1,169
7,465		
1,812 × 20% (savings)		362
9,277		
Less: MCAA (Note (3)) (588 × 10%)	(59)	
Income Tax Liability	3,916	1,746
Less: Tax credits (1,850 + 400 + 2,625) (Note (1))	(4,875)	
(1,384 + 362)		(1,746)
Income tax repayable	(959)	Nil

Notes

(1) **Treatment of interest received from Quercus Ltd**

An individual receives interest from a company net of 20% tax. The gross amount of £2,000 is assessed as savings income.

A tax credit of £400 can be deducted from Fagus' income tax liability.

(2) **Treatment of loan interest paid**

For loan interest paid to qualify as an allowable charge on income, the loan on which interest is paid must be for a qualifying purpose. This includes loans which are lent onwards for trading purposes to a close company in which the taxpayer paying the interest either (i) owns a material interest (more than 5%) or (ii) holds some ordinary share capital and works full time as a manager or director of the company.

Whilst Fagus does not work for Quercus Ltd, because he owns 10% of the ordinary shares in this company he does own a material interest. Further Quercus Ltd is a close company being controlled by five or fewer participators and the loan it received from Fagus, being used to acquire plant and machinery used in its trade, is for a trading purpose.

The interest paid on the loan relating to Quercus Ltd therefore qualifies as a charge on income.

(3) **Allowances available to Fagus**

Personal age allowance

Fagus is aged 72 at the end of the 2006/07 tax year and is therefore entitled to the higher personal allowance of £7,280. However, as Fagus' statutory total income exceeds the abatement threshold of £20,100 for this tax year, the allowance is reduced by £1 for every £2 of income over this threshold.

Fagus' personal allowance therefore becomes £5,035 [(38,700 – 20,100) × ½ = £9,300 reduction, but restricted to £2,245 to leave the basic personal allowance of £5,035].

Married couples allowance

As Fagus was born before 6 April 1935 he is entitled to the married couples age allowance (MCAA) tax reducer of £6,065. This will be restricted because of his income level and the fact that marriage occurred in the tax year as follows:

	£
	6,065
...atement (restricted) (see below)	(3,715)
	2,350
...Reduction for complete tax months not married 9/12 × 2,350)	(1,762)
...MCAA	588

...tement of MCAA:

...ver of   (i)   remaining abatement (9,300 – 2,195) = £7,105, and

         (ii)   £3,715 (as the MCAA cannot be reduced below £2,350 for 2006/07 tax year).

(c)   **Notes for a meeting with Fagus**

   (i)   **Position with capital taxes**

       Capital gains tax:

The disposal of an asset by one spouse to another is treated as being for such consideration as gives rise to neither a capital gain or loss. Effectively, therefore, chargeable assets will be acquired at the base cost of the disposing spouse.

For this rule to apply the couple must be married (i.e. spouses) or civil partners and living together.

Gifts prior to marriage will therefore be subject to normal capital gains tax rules. Such gifts will be treated as not having been made at arms length, and therefore the deemed proceeds will be equal to the asset's market value at the date of gift.

Inheritance tax:

Again only gifts of assets between *spouses* or civil partners are exempt from IHT.

Gifts prior to marriage will therefore be subject to normal IHT rules (i.e. the gifts between individuals will be treated as potentially exempt transfers subject to the seven year survivorship rule).

An outright exemption of up to £2,500 will, however, be possible for gifts, made in consideration of marriage, between the parties to the marriage.

Stamp duties:

Gifts *inter vivos* (i.e. during lifetime) are exempt from *ad valorem* duty and, if properly certified, they will also be exempt from the fixed duty of £5.

   (ii)   **Measures aimed at reducing couple's income tax liabilities**

To reduce the couple's income tax liabilities, they should try to maximise the use of personal allowances and tax reducers whilst minimising the incidence of taxable income exceeding the higher rates tax threshold.

This would be achieved if Fagus reduces his taxable income by transferring income bearing assets to Ulmus.

Assuming income levels remain the same as in 2006/07 Fagus could unconditionally transfer 'income' up to £24,023 (W) to Ulmus.

The simplest way of achieving this would be for Fagus to either transfer (after marriage)

     (a)   all of his deposit/loan funds and some shares in Quercus Ltd or;

     (b)   purely some shares in Quercus Ltd.

It would probably be preferable and administratively simpler if Fagus were to only gift shares. This is because following the gift(s), with the available tax credits, it is likely that Fagus will be in a tax overpayment position from 6 April 2007 and tax credits associated with dividends are not refundable.

It should be noted that this will not impact on Fagus's ability to claim relief for the eligible loan interest paid as a charge on income, as the holdings of associates (which includes his spouse and son) are taken into account in satisfying the 'material interest' condition.

The effects of the transfer of shares would be as follows:

(1)   Ulmus's tax payable would still remain nil as her tax credits will still exactly match her tax liability.

(2)   Fagus's statutory total income will fall to £14,677 (38,700 – 24,023). He will therefore become entitled to the higher personal allowance of £7,280 in full as his statutory total income does not exceed the abatement threshold of £20,100.

(3)   Fagus's entitlement to MCAA would not be abated by reference to income.

(4)   Fagus would become entitled to a tax refund (detailed calculations are not required).

Working: **Transfer of income**

	£
Higher rate threshold	33,300
Ulma's taxable income	(9,277)
Transfer of income	24,023

Tutorial note: A detailed calculation of the refund to which Fagus will become entitled to is not required by the question but is produced here for tutorial purposes.

Assuming that the measures noted above had been in place throughout the 2006/07 tax year and also that the couple were married throughout this tax year, the refund is calculated as follows:

	£
Revised statutory total income (38,700 – 24,023)	14,677
Less: Revised personal allowance	(7,280)
Taxable income	7,397

Analysis of income:
Dividends £2,227 (26,250 – 24,023), Savings £5,170

Income Tax

£	
2,150 × 10%	215
3,020 × 20%	604
5,170	
2,227 × 10%	223
7,397	1,042
Less: MCAA (6,065 × 10%)	(607)
Income tax liability	435
Less: Tax credits – dividends	(223)
– savings	(2,250)
Income tax refundable	(1,838)

Clearly the position in reality going forward is likely to differ if only because the furnished holiday letting loss arising in 2006/07 is unlikely to repeat itself on an annual basis.

				Marks
(a)		FHL conditions		2.0
		FHL conclusion		1.0
		Loss relief		1.0
		Calculation		<u>1.0</u>
			Max	<u>4.0</u>
(b)		Income tax liabilities		
		Fagus		
		Pension		0.5
		Building Society interest		0.5
		Interest from Quercus Limited		0.5
		Dividends		0.5
		Charge on income (see below)		0.5
		Loss relief (from (a))		0.5
		PAA (see below)		0.5
		Income tax calculation		2.0
		MCAA (see below)		0.5
		Income tax payable		1.0
		Ulmus		
		Employment income		0.5
		Building Society interest		0.5
		PA		0.5
		Income tax calculation		1.5
		Income tax payable		1.0
		Charge on income		
		Qualifying conditions		2.5
		Quercus Limited – position		1.0
		Allowance and Tax Reducers		
		Higher personal allowance		0.5
		Abatement		1.5
		Married Couples Age Allowance		0.5
		Restriction – marriage in tax year		1.0
		– abatement position		<u>1.5</u>
			Max	<u>17.0</u>
(c)	**(i)**	Capital taxes		
		CGT No gain/No loss		1.0
		Position prior to marriage		1.0
		IHT Exemption		0.5
		Position prior to marriage		1.5
		Stamp Duty		1.0
	(ii)	Reducing Income Tax		
		Principle		1.0
		Higher rate threshold		1.0
		Gifting shares/non-refundable tax credits		1.5
		Personal allowance		1.0
		MCAA		1.0
		Tax refund (detailed calculation not required)		<u>1.0</u>
			Max	<u>9.0</u>
Total				<u>30.0</u>

INCOME TAX ON INCOME FROM EMPLOYMENT

4   TARIKI PUTIN

(a)   **Income tax computation for 2006/07**

	£
Salary from A V Ltd	29,500
Video camera (W1)	1,400
Car expenses (W2)	(285)
Occupation pension contributions (29,500 × 2%)	(590)
Employment income = STI	30,025
Personal allowance	(5,035)
Taxable income	24,990

Income tax
£

2,150 at 10%	215
22,840 at 22%	5,025
24,990	5,240

(b)   (i)   **Vladimir Putin**
Inheritance tax on death estate

	£
House in Bristol	270,000
House in Padua (see below)	Nil
Quoted shares	135,000
Shares in ISAs	32,200
Cash	7,600
Car and chattels	36,800
Funeral expense	(2,700)
Chargeable estate	478,900
Nil rate band available (no lifetime gifts)	(285,000)
Taxable amount	193,900
IHT (193,900 × 40%)	77,560

Estate rate $\dfrac{77,560}{478,900} = 16.195\%$

Contentious issues

It has been assumed that Vladimir is domiciled in Padua and therefore only UK assets have been brought into the estate.

This is far from certain but is indicated by his apparent desire to return there and the fact that he has retained property in the country.

Vladimir will not be deemed domiciled in the UK for inheritance tax purposes as he has not been resident in the UK for at least 17 out of the previous 20 tax years.

The house in Padua is an overseas asset and is not chargeable to inheritance tax if Vladimir is not domiciled in the United Kingdom.

(ii) **Payment by instalments**

The tax due on the house in Bristol can be paid in ten equal annual instalments starting on 31 October 2007.

Each instalment is £4,373 (270,000 × 16.195% ÷ 10)

Interest is charged on the whole of the outstanding balance as well as any payments made late. Note that the whole of the tax due on the house becomes payable if Tariki sells the property.

The remainder of the IHT liability, £33,830 (77,560 – 43,730), is due on 31 October 2007.

(c) **Investment income**

The rent from the Bristol house will be taxed under the property income rules on the accruals basis. Part of the rent will fall into the basic rate tax band and will be taxed at 22%. The balance will be taxed at 40%.

The bank interest will be received net of 20% tax. The amount received must be grossed up at 100/80 and will be taxed at 40% with a credit available for the tax suffered.

Dividends are received net of a notional 10% tax credit. The amount received must be grossed up at 100/90 and will be taxed at 32.5% with a 10% tax credit.

The rent from the house in Padua will be taxed as property income on the accruals basis, inclusive of the Paduan tax suffered. The gross amount will be taxed at 40% and a credit will be given for the lower of the tax suffered in Padua or the UK income tax in respect of that income.

Additional tax due on investment income

	£
Bristol house rental income (12 × 950)	11,400
Bank interest (880 × 100/80)	1,100
Dividends (5,940 × 100/90)	6,600
Padua house rental income (12 × 300)	3,600
Additional taxable income	22,700

Analysis of additional income:

Savings £1,100, Dividends £6,600, other income £15,000.

Basic rate band remaining (assuming employment income and the tax rates and allowances for 2006/07 continued to apply) = (33,300 – 24,990) = £8,310.

Additional income tax	£
£	
8,310 × 22% (other – Bristol house)	1,828
3,090 × 40% (other – Bristol house)	1,236
3,600 × 40% (other – Padua house)	1,440
_____	
15,000	
1,100 × 40% (savings)	440
6,600 × 32½% (dividends)	2,145
_____	
22,700	
_____	_____
	7,089

Less Double taxation relief
Lower of   (1)   overseas tax
                        (3,600 × 15%) = 540   (540)
              (2)   UK tax = 1,440 (above)

Additional income tax liability	6,549
Less Tax credits	
– on dividends (6,600 × 10%)	(600)
– on savings (1,100 × 20%)	(220)
	_____
Additional income tax payable	5,669

(d)   (i)   Transfer of investments to Juliette

Income tax

The main advantage of transferring investments to Juliette is that the income generated will be taxed in her hands rather than Tariki's. This will reduce the couple's income tax liability, as Juliette is not using her personal allowance or the lower and basic rate tax bands whereas Tariki is a 40% taxpayer.

Capital gains tax

The transfer of an asset between spouses takes place at no gain, no loss. Accordingly the transfer can be carried out with no tax cost.

On a future sale of an investment, the taper relief will be computed by reference to the ownership periods of both Tariki and Juliette. This means that the transfer is not disadvantageous from the point of view of taper relief.

A further advantage may arise on a sale in the future, as any gain will be taxed in the hands of Juliette and not Tariki. Whether this is advantageous or not will depend on the circumstances but it is likely that Juliette will not have used her annual exemption and that part of the gain will be taxed at 20%.

Inheritance tax

The transfer of an asset between spouses is exempt from inheritance tax. Accordingly, as with capital gains tax, the transfer can be carried out with no tax cost.

Tariki and Juliette should ensure that they each own assets equal to the nil rate band, £285,000; transferring the property may be helpful in this respect.

Summary

The transfer would save income tax, and have possible capital gains tax and inheritance tax advantages, with no tax downside.

(ii) **ISAs**

The maximum investment is £7,000 per annum. Of this, a maximum of £3,000 can be held as cash. The balance is invested in quoted shares or insurance.

Income and gains generated by the investments held in the ISA are tax free.

Workings

(W1) **Video camera**

In 2006/07 there are two benefits: one for the use of the camera until 10 October 2006 and one for the sale of the camera.

	£	£
Benefit for use (2,200 × 20% × 6/12)		220
Benefit for sale of camera		
Higher of:		
(i) Market value when first made available to Tariki	2,200	
Benefit assessed in 2004/05 (2,200 × 20% × 3/12)	(110)	
2005/06 (2,200 × 20%)	(440)	
2006/07 (above)	(220)	
	1,430	
Less Price paid	(250)	
	1,180	1,180
(ii) Market value as at 1 October 2006	250	
Less Price paid	(250)	
	Nil	
Total benefits		1,400

(W2) **Car expenses**

	£
Tax allowable using AMAPs (5,700 × 40p)	2,280
Received from A V Ltd (5,700 × 35p)	(1,995)
Deductible expense for employment income	285

5 LANDSCAPE LTD

(a) **Peter Plain**

It is necessary to consider the essential distinction between a contract of service (employed) and a contract for services (self-employed). The relevant tests point towards a contract of service:

The control test: Peter works at Landscape Ltd's offices for five days each week, so the company appears to have control over the way he performs his work.

The mutual obligations test: Peter's only client is Landscape Ltd, so there appears to be an obligation for the company to provide work, and an obligation for him to do the work provided.

The economic reality test: Peter's activities do not appear to form a profession in their own right, since he uses Landscape Ltd's offices and computer equipment, and is paid an hourly rate. There is no indication that Peter has assumed any financial risk by becoming 'self-employed'.

The integration test: The computer function (and hence Peter) is an integral part of Landscape Ltd's business operations.

HMRC are therefore almost certain to contend that Peter is in fact still 'employed' by Landscape Ltd.

(b) **Richard Rosland**

The maximum market value of shares that can be allocated to Richard in any year of assessment is £3,000. He will therefore have received 2,000 (3,000/1.50) shares during 2003/04.

The 1,000 (2,000/2) shares sold on 31 January 2007 have not been held for the required five years but have been held for three years. Richard will therefore be assessed in 2006/07 to an employment income charge based on the initial market value of £1,500 (3,000/2), since this is lower than the sale proceeds of £2,800.

(c) **Simon Savannah**

The statutory redundancy payment of £2,400 is exempt income. The holiday pay of £1,500 and the restrictive covenant of £5,000 are both taxable as employment income in 2006/07.

The treatment of the balance of the lump sum redundancy payment of £46,100 (55,000 - 2,400 - 1,500 - 5,000) is unlikely to be fully taxable provided it is a genuine redundancy payment.

Assuming that this is the case Simon will be entitled to the exemption of £30,000, although this is reduced by the statutory redundancy payment.

This payment is assessed on a receipts basis as follows:

	£
Exempt limit	30,000
Statutory redundancy pay	(2,400)
Reduced limit	27,600
Balance of lump sum	46,100
Reduced exempt limit	(27,600)
Taxable amount	18,500
Assessed in 2006/07	8,500
2007/08	10,000

(d) **Trevor Tundra**

Provision of car

Trevor is a participator (i.e. a shareholder) of Landscape Ltd, but he is neither a director nor an employee of the company. The provision of a company motor car to Trevor is therefore treated as a distribution.

The amount of the net distribution for 2006/07 is £4,185 (W1) being the benefit that would have been assessed on him had he been a P11D employee. The gross income of £4,650 (4,185 × 100/90) is assessed on Trevor, with a related tax credit of £465 (4,650 × 10%).

The loan of £40,000 to Trevor is interest free. Under the beneficial loan rules, Trevor is treated as receiving a net distribution equal to the normal beneficial loan benefit rules, calculated using the official interest rate. The interest calculated on a strict basis is £727 (W2) net, equivalent to gross income of £808 (727 × 100/90), with a related tax credit of £81 (808 × 10%).

When the loan is written off, Trevor will be assessed on gross income of £15,000 (40,000 - 26,500 = 13,500 × 100/90) in 2006/07. The related tax credit is £1,500 (15,000 × 10%).

In each case, Trevor will only have an additional income tax liability to pay if he is a higher rate taxpayer.

Workings

(W1) **Car benefit = net distribution**

CO_2 emissions 221 g/km, available all year

Appropriate % = 15% + (220 – 140) × $\frac{1}{5}$ = 31%

Car benefit = 13,500 × 31% = £4,185

(W2) **Beneficial loan interest**

	£
40,000 × $\frac{2}{12}$ × 5%	333
13,500 × $\frac{7}{12}$ × 5%	394
	727

(e) **Ursula Upland, Violet Veld and Wilma Wood**

All three employees are attending Cambridge in the performance of their duties. Relief will therefore be given for the cost of travel between home and Cambridge, provided this qualifies as a temporary place of work.

A place of work is classed as a temporary workplace if an employee does not work there continuously for a period that lasts (or is expected to last) more than 24 months.

Ursula:

All of her journeys to Cambridge qualify for relief. The mileage allowance received will be tax free, and she can make the following expense claim for 2006/07:

	£
AMAP: 4,800 miles (120 days × 40 miles) at 40p	1,920
Mileage allowance received (4,800 at 36p)	(1,728)
Expense claim against employment income	192

Violet:

From 1 October to 31 December 2006, Cambridge will be treated as a permanent workplace since Violet's assignment is expected to exceed the 24-month limit.

No relief for travel costs during this period is given, so she will be assessed on employment income on a benefit of £1,800 (120 × 3/6 x £30) for 2006/07. However, relief will be given from 1 January 2007 onwards, since she no longer expects to exceed the 24-month limit.

Wilma:

All of her journeys to Cambridge should qualify for relief. Although Wilma passes her normal permanent workplace on the way to Cambridge, full relief will be available provided she does not stop at the London shop (or any stop is incidental, i.e. to pick up some papers).

Wilma will travel 18,000 miles (120 days × 150 miles) in 2006/07 and be assessed on an employment income benefit for 2006/07 as follows:

	£
10,000 miles at 40p	4,000
8,000 miles at 25p	2,000
AMAP	6,000
Mileage allowance received (18,000 at 36p)	(6,480)
Assessable benefit	480

Key answer tips

This involves a series of points on benefits and expenses. Consider each separately from the recipient's view.

6   WORKOUT PLC

Company motorcar

Gareth will be assessed on employment income on a car benefit of £3,126 (W1) and a fuel benefit of £3,312 (W1).

The additional income tax liability is £2,575 (3,126 + 3,312 = 6,438 at 40%).

Cash alternative

The additional salary of £500 per month will be taxed as employment income.

Gareth will be paid an allowance of 30p per mile for 12,600 (1,750 × 12 × 60%) business miles. The mileage allowance received will be tax free, and Gareth can make the following expense claim:

	£
10,000 miles at 40p	4,000
2,600 miles at 25p	650
AMAP	4,650
Mileage allowance received (12,600 at 30p)	(3,780)
Expense claim against employment income	870

Relocation costs

As the £8,000 limit is not exceeded, there should not be a taxable benefit in respect of the relocation costs paid for by Workout plc. This is because Gareth does not live within a reasonable daily travelling distance of where he is to be employed.

The exemption covers such items as legal and estate agents' fees, stamp duty, removal costs, and the cost of new domestic goods where existing goods are not suitable for the new residence. The expenses must be incurred by 5 April 2008.

Beneficial loan

Gareth will be assessed on the difference between the interest paid on the loan and the official rate of interest as an assessable benefit of employment. The 'average' method of calculation give a taxable benefit for 2006/07 of £4,200 (W2). The additional income tax liability is therefore £1,680 (£4,200 at 40%).

The balance at 5 April 2007 is after taking account of 12 monthly repayments of £1,000. The taxable benefit will be the same if calculated using the actual basis.

Living accommodation

Gareth will be assessed on the provision of the living accommodation provided to him as an assessable benefit of employment. There will be an additional benefit based on the market value of £135,000, since the house cost is in excess of £75,000 and the house was purchased more than six years before first being provided.

The taxable benefit will be:

	£
Rateable value	7,700
Additional benefit (135,000 - 75,000) × 5%	3,000
Furniture (12,400 × 20%)	2,480
Running costs	3,900
Total accommodation benefits	17,080

The additional income tax liability is £6,832 (17,080 at 40%).

Mobile telephone

The provision of one mobile telephone per employee does not give rise to a taxable benefit, even if there is private use.

Fixed telephone

If Gareth receives £75 per month towards his home telephone, he will assessed on a taxable employment benefit of £900 (12 × 75). However he will be able to make an expense claim of £650 in respect of the expenditure on business telephone calls.

The additional income tax liability is therefore £100 (900 - 650 = 250 × 40%).

Health club

The cost of the provision of free membership to the health clubs in which the managers work will be assessed on Gareth as a taxable benefit of employment.

As per the case of *Pepper v Hart* (1992), 'cost' for this purpose is the marginal cost of providing the benefit. The budgeted number of members has been exceeded, and so the fixed costs should be fully recovered. Since Gareth is utilising surplus capacity, the taxable benefit would appear to be £140 (40 + 100) being the extra costs incurred by Workout plc in the provision of the free membership.

The additional income tax liability is £56 (140 × 40%).

Golf club

Gareth will be assessed on a taxable benefit of employment of £800 if his golf membership is paid. The additional income tax liability is £320 (800 × 40%).

Share incentive plan

The maximum market value of shares that can be allocated to Gareth in any year of assessment is £3,000. He will therefore receive 1,000 (3,000/3) shares during 2006/07.

Provided the shares are held for the required five years, no charge to income tax will arise. There may, however, be a liability to CGT.

If the shares are sold after five years, Gareth would have a capital gain of £3,750 (W3). This gain may be reduced by taper relief.

Share options

There will be no income tax charge until the options are exercised in five years' time. The income tax charge will then be based on the market value of the shares at that date, less the amount paid for the shares.

Gareth will therefore be assessed to income tax on £49,500 (W4). The additional income tax liability is £19,800 (49,500 × 40%). When the shares are subsequently sold, any CGT liability will be calculated using a base cost of £6.75 per share.

Key answer tips

You were required to explain the tax implications for Gareth only, but were not required to advise him which options to choose.

Workings

(W1) **Car and fuel benefit**

CO_2 emissions = 182 g/km, available all year

Appropriate % = 15% + (180 – 140) × $\frac{1}{5}$ = 23%
MLP = (£19,200 - £3,000 Capital contribution) = £16,200

	£
Car benefit = (16,200 × 23%)	3,726
Less Monthly contribution (50 × 12)	(600)
Car benefit	3,126
Fuel benefit (14,400 × 23%)	3,312

(W2) **Beneficial loan**

	£
Loan at start of year	90,000
Loan at end of year	78,000
	168,000

Average loan = (168,000 ÷ 2) = £84,000

Assessable benefit (84,000 × 5%)	4,200

(W3) **Share incentive plan**

	£
Sale proceeds (1,000 × £6.75)	6,750
Cost of shares (1,000 × £3)	(3,000)
Capital gain	3,750

No indexation allowance available as shares acquired after April 1998.

(W4)   **Share option scheme**

	£
On exercise of shares	
MV @ date of exercise (10,000 × £6.75)	67,500
Cost of shares (10,000 × £3 × 60%)	(18,000)
Charged to income tax	49,500

7   ALFIE

(a)   **The tax implications of Alfie acquiring a car**

Car Acquired Personally

Alfie's Position

Authorised Mileage Allowance Payments (AMAPs) paid for business travel up to the limits of 40p per mile for the first 10,000 business miles and 25p per mile thereafter can be paid tax free to Alfie.

If the allowances paid by the limited company are less than the AMAPs, he can claim for the difference to be allowed as an employment income expense deduction. If the rates paid exceed these limits the excess is subject to income tax and Class 1 employee National Insurance contributions ('NICs') under PAYE procedures.

In these circumstances because Alfie is a higher rate taxpayer the income tax will be at 40%. Employees Class 1 NIC would be due at 1% as Alfie's salary already exceeds the annual upper earnings threshold of £645 per week.

The running and capital costs of the car will need to be met from the allowances paid.

Limited Company's Position

Providing payments for business mileage do not exceed the AMAP limits there will be no need to report allowances paid on end of year PAYE Form P11D. If the rates paid exceed these limits then employers Class 1 NIC at the rate of 12.8% will be due under PAYE procedures.

The company will be able to claim a deduction against trading profits or any mileage allowances paid in its corporation tax computations either as a travel cost or employee cost (if rates are paid in excess of the authorised limits).

The company will also be able to recover input VAT on the fuel element only of the allowances paid.

Car Acquired by Limited Company

Alfie's Position

If the car is acquired by the limited company which will meet all the running costs, including fuel, then Alfie will be assessed on the following benefits:

Car benefit	£15,000 × 19% (W)	=	£2,850
Fuel benefit	£14,400 × 19%	=	£2,736

These benefits will be subject to income tax at the rate of 40% but no employee NICs payable on benefits.

Limited Company's Position

The company will need to report the assessable benefits to HMRC at the end of the tax year via a Form P11D. It will also have to account for Class 1A NIC on the value of these benefits at the rate of 12·8%. This needs to be paid by 19 July following the end of the tax year.

The company will be able to claim a deduction against trading profits for all of the net of VAT running costs it pays. The related input VAT will be recoverable via its VAT Returns. A VAT fuel scale charge will apply at the appropriate rate per quarter because all fuel, including that used privately, is paid for by the company.

The company will not be able to recover VAT on the purchase price of the car.

The company will also be able to claim a deduction against trading profits for capital allowances on the purchase price, including VAT, for the car. Because the cost of the car exceeds £12,000 writing down allowances will be restricted to £3,000 in the company's first corporation tax computation. This car will not enter the general capital allowances pool but rather will be dealt with separately as an expensive car.

Working – Car benefit

CO2 emissions 160 g/km, available all year

Appropriate % = 15% + (160 – 140) × $\frac{1}{5}$ = 19%

(b)   **The tax implications of Alfie acquiring a van**

Van acquired personally

If the vehicle acquired is a van the position remains the same as above if this is acquired personally by Alfie.

Van acquired by limited company

If, however, the van is acquired by the limited company the above answer will need to be modified as follows:

Alfie's position

Assuming Alfie's private use of the van is more than just commuting to work, then the benefit taxable upon Alfie will become a fixed amount of £500 which will again be liable to Class 1A NIC. No separate fuel benefit will apply.

Limited company's position

The limited company will be able to recover VAT on the purchase price of the van. This amounts to £2,234 (15,000 × 17.5/117.5).

Capital allowances will be calculated on £12,766 (15,000 – 2,234), the net of VAT cost of the van. Because the limited company is likely to be a small enterprise the van will be eligible for a first year allowance of 50% with the balance entering the general pool.

(c)   **Advice on tax efficiency of two alternatives**

Car Acquired Personally

Limited Company

	£	£
Business mileage (10,000 × 0.4)	4,000	
(10,000 × 0.25)	2,500	
	———	
Mileage allowance paid to Alfie	6,500	
= Trading profit deduction	———	(6,500)
Corporation tax saving (6,500 × 19%)		1,235

Alfie

	£
Mileage received	6,500
Less: Costs (500 + 500 + 100)	(1,100)
Fuel (22,000/40 × 3)	(1,650)
Capital cost	(3,000)
	———
Net Cost	(4,515)
	———

Car Acquired by Limited Company

Limited Company

	£	£
Costs (3,000 + 500 + 500 + 100 + (fuel) 1,650)		(5,750)
Insurance	500	
Repairs	500	
Road fund licence	100	
Fuel	1,650	
Class 1A NIC (2,850 + 2,736) × 12.8%	715	(715)
Capital allowances	3,000	
	———	
Trading deduction	6,465	
Corporation tax saving × 19%	———	1,228

Alfie

	£
Income tax benefits – car (2,850 × 40%)	(1,140)
– fuel (2,736 × 40%)	(1,094)
	———
Net Cost	(7,471)
	———

Conclusion

On the basis of the information provided it would appear more tax efficient if the car is acquired by Alfie personally.

ACCA marking scheme			
			Marks
(a)	Personally		
	Alfie	Mileage allowances	3.0
	Limited company	P11D	0.5
		Employers Class 1 NIC	1.0
		Mileage allowances	0.5
		VAT recovery	1.0
	Limited company		
	Alfie	Benefits	1.0
	Limited company	P11D	0.5
		Class 1A NIC	1.0
		Running costs	0.5
		VAT recovery – running costs	0.5
		– vehicles	1.0
		Fuel scale charge	0.5
		Capital allowances	1.0
		Available	12.0
		Maximum	11.0
(b)	Benefit		1.0
	VAT recovery on van		1.0
	Capital allowances		1.0
		Available	3.0
		Maximum	3.0
(c)	Car acquired personally:		
	Mileage allowance		1.0
	Corporation tax saving		1.0
	Personal net costs		2.0
	Acquired by Limited Company:		
	Costs		1.0
	Capital allowances		0.5
	Class 1A NIC		1.5
	Trading profit deduction		1.5
	Corporation tax saving		0.5
	Benefits		1.0
	Conclusion		1.0
		Available	11.0
		Maximum	11.0
Total			25.0

8 ADVANCED TECHNOLOGIES LTD

(a) (i) **Tax implications of engaging Bill**

Implications for Bill:

Employee

As an employee Bill will receive the following amounts from Advanced Technologies Limited ('ATL') during 2007/2008.

	£
Salary	39,000
Mileage allowance (4,160 + 1,560) × 60 pence	3,432
Home-working contribution	120
	42,552

Bill will be liable to income tax on his salary.

Mileage allowances of up to 40 pence per mile for business mileage (up to 10,000 miles and 25 pence per mile thereafter) can be received tax free. The travelling to the client will be permissible business mileage but the travelling to ATL's premises will not. Bill will therefore be liable to further income tax on the allowances paid for travelling to the premises of ATL and also for the fact that he is receiving an excess of 20 pence per mile for each mile paid.

Both the income tax on his salary and excess mileage allowances paid will be collected under the PAYE scheme operated by ATL.

With regards the home-working contribution HMRC will allow, without supporting documentation, up to £104 per year. As the amount of £120 paid by ATL is only slightly in excess of this it is likely that all of this will be allowed tax-free.

As an employee Bill will be liable to Class 1 National Insurance contributions ('NIC') at the rate of 11% on his earnings (comprising salary and excess mileage allowances) above the lower earnings threshold of £5,035. Any earnings exceeding the upper earnings threshold of £33,540 will also be liable to Class 1 NIC at the rate of 1%.

Self-employed

If Bill works on a self-employed basis he will be assessed to income tax on his trading income. As his business will run from 6 April 2007 to 5 April 2008 he will be assessed on the net profits for this period in his 2007/2008 self-assessment tax return.

In arriving at his assessable profit figure, based upon the information provided, Bill will be able to claim the following:

– The business proportion of his vehicle expenses incurred in this period. As an alternative for a small business HMRC will accept a claim based upon business mile multiplied by the tax free mileage rates (i.e. 40 pence per mile for the first 10,000 business miles and 25 pence per mile thereafter).

– The other allowable business expenses of £500.

– A first year allowance of 50% for the computer equipment purchased and used exclusively for business purposes, provided it is purchased before 31 March 2007 (40% if after that date).

– A writing down allowance of £3,000 multiplied by the business use fraction for his vehicle (but see tutorial note below).

Bill will also be liable to pay Class 2 NIC of £109 for 2007/08 and Class 4 NIC at the rate of 8% on net profits between £5,035 and £33,540 and 1% on any profits in excess of £33,540.

To avoid any penalties Bill will need to inform HMRC by 5 October 2007 of his self-employed income source and by 5 July 2007 for Class 2 NIC purposes.

Tutorial note: The writing down allowance on the vehicle is not available if Bill claims for business mileage using the tax free authorised mileage rates.

Implications for ATL

Employed

Any salary, mileage allowance and home-working contributions paid to Bill by ATL will be deductible for corporation tax purposes. In addition the company will be able to claim a 50% first year allowance for the computer equipment.

ATL will be responsible for operating PAYE on any 'earnings' (including excess mileage allowances) paid to Bill. As part of this ATL will need to pay employer's Class 1 NIC at the rate of 12.8% on any earnings paid over the lower threshold of £5,035. Employer's Class 1 NIC is also deductible for corporation tax purposes.

Self-employed

If Bill is self-employed ATL will be able to claim a deduction for corporation tax purposes on the accruals basis for any invoices raised by Bill for services performed.

Providing HMRC accept that Bill is self-employed, ATL will have no responsibility for operating PAYE on such payments.

(ii) **The most beneficial treatment from the company perspective**

Employed

If Bill is employed, ATL's after tax cashflows will be as follows:

	£
Payments to Bill (part (a) (i))	42,552
Class 1 NIC (W1)	4,574
	47,126
Corporation tax savings (47,126 × 19%)	(8,954)
Computer equipment	5,000
Tax saving (W3)	(475)
Net of tax cashflows	42,697

Self-employed

If Bill is self-employed, ATL's after tax cashflows will be as follows:

	£
Payments to Bill	48,000
Corporation tax savings (48,000 × 19%)	(9,120)
Net of tax cashflows	38,880

Conclusion

ATL will therefore save £3,817 (42,697 – 38,880) if it can treat Bill on a self-employed basis.

Workings

(W1)   Class 1 NICs

	£
Salary	39,000
Excess mileage allowance (W2)	1,768
	40,768
Less Threshold	(5,035)
Class 1 NICs	35,733 × 12.8% = £4,574

(W2)   Excess mileage allowance

	£
Allowance received (5,720 miles × 60p)	3,432
AMAPs (4,160 × 40p)	(1,664)
Excess allowances	1,768

(W3)   Computer equipment tax saving

	£
Cost	5,000

Assuming the computer is acquired before 31 March 2007, a 50% FYA is available

Capital allowances (50% × 5,000)	2,500
Corporation tax saving @ 19%	475

(b)   (i)   **Factors to consider in determining self-employed status**

The distinction between employment and self-employment turns on whether Bill will have a contract of service (employee) or contract for services (self-employed).

The main factors that will be considered in determining which applies are:

1   The degree of 'day to day' control exercised over Bill. Note this does not have to be actual control, merely the right to exercise this level of control.

2   Whether Bill must work exclusively for ATL.

3   Whether ATL must provide further work and Bill accept further work.

4   Whether the work performed by Bill is an integral part of the business and not merely an accessory to it.

5   Whether Bill takes financial risk and has the ability to profit from sound management.

6   Whether Bill has the right to employ his own resources (e.g. hire staff, use his own equipment).

7   Whether Bill can decide when he works to complete the project.

In the context of Bill's proposed engagement on a 'self-employed' basis with ATL, it would appear that whilst the work may form an integral part of ATL's business, the other factors appear favourable to the conclusion that he is correctly to be treated as self-employed rather than employed.

Providing the project is completed to schedule Bill can choose to work when he pleases. As well as satisfying point (7) above this also suggests that ATL do not have the right to exercise 'day to day' control over Bill. There is no requirement for Bill to work exclusively for ATL.

In addition Bill has the right to delegate the work to his own staff and will use his own equipment (computer and vehicle) over the course of the assignment.

He also has the ability to profit from sound management in so far as he is working to a fixed price and can therefore benefit financially from early successful completion of the project. Equally a fixed price implies financial risk in that should the project take longer than anticipated Bill will need to expend further resources to complete the project.

On balance it would appear that in this case the evidence points towards self-employment, although ATL would be well advised to seek agreement to this treatment from HMRC at the outset.

(ii) **Potential tax savings of operating through a company**

If Bill were to perform the assignment through a limited company rather than as a sole trader, tax savings could be achieved because:

(1) The first £300,000 of profits made by a limited company have a 19% corporation tax rate with profits in excess of this being taxed at a marginal rate of 33.75% until profits exceed £1.5 million where upon a 30% tax rate applies. Based upon the level of profits anticipated, however, as a sole trader his marginal income tax rate would be 40%.

In addition he would have to pay Class 2 NIC of £109 and Class 4 NIC at the rate of 8% of assessable profits between £5,035 and £33,540 and 1% of profits in excess of £33,540.

(2) To take advantage of the lower corporation tax rates Bill will need to take the bulk of his remuneration in the form of dividends.

A simple strategy would be to pay himself a salary of £5,035 to make use of his personal allowance and enable him to be credited with some NIC payments (even though no NICs are actually payable unless his salary exceeds £5,035).

The balance of remuneration would then be drawn in the form of dividends which are taxed at a maximum of 32½% and have a deemed tax credit of 10%. Providing the dividends do not take Bill's income over the higher rate tax threshold he will have no further personal tax to pay in respect of them.

In addition, dividends do not attract a Class 1 NIC liability.

If Bill wishes to adopt this strategy of operating through a company he should be aware of the 'IR35' personal service company legislation.

This states that if Bill would have been regarded as an employee if engaged directly by ATL the income received by his limited company will be treated as if it had been paid as a salary to him (irrespective of whether it actually has).

The effect would be a much higher level of overall taxation for Bill and his limited company because

(i)   employee's and employer's Class 1 NIC will apply to the deemed payment, and

(ii)   his deemed salary is likely to make Bill a 40% higher rate taxpayer.

Bill needs to be aware that if he chooses to perform his services through a limited company the 'risk' of determining employment status passes from ATL to him and his company. Whilst on the evidence it appears that this would be a genuine self-employment, in these circumstances Bill would be well advised to seek agreement from HMRC that the 'IR 35' provisions will not apply at the outset.

		ACCA marking scheme			*Marks*
(a)	(i)	Implication for Bill			
		Employee	salary		0.5
			mileage allowances		1.0
			tax collection through PAYE		0.5
			home-working contribution		0.5
			Class 1 NIC		1.0
		Self-employed	trading income/self assessment		1.0
			deductions		2.0
			Class 2 NIC/Class 4 NIC		1.0
			notification		1.0
		Implication for ATL			
		Employee	corporation tax deductions		0.5
			Class 1 NIC		1.0
		Self-employed			0.5
				Available	10.5
				Maximum	10.5
	(ii)	Employed	Net cash outflows		
			payments to Bill		0.5
			computer equipment		1.0
			Class 1 NIC		1.5
			tax savings		0.5
		Self-employed	Net cash outflows		1.0
		Conclusion			0.5
				Available	5.0
				Maximum	5.0
(b)	(i)	Contract of vs for service			0.5
		Factors			2.5
		Discussion/conclusion			2.5
				Available	5.5
				Maximum	5.0
	(ii)	Marginal tax rates			1.5
		Remuneration strategy			1.5
		IR 35 provisions			1.5
		Conclusion			1.0
				Available	5.5
				Maximum	5.0
Total					25.0

9   OLIVER

(a)   **Employment v self employment**

Employment represents a contract of service as opposed to a contract for services. In looking at the status of an individual HMRC will consider the following criteria:

- The degree of day to day control exercised.

- The degree of exclusivity.

- The mutuality of obligation between the two parties.

- Whether the work done by the individual is an integral part of the business and not an accessory to it.

- The financial risk and reward.

- The ability to employ his/her own resources.

- The individual's ability to decide where and when he /she works to complete the project.

In Oliver's case, he appears to be able to control his work, can work for others, has the ability to profit from his own enterprise, and can work at home when he wants.

Therefore it is likely that Oliver will be treated as self-employed.

(b)   **The cash impact of accepting Easylife's contract**

Tutorial note:

To compare the two options available it is necessary to calculate the net cash flow of continuing in employment with Hardlife Ltd or accepting the new contract with Easylife Ltd.

Comparison of options

	Hardlife Ltd £	Easylife Ltd £
Cash received		
– Salary	62,000	
– Easylife contract (£3750 × 12)		45,000
– Other contracts		10,000
– Mileage allowance (13,000 × 35p)		4,550
	62,000	59,550
Cash out		
– Income tax (Notes (i) (ii))	(26,951)	(12,934)
– NICs (Notes (i) (ii))	(3,421)	(2,602)
– Car running costs (£6,000 + £3,000)	-	(9,000)
Net cash flow	31,628	35,014

Conclusion

Oliver should accept the Easylife contract and move to a consulting role.

Note (i)   **Assuming Oliver continues to work for Hardlife Ltd.**

Income tax calculation – 2007/08

	Workings	£
Employment income		
Salary		62,000
Assessable benefits:		
Company car	(1)	9,212
Fuel benefit	(2)	5,040
Accommodation	(3)	13,590
Car parking	(4)	–
Statutory total income		89,842
Less: Personal allowance		(5,035)
Taxable income		84,807

Income tax:

		£
2,150 × 10%		215
35,150 × 22%		7,733
37,300 Extended basic rate band	(5)	
47,507 × 40%		19,003
84,807		
Income tax liability		26,951

National Insurance contributions (NIC)

	£
(£33,540 – £5,035) × 11%	3,136
(£62,000 – £33,540) × 1%	285
	3,421

Note (ii)   **Assuming Oliver takes the consulting role.**

Income tax calculation – 2007/08

	Workings	£
Trading profit		
((3,750 × 12) + 10,000)		55,000
Mileage claim	(6)	(200)
Statutory total income		54,800
Less: Personal allowance		(5,035)
Taxable income		49,765

Income tax:

		£
2,150 × 10%		215
35,150 × 22%		7,733
37,300 Extended basic rate band	(5)	
12,465 × 40%		4,986
49,765		
Income tax liability		12,934

National insurance contributions (NIC):	£
Class 2 (£2.10 × 52)	109
Class 4 (£33,540 – £5,035) × 8%	2,280
(£54,800 – £33,540) × 1%	213
	2,602

Workings:

(1)   *Company car*

The price for tax purposes ignores discounts, but includes optional extras at cost. The list price therefore is £22,870 + £3,450 = £26,320.

CO_2 emission level of car 237 g/km

The base CO_2 emission level for 2006/07 is 140 g/km.

$$\text{Appropriate \%} = 18\% \text{ (diesel)} + (235 - 140) \times \tfrac{1}{5}$$
$$= 37\%, \text{ restricted to } 35\%$$

Car benefit = £26,320 × 35% = £9,212

(2)   *Fuel benefit*

Base figure for 2006/07 = £14,400
Fuel benefits £14,400 × 35% = £5,040

(3)   *Accommodation*

(a)   The property is owned by Hardlife Ltd, so the market rent is not relevant and the annual amount is equal to the rateable value of £7,200.

(b)   In addition, as the property cost exceeds £75,000 there is an additional benefit equal to the official rate of interest on the excess of £4,750 (£170,000 - 75,000 x 5%).

(c)   Council tax is paid by the company, so is a benefit: £1,400.

(d)   The use of the TV benefit is £240 (20% x £1,200).

Total accommodation benefits are thus:

(£7,200 + £4,750 + £1,400 + £240) = £13,590

(4)   *Car parking*

Car parking is not a taxable benefit.

(5)   *Pension contribution*

The payment of £3,120 is net of income tax and is equivalent to (£3,120/0.78) = £4,000 gross.

Higher rate relief is given by the extension of the basic rate band to £37,300 (33,300 + 4,000).

(6)   *Mileage claim*

	Paid	*Allowable*	*Taxable/Relief*
	£	£	£
First 10,000 miles	3,500	4,000	(500)
Next 3,000 miles	1,050	750	300
	4,550	4,750	
Total taxable / (relievable)			(200)

(c) **Working from home**

Income tax implications

Oliver should be able to offset several house related expenses against his taxable trading income. For expenditure which depends on usage (such as electricity, heating etc), he can apportion the total cost on a reasonable basis (for example, heating based on volume of study compared to the total house volume).

Loan interest, for example, on a mortgage on the house, can also be apportioned, but only if part of the property is used exclusively for business purposes.

Capital gains tax implications

Caution should be exercised where a room is used wholly and exclusively for business purposes as this will result in a restriction of Oliver's principal private residence (PPR) exemption for capital gains tax.

However, business asset taper relief would be available on that part of the gain.

(d) **Maximum personal pension contributions**

The maximum gross personal pension contributions that Oliver can obtain tax relief for is the higher of

(i)   £3,600

(ii)   100% of earned income = £54,800

To obtain the maximum relief of £54,800, Oliver would need to pay £42,744 (£54,800 × 78%) into the scheme before 6 April 2007.

ACCA marking scheme			
			Marks
(a)	Contract for/of services		1.0
	Parameters (0.5 each)		3.5
	Application to Oliver		2.0
		Max	6.0
(b)	Personal allowance		0.5
	Extend basic rate band (pension)		0.5
	Tax at graduated rates		0.5
	Class 1 National insurance calculations		0.5
	Calculation of after-tax income		0.5
	Car price		1.0
	Car benefit		1.0
	Fuel benefit		0.5
	Accommodation annual value		1.0
	Expensive accommodation charge		1.0
	Council tax		0.5
	Television benefit		0.5
	Pension gross-up		0.5
	Total Trading Income		0.5
	Mileage allowance adjustment:		
	10,000 mile comparison		0.5
	3,000 mile comparison		0.5
	result (tax relief)		0.5
	Tax at graduated rates		0.5
	Class 2 national insurance		0.5
	Class 4 national insurance		0.5
	Calculation of after-tax income		1.0
	Conclusion		0.5
		Max	13.0

(c)	Expense offset		0.5
	Interest deduction		1.0
	Loss of principal private residence relief		0.5
	Availability of business taper relief		1.0
		Max	3.0
(d)	Contribution for 2007/08		2.0
	Paid net		0.5
	Payment date		0.5
Total			25.0

10   JAN

(a) **Income tax computation – 2006/07**

Tutorial note: As Jan is not domiciled in the UK, he is taxed on his overseas income on the remittance basis.

	Notes	Total £	Other income £	Savings £	Dividends £
Employment income:					
Salary (pro rated)		68,530			
Benefits: car	(1)	10,850			
Benefits: fuel	(1)	3,672			
Benefits: other		3,965			
		87,017	87,017		
Dividends	(2)	3,600			3,600
ISA interest	(3)	–		–	
Bank interest	(4)	925		925	
Overseas property income	(5)	8,360	8,360		
Overseas interest	(6)	6,000		6,000	
Statutory Total Income		105,902	95,377	6,925	3,600
Less: Personal allowance		(5,035)	(5,035)		
Taxable income		100,867	90,342	6,925	3,600

Income tax £	£
2,150 × 10% (other income)	215
31,150 × 22% (other income)	6,853
57,042 × 40% (other income)	22,817
90,342	
6,925 × 40% (savings)	2,770
3,600 × 32.5% (dividends)	1,170
100,867	
	33,825
DTR on property income (8)	(3,344)
DTR on interest income (9)	(900)
Income tax liability	29,581
Tax credit on dividend income	(360)
Tax credit on bank interest	(185)
Income tax payable	29,036

Notes:

(1) **Car and fuel benefit**

CO_2 emission 237 g/km, available for 9 months

Appropriate % = 15% + (235 – 140) × $\frac{1}{5}$ = 34%

Car benefit = £42,550 × 34% x 9/12 = 10,850

Fuel benefit = 14,400 × 34% × 9/12 = 3,672

(2) **Dividends**

3,240 × (100/90) = 3,600

(3) **ISA interest**

Interest on ISA accounts is not taxable.

(4) **Bank interest**

740 × (100/80) = 925

(5) **Overseas property income**

Rental income is received net of 45% overseas tax.

Gross income = 4,598 × (100/55) = £8,360

Overseas tax suffered = 8,360 × 45% = £3,762

(6) **Overseas interest**

Interest is received net of 15% overseas tax

Gross income = 5,100 × (100/85) = £6,000

Overseas tax suffered = 6,000 × 15% = £900

(7) **Double tax relief on rental income**
Lower of
(a) UK income tax = 40% × £8,360 = £3,344, and
(b) overseas tax = £3,762

(8) **Double tax relief on interest**
Lower of
(a) UK income tax = 40% × £6,000 = £2,400, and
(b) overseas tax = £900

(b) **Taxable benefit – accommodation**

If Jan accepts the offer, he will occupy the building for a period of eight months in the tax year 2007/08 (from 6 August 2007 – 5 April 2008). The company will pay the rent for six months and the benefit will therefore last for six months.

The taxable benefit is the higher of: £

(i) The rent borne by the company = 600 × 6 = 3,600

(ii) The annual (rateable) value = 6,000 × 6/12 = 3,000

The benefit is therefore £3,600.

There is no additional 'expensive accommodation' benefit as the company rents the property and therefore does not own the property.

(c)   (i)   **Paper for paper exchange rules**

The proposed transaction broadly falls under the 'paper for paper' exchange rules. Where this is the case, chargeable gains do not arise. Instead, the new holding stands in the shoes (and inherits the base cost) of the original holding.

The company issuing the new shares must:

(i)   as a result of the transaction end up with more than 25% of the ordinary share capital (or a majority of the voting power) of the old company, or

(ii)   make a general offer to shareholders in the other company with a condition that, if satisfied, would give the acquiring company control of the other company.

The exchange must be for *bona fide* commercial reasons and must not have as its main purpose (or one of its main purposes) the avoidance of CGT or corporation tax. The acquiring company can obtain advance clearance from HMRC that the conditions will be met.

If part of the offer consideration is in the form of cash, a gain must be calculated using the part disposal rules.

If the cash received is not more than the higher of £3,000 or 5% of the total value on takeover, then the amount received in cash can be deducted from the base cost of the securities under the small distribution rules.

(ii)   **Capital gain arising on the takeover**

The cost and indexation details for the 1985 pool are as follows:

	No of shares	Cost £	Indexed cost £
August 1986: acquisition	2,500	10,175	10,175
January 1994: bonus issue	22,500	Nil	Nil
	25,000	10,175	10,175
Indexation: $\dfrac{162.6 - 97.82}{97.82}$			6,738
Balance @ takeover	25,000	10,175	16,913

Note that indexation is calculated only up to 1998, as Jan is an individual. Indexation in the 1985 pool is not rounded to three decimal places.

The takeover consideration is forecast to be:	£
Shares (25,000 × 3/5 × 3.55)	53,250
Cash (25,000 × 0.25)	6,250
Takeover consideration	59,500

The cash of £6,250 exceeds £3,000 and £2,975 (5% × £59,500 takeover value), so there is a part disposal gain to calculated.

		£
Disposal proceeds = cash received		6,250
Apportioned cost:		
10,175 × (6,250/59,500)		(1,069)
Unindexed gain		5,181
Less: Indexation allowance		
6,738 × (6,250/59,500)		(708)
Indexed gain before taper relief		4,473
Business asset taper relief (75%) (Note)		(3,355)
Chargeable gain (25%)		1,118

Note: the shares are qualifying business assets for taper relief purposes and have been owned for more than 2 years. The gain is therefore 25% chargeable.

(iii) **Qualifying corporate bond**

A qualifying corporate bond ('QCB') is a security that represents a normal commercial loan. This excludes bonds that can be converted into shares. The security cannot carry a right to excessive interest, or interest which depends on the result of the owner's business.

The security must be expressed in sterling. There can be no provision for conversion into or redemption in another currency. The security must have been acquired (by the person disposing of it) after 13 March 1984.

If Jan received a QCB instead of cash, the gain will be apportioned between the shares and the loan stock in the same way as for cash above.

The new shares will inherit the base cost of the old shares, and any gain will only arise on the subsequent disposal of the new shares, as explained above.

However, unlike with cash consideration received, there is no chargeable gain arising at the time of the takeover in respect of receiving the QCB.

Instead, the gain apportioned to the loan stock is calculated as for cash consideration and will be £1,118 as above, however the gain is not taxed, it is 'frozen' and deferred until the loan stock is disposed of. At that time, the held over gain becomes chargeable.

The increase in value of the QCBs from the takeover to the date of sale is exempt from CGT as QCBs are exempt assets for individuals. Only the 'frozen' deferred gain becomes chargeable.

<table>
<tr><td colspan="4" align="center">**ACCA marking scheme**</td></tr>
<tr><td></td><td></td><td></td><td align="right">*Marks*</td></tr>
<tr><td>(a)</td><td colspan="2">Prorated salary</td><td align="right">0.5</td></tr>
<tr><td></td><td colspan="2">Other benefit</td><td align="right">0.5</td></tr>
<tr><td></td><td colspan="2">Dividend (gross up)</td><td align="right">0.5</td></tr>
<tr><td></td><td colspan="2">ISA interest not taxable</td><td align="right">0.5</td></tr>
<tr><td></td><td colspan="2">Bank interest gross up</td><td align="right">0.5</td></tr>
<tr><td></td><td colspan="2">Overseas income gross up (0.5 each)</td><td align="right">1.0</td></tr>
<tr><td></td><td colspan="2">Personal allowance</td><td align="right">0.5</td></tr>
<tr><td></td><td colspan="2">Graduated rates of income tax</td><td align="right">1.0</td></tr>
<tr><td></td><td colspan="2">Rate for savings income</td><td align="right">0.5</td></tr>
<tr><td></td><td colspan="2">Separate rate for dividends</td><td align="right">0.5</td></tr>
<tr><td></td><td colspan="2">Tax credit on dividend</td><td align="right">0.5</td></tr>
<tr><td></td><td colspan="2">Tax credit on interest</td><td align="right">0.5</td></tr>
<tr><td></td><td colspan="2">Car benefit percentage</td><td align="right">0.5</td></tr>
<tr><td></td><td colspan="2">Calculation / pro rating of car benefit (0.5 each)</td><td align="right">1.0</td></tr>
<tr><td></td><td colspan="2">Fuel benefit / pro rating of benefit (0.5 each)</td><td align="right">1.0</td></tr>
<tr><td></td><td colspan="2">Double tax relief lower of two figures (£3,344)</td><td align="right">0.5</td></tr>
<tr><td></td><td colspan="2">Double tax relief: UK tax</td><td align="right">0.5</td></tr>
<tr><td></td><td colspan="2" align="right">Overseas tax</td><td align="right">0.5</td></tr>
<tr><td></td><td colspan="2">Repeat calculation for offshore interest (£900)</td><td align="right">0.5</td></tr>
<tr><td></td><td colspan="2">Max</td><td align="right">11.0</td></tr>
<tr><td>(b)</td><td colspan="2">Benefit: rent</td><td align="right">0.5</td></tr>
<tr><td></td><td colspan="2" align="right">Rateable value</td><td align="right">0.5</td></tr>
<tr><td></td><td colspan="2" align="right">Select higher</td><td align="right">0.5</td></tr>
<tr><td></td><td colspan="2">Identify £75,000</td><td align="right">0.5</td></tr>
<tr><td></td><td colspan="2">time-apportioned benefit</td><td align="right">0.5</td></tr>
<tr><td></td><td colspan="2">comment re: 'expensive accommodation'</td><td align="right">0.5</td></tr>
<tr><td></td><td colspan="2">Max</td><td align="right">3.0</td></tr>
<tr><td>(c)</td><td>(i)</td><td>No chargeable gains on share for share</td><td align="right">0.5</td></tr>
<tr><td></td><td></td><td>New holding stands in shoes of old holding</td><td align="right">0.5</td></tr>
<tr><td></td><td></td><td>Conditions: more than 25% share capital</td><td align="right">0.5</td></tr>
<tr><td></td><td></td><td align="right">General offer to shareholders</td><td align="right">0.5</td></tr>
<tr><td></td><td></td><td align="right">Gaining control if offer accepted</td><td align="right">0.5</td></tr>
<tr><td></td><td></td><td>*Bona fide* commercial reasons</td><td align="right">0.5</td></tr>
<tr><td></td><td></td><td>Not for avoidance of CGT/CT</td><td align="right">0.5</td></tr>
<tr><td></td><td></td><td>Advance clearance available</td><td align="right">0.5</td></tr>
<tr><td></td><td></td><td>Part disposal rules of part cash</td><td align="right">0.5</td></tr>
<tr><td></td><td></td><td>*De minimus:* higher of 5%/£3,000</td><td align="right">0.5</td></tr>
<tr><td></td><td></td><td>Max</td><td align="right">4.0</td></tr>
<tr><td></td><td>(ii)</td><td>Bonus issue has no effect</td><td align="right">0.5</td></tr>
<tr><td></td><td></td><td>Indexation</td><td align="right">0.5</td></tr>
<tr><td></td><td></td><td>Calculation of consideration (0.5 for each)</td><td align="right">1.0</td></tr>
<tr><td></td><td></td><td>Part disposal: apportioned cost</td><td align="right">0.5</td></tr>
<tr><td></td><td></td><td align="right">Apportioned indexation</td><td align="right">0.5</td></tr>
<tr><td></td><td></td><td>Taper relief: business rates</td><td align="right">0.5</td></tr>
<tr><td></td><td></td><td align="right">75% reduction</td><td align="right">0.5</td></tr>
<tr><td></td><td></td><td>Max</td><td align="right">4.0</td></tr>
<tr><td></td><td>(iii)</td><td>Normal commercial loan</td><td align="right">0.5</td></tr>
<tr><td></td><td></td><td>Interest rate not related to success of business</td><td align="right">0.5</td></tr>
<tr><td></td><td></td><td>No right to excessive interest</td><td align="right">0.5</td></tr>
<tr><td></td><td></td><td>Identify 1984 date</td><td align="right">0.5</td></tr>
<tr><td></td><td></td><td>Expressed in sterling</td><td align="right">0.5</td></tr>
<tr><td></td><td></td><td>Cannot convert to/redeem in another currency</td><td align="right">0.5</td></tr>
<tr><td></td><td></td><td>Still need to apportion</td><td align="right">0.5</td></tr>
<tr><td></td><td></td><td>Exempt from capital gains tax</td><td align="right">0.5</td></tr>
<tr><td></td><td></td><td>Gain frozen</td><td align="right">0.5</td></tr>
<tr><td></td><td></td><td>Identify when held over gain chargeable</td><td align="right">0.5</td></tr>
<tr><td></td><td></td><td>Max</td><td align="right">3.0</td></tr>
<tr><td colspan="3">Total (Max)</td><td align="right">25.0</td></tr>
</table>

11   JOANNE

(a)   **Residence status**

As Joanne has stated her intention to move permanently to the UK, she will be treated as UK resident from the day she arrives in the UK. Her income from this point will be taxable in the UK, and she will receive a full personal allowance (unapportioned) for the year.

Income earned in the UK will be taxable, but income earned abroad in Germany will not be taxed unless it is remitted to the UK.

Although Joanne is UK resident, she is not UK domiciled. Thus, while capital gains on UK assets will be taxable, gains on assets held overseas are taxable only to the extent that the proceeds of the sale are remitted to the UK. As Joanne intends to remit the proceeds from selling her shares in Germany and reinvest them in the UK, the gain will be taxable in the UK.

(b)   **Letter to Joanne concerning VAT matters**

[Joanne's address]   [Firm's address]

Dear Joanne   5 February 2007

I am writing to you in order to set out the value added tax (VAT) issues you face on registering your trade, together with some other aspects of VAT that are relevant to you.

Registration

VAT registration is compulsory once taxable supplies exceed £61,000. This turnover figure is based on the value of your cumulative taxable supplies in the previous 12 months. You have an obligation to inform HMRC within 30 days of the end of the month in which the annual limit is exceeded. Registration will become effective on the first day of the following month.

VAT registration is also required if there are reasonable grounds for believing that the taxable supplies in the following 30 days will exceed £61,000. In such cases, notification is required by the end of that 30 day period with registration being effective from the start of that period.

Based on your estimates of taxable supplies, you will exceed the annual limit at the end of October 2007 when your cumulative turnover will be £62,000. You will therefore have to inform HMRC by the end of November 2007. Your registration will be effective as of 1 December 2007.

You also have the option of voluntarily registering prior to date of compulsory registration. In this case you will normally become registered from the date you applied. This is useful where your sales are to VAT registered customers for whom the extra VAT would not be a cost.

You would then be able to recover VAT on your attributable costs. However, you will have to comply with the VAT administrative requirements.

Recovery of pre-registration VAT

It is possible to claim the recovery of VAT incurred prior to registering for VAT, however subject to conditions being satisfied.

The costs of the goods or services must have been incurred for the purpose of the business within permitted time limits. VAT on capital assets (such as your computer) can be recovered provided they were not acquired more than three years before the date of registration. VAT on services however (such as the consultancy fees) can only be recovered if the services were provided in the 6 months prior to registration.

As a result, I would recommend that you apply for voluntary registration as soon as possible, as registering after 22 April 2007 will mean that you will be unable to reclaim the VAT on your consultancy fees.

I hope the above information is useful to you.

Yours sincerely,

A. Consultant.

(c) (i) **Income tax computation – 2006/07**

	£
Employment income (Note 1)	25,000
Trading income (Note 2)	5,070
Statutory total income	30,070
Less: Personal allowance	(5,035)
Taxable income	25,035

Income tax

£		£
2,150 × 10%		215
22,885 × 22%		5,035
25,035		

	£
Income tax liability	5,250
Less: Paid under PAYE	(4,000)
Income tax payable	1,250

Notes:

(1) **Employment income**

Joanne is taxable on her two months salary for October and November 2006.

In addition, the payment made to Joanne for the notice period of three months will be taxable as it derives from her contract of employment.

She will therefore be taxed on 5 months salary = 5 × £5,000 = £25,000.

(2) **Trading income**

Joanne's first accounting period is the four months to 31 March 2007. Her basis period for 2006/07 is 1 December 2006 to 5 April 2007.

As Joanne is not registered for VAT in this period, her trading income for the year includes VAT on all costs, and is calculated as follows:

	£
Income (£2,000 + £3,000 + £4,000 + £5,000)	14,000
Expenses (5,000 × 1.175) + (4 × £400 × 1.175))	(7,755)
Capital allowances: FYA (2,000 × 1.175 × 50%)	(1,175)
Trading income	5,070

The tax written down value at 31 March 2007 is £1,175 (2,350 – 1,175)

Capital gains tax – 2006/07

As Joanne is not paying higher rate tax for the year, the first £8,265 (33,300 – 25,035) of any taxable gains will be taxed initially at 20%.

	£
Sale proceeds (March 2007)	21,500
Less Cost (September 1986)	(3,500)
Unindexed gain	18,000
Indexation: $\frac{162.6 - 98.3}{98.3}$ (Note)	(2,289)
Indexed gain	15,711

As a non-business held for 9 qualifying years (including the bonus year), the gain is 65% chargeable.

	£
Chargeable gain (15,711 × 65%)	10,212
Less: Annual exemption	(8,800)
Taxable gain	1,412
Capital gains tax at 20%	282

Note: The shares were acquired in September 1986 and will therefore form part of the 1985 pool. Indexation in the pool is not rounded to three decimal places.

(ii)   **Income tax computation – 2007/08**

	£
Trading income (Note)	79,149
Less: Personal allowance	(5,035)
Taxable income	74,114

Income tax

£	£	£
2,150 × 10%		215
31,150 × 22%		6,853
40,814 × 40%		16,326
74,114		
Income tax liability		23,394

National insurance – 2007/08

		£	£
Class 2:	£2.10 × 52		109
Class 4:	(33,540 – 5,035) × 8%	2,280	
	(79,149 – 33,540) × 1%	741	3,021
Total NIC liability			3,130

Total income tax and Class 4 NICs payable by self assessment

= (23,394 + 3,021) = £26,415

Note: **Trading income**

Joanne's basis period for 2007/08 is the year ended 31 March 2008. As Joanne has registered for VAT from 1 April 2007, all amounts are net of VAT.

For capital allowance purposes the VAT refund on the computer of £350 (£2,000 × 17½%) is treated as disposal proceeds and deducted from the general pool.

Joanne's trading income is calculated as follows:

	£
Income (£6,000 + (11 × £7,000))	83,000
Expenses (12 × £400)	(4,800)
Refund of VAT (taxable) (7,755 × 17.5/117.5)	1,155
Capital allowances (£1,175 − £350) × 25%	(206)
Trading income	79,149

(iii) **Schedule of payments for 2006/07 and 2007/08**

The tax payments are due as follows:

2006/07

Type of tax payment	Due date	£
Income tax balancing payment (net of £4,000 PAYE)	31 January 2008	1,250
Capital gains tax	31 January 2008	282
		1,532

2007/08

As Joanne paid more than £500 to HMRC and did not pay at least 80% of her income tax through PAYE or other deduction at source in 2006/07 (she paid 76.2% = 4,000 ÷ 5,250), she will be required to make payments on account (POAs) in 2007/08.

POAs are based on the tax not deducted at source (excluding capital gains) in 2006/07 (totaling £1,250). Two payments each representing 50% of this sum (i.e. £625) will be payable on 31 January 2008 and 31 July 2008 respectively.

The balance of the income tax and Class 4 National Insurance will be payable on 31 January 2009.

Class 2 National Insurance is usually paid monthly by direct debit, or by quarterly invoicing.

Type of tax payment	Due date	£
Income tax payments on account	31 January 2008	625
	31 July 2008	625
balancing payment	31 January 2009	25,165
Total income tax and Class 4 NICs (part (c) (ii))		26,415

		ACCA marking scheme	
			Marks
(a)		Date of becoming UK resident	0.5
		Taxed from becoming UK resident	0.5
		Full personal allowances given	0.5
		Overseas income not taxable unless remitted	0.5
		Capital gains on UK assets taxable	0.5
		Overseas capital gains not taxable unless remitted	0.5
		Max	3.0
(b)		Registration:	
		– Required if taxable turnover exceeds £61k	0.5
		– 30 days to notify HMRC	0.5
		– Registration effective on day 1, following month	0.5
		– Retrospective & prospective tests	0.5
		Application to Joanne	1.0
		Ability to voluntarily register	0.5
		Reason(s) why Joanne would wish to do so	0.5
		Recovery of VAT:	
		– business requirement	0.5
		– time limits re services/fixed assets (2×0.5)	1.0
		Voluntarily register before 22.4.07 to recover VAT re fees	1.0
		Presentation and format	2.0
		Max	7.0
(c)	(i)	Notice period pay taxable	0.5
		Trading income basis period	0.5
		APE 31/3/07 adjusted profit	
		revenue	0.5
		costs/fees incl. VAT (2×0.5)	1.0
		FYA computer 50%	0.5
		Personal allowance	0.5
		Tax rates	0.5
		Capital gain: cost	0.5
		indexation	0.5
		taper relief: non-business asset	0.5
		correct number of years/rate	0.5
		annual exemption	0.5
		tax at 20%	0.5
		Max	6.0
	(ii)	Trading income basis period	0.5
		APE 31/3/08: expense net of VAT	0.5
		Computer: adjust WDV re VAT reversal	0.5
		VAT adjustment for earlier expenses	0.5
		WDA at 25%	0.5
		Personal allowance	0.5
		Income tax calculation	0.5
		Class 2 NIC	0.5
		Class 4 NIC	0.5
		Max	4.0

(iii) 2006/07:		
	Balancing payment 31 January 2008	0.5
	Net of PAYE	0.5
	Amount includes CGT	0.5
	Class 2 payable quarterly/direct debit	0.5
2007/08:		
	Why payments on account required	1.0
	Basis for payments on account – income tax only	0.5
	Payment 31 January 2008 (50%)	0.5
	Payment 31 July 2008 (50%)	0.5
	Balancing payment 31 January 2009	0.5
	Amount includes Class 4 NIC	0.5
	Max	5.0
Total		25.0

12 ALASDAIR

(a) **Extraction of funds from Beezer Ltd**

Alasdair will be taxed in 2007/08 as follows for the two alternative suggestions:

(i) **Dividend**

In 2007/08 Alasdair already has taxable income of £24,965 (30,000 – 5,035) from his partnership interest. The remaining basic rate band is therefore £8,335 (33,300 – 24,965).

		£	£
Dividend received (120,000 × 100/90)			133,333
Income tax: £			
8,335	at 10%	834	
124,998	at 32.5%	40,624	41,458
133,333			
Less: Tax credit			(13,333)
Income tax payable			28,125
Cash remaining after tax (120,000 – 28,125)			91,875

(ii) **Liquidation**

The liquidation of Beezer will give rise to a capital gain, based on the excess of the distribution of assets over the original capital value of the shares.

The shares qualify for full business asset taper relief but only for part of the period. When Alasdair ceased trading on 1 January 2007, his business asset taper relief ceased. Only non-business asset taper relief will apply thereafter until the date of disposal.

Actual period of ownership	107 months
Qualifying business asset	92 months
Non-business asset	15 months
Complete years of ownership	8 years

The gain is apportioned and the appropriate taper relief percentage applied to each part of the gain based on 8 complete years ownership for both the business and non-business portion.

There is no bonus year for the non-business portion as the shares are not owned on 17 March 1998.

	£
Gross distribution (March 2008)	120,000
Less: Liquidator's costs	(5,000)
Net proceeds	115,000
Less Cost of shares (May 1999)	(1,000)
Gain before taper relief	114,000

There is no indexation allowance as the shares were acquired after April 1998.

Chargeable gain:

		£
Business:	92/107 × 114,000 × 25% chargeable	24,505
Non-business:	15/107 × 114,000 × 70% chargeable	11,187
Total chargeable gain		35,692
Less: Annual exemption		(8,800)
Taxable gain		26,892

As £8,335 of the basic rate band remains the CGT payable is calculated as follows:

£	£
8,335 × 20%	1,667
18,557 × 40%	7,423
26,892	9,090

Cash remaining after tax (£115,000 – £9,090)	105,910

Conclusion

As a result, Alasdair is better off liquidating the company as this gives £14,035 (105,910 – 91,875) extra cash after tax.

(b) (i) **Tax implications attached to property investments**

Income tax: Direct investment in residential or commercial property

The income received will be taxed as property business income for both residential and commercial property investment and treated as non-savings income taxed at the normal rates (10/22/40%) as appropriate.

Expenses can be offset against income under the normal trading rules. These will include interest charges incurred in borrowing funds to acquire the properties.

Property business losses are restricted to use against future property business profits, with the earliest profits being relieved first.

When acquiring commercial properties, it may be possible to claim capital allowances on the fixtures and plant held in the building. In addition, industrial buildings allowances (IBA) may also be available if the property qualifies as an industrial building.

Capital allowances are not normally available for fixtures and fittings included in a residential property. Instead, a wear and tear allowance can be claimed if the property is furnished. This is equal to 10% of the rental income after any tenants cost (for example, council tax) paid by the landlord.

Income tax: Real Estate Investment Trust

A REIT is a quoted property investment trust. UK resident listed companies carrying on a property rental business can elect to become a REIT with effect from 1 January 2007.

Dividends received by an individual out of the profits of a REIT are not treated as normal dividend income.

The dividends are treated as property income received net of 22% tax and are taxed on the individual as non-savings income at 10/20/40% as appropriate.

Income tax: Shares in a property investment company or unit trust

With collective investments such as property investment companies and unit trusts, the investor either buys shares in an investment company or units in an equity unit trust.

The income tax treatment of both is the same in that the investor receives dividends. These are taxed in the normal way as dividends at 10% and 32.5% respectively (for basic and higher rate taxpayers).

However, note that investors are not able to claim income tax relief on either interest costs of borrowing or any other expenses.

Capital gains tax (CGT):

The normal rules apply for CGT purposes in all situations.

Property investments do not normally qualify for business rates of taper relief unless they are furnished holiday lets or in certain circumstances, commercial property.

Investments in unit trusts or shares in REITs or property investment companies will never qualify for business taper rates.

It is possible to use an individual savings account (ISA) to make collective investments. If this is done, income and capital gains will be exempt from tax.

Other taxes: VAT and stamp duty

New commercial property is subject to value added tax (VAT) at the standard rate, but new residential property is subject to VAT at the zero rate.

If a commercial building is acquired second hand as an investment, VAT may be payable if a previous owner has opted to tax the property. If this is the case, VAT at the standard rate will be payable on the purchase price, and rental charges to tenants will also be subject to VAT, again at the standard rate.

The acquisition of shares is not subject to VAT.

Stamp duty land tax (SDLT) will be payable broadly on the direct acquisition of any property. The rates vary from 0 to 4% depending on the value of the land and building and its nature (whether residential or non-residential).

Stamp duty is payable at a rate of 0.5% on the acquisition of shares.

Investment risks/benefits

Direct investment in residential or commercial property

Investing directly in property represents a long term investment, and unless this is the case, investment risks are high.

Substantial initial costs (such as SDLT, VAT and transactions costs) are incurred, and ongoing running costs (such as letting agents' fees and vacant periods) can be significant. The investments are illiquid, particularly commercial properties which can take months to sell.

All types of properties are dependent on a cyclical market, and the values of property investments can vary significantly as a result. However, residential property has (on a long term basis) proven to be a good hedge against inflation.

Collective investments

The nature of collective investments is that the investor's risk is reduced by the investment being spread over a large portfolio as opposed to one or a few properties.

In addition, investors can take advantage of the higher levels of liquidity afforded by such vehicles.

(ii) **IHT and CGT tax reliefs available for the warehouse**

Apart from the fact that Alasdair works for Gallus & Co. and can keep an eye on his tenant, the main advantages of leasing the warehouse to the partnership rather than an unconnected tenant are twofold:

IHT: If the firm are the tenants, the property will be land and buildings used in a business carried on by a partnership in which the donor is a partner.

As a result, Alasdair will be able to claim business property relief (BPR) at a rate of 50% on the warehouse so long as he remains a partner in the firm.

However, this relief would not be available until Alasdair has owned the property for at least two years from his firm taking up the tenancy.

CGT: As Alasdair is a partner in the firm using the building, it will also be a qualifying asset for the purposes of rollover relief on any gains arising from the disposal of the property.

Assuming that Alasdair acquires a replacement asset which will be used in the trade, the gain on sale can be deferred against the tax base cost of the replacement asset.

In the event that rollover relief cannot be used, any gains on disposal will be subject to business asset taper relief.

(c) **Tax consequences of a loan to a participator in a close company**

All of the shares of Glaikit Limited are held by two individuals. The company is therefore a close company for corporation tax purposes.

Alasdair is not employed, nor is he a director, of Glaikit Limited. However, as he holds 25% of the shares in Glaikit Limited, he is a participator in a close company and therefore the special close company provisions will apply.

Alsadair will be taxed under the 'loans to participator' rules if he borrows from the company.

Tax consequences for Alasdair

When the loan is written off, the amount waived will be treated as a gross distribution of £16,667 (£15,000 × 100/90). This will be assessed in the tax year in which the loan is written off (expected to be 2008/09 or 2009/10). To the extent that this additional income makes Alasdair a higher rate taxpayer in that year, he will have to pay additional income tax of 32.5% of the gross amount, less the available 10% tax credit.

As the loan is tax free, HMRC may also seek to tax Alasdair under the beneficial loan rules. If HMRC were to seek an assessment in this manner, the value of the benefit would be calculated and taxed as a deemed distribution. However, as Alasdair has no connection with the company other than as an investor, it is unlikely that the beneficial loan benefit will lead to such a deemed distribution.

Tax consequences for the company

From the company's perspective, Glaikit Limited will have to pay 25% of the net value of any loan made to Alasdair which has not been repaid to the company (or written off) within nine months of the year end.

As the loan will remain outstanding as at 31 March 2008, Glaikit Limited will have to pay £3,750 (25% × £15,000) to HMRC by 1 January 2009. This amount will not be repaid until the loan is repaid or written off. This repayment usually takes place nine months after the year end in which the loan is written off, so Glaikit Limited should ensure that any write-off occurs prior to 31 March 2009, or else the repayment may be delayed for up to one year.

	– commercial property: possibly claim plant allowances	0.5
	– residential property: wear & tear allowance (furnished)	0.5
	– normal tax rates (10/22/40%)	0.5
	Income Tax: Collective investment	
	– REITs explanation	1.5
	– distributions taxed at 10/32.5% with tax credit	0.5
	– no relief for interest or other expenses	0.5
	CGT:	
	– normal rules apply	0.5
	– not normally a business asset	0.5
	– collective investment may be ISA'd	0.5
	VAT position on purchase	
	– new, commercial/residential	0.5
	– second hand, commercial	0.5
	Stamp Duty Land Tax/Stamp Duty	0.5
	Investment risks/benefits: Direct Investment	
	– high risk other than long term	0.5
	– substantial initial costs	0.5
	– significant ongoing running costs	0.5
	– illiquid investment (particularly commercial property)	0.5
	– cyclical market	0.5
	– residential property historically good inflation hedge	0.5
	Investment risks/benefits: Collective Investment	
	– reduced risks via diversification through large portfolio	0.5
	– more liquid investment	0.5
	Max	9.0

Note: additional half marks up to the maximum will be given for other relevant points.

(ii)	Availability of BPR	1.0
	Rate of BPR	0.5
	Two year ownership condition	0.5
	Availability of rollover relief	1.0
	Operation of rollover relief	0.5
	Requirement for replacement asset	0.5
	Availability of business asset taper relief	0.5
	Max	4.0

(c)	Alasdair is a participator in a close company	0.5
	Deemed distribution on write off	0.5
	Additional tax as higher rate taxpayer	0.5
	Glaikit to pay 25% of net loan	0.5
	Timing of payment	0.5
	Refund when written off	0.5
	Possibly taxed under beneficial loan rules	0.5
	Max	3.0
Total		25.0

INCOME TAX ON INCOME FROM SELF-EMPLOYMENT

13   THE BARTON PARTNERSHIP

(a)   **Assessable profits for 2006/07**

Profits are allocated to the partners according to the partnership agreement in the accounting period.

The basis of assessment for the closing year 2006/07 is from the end of the penultimate year assessment to the date of cessation (i.e. from 1 June 2005 to 30 November 2006) less the overlap profits.

Allocation of profits	Total £	Eric £	Fred £	George £
y/e 31 May 2006				
Salary	8,000		8,000	
Balance (50:25:25)	33,200	16,600	8,300	8,300
	41,200	16,600	16,300	8,300
p/e 30 Nov 2006				
Salary (6 months)	4,000		4,000	
Balance (50:25:25)	8,800	4,400	2,200	2,200
	12,800	4,400	6,200	2,200

Trading income assessments – 2006/07

	Eric	Fred	George
1 June 2005 to 30 Nov 2006			
y/e 31 May 2006	16,600	16,300	8,300
p/e 30 Nov 2006	4,400	6,200	2,200
	21,000	22,500	10,500
Less Overlap profits	(12,000)	(8,000)	(14,000)
Profits/(loss) (see tutorial note)	9,000	14,500	(3,500)
Trading income assessment	9,000	14,500	Nil

George has a trading loss for 2006/07 of £3,500, which is also a terminal loss.

The loss can be relieved in the following ways.

(i)   by offset against statutory total income of 2006/07 and/or 2005/06 under s380 ICTA 1988.

(ii)   following a claim under (i), any remaining loss can be offset against capital gains of the year of claim under s72FA 1991.

(iii)   by offset against George's trading profit of 2005/06 under a terminal loss claim. There are insufficient losses to carry back prior to 2005/06.

(iv)   by carried forward for relief against income derived by George from BPK Ltd.

Tutorial note: In practice, where one partner is allocated a loss and the other partners allocated profits, the loss is shared between the other partners. This topic is, however, outside the scope of the syllabus.

(b) (i) **Capital gains tax payable**

	Eric £	Fred £	George £
Gains split (50:25:25)	187,500	93,750	93,750
Incorporation relief (Note 1)	(150,000)	(75,000)	(75,000)
Gain before taper relief	37,500	18,750	18,750
Taper relief (Note 2)	(28,125)	(14,063)	(14,063)
Chargeable gain (25%)	9,375	4,687	4,687
Capital gain tax at 40% (Note 3)	3,750	1,875	1,875

Notes:

1   The consideration consists of shares worth £672,000 (537,600 × 1.25) representing 80% of the value of the business. Accordingly, 80% of the gains can be rolled over against the base cost of the shares with a claim for incorporation relief. The remaining gain relating to the loan note consideration received is taxable in 2006/07.

2   Eric and Fred qualify for eight years taper relief. George qualifies for 2 years taper relief. As a partnership interest is a business asset, all of the gains are 25% chargeable.

3.   The question states that all three individuals are 40% tax payers and that the annual exemptions have been used against other gains.

Base cost of shares held in BPK Ltd

	Eric £	Fred £	George £
Value of shares received (537,600 × 1.25) (50:25:25)	336,000	168,000	168,000
Incorporation relief	(150,000)	(75,000)	(75,000)
Base cost	186,000	93,000	93,000

(ii) **Tax advice for Eric's sale of shares**

If Eric sells his shares before 5 April 2007 he will receive no taper relief on the gain as he has held the shares for less than a year. Only 50% taper relief is available if he delays the sale for over a year after incorporation.

He should therefore elect to disapply incorporation relief, so that he will obtain 75% taper relief on the gain on incorporation.

If Eric uses his incorporation relief

With incorporation relief Eric will pay capital gains tax in 2006/07 of £129,350 calculated as follows:

	£
Capital gains tax on sale of shares:	
Sale proceeds (April 2007)	500,000
Base cost of shares	(186,000)
Gain on sale of shares (100% chargeable)	314,000
Capital gains tax at 40%	125,600
Capital gains tax on incorporation	3,750
Total capital gains tax for 2006/07	129,350

If Eric elects to disapply incorporation relief

If Eric elects to disapply incorporation relief he will pay capital gains tax in 2006/07 of £84,350 as follows:

Capital gains tax on incorporation	£	£
Share of gains arising on incorporation	187,500	
Taper relief (75%)	(140,625)	
	————	
Chargeable gain on incorporation	46,875	
	————	
Capital gains tax at 40%		18,750
Capital gains tax on sale of shares:		
Sale proceeds (April 2007)	500,000	
Base cost of shares	(336,000)	
	————	
Gain on sale of shares	164,000	
Capital gains tax at 40%	————	65,600
		————
Total capital gains tax for 2006/07		84,350
		————

By electing to disapply incorporation relief Eric will save capital gains tax of £45,000 (£129,350 – £84,350).

The election must normally be submitted by the second anniversary of 31 January following the tax year in which the incorporation takes place ie. 31 January 2010.

If the shares have been sold before the end of the tax year following that in which incorporation took place then the deadline is brought forward by one year. Eric must therefore submit the election by 31 January 2009.

(c) **VAT implications on the sale of the business**

The sale of a business is a supply of goods and output tax would normally be charged.

However, where a business is being transferred as a going concern to a taxable person the supply is outside the scope of VAT and no VAT should be charged.

For this to apply, BPK Ltd must be registered for VAT and must continue the trade previously carried on by the partnership without a significant break.

14 ALPHABET ENGINEERING

(a) **Assessable trading income for each partner in 2006/07**

Each partners assessment for 2006/07 will include their share of the tax adjusted trading profit for the year ended 31 December 2006:

	£	£
Net profit per accounts		158,500
Add: Depreciation		5,400
Amortisation of lease		2,500
		————
		166,400
Less: Capital allowances (W1)	8,750	
Lease deduction (W2)	2,050	
	————	
		(10,800)
		————
Tax adjusted trading profit		155,600
		————

Allocation	Alfred – 50%	77,800
	Bertie – 30%	46,680
	Claude – 20% × 6/12	15,560
	Daniel – 20% × 6/12	15,560

Partners' 2006/07 Trading income assessments

	£	£
Alfred		
CYB - (year ended 31.12.06)		77,800
Bertie		
CYB - (year ended 31.12.06)		46,680
Claude		
Closing year rules (1.1.06 – 30.6.06)	15,560	
Less: Overlap relief (W3)	(6,100)	
		9,460
Daniel		
Opening year rules (Actual 1.7.06–5.4.07)		
1.7.06–31.12.07	15,560	
1.1.06–5.4.07 (190,000 × 20% × 3/12)	9,500	
		25,060

Key answer tips

The cessation rules apply to Claude who resigned as a partner on 30 June 2006, and the commencement rules apply to Daniel who joined the partnership on 1 July 2006.

Workings

(W1) **Capital allowances – year ended 31 December 2006**

	Pool	Alfred	Motor cars Bertie	Motor cars Claude	Daniel	Allowances
	£	£	£	£	£	£
WDV b/f	22,000	14,500	8,000	15,000		
Addition					10,000	
Deemed proceeds				(13,500)		
				————		
Balancing allowance				1,500 ×20%		300
				————		
WDA – 25%	(5,500)					5,500
WDA – Restricted		(3,000) ×60%				1,800
WDA – 25%			(2,000)× 20%			400
WDA – 25%					(2,500) ×30%	750
	————	————	————		————	
WDV c/f	16,500	11,500	6,000		7,500	
	————	————	————		————	
Total allowances						8,750
						————

(W2) Lease deduction

The income proportion of the premium assessed on the owners will be deductible against the partnership's trading income assessment over the period of the lease.

	£
Premium paid	25,000
Less: $25{,}000 \times 2\% \times (10 - 1)$	(4,500)
Income portion of premium	20,500
Allowance deduction for partnership (20,500/10 years)	2,050 pa

(W3) Overlap relief

Claude will have overlap profits for the period 1 January 2005 to 5 April 2005 as follows:

$(122{,}000 \times 20\% \times 3/12) = £6{,}100$

(b) **Tax implications from the sale of the leasehold workshop**

The disposal of the leasehold property will result in a capital gain as follows:

	£
Sale proceeds	45,000
Cost $\quad 25{,}000 \times \dfrac{35.414}{46.695}$	(18,960)
Capital gain (see key answer tips)	26,040

Allocation:		
	Alfred – 50%	13,020
	Bertie – 30%	7,812
	Daniel – 20%	5,208

Each partner will be assessed to his share of the capital gain for 2007/08.

Alternatively, it will be possible for a partner to rollover his share of the gain against his share of the cost of the freehold workshop, since all of the proceeds from the disposal of the leasehold workshop have been re-invested.

Any gain that remains will be chargeable after taper relief. The gain will be 25% chargeable for Alfred and Bertie and 50% chargeable for Daniel as Daniel has only had an interest in the leasehold property for one year.

Tutorial note: Daniel is treated as if he had acquired his share of the leasehold from Claude on 1 July 2006. Assuming the premises were not revalued in the accounts, he takes over Claude's base cost.

Purchase of freehold workshop

Industrial buildings allowance of £2,600 pa (65,000 at 4%) will be available, commencing in the period of account during which the workshop is brought into use.

Key answer tips

The original answer reduced the lease by £6,150 (2,05 × 3) being the allowable deductions obtained in the past against trading profits for the use of the property as business premises. To prevent relief being given twice, the CGT cost is reduced. However, this lease deduction is a specialised point and therefore not shown in the answer. Making the point would obtain a bonus mark in the exam.

15   MING AND NINA

(a)   (i)   Allocation of adjusted trading loss

The partnership's capital allowances for the 15 month period to 31 July 2007 are £43,200 calculated as follows:

	Pool
	£
Additions	
Recording equipment	48,700
Electrical system	19,400
Sound insulation	34,800
Heating system	5,100
	108,000
FYA (50%)	(54,000)
WDV carried forward	54,000

Key answer tips

FYAs are not increased pro-rata in a long period of account. It is reasonable to assume that the business qualifies as small for capital allowance purposes and is therefore eligible for FYAs at 50%.

The tax adjusted trading loss is therefore £105,000 (51,000 + 54,000), and this is allocated between Ming and Nina as follows:

	Total	Ming	Nina
15 m/e 31 July 2007	£	£	£
Loss (60:40)	105,000	63,000	42,000

Trading income assessments and allowable losses

	Ming		Nina	
	Assessment	Available loss	Assessment	Available loss
2006/07	£	£	£	£
Actual basis				
1-5-06 to 5-4-07				
11/15 × 63,000/42,000	Nil	46,200	Nil	30,800
2007/08				
Balance of loss	Nil	16,800	Nil	11,200
		63,000		42,000

(ii)   Options for relieving the trading losses

Each partner can utilise their share of the partnership losses in the most tax efficient manner according to their personal circumstances.

The options available for the use of the trading loss are as follows:

- Carrying the full amount of the loss forward under s385 ICTA 1988 against future trading profits.

- Claiming relief against statutory total income under s380 ICTA 1988. The loss for 2006/07 can be set against total income for 2006/07 and/or 2005/06, and the loss for 2007/08 can be set against total income for 2007/08 and/or 2006/07. A claim could then be made under s72 FA 1991 to extend the set off to chargeable gains of the same year.

- Since the loss is incurred in the first four years of trading, Ming and Nina can claim loss relief under s381 ICTA 1988 against their total income of the three years preceding the year of the loss, earliest year first.

(b) **Most beneficial use of trading losses**

Ming Khan

In 2004/05 and before Ming had a salary of £42,000. In 2006/07 and 2007/08 she had no income but in 2005/06 she had a salary and a termination payment.

Ming should claim under s380 ICTA 1988 to set the loss of £46,200 for 2006/07 against her total income for 2005/06. The tax refund will be £15,594 as follows:

	£	£
Employment income		
Salary (42,000 × 11/12)		38,500
Compensation	60,000	
Exemption	(30,000)	
		30,000
STI		68,500
Loss relief - s380 ICTA 1988		(46,200)
Revised STI		22,300
Personal allowance		(5,035)
Taxable income		17,265

Tax refund:	£	
(33,300 – 17,265) =	16,035 at 22%	3,528
(46,200 – 16,035) =	30,165 at 40%	12,066
	46,200	15,594

Ming does not have any income for 2006/07 or 2007/08, and so a claim under s380 ICTA 1988 in respect of her loss for 2007/08 is not available.

She should therefore make a claim under s381 ICTA 1988 against her total income for 2004/05. The tax refund will be £4,356 as follows:

	£
Employment income – salary	42,000
Loss relief - s381 ICTA 1988	(16,800)
Revised STI	25,200
Personal allowance	(5,035)
Taxable income	20,165

Tax refund:	£	
(33,300 – 20,165)	13,135 at 22%	2,890
(16,800 – 13,135)	3,665 at 40%	1,466
	16,800	4,356

Neither claim will waste personal allowances, and Ming's 40% tax liability will be eliminated for 2004/05 and 2005/06.

Nina Lee

As a student, Nina's taxable income for 2003/04 and 2004/05 was only £1,485 (6,520 – 5,035), and so a claim under s381 ICTA 1988 does not appear to be beneficial, especially since the tax credits on dividends is not repayable.

She should therefore utilise her loss of £30,800 for 2006/07 by claiming under s380 ICTA 1988 against her total income for 2005/06, and then extend the claim under s72 FA 1991 against her chargeable gain for the same year.

The total tax refund will be £5,021 as follows:

	Before loss relief £	After loss relief £
Income tax		
Dividends	6,520	6,520
Loss Relief - s380 ICTA 1988	(-)	(6,520)
	6,520	Nil
Personal allowance	(5,035)	(wasted)
Taxable income	1,485	Nil
Income tax refund: (Dividend tax credits are not recoverable)		Nil
Capital gains tax		
Chargeable gain	40,700	40,700
Loss relief - s72 FA 1991 (30,800 - 6,520)	-	24,280
	40,700	16,420
Annual exemption	(8,800)	(8,800)
Taxable amount	31,900	7,620

CGT liability:

	£		
(2,150 – 1,485) =	665 at 10%	66	
	31,150 at 20%	6,230	
	85 at 40%	34	
	31,900		
	2,150 at 10%		215
	5,470 at 20%		1,094
	7,620		
		6,330	1,309
Capital gains tax refund			5,021

Nina's loss of £11,200 for 2007/08 should be carried forward under s385 ICTA 1988 against her trading profits for 2008/09 (year ended 31 July 2008).

Key answer tips

Identify the tax years where there is income or capital gains so that you can select from the loss options you have already discussed.

(c)   **Income tax and VAT implications**

Irrecoverable debts

For income tax purposes, relief will be given in the period of account when the irrecoverable debt is either written off or provided for by a specific provision. The relief will be for £20,000 (23,500 × 100/117.5) less any amount that is recoverable.

For VAT purposes, relief will be given on the appropriate VAT return when the date on which payment of the debt was due is over six months old, and the debt has been written off. The relief will be for £3,500 (23,500 × 17.5/117.5). However, if the partnership operates the cash accounting scheme, then relief is automatic, since output VAT would not have been paid to HMRC in respect of the original invoice.

Digital recording equipment – hire purchase

The partnership will be able to claim capital allowances on the cost of the equipment of £52,000 (61,100 × 100/117.5). Since the equipment is to be worthless and replaced in three years time, it will be beneficial to make a claim for treatment as a short-life asset. Capital allowances of £52,000 will then be given over the three years.

The finance charge of £20,000 (36 payments at £2,000 = 72,000 – 52,000) will be a deductible expense for the partnership, and will be allocated to periods of account using normal accounting principles.

The input VAT of £9,100 will be reclaimed on the VAT return for the period in which the recording equipment is purchased.

Digital recording equipment – Leasing

The lease rental payments of £24,000 pa (28,200 × 100/117.5) will be a deductible expense for the partnership, and will be allocated to periods of account in accordance with the accruals concept.

The input VAT of £4,200 (28,200 × 17.5/117.5) included in each lease rental payment will be reclaimed on the tax return for the period during which the appropriate tax point occurs.

Key answer tips

The question itself prompts you to consider VAT as well as income tax.

---

16   BASIL AND SYBIL PERFECT

(a)   (i)   **Trading income assessments**

Basil

As he is continuing in business, Basil will be treated as changing his accounting date. The change will allow all of the brought forward overlap profits to be offset.

	£
2006/07	
Year ended 30 June 2006	49,920
Period ended 31 March 2007	47,700
	97,620
Relief for overlap profits	
2004/05 (1.7.04 – 5.4.05) (38,640 × 9/12)	(28,980)
	68,640

2007/08
Year ended 31 March 2008 (80,000 × 75%)   60,000

Sybil
Sybil has just commenced to trade.
Her trading income assessments are therefore as follows:

                                                              £
2006/07
Actual basis (1.6.06 – 5.4.07)   11,100

2007/08
Year ended 31 March 2008 (80,000 × 25%)   20,000

(ii)   **Choice of Accounting date**

The advantages and disadvantages of an accounting date of 31 March (or 5 April) as compared to 30 June (or any date early in the tax year) are as follows:

- The calculation of assessable profits is simplified with an accounting date of 31 March (there are no overlap profits).

- An assessment of up to 21 months' profits may arise in the year of cessation with an accounting date of 30 June. This is not the case with 31 March.

- An accounting date of 30 June will mean that the interval between earning profits and paying the related tax liability is nine months longer than with an accounting date of 31 March. This is advantageous where profits are rising. There is also longer to prepare the related tax return.

(b)   (i)   **Additional VAT payable as a partnership**

As a sole trader, Basil would have to pay output VAT of £2,625 (15,000 × 17.5%) on the supply to Sybil. She could not recover this as input VAT. No such charge will be necessary if a partnership is formed.

Output VAT will have to be charged on Sybil's income. Since supplies are to the general public in a competitive market, this will have to be absorbed by the partnership. The cost is £7,000 (47,000 × 17.5/117.5), but input VAT of £1,925 (26,000 - 15,000 = 11,000 × 17.5%) can be reclaimed on the related expenses.

Basil is partially exempt (the de minimis limit of £625 per month on average is exceeded), and the inclusion of Sybil's standard rated sales will improve the recovery of input VAT on expenses that are not directly attributable.

As a sole trader the recovery is restricted to 60% calculated as follows:

Taxable supplies: £170,000

Total supplies: £285,000 (170,000 + 115,000)

Partial exemption recovery percentage: $\frac{170,000}{285,000} = 59.6\%$, rounded up to 60%

This recovery rate will increase to 63% if a partnership is formed, calculated as follows:

Taxable supplies: £195,000 (170,000 -15,000 + 47,000 - 7,000)

Total supplies: £310,000 (195,000 + 115,000)

Partial exemption recovery percentage: $\frac{195,000}{310,000} = 62.9\%$, rounded up to 63%

The additional recovery is £378 (W1). The recovery relating to directly attributable expenses is not affected.

The additional VAT payable for the year ended 31 March 2008 as a result of forming a partnership is therefore £2,072 (W2).

Workings

(1) **Additional VAT recovery on partial exemption rules**

Input VAT directly attributed to taxable supplies = 25%

Input VAT directly attributed to exempt supplies = 30%

Input VAT not directly attributable

$= (160,000 \times 17\frac{1}{2}\% \times 45\%) = 12,600$

Improved recovery of non-attributable VAT

$(63\% - 60\%) = 3\% \times 12,600 = £378$

(2) **Additional VAT payable**	£
Output VAT on Sybil's supplies to be absorbed	7,000
Output VAT on sales to Sybil not required	(2,625)
Input VAT claimable on Sybil's expenses	(1,925)
Additional recovery from partial exemption rules	(378)
	2,072

(ii) **Direction under the disaggregation rules**

HMRC will apply the disaggregation rules where Sybil's business is effectively an extension of Basil's business.

The decision will be based on financial links (for example, Sybil may have received financial support from Basil), economic links (for example, both Sybil and Basil may supply the same customers), and organisational links (for example, Sybil and Basil may use the same employees, premises or equipment).

Key answer tips

It seems odd to refer to 'disaggregation' when the opposite is intended but this is the examiner's convention. HMRC normally seek to 'aggregate' two businesses even where they were never originally together if it is appropriate.

(c) **Alternative profit sharing arrangements**

Income tax

Under either arrangement Sybil will remain a basic rate tax payer.

Basil will make the pension contribution net of basic rate tax (22%). The gross pension contribution will be £19,500 ($15,210 \times {}^{100}/_{78}$). Basil will obtain tax relief for pension contributions made up to an amount equal to 100% of his earnings. Regardless of the profit split, Basil will therefore obtain relief for the £19,500 contribution. Accordingly, Basil's higher rate threshold is increased from £33,300 to £52,300.

If there is a 75:25 profit split, Basil will pay higher rate tax on £2,165 (W1). No higher rate tax will be paid on a 60:40 profit split. The alternative split therefore achieves an income tax saving of £390 (W1).

Class 4 NIC

However, a 60:40 profit split will increase Sybil's profits liable to Class 4 NIC from £20,000 to £32,000. This will increase her Class 4 NIC liability by £960 (1,200 × 8%).

Basil's profits liable to Class 4 NIC will decrease from £60,000 to £48,000. This will reduce his Class 4 NIC liability by £120 (60,000 – 48,000 at 1%).

Conclusion

A profit sharing basis of 60:40 increases the overall tax and Class 4 by £450 (W2).

Workings

(W1) **Basil's income tax**

	75:25 split of income	60:40 split of income
	£	£
Profit share	60,000	48,000
Personal allowance	(5,035)	(50,35)
Taxable income	54,965	42,965
HR threshold	52,800	52,800
HR tax payable on	2,165	Nil

Income tax saving: 2,165 × (40% – 22%) = £390

(W2) **Overall tax increase**

	£
Income tax saving – Basil (W1)	(390)
Class 4 NIC increase – Sybil	960
Class 4 NIC decrease – Basil	(120
	450

17 NURTURE AND OVERSEE

(a) **Partners' Trading income assessments - 2006/07**

		£	£
Michael			
Final fiscal year			
(1.1.06 to 30.9.06)			
(420,000 × 1/3 × 9/12)		105,000	
Overlap relief (W)		(29,500)	
			75,500
Nigel			
CYB (420,000 × 1/3)			140,000
Onika			
CYB (420,000 × 1/3)			140,000
Petra			
Opening year (actual 1.10.06 – 5.4.07)			
1.10.06 – 31.12.06	(420,000 × 1/3 × 3/12)	35,000	
1.1.07 – 5.4.07	(450,000 × 1/3 × 3/12)	37,500	
			72,500

Key answer tips

The cessation rules apply to Michael who resigned as a partner on 30 September 2006, and the commencement rules apply to Petra who joined the partnership on 1 October 2006.

Working – Overlap relief

Michael will have overlap profits of £29,500 ($354,000 \times 1/3 \times 3/12$) for the period 1 January 2004 to 5 April 2004.

(b) **Incorporation of the partnership**

Income tax and NIC liability of the partners if the business is not incorporated

Each of the three partners will be assessed on tax adjusted trading profits of £150,000 ($450,000 \times 1/3$) for 2007/08.

Their income tax and NIC liability is therefore as follows:

	£	£
Income tax (150,000 at 40%)		60,000
Class 2 NIC (52×2.10)		109
Class 4 NIC (33,540 – 5,035) at 8%	2,280	
(150,000 – 33,540) at 1%	1,164	3,444
		63,553

Corporation tax liability of NOP Ltd if the business is incorporated

The corporation tax liability of NOP Ltd for the year ended 31 December 2007 is as follows:

	£	£
Trading profit		450,000
Directors' remuneration ($3 \times 100,000$)	300,000	
Employer Class 1 NIC (W)	36,468	
		(336,468)
PCTCT		113,532
Corporation tax at 19%		21,571

Income tax and NIC liability of the directors

The income tax and NIC liability of each director for 2007/08 is as follows:

	£	£
Income tax (100,000 at 40%)		40,000
Employees' Class 1 NIC (33,540 – 5,035) at 11%	3,136	
(100,000 – 33,540) at 1%	665	3801
		43,801

Due dates

Each partner's income tax and Class 4 NIC liability will be due on 31 January 2009, with payments on account being made on 31 January and 31 July 2008.

Class 2 NIC is normally paid on a monthly basis by direct debit or by quarterly invoicing.

NOP Ltd's corporation tax liability will be due on 1 October 2008.

The company will account for income tax and Class 1 NIC on a monthly basis under the PAYE system.

Conclusion

If the business is not incorporated, the total tax liability of the three partners for 2007/08 is £190,659 (3 × 63,553).

If the partnership is incorporated the total tax liability is £189,442 (W2).

Incorporation therefore saves tax of £1,217 (190,659 – 189,442), although the due dates of the tax liabilities may be earlier.

Workings

(W1) **Employers Class 1 NIC**

Per director: (100,000 – 5,035) × 12.8% = £12,156

For three directors: (3 × 12,156) = £36,468

(W2) **Total tax liabilities as a company**

	£
Corporation tax	21,571
Employers Class 1 NIC	36,468
Directors income tax and Class 1 NIC (3 × 43,801)	131,403
	189,442

Key answer tips

The question guides you through the calculations to enable you to identify where any tax saving lies.

(c)   (i)   **Conditions for a valid change of accounting date**

For a change of accounting date to be valid there must not have been a change of accounting date within the preceding five tax years. However, this condition does not apply if the present change is made for genuine commercial reasons.

The change must be notified to HMRC by 31 January following the year of change, and the first accounts to the new accounting date must not exceed 18 months in length.

Partners' Trading income assessments - 2007/08

For Nigel and Onika the basis of assessment for 2007/08 is the fifteen-month period to 31 March 2008. They will therefore each be assessed on trading profits of £190,000 (450,000 + 120,000 = 570,000 × 1/3), and can offset the three months of overlap profits of £29,500 that arose on the commencement of trading.

Trading income assessments for Nigel and Onika are therefore £160,500 (190,000 - 29,500).

Petra who is being assessed on her second fiscal year, will be assessed on trading profits of the twelve month period to 31 March 2008, and will therefore not have any overlap profits.

Her assessment will be £152,500 (W).

(ii) **Advantages and disadvantages**

The main advantage of the partnership changing its accounting date from 31 December to 31 March is that the calculation of assessable profits is simplified (there are no overlap profits). This will be particularly relevant should new partners join the partnership.

In addition, the maximum assessment in the year of cessation will be for twelve months, and the partners' existing overlap relief will be fully utilised.

The main disadvantage is that the interval between earning profits and paying the related tax liability will be three months shorter than previously.

Working: Petra's second year assessment

	£
$^9/_{12}$ of y/e 31 Dec 2007 (450,000 x $^9/_{12}$)	337,500
3 m/e 31 March 2008	120,000
3 m/e 31 March 2008	457,500
$^1/_3$rd share	152,500

18   DAVID AND PATRICIA

(a)   (i)   **Taxation implications for David of involving his wife in the business**

Employing Patricia

If David employs his wife, he is only able to claim a tax deduction for the salary paid if he pays her the market rate. As she was earning £12,000 as a bookkeeper previously, this would appear to be the market rate.

The business must pay employers' National Insurance Contributions (NIC) at 12.8% on her gross salary in excess of £5,035 per annum.

The salary and NICs will both be tax deductible expenses for the business.

Patricia will have to pay NICs at 11% as an employee, and will be taxed on her salary under PAYE.

Setting up a partnership

If David and Patricia are in partnership, then the profit sharing ratios can be in any proportion they decide. The ratio does not have to reflect their respective input to the business provided there is a proper partnership agreement and Patricia takes an active part in the business.

The ratio can therefore be chosen so as to reduce their overall tax liability, and may even be changed at a later date if their circumstances change.

David has property business income of £40,000 from 2007/08 onwards and so he will be a higher rate taxpayer. Patricia has no other income. The maximum income tax saving will therefore be generated where Patricia's share equates to £38,335 (that is, equivalent to the personal allowance £5,035 plus the starting and basic rate bands £33,300).

This would imply a profit sharing ratio of 3:7 (David:Patricia) as £38,335 is approximately 70% of £54,500.

In addition, Patricia will pay NIC at a maximum rate of 8%, compared to 11% for her and 12.8% by the business, as an employee.

Calculation of income tax and NICs under each option

1   Patricia as an employee

Employment costs relating to Patricia

	£
Salary	12,000
Employers' NIC (12,000 − 5,035) × 12.8%	892
Employment costs	12,892

This amount is tax deductible for the business.

Income tax and NIC payable by David

	£	£
Trading income (54,500 − 12,892)		41,608
Income tax (41,608 × 40%)		16,643
Class 2 NIC (52 × £2.10)		109
Class 4 NIC (33,540 − 5,035) × 8%	2,280	
(41,608 − 33,540) × 1%	81	
		2,361
Total income tax and NIC		19,113

Income tax and NIC payable by Patricia

	£
Salary	12,000
Less: Personal allowance	(5,035)
Taxable income	6,965

Income tax £	
2,150 × 10%	215
4,815 × 22%	1,059
6,965	
Income tax liability	1,274
Class 1 NICs (12,000 − 5,035) × 11%	766
Total income tax and NIC	2,040
Total tax payable by the couple (19,113 + 2,040 + 892)	22,045

2   Patricia as a partner, sharing profits 3:7 (David:Patricia)

The profits for a full year will be allocated £16,350 (54,500 × 30%) to Daivd and £38,150 (54,500 × 70%) to Patricia.

Income tax and NIC payable by David

	£
Income tax (16,350 × 40%)	6,540
Class 2 NIC (52 × £2.10)	109
Class 4 NIC (16,350 − 5,035) × 8%	905
Total income tax and NIC	7,554

Income tax and NIC payable by Patricia	£	£
Trading income		38,150
Less: Personal allowance		(5,035)
Taxable income		33,115

Income tax   £

2,150 × 10%		215
30,965 × 22%		6,812
33,115		
Income tax liability		7,027
Class 2 NIC (52 × £2.10)		109
Class 4 NIC (33,540 – 5,035) × 8%	2,280	
(38,150 – 33,540) × 1%	46	
		2,326
Total income tax and NIC		9,462
Total tax payable by the couple (7,554 + 9,462)		17,016

Conclusion

By operating as a partnership the couple can achieve a tax saving of £5,029 (22,045 – 17,016).

Tutorial note:

The (3:7) profit sharing ratio is not the only answer that would have been acceptable. Candidates will be given credit for the recognition that an unequal split of profits between David and Patricia would reduce, firstly the income tax payable by the couple (using Patricia's lower rate bands) and secondly, the NIC payable by David (paying at the 1% rate in Patricia's hands and at the 8% rate in David's).

(ii)   **Tax administration**

Notification of new source of income

For income tax purposes HMRC should be notified within six months from the end of the tax year in which the liability on the new source of income arises, i.e. by 6 October 2007.

Submission of tax return

David's self assessment income tax return for 2006/07 is due on the later of: 31 January 2008, and 3 months after the notice to file the return was issued.

If submitted by 30 September 2007, HMRC will calculate his tax liability for him.

Payment dates

Income tax is normally payable as follows:

31 January in the tax year	⎫	
31 July following the tax year	⎬	Payments on account
31 January following the tax year		Balancing payment

However, as the payments on account are each based on 50% of the previous year's income tax and NIC liability, this is not possible in the first tax year.

Thus, if the business starts to trade on 1 January 2007, the first payment on account is due on 31 January 2007, but no payment will be made, as trade has just commenced. The second payment on account is due on 31 July 2007, but again, it is unlikely that any payments will be made. The balancing payment is due on 31 January 2008, and the total liability will be paid on that date.

(b)   **Loss reliefs available to David**

The loss relief options available to David are as follows:

(1)   Relief against Statutory Total Income (STI) of the previous three tax years on a first in first out (FIFO) basis (S.381).

(2)   Relief against STI (and gains, if required) of the current tax year and/or the previous tax year (S.380).

(3)   Relief by carried forward against future trading profits of the same trade (S.385).

When deciding which loss relief to take, consideration should be given to the rate of tax saved, to the timing of any relief/repayment and to avoiding the loss of personal allowances.

The profit sharing ratio is 50:50, so the loss arising to David (and Patricia) in 2006/07 is £20,000 each.

David – the most beneficial claim

David has had employment income of £42,000 per annum since 1998, with £31,500 (3,500 × 9 months) in 2006/07. David will also have taxable income of £67,250 (£40,000 property income + £27,250 equal share of trading profits) from 2007/08 onwards.

The tax savings achieved under each option is as follows:

(1)   Carry the loss back (s.381) to the tax year 2003/04 and receive a repayment of income tax of £5,060 (W1)

(2)   Use the loss in 2006/07 (s.380) resulting in an additional tax repayment of £4,400 (W2); or (3) carry forward the loss to 2007/08 (s.385) saving tax of £8,000 (W3).

Ignoring the timing of tax saving, the greatest tax is saved if the loss is carried forward to 2007/08.

Workings

(W1)   **Using the loss in 2003/04 (s.381)**

	Before loss relief £	*After loss relief* £
Employment income	42,000	42,000
Less: Loss relief	-	(20,000)
Less: Personal allowance	(5,035)	(5,035)
Taxable income	36,965	16,965

Tax saved	£		£
(36,965 – 33,300) 3,665 × 40%			1,466
(20,000 – 3,665) 16,335 × 22%			3,594
	20,000		5,060

(W2) Using the loss in 2006/07 (s.380)

	Before loss relief £	*After loss relief* £
Employment income (9 × 3,500)	31,500	31,500
Trading profit	Nil	Nil
Less: Loss relief	-	(20,000)
Less: Personal allowance	(5,035)	(5,035)
Taxable income	26,465	6,465
Tax saved: (£20,000 × 22%)		£4,400

(W3) Using the loss in 2007/08 (s.385)

	Before loss relief £	*After loss relief* £
Trading profit	26,000	26,000
Less: Loss relief	-	(20,000)
	26,000	6,000
Property income	40,000	40,000
Less: Personal allowance	(5,035)	(5,035)
Taxable income	60,965	40,965
Tax saved: (£20,000 × 40%)		8,000

			Marks
ACCA marking scheme			
(a)	(i)	Market rate	0.5
		Consequences for employer (tax/NIC)	1.0
		Consequences for employee (NIC/PAYE)	0.5
		Partnership share can be in any proportion, provided partnership is 'real'	1.5
		NIC lower if partner	0.5
		Potential savings arising from greater share to Patricia	1.5
		Calculations as employee:	
		Employer's NIC	0.5
		Patricia – IT	0.5
		– NIC	0.5
		David – IT (½ + ½)	1.0
		– NIC	1.0
		Calculations as partner:	
		Patricia – IT	1.0
		– NIC	1.0
		David – IT	0.5
		– NIC	1.0
		Savings	0.5
			13.0
	(ii)	Six months/6 October	0.5
		31 January/three months	1.0
		30 September	0.5
		31 January/31 July	0.5
		Balancing payment/31 January	0.5
		Position in first year	1.5
			4.5
(b)		Identify reliefs (3 × ½)	1.5
		Factors to consider	1.0
		Loss available (£20,000)	0.5
		Relief available s.381	2.5
		Relief available s.380	2.0
		Relief available s.385	2.0
		Identify best option	0.5
			10.0
Total available (vs a maximum of 25)			27.5

Based on ½ mark for correct Y/A and remaining 2/1 ½ marks for the calculation of the tax saving/repayment in each case

19   LINDA

(a)   **Advice concerning choice of tenants for the factory**

The two tenants will provide Linda with rental property income which will be taxable at 40%. However, it may be possible to claim IBAs against the rental income and therefore save tax at 40%.

Of the two tenants, Murcia does not carry on a qualifying activity therefore IBAs could not be claimed. However, Navarra's trade will qualify for IBAs, as manufacturing is usually a qualifying activity. The tax effect, of IBAs therefore needs to be taken into account.

	Murcia	Navarra	
	£	£	£
Annual rental income	20,000	17,000	17,000
Capital allowances (W)	–	(9,475)	
	20,000	7,525	
Tax at 40%			
(higher rate taxpayer)	(8,000)	(3,010)	(3,010)
Cash received after tax	12,000		13,990

Although the rent received from Murcia is greater, the IBAs available if Navarra uses the factory are significant enough to reduce Linda's tax liability so that, despite the lower rent, Linda receives more cash.

As the property is to be kept until after its tax life expires, the allowances should be permanent (i.e. there will be no clawback on disposal).

Conclusion

As a result, Linda should choose Navarra as her tenant.

Working

Industrial Buildings Allowances

The building has a history of industrial buildings allowances (IBAs). A calculation is required to work out the balance that is available to Linda if she acquires the factory.

The original IBA qualifying cost was £190,000, being as follows:

	Qualifying	Non-qualifying	Plant and machinery
	£	£	£
Land		75,000	
Land preparation	25,000		
Building	165,000		
Fixtures			35,000
	190,000	75,000	35,000

Previous allowances claimed would have been as follows:

Year ended 31 December	IBA (4%) £	Notional IBA (4%) £	TWDV £
2001	7,600		190,000
2002	7,600		(7,600)
2003	7,600		(7,600)
2004	7,600		(7,600)
2005		7,600	(7,600)
2006	7,600		(7,600)
Total allowances	38,000	7,600	144,400

Linda proposes to pay £235,000 for the qualifying building, which is more than the cost of £190,000.

Therefore a balancing charge will arise equal to the allowances claimed to date of £38,000.

Allowances available to Linda as the second user are: $\dfrac{\text{Residue after sale}}{\text{Remaining tax life}}$

Remaining tax life: 19 years 3 months (231 months)

Residue after sale (RAS):

	£
TWDV before sale	144,400
Plus balancing charge	38,000
RAS	182,400

$$\text{WDA} = \frac{182,400}{19^3/_{12}} \qquad 9,475 \text{ p.a.}$$

(b) **Assignment of Lease**

Where a lease with less than 50 years to run is assigned, the cost is restricted.

A fraction, X/Y, is applied by reference to a lease table.

X = % for the years left at the date of assignment = % for 38 years

Y = % for the years left at the date of acquisition by the seller (Linda) = % for 45 years

The calculation is as follows:

	£
Premium received	115,000
Less: Cost £100,000 × $\left(\dfrac{94.189}{98.059}\right)$	(96,053)
Gain before taper relief	18,947

There is no indexation allowance as the lease was acquired after April 1998.

As a business asset held for more than 2 years, the gains is 25% chargeable.

Chargeable gain (25%)   4,737

(c)   **Linda's tax liabilities for 2006/07**

Income tax computation - 2006/07

	Notes	£	£	£
Property business				
Rental income				251,000
Expenses:				
Interest			115,425	
Other costs		43,540		
Less Disallowable items:				
Survey fee	(1)	(940)		
Fees relating to new lease	(2)	(750)		
			41,850	
Capital allowances	(4)		21,356	
				(178,631)
Property business income for the year				72,369
Less: Property business losses brought forward				(7,500)
Statutory total income				64,869
Personal allowance				(5,035)
Taxable income				59,834

Income tax:

£	
$2,150 \times 10\%$	215
$31,150 \times 22\%$	6,853
$26,534 \times 40\%$	10,614
59,834	
Income tax liability	17,682

Notes:

(1)   The survey fee related to a capital item and so is not an allowable expense.

(2)   Fees relating to the creation/acquisition of a lease are capital and not an allowable expense. Fees relating to the renewal of an existing short lease (less than 50 years) are however allowable.

(3)   The bank fee is allowable as a cost of obtaining loan finance.

(4)   Capital allowances = £85,424 x 25% WDA = £21,356.

National insurance contributions (NIC) - 2006/07

Class 2 NIC: $£2.10 \times 52$		109
Class 4 NIC: $(£33,540 - £5,035) \times 8\%$	2,280	
(see note) $(£64,869 - £33,540) \times 1\%$	313	2,593
		2,702
Total income tax & NIC (17,682 + 2,702))		20,384

Note: The calculation of Class 4 NIC assumes that Linda will be classed as running a trade of property letting, and, as such, her rental profits will be subject to Class 4 NIC.

Capital gains tax (CGT) computation - 2006/07

	£
Gain on Birmingham property	4,737
Other gains	6,800
Total chargeable gains	11,537
Less: Annual exemption	(8,800)
Taxable gain	2,737
Capital gains tax at 40%	1,095

(d)   Key features of a self invested personal pension scheme (SIPP)

A self invested personal pension scheme (SIPP) is a pension scheme which allows an individual to have control over his investment by directing where the funds are to be invested, although the individual will need to appoint an investment manager.

SIPPs can invest in a wide range of assets, including options, futures and commercial property. The SIPP can also take out a loan (to acquire property) of up to 75% of the purchase price. In all other respects, a SIPP is governed by the same rules as other personal pensions schemes.

A SIPP is particularly useful for a self-employed individual who wishes to invest in commercial property as once the property is transferred into the SIPP, neither the income arising in the form of rents, nor any gains arising on disposal, are subject to tax.

Suitability of the two proposed properties

Neither of the two proposed properties is really suitable for Linda to put into her SIPP. Although a property with high growth potential would normally be ideal for this purpose, a SIPP cannot invest in property acquired from a scheme member.

As such, any property currently owned by Linda would be ineligible.

Also, by putting the factory into the scheme, the benefit of the available capital allowances would be wasted.

ACCA marking scheme			Marks
(a)		Qualifying cost for IBA	1.0
		Allowances to date / TWDV	1.0
		Balancing charge	0.5
		Allowances available to Linda	0.5
		Remaining life	0.5
		Allowances: per year	0.5
		Allowances 'rump' period	0.5
		Murcia non qualifying so no IBA	0.5
		Navarra the opposite	0.5
		Compare net of tax income	1.5
		Conclusion	1.0
	Max		8.0
(b)		Proceeds	0.5
		Cost = original × X / Y	1.5
		No indexation	1.0
		Business asset taper relief	1.0
	Max		4.0
(c)		Income	0.5
		Interest	0.5
		Other costs	0.5

	Survey add back plus reason	1.0
	Professional fee add back plus reason	1.0
	Bank fees reason	0.5
	Amended lease cost reason	0.5
	Loss relief	0.5
	Capital allowances	0.5
	Personal allowance	0.5
	Income tax	0.5
	Class 2 NIC	0.5
	Class 4 NIC	0.5
	CGT: Total gains	0.5
	Annual exemption	0.5
	Tax at 40%	0.5
	No NIC	0.5
	Max	9.0
(d)	Can direct how funds invested	0.5
	Needs investment manager	0.5
	Same general rules as other PPS	0.5
	Wider range of investments	0.5
	Including commercial property	0.5
	Loan to buy up to 75%	0.5
	Cannot be acquired from scheme member	0.5
	Income and gains tax free	0.5
	Why existing property not suitable	0.5
	Why factory not suitable	1.0
	Max	4.0
Total		25

20   BOB

(a)   **Evidence of trading**

[Client address]

[Own address]

[Date]

Dear Bob,

I note that you have been selling some books in order to raise some extra income.

While you believe that the sums are not taxable, I believe that there may be a risk of the book sales being treated as a trade, and therefore subject to income tax as trading income. We need to refer to guidance in the form of a set of principles known as the 'badges of trade'. These help determine whether or not a trade exists, and need to be looked at in their entirety.

The badges of trade are as follows:

1. *The subject matter*

    Some assets can be enjoyed by themselves as an investment, while others (such as large amounts of aircraft linen) are clearly not. It is likely that such assets are acquired as trading stock, and are therefore a sign of trading. Sporting books can be an investment, and so this test is not conclusive.

2. *Frequency of transactions*

    Where transactions are frequent (not one-offs), this suggests trading. You have sold several books, which might suggest trading, although you have only done this for a short period of between one and two years.

3.   *Length of ownership*

Where items are bought and sold soon afterwards, this indicates trading. You bought your books in the 1990s, and the length of time between acquisition and sale would not suggest trading.

4.   *Supplementary work and marketing*

You are actively marketing the books on your internet website, which is an indication of trading.

5.   *Profit motive*

A motive to make profit suggests trading activity. You sold the books to raise funds for your property business, and not to make a profit as such, which suggests that your motive was to raise cash, and not make profits.

6.   *The way in which the asset sold was acquired*

Selling assets which were acquired unintentionally (such as a gift) is not usually seen as trading. You acquired the books for your collection over a period of time, and while these were intentional acquisitions, the reasons for doing so were for your personal pleasure.

By applying all of these tests, it should be possible to argue that you were not trading, merely selling some assets in order to generate short-term cash for your business.

The asset disposals will be taxed under the capital gain tax rules, but as the books are chattels and do not form part of a set, they will be exempt from capital gains tax.

Yours sincerely

A N. Accountant

(b)   **Calculation of taxable income and gains**

The trading income assessments are based on the rules relating to the commencement of trade, and are as follows (before loss utilisation);

	£	Tax adjusted trading profit/loss £	Trading income assessment £
2003/04 (basis period 1.10.03 – 5.4.04)			
£3,500 × 6/7		3,000	3,000
2004/05 (basis period: first 12 months)			
£3,500 × 7/7 Profit	3,500		
£(18,000) × 5/12 Loss	(7,500)	(4,000)	Nil
2005/06 (basis period: year to 30 April 2005)			
(£18,000) Loss	(18,000)		
Less 5/12 × (18,000) utilised in 2004/05	7,500	(10,500)	Nil
2006/07 (basis period: year to 30 April 2006)		28,000	28,000

Bob has two losses available for relief: £4,000 in 2004/05 and £10,500 in 2005/06.

The loss relief options available are as follows:

Losses can be relieved against statutory total income of the year of loss (s.380) and/or the statutory total income of the prior year. Unused losses can be carried forward against the first available future trading profits from the same trade (s.385).

A loss relief claim against statutory total income (s.380) can also be extended to include set-off against capital gains in either the year of loss or the previous year. However, Bob has no chargeable gains until 2006/07, which is after the years of the loss.

As this is a new business, relief is also available against income in the three years prior to the year of first loss under s.381, but Bob has not earned any income in the three years prior to the start of his business, and his 2003/04 trading profits are covered by his personal allowance.

The most beneficial way for Bob to use the losses incurred is to carry them forward to 2006/07 as this will relieve tax at the highest rate. Bob's marginal rate of income tax is 22% in 2005/06 and 40% in 2006/07.

His taxable income and gains for the years in question will therefore be as follows:

Taxable income and gains	2003/04	2004/05	2005/06	2006/07
	£	£	£	£
Employment income	Nil	3,150	12,600	12,600
Trading income	3,000	Nil	Nil	28,000
Less relief for losses b/f	Nil	Nil	Nil	(14,500)
Statutory total income	3,000	3,150	12,600	26,100
Less: Personal allowance	(5,035)	(5,035)	(5,035)	(5,035)
Taxable income	Nil	Nil	7,565	21,065
Taxable gains (23,720 – 8,800)				14,920
Total taxable income and gains	Nil	Nil	7,565	35,985

Loss memorandum	2004/05	2005/06	2006/07
	£	£	£
Losses brought forward		4,000	14,500
Losses arising in the year	4,000	10,500	
Loss relief utilised (s.385)			(14,500)
Losses carried forward	4,000	14,500	Nil

(c) **Claims for capital losses**

Where the value of shares (a chargeable asset) has become negligible (defined as <5% of the original cost), a claim can be made to treat the asset as though it was sold and then immediately reacquired for its current market value. This is known as a negligible value claim.

The sale and reacquisition is treated as taking place at the time that the claim is made or at a specified time (up to 2 years before the start of the tax year in which the claim was made) if the asset was of negligible value at that time.

As the loss is on unquoted shares, a further relief (s.574 ICTA 1988) allows the loss to be relieved against the total income of the taxpayer for the year in which the loss arose, and/or against the total income of the previous year.

Losses are first relieved against current year income, with any excess being available for offset against the prior year's income.

Bob can therefore make a negligible value claim as at 1 December 2006. This will give rise to a loss of £14,500 (£500 – £15,000) which will be deemed to arise in the year 2006/07. By doing so, his taxable income and gains for that year will be reduced from £3635,985 to £21,485.

ACCA marking scheme		
		Marks
(a)	Identification of badges (6 × 0.5)	3.0
	Commentary on each (6 × 0.5)	3.0
	Presentation	2.0
	Summary of application to Bob	1.0
	Discuss how profits will be taxed	1.0
	Max	9.0
(b)	03/04: basis period	0.5
	assessment	0.5
	04/05: basis period	0.5
	offset of losses	0.5
	assessment	0.5
	05/06: basis period	0.5
	Losses used against tax at highest rates	0.5
	Current year relief (s.380)	0.5
	Prior year relief (s.380)	0.5
	Carry forward of unused losses (s.385)	0.5
	Use losses v capital gains (s.72)	0.5
	Other loss relief available (s.381)	0.5
	No income for s.381 except for 03/04	0.5
	03/04 income covered by personal allowance	0.5
	Carry forward is best option	0.5
	Relief at highest rates if carry forward	0.5
	Compare income tax rates to justify	0.5
	Calculation of employment income	1.0
	Use of losses b/fwd (s.385)	0.5
	Personal allowance	0.5
	Taxable income: 05/06	0.5
	06/07	0.5
	Loss relief: 04/05	0.5
	03/04	0.5
	Deduction of capital gains annual allowance	0.5
	Max	12
(c)	Asset becoming negligible	0.5
	Treated as sold and immediately reacquired	0.5
	Timing of sale and reacquisition (2 × 0.5)	1.0
	Loss relief v total income	0.5
	Years of income to offset loss against (2 × 0.5)	1.0
	Order of set-off	0.5
	Calculation of claim	0.5
	Identify tax saved	0.5
	Max	4
Total (Max)		25

21 DONALD

(a) (i) **Tax position for the year ended 31 March 2008**

Sole trader

As a sole trader, Donald will pay income tax on the profits earned. He will also be required to pay both Class 2 and Class 4 National Insurance Contributions (NIC).

Based on his estimates, the income tax computation will be as follows:

	£
Trading profits	47,500
Less: Personal allowance	(5,035)
Taxable income	42,465

Income tax		£
£		
2,150 at 10%		215
31,150 at 22%		6,853
9,165 at 40%		3,666
42,465		
Income tax liability		10,734

National insurance:		
Class 2 (52 × £2.10)		109
Class 4 (33,540 – 5,035) × 8%	2,280	
(47,500 – 33,540) × 1%	140	2,420
Total income tax and national insurance		13,263
Income after all taxes (47,500 – 13,263)		34,237

Company

Any payment of salary above £5,035 will attract employers' National Insurance Contributions at a rate of 12.8%. Both salary and employers' National Insurance Contributions will be tax deductible for corporation tax purposes.

The total wage cost for the company is as follows:

	£
Salary	42,681
Class 1 employers' National Insurance:	
(42,681 – 5,035) × 12.8%	4,819
Total employment cost	47,500
Taxable profit (47,500 – 47,500)	Nil
Corporation tax	Nil

	£
Employment income	42,681
Less: Personal allowance	(5,035)
Taxable income	37,646

Income tax:

£		£
2,150 at 10%		215
31,150 at 22%		6,853
4,346 at 40%		1,738
37,646		
Income tax liability		8,806

National insurance:

Class 1 (33,540 – 5,035) × 11%	3,136	
(42,681 – 33,540) × 1%	91	3,227
Total income tax and national insurance		12,033
Income after all taxes (42,681 – 12,033)		30,648

Conclusion

On the basis of the above figures, Donald will be £3,589 (34,237 – 30,648) better off by operating as a sole trader.

(ii) **Corporation tax payable for year ended 31 March 2008**

	£
Salary	31,000
Class 1 employers' National Insurance:	
(31,000 – 5,035) × 12.8%	3,324
Total employment costs	34,324

	£
Taxable profit	47,500
Less: Employment costs	(34,324)
Profits chargeable to corporation tax	13,176
Corporation tax at 19%	2,503

(iii) **Cash remaining in company**

		£
Cash/profits for year		47,500
Less:	Salary and National Insurance	(34,324)
	Dividend payment	(10,000)
	Corporation tax	(2,503)
Cash/profit retained in company		673

(b) (i) **Chargeable gain on the disposal of the painting**

	£
Disposal proceeds	8,600
Less: Commission	(516)
Net disposal proceeds	8,084
Less: cost (probate value)	(3,200)
Unindexed gain	4,884
Less: Indexation allowance	
$162.6 - 159.5/159.5 = 0.019 \times 3,200$	(61)
Indexed gain before taper relief	4,823

The indexed gain cannot exceed

$5/3 \times (8,600 - 6,000)$	4,333

As a non-business asset held for 10 qualifying years (including the bonus year), the gain is 60% chargeable.

Chargeable gain ($4,333 \times 60\%$)	2,600

(ii) **Letter concerning the tax efficient utilisation of trading losses**

[Donald's address]	[Firm's address]
Dear Donald	[Date]

Utilisation of trading losses

I understand that you have incurred a tax loss in your first year of trading.

The following options are available in respect of this loss.

1. *Claim under S380 for relief in the current year*

    The first option is to use the trading loss against other forms of income in the same year. If such a claim is made, losses are offset against income before personal allowances.

    Any excess loss can still be offset against capital gains of the year. However, any offset against capital gains is before both taper relief and annual exemptions.

    As you have no income in the tax year 2007/08, no relief is obtained against income in that year, however the trading losses can still be used against the capital gains. At the moment, your capital gains *situation in 2007/08 is as follows:*

	Painting	*Other gains*	*Total*
	£	£	£
Total chargeable gains	2,600	8,775	11,375
Less: Annual exemption			(8,800)
Taxable gains			2,575

Capital gains tax:	£	
	2,150 at 10%	215
	425 at 20%	85
	2,575	300

However, if loss relief is claimed against gains, the £8,000 loss will be used against the gains before taper relief, totalling £14,083 (4,333 + 9,750).

This leaves chargeable gains of £6,083. While these are covered by the annual exemption thereby saving tax of £300, part of the annual exemption (as well as the taper relief) is wasted as a result.

2. *Claim under S380 and S381 for relief in previous years*

It is also possible to offset a trading loss against the income of the previous year, and in the case of losses incurred in the first four years of a business, against the income of the three years prior to the year of loss taking the earliest year first. Again, the loss is offset against income before the deduction of personal allowances.

However, your part-time income at university is already covered by your personal allowance for each year, and therefore no tax would be saved by making such loss claims.

3. *Carry losses forward against trading income*

If you do not choose to offset your loss against your other income/gains as stated above, your trading loss will instead be carried forward and offset against future trading income.

On the basis of your current trading forecasts, you should be able to use all of your losses against the predicted profits in the year ended 31 March 2009. The tax saved will be £1,760 (£8,000 × 22%).

The advantage of doing this is that you do not waste any of your capital gains annual exemption in the current year. However, the disadvantage is that you will still pay capital gains tax of £300 in the current year, and the tax relief for the losses will be deferred by one year.

Conclusion

The most tax efficient way of relieving your losses is to carry them forward and offset them against future trading income. By doing so, you maximise the use of your 2007/08 capital gains annual exemption, and can use the losses against income taxed at 22% in 2008/09 (as opposed to a combination of 10% and 20% in 2007/08).

This will save tax of £1,760 in 2008/09, an improvement of £1,460 (1,760 − 300) compared to the alternative situation.

Yours sincerely

A. N. Advisor

		ACCA marking scheme	
			Marks
(a)	(i)	Sole trader:	
		– Income tax on profits	0.5
		– Requirement to pay Class 2 and 4 National Insurance	0.5
		– Personal allowance	0.5
		– Income tax charge	0.5
		– Class 2 NIC	0.5
		– Class 4 NIC	0.5
		– Calculation of remaining cash	0.5
		Company:	
		– Salary and employers' NIC deductible for CT purposes	0.5
		– Employers' NIC: identify as payable	0.5
		correct rate/calculation	0.5
		– Taxable profit/corporation tax	0.5
		– Personal allowance	0.5
		– Income tax payable	0.5
		– Employees' NIC	0.5
		– Calculation of remaining cash	0.5
		Comparison of two options	0.5
		Max	8.0
	(ii)	Employers' NIC	1.0
		Company PCTCT	1.0
		Corporation tax at 19%	0.5
		Max	2.0
	(iii)	Deduction of salary and NIC	1.0
		Deduction of dividend	0.5
		Deduction of corporation tax	0.5
		Max	2.0
(b)	(i)	Correct calculation of gross proceeds	0.5
		Deduction of cost	0.5
		Indexation allowance	0.5
		Application of 5/3 limit, using gross proceeds (2 × 0.5)	1.0
		Choose lower gain	0.5
		Taper relief: non-business asset	0.5
		correct number of years/rate	0.5
		Max	4.0
	(ii)	Availability of loss relief in current year	0.5
		Gains as well as income	0.5
		Income before personal allowance	0.5
		Gains before annual exemption and taper relief (2 × 0.5)	1.0
		Calculation of tax payable/saveable	1.0
		Effect of the loss relief offset before taper relief	0.5
		Would waste part of annual exemption	0.5

Availability for earlier year loss offset	0.5	
Waste of personal allowance/no tax saved	1.0	
Carry forward of losses v future trading profits	0.5	
Full relief at 22% 0.5		
Does not affect use of AE/PA	0.5	
Deferral of tax relief to y/e 31/03/08	0.5	
Calculation of additional tax saving	0.5	
Presentation	2.0	
	Max	9.0
Total		25.0

CAPITAL GAINS TAX

22 TAHOA

(a) (i) **Capital gains tax implications of Tahoa's disposals**

Sale of the apartment in Lilliput

The indexed gain arising on the apartment is £75,080 (W1).

The disposal qualifies for nine years of taper relief (including the bonus year).

Capital gains tax of £19,521 ($75,080 \times 65\% \times 40\%$) (ignoring the annual exemption) is due on 31 January 2008.

The disposal is also liable to £12,300 overseas capital taxes. Double taxation relief is available for the lower of the non CGT (£19,521) or overseas capital tax (£12,300).

Gift of BTP plc shares

For capital gains purposes, the deemed sales proceeds on a gift is the market value of the assets gifted. Quoted shares are valued at the lower of the quarter up method = £2.72 [£2.70 + (¼ (2.78 – 2.70))] or and the mid-bargain price of £2.73 [½ × (2.68 + 2.78)]. Therefore the shares are valued at £2.72 each.

The shares sold are matched with the acquisition post 5 April 1998 and then the 1985 pool. The shares are non-business assets as they are quoted shares, Tahoa owns less than 5% and has never been an employee of the company.

The post 5 April 1998 disposal does not qualify for taper relief as the shares have been held for less than three years. The disposal from the 1985 pool qualifies for nine years of taper relief.

Gift relief is not available as the shares are not qualifying assets for gift relief purposes. This is because Tahoa owns less than 5% and they are quoted shares.

The total chargeable gains on the disposal of shares is £77,166 (W2).

The tax due on 31 January 2008 is £30,866 ($77,166 \times 40\%$).

Gift of Necklace

The necklace is a non-wasting chattel and therefore a gain arises as it has a market value in excess of £6,000 at the date of the gift. An indexed gain of £3,049 (W3) arises but is restricted to £2,333 [$5/3 \times (7,400 - 6,000)$]

The necklace is a non-business asset and the disposal qualifies for nine years of taper relief.

Capital gains tax of £607 (2,333 × 65% × 40%) is therefore due on 31 January 2008.

Gift relief is not available as a necklace is not a qualifying asset.

Gift of AJB Ltd shares

Tahoa owns a $^1/_6$th interest in the company (i.e. 16.667%) and therefore the shares are valued at £14,40 each. Tahoa has given the trustees all 16.67% of AJB Ltd. The indexed gain of £516,000 (W4) can be held over, as the transfer is immediately chargeable to inheritance tax. This requires an election by Tahoa.

The indexed gain of £516,000 is deferred against the base cost of the shares to the trustees. Any accrued taper relief by Tahoa is lost. Tahoa will not have a chargeable gain on these shares in 2006/07.

(ii) **Payment by instalments**

Capital gains tax can be paid by instalments where the consideration is being paid over a period of more than 18 months or where there is a gift of qualifying assets on which gift hold over relief cannot be claimed.

Qualifying assets consist of land, controlling shareholdings and unquoted shares.

Accordingly, none of the tax due can be paid in instalments for the following reasons:

- the apartment was sold

- the shareholding in BTP plc is not a controlling holding

- hold over relief can be claimed on the gift to the trust.

(b) **Inheritance tax implications of lifetime gifts**

BTP plc shares

The gift is a PET of £217,600 (80,000 × £2.72). No tax will be charged at the time of the gift as it is a PET and no tax will be charged unless Tahoa dies before 22 December 2013. Any tax due on death will be reduced by taper relief by reference to the time between the date of the gift and the date of death.

Necklace

The gift of the necklace is a PET of £7,400 from which the marriage exemption of £5,000 can be deducted. No IHT is payable at the time of the gift as it is a PET. No tax will be charged unless Tahoa dies before 18 November 2013. Any tax due on death will be reduced by taper relief as explained above.

AJB Ltd shares

The gift is a chargeable lifetime transfer. IHT is payable when the shares are put into the trust provided the value exceeds the nil rate band (£285,000). The value of the CLT is £744,000 (W5) using the related property rules.

As Tahoa pays the IHT, it is a net gift which is taxed at 25% on the excess over the nil rate band.

Lifetime IHT of £114,750 ((744,000 – 285,000) × 25%) is due by 30 September 2007.

No further IHT is payable unless Tahoa dies before 4 March 2014.

(c)   **Income tax**

BTP plc shares

Where a parent transfers capital to a child which gives rise to income of more than £100 in a tax year, the income is treated as that of the parent rather than the child.

Tirua is a minor as he is still at school. Accordingly, any income arising in respect of the shares will be included in the income tax computation of his father, Tahoa, unless it is less than £100 in the tax year.

AJB Ltd shares

Dividends arising on the shares will be taxed in the hands of the trustees at 32½%, as it is a discretionary trust.

Workings

(W1) **Sale of the apartment in Lilliput**

	£
Sale proceeds (October 2006)	128,000
Cost (February 1983)	(27,000)
	101,000
Indexation allowance to April 1998 (27,000 × 0.960)	(25,920)
Indexed gain	75,080

(W2) **Gift of the BTP shares**

Disposal of shares acquired 11 January 2005

	£
Market value (£2.72 × 30,000)	81,600
Cost (January 2005)	(56,000)
Chargeable gain (100%)	25,600

No taper relief available as held for 1 year

Disposal of 50,000 shares in 1985 pool

	£
Market value (£2.72 × 50,000)	136,000
Indexed cost (68,000 × 50/60)	(56,667)
Indexed gain	79,333
Taper relief (35%)	(27,767)
Chargeable gain (65%)	51,566
Total chargeable gains (25,600 + 51,566)	77,166

(W3) **Gift of necklace**

	£
Market value (November 2006)	74,000
Cost (probate value) (May 1997)	(4,200)
Unindexed gain	3,200
Indexation (4,200 × 0.036)	(151)
Indexed gain	3,049

(W4) Gift of Gain as the AJB Ltd shares

	£
Market value (40,000 × £14.40) (March 2007)	576,000
Indexed cost	(60,000)
Indexed gain	516,000

(W5) IHT value of AJB Ltd shares put into discretionary trust

The value of the chargeable lifetime transfer (CLT) is the diminution in value of Tahoa's estate (i.e. from a 16.667% holding to a Nil holding). However, his shares must be valued taking account of related property (i.e. taking account of the shares held by both Tahoa and his wife) as follows:

	Before gift	*After gift*
Tahoa	40,000	Nil
Wife	40,000	40,000
	80,000	40,000
	33.33%	16.667%

	£
Value of Tahoa's estate before gift (40,000 × £18,60)	744,000
Value of Tahoa's estate after gift	(Nil)
Transfer of value	744,000
BPR (Investment company)	(Nil)
Annual exemptions (to be ignored)	(Nil)
CLT	744,000

23   DELIA JONES

(a)   (i)   **Trading income assessment for 2006/07**

The disposal of the fixtures and fittings will result in a balancing charge of £95,000 as follows:

	£
WDV brought forward at 31 August 2006	114,000
Additions – December 2006	31,000
	145,000
Disposal proceeds	(240,000)
Balancing charge	(95,000)

Delia and Fastfood Ltd are not connected persons, and so they cannot elect to transfer the fixtures and fittings at their written down value.

Delia's 2006/07 trading income assessment is £206,500 as follows:

	£	£
Year ended 31 August 2006		77,200
Period ended 31 March 2007	58,500	
Balancing charge	95,000	
		153,500
		230,700
Relief for overlap profits		(24,200)
Trading income assessment		206,500

(ii) **Capital gains tax liability for 2006/07**

Delia's disposal of her business on 31 March 2007 will result in a CGT liability of £37,060 as follows:

	£	£
Goodwill (125,000 - Nil cost)		125,000
Freehold property (A) (462,000 - 230,000)		232,000
Freehold property (B) (118,000 - 94,000)	24,000	
Capital loss brought forward (Note)	(12,400)	
		11,600
Total gain before taper relief		368,600
Chargeable gains (working)		100,850
Annual exemption		(8,800)
Taxable gains		92,050
Capital gains tax at 40%		36,820

Note: Taper relief is maximised by setting the capital loss brought forward of £12,400 against the capital gain of £24,000 arising on freehold property (B) which has been owned for less than one year and does not qualify for taper relief. The net gain of £11,600 is 100% chargeable.

Working:

Goodwill and freehold property A are business assets held for more than two years, therefore the gains are 25% chargeable.

	£
Goodwill + freehold property A (125,000 + 232,000) × 25%	89,250
Freehold property B (100% chargeable)	11,600
Total chargeable gains	100,850

(iii) **Value added tax implications of sale**

Output VAT will not have to be charged on the value of stocks and other assets on which VAT has been claimed, since Delia's business is being transferred as a going concern.

Delia will have to inform HMRC by 30 April 2007 that she has ceased to make taxable supplies. They will then cancel her VAT registration as from 31 March 2007.

(b) (i) **Disposal on 30 April 2007**

Income tax implications

Delia's trading income assessments will be as follows:

		£	£
2006/07	Year ended 31 August 2006		77,200
2007/08	Period ended 30 April 2007		
	(58,500 + 9,000)	67,500	
	Balancing charge	95,000	
		162,500	
	Relief for overlap profits	(24,200)	
			138,300

The balancing payment of the related income tax liability will be due on 31 January 2009 rather than on 31 January 2008, although payments on account will be required on 31 January and 31 July 2008 based on the 2006/07 assessment.

National insurance implications

Delia will have to pay the higher rate (8%) of Class 4 NIC contributions on profits between £5,035 and £33,540 for 2006/07 and 2007/08 rather than just for 2006/07.

This is an additional cost of £1,995 ((33,540 - 5,035) at 7% (8% − 1%)).

Capital gains tax implications

Taper relief will not be affected. Maximum taper relief is already available on the goodwill and freehold property A, and 50% taper relief would only be available on property B if the sale were delayed until July 2007.

The CGT liability will be due on 31 January 2009 rather than on 31 January 2008.

Conclusion

A disposal date of 30 April 2007 therefore appears to be beneficial.

Key answer tips

The main benefit of delaying the sale derives from the postponement of the payment of a substantial proportion of the tax by one year.

(ii) **Consideration as ordinary shares in Fastfood Ltd**

If the consideration is in the form of ordinary shares then the total indexed gains (before taper relief) of £381,000 (125,000 + 232,000 + 24,000) will automatically be rolled over against the base cost of the shares in Fastfood Ltd.

This is because Delia's business is transferred as a going concern, and all of the business assets are being transferred and accordingly incorporation relief applies.

The fact that Delia does not become an employee or director of Fastfood Ltd is irrelevant. The base cost of her shares in fastfood Ltd will be £469,000 (850,000 - 381,000).

On a subsequent disposal of the shares in Fastfood Ltd, only the period of ownership of the shares will count in deciding how much taper relief is due.

The shares will be treated as a business asset for taper relief purposes as they are unquoted trading company shares. This includes AIM companies. The maximum taper relief reduction is therefore 75% (100% - 25%) and will be available if the shares are held for two complete years.

From a tax point of view, taking the consideration in the form of shares appears to be beneficial since the CGT liability is postponed until such time as the shares are sold and the full business taper relief is available after only two years. This must be balanced against the relatively risky nature of holding an investment quoted on the AIM.

If the shares should be sold within two years of the transfer, Delia can elect to disapply incorporation relief. She would then benefit from the taper relief on the transfer of the goodwill and freehold property A.

Key answer tips

Remember to take commercial and investment factors into account when giving advice.

The election to disapply incorporation relief could be deferred until the shares are sold, so that Delia can minimise her gains with the benefit of hind sight.

24 ARMADA ENTERPRISES

(a) **Disposal of shares in June 2003**

The share matching rules will apply to the disposal of Basil's holding of 12,000 shares in Moonbeam plc in June 2003. These rules state that share disposals are first matched with acquisitions (on a LIFO basis) made after 5 April 1998 and then with shares acquired in the 1985 pool.

Disposal of shares acquired in May 2003

	£
Proceeds (2000/12,000 × 78,000)	13,000
Less: Cost	(10,500)
Gain before taper relief	2,500
Less: Taper relief (see below)	Nil
Chargeable gain	2,500

Note: No indexation allowance is available as the shares were acquired after April 1998. Taper relief at the non-business asset rate only is available. As the shares were acquired in May 2002 they have not been held for at least three years, so no taper relief is available. The gain is 100% chargeable.

Disposals from the 1985 Pool

This is more complicated because of the interaction with the inter-spouse no gain/no loss provisions and the death of Basil's wife.

The transfer of 10,000 Moonbeam plc shares into joint ownership in December 1993 effectively amounts to a disposal of 50% of the shares by Basil's wife. This transfer will be subject to the no gain/no loss provisions which state that the disposal will be at such a value that does not result in a capital gain or an allowable loss – i.e. at indexed cost. Basil will therefore acquire this interest at the following base cost:

	£
Cost (April 1986)	50,000
Indexation to December 1993	
((141.9–97.87)/97.87) × 50,000 (Note (i))	22,494
Indexed cost	72,494
Basil's 50% share (Note (ii))	36,247

Note:

(i) These shares are 1985 pool shares, therefore the indexation factor is not rounded to three decimal places.

(ii) The make up of Basil's 50% share is £25,000 cost and £11,247 indexation allowance.

Death results in a tax free uplift in base cost. This means that upon his wife's death in September 1997 Basil will acquire the remaining 50% interest in these shares at their probate value on the date of his wife's death.

Using the quarter-up method these shares were valued at death at 990p per share (988 + (996 – 988)/4) giving a valuation of the 50% interest of £49,500 (5,000 × 990 p).

The total base cost of the 1985 holding before indexation is therefore £74,500 (25,000 + 49,500) and after indexation is £85,747 (36,247 + 49,500).

The disposal of the 1985 holding of shares therefore results in the following position:

	£
Sale proceeds (10,000/12,000 × 78,000)	65,000
Less Cost (25,000 + 49,500)	(74,500)
Allowable loss	(9,500)

Indexation allowance cannot be used to create or increase a loss.

Overall result of disposing of shares in June 2003

The net position for 2003/04 is therefore net losses of £7,000 (9,500 – 2,500) to carry forward for use against future capital gains.

Tutorial note:

Indexation allowance of £11,247 is available on the shares acquired by inter-spouse transfer up to December 1993, and further indexation is available based on the base cost of the shares from December 1993 to April 1998. Indexation is also available on the shares acquired on his wife's death from September 1997 to April 1998. However, the amount of the indexation allowance need not be calculated as an allowable loss arises on the disposal of the shares and indexation cannot increase a capital loss.

(b) (i) **Incorporation relief - conditions**

The principal conditions that need to be satisfied for the incorporation of Armada Enterprises to qualify for rollover relief are as follows:

– The transferor must be a person who is not a company – Basil is an individual and will therefore qualify.

– Armada Enterprises needs to be a going concern. The fact that its goodwill value has increased over time suggests that this condition should not be a problem.

–   The transfer needs to comprise all the assets of the business. The only exception to this is cash. Liabilities do not need to be transferred to qualify for this type of relief.

–   The transfer needs to be wholly or partly in exchange for shares which will be issued by the limited company to Basil.

(ii)   **Maximum cash consideration to accept**

When some of the consideration is in the form of cash and some in the form of shares, the gain is apportioned. The gain eligible for rollover relief is calculated using the formula:

Total gains × Value of shares issued/Total consideration

The gain relating to the cash consideration is chargeable at the time of incorporation.

It is therefore possible to calculate the maximum cash consideration without giving rise to CGT as follows.

Note that it is only the capital gains arising from the disposal of chargeable assets that are relevant. In this respect only the freehold land & buildings and goodwill are chargeable assets. It should also be noted that Basil will lose any entitlement to taper relief on any portion of the gain to which rollover relief applies.

The capital gains arising are:

	Freehold land & buildings £	*Goodwill* £
Proceeds	80,000	40,000
Less: cost	(50,000)	(25,000)
Capital gains	30,000	15,000

No indexation allowance available as the assets are acquired after April 1998.

Basil's annual exemption is £8,800. He also has an unused capital loss brought forward of £7,000 relating to the disposal of his Moonbeam plc shares (part (a)) and will be entitled to business asset taper relief of 75% on any gains remaining chargeable after incorporation rollover relief and the brought forward loss has been deducted.

The order of offset is important, with incorporation rollover relief being relieved first, then the brought forward loss, then taper relief and finally the annual exemption.

Working backwards from a required taxable amount of £Nil:

	Step	£
Total capital gains on disposal of business (30,000 + 15,000)		45,000
Gain required re-share consideration (i.e. incorporation relief required)	(Bal fig)	(2,800)
Gain required re-cash consideration	(5)	42,200
Less Brought forward capital loss	(4)	(7,000)
Net gain before taper relief (8,800 ÷ 25%)	(3)	35,200
Required chargeable gain after tape relief		8,800
Annual exemption	(2)	(8,800)
Taxable amount	(1)	Nil

The required incorporation relief is £2,800 which means that the value of the shares needs to be £8,898 calculated as:

$$£2,800 = \frac{\text{Value of shares}}{£143,000} \times £45,000$$

Value of shares = £8,898

Therefore the cash consideration should be restricted to £134,102 (£143,000 - £8,898).

(iii) **Taxation disadvantages of incorporation rollover relief**

The following are disadvantages of incorporation relief:

– The need to transfer all business assets to the limited company. This could lock, for example, the freehold property into the limited company. This may lead to a double tax charge situation in the future when the property is disposed of (once when the property is disposed of by the limited company, and again when Basil tries to extract any sale proceeds from the company).

It can also be tax efficient retain the property personally and then to rent the property to the limited company. This is because the limited company will obtain a corporation tax deduction for its rental payments which are treated as investment income in the hands of Basil and therefore not liable to Class 1 NIC. The benefit can be enhanced if the property is transferred to a small self administered pension fund as in these circumstances the rental income received should not be taxable.

– Loss of taper relief accrued on the gains arising upon incorporation.

– The relief is only a deferral mechanism, it does not exempt the gains from tax. The rolled over gain is deducted in calculating the base cost of the shares received. The gains will therefore become chargeable in the future when Basil disposes of his shares.

ACCA marking scheme		
		Marks
(a) Share matching rules		1.0
May 2003 holding		1.5
1985 holding – inter-spouse rule/application		2.0
– death rule/application		2.5
– disposal		1.5
– net position		0.5
	Maximum	9.0
	Available	8.0
(b) (i) Conditions		3.0
(ii) Formula/gains		1.5
Availability of loss brought forward, taper relief and annual exemption		1.5
Order of offset		1.0
Calculation		3.5
(iii) Locking assets/discussion of property		3.0
Taper relief		0.5
Deferral relief only		0.5
	Maximum	13.0
	Available	14.5
Total		21.0

UL AND SUSAN

(i) **Furnished holiday accommodation - conditions**

Furnished holiday accommodation is furnished property in the UK, let on a commercial basis with a view to the realisation of profits.

In addition it must satisfy the following:

(1) It is available for commercial letting for at least 140 days in the tax year.

(2) It is actually let for at least 70 days.

(3) It must not be let for periods of long term occupation totalling in excess of 155 days in the relevant 12 month period.

Long term occupation is a period of more than 31 consecutive days let to the same person.

(ii) **Paul – Taxable income - 2006/07**

	£
Employment income	40,000
Property business income (W1)	Nil
Dividend income ((6,000 + 9,750) × 100/90)	17,500
	57,500
Less: Furnished holiday letting loss (W2)	(1,700)
STI	55,800
Less: Personal allowance	(5,035)
Taxable income	50,765

Workings

(W1) Property business income

The property income assessments on Property A and Property B must be calculated separately as Property A is a furnished holiday letting and treated as earned income.

Property B	£
Income	4,000
Less: Management expenses	(700)
Less: Wear and tear allowance (10% × 4,000)	(400)
Property profit	2,900
Less: Property business loss brought forward	(2,900)
Assessable in 2006/07	Nil
Property business loss carried forward (3,000 – 2,900)	£100

Note: There was no need to calculate the loss to carry forward, this is shown for tutorial purposes only.

(W2) **Furnished holiday letting loss**

Property A	£
Income	2,000
Less: Management expenses	(1,500)
Capital allowances	(1,200)
Interest	(1,000)
Allowable trading loss	(1,700)

Paul should claim relief for this loss, as if it were a trading loss, against his Statutory Total Income for the year.

(b) (i) **Paul – Capital gains tax liability - 2006/07**

	£
Vintage car (exempt asset)	Nil
Racehorse (wasting chattel – exempt)	Nil
Painting (non-wasting chattel sold at a gain with proceeds of less than £6,000 – exempt)	Nil
Antique vase (W1)	(1,250)
Diamond ring (W2)	1,000
Capital loss – carried forward	(250)
Capital gains tax liability	Nil

Workings

(W1) **Antique vase**	£
Proceeds (deemed)	6,000
Less: Cost	(7,250)
Capital loss	(1,250)

(W2) **Diamond ring**	
Proceeds	6,600
Less: Cost	(5,400)
Gain	1,200

No indexation allowance as acquired after April 1998.
Restricted to a maximum of

$5/3 \times (6,600 - 6,000)$	1,000

(ii) **Taxation implication of gifting shares in Alpha plc and Beta ltd**

Gifting 4% holding in Alpha plc

Inheritance tax

The gift will potentially exempt transfer (PET) on 3 April 2007 with the following value:

	£
Transfer of value	100,000
Less: Annual exemption 2006/07	(3,000)
PET	97,000

The 2005/06 annual exemption and the nil band have been used by the chargeable lifetime gift to his daughter in March 2006. As a PET, there is no lifetime IHT payable and the PET will only become chargeable if Paul dies within seven years of April 2007.

If so, his son will be liable for any IHT payable.

Business property relief will not be available for this gift as the shares are in a quoted company and Paul does not have a controlling interest.

Capital gains tax

The gift is a chargeable disposal at market value, The gain arising is calculated as follows:

	£
Proceeds – market value	100,000
Less: Cost	(65,000)
Unindexed gain	35,000
Less: Indexation allowance	
$65,000 \times (162.6 - 134.1)/134.1$	(13,814)
Indexed gain	21,186
Less: Capital loss (from b(i)) (see note below)	(250)
Net indexed gain	20,936

The holding in Alpha plc does not qualify for gift relief, as it is not a holding of at least 5% in a quoted company.

The shares are a non-business asset for the purposes of taper relief. The qualifying period is nine years (6.4.98 to 3.4.06 being eight complete years plus one year for ownership on 17.3.98).

The chargeable gain is therefore £13,608 (£20,936 × 65%).

The 2006/07 annual exemption of £8,800 is available to set against this, leaving a taxable amount of £4,808 (13,608 – 8,800).

As Paul's taxable income is £50,765, capital gains tax will be payable at 40%, amounting to £1,923 (4,808 × 40%).

Tutorial note: The capital loss of £1,250 in 2006/07 will be set in preference against the gain on the diamond ring, as this asset was purchased in January 1999 and is therefore not eligible for the bonus year of taper relief. The gain is 70% chargeable (held for eight complete years).

Gift of 15% holding in Beta Ltd

Inheritance tax

The gift will be a PET on 3 April 2007, valued using the related property rules as follows:

	£
Before transfer	
£765,000 × 30%/(30% + 55%)	270,000
After transfer	
£490,000 × 15%/(15% + 55%)	(105,000)
Value transferred	165,000

Business property relief (BPR) of 100% is available as the shares are unquoted trading company shares.

As a PET, there is no lifetime IHT payable and the PET will only become chargeable if Paul dies within seven years of April 2007. If so, to continue to qualify for BPR the shares must still be owned by his son on the date of Paul's death. Otherwise, the gift will be chargeable as follows:

	£
Value transferred	165,000
Less: Annual exemption 2006/07	(3,000)
PET	162,000

Capital gains tax

The gift is a chargeable disposal at market value. The gain arising is calculated as follows:

	£
Proceeds – market value	100,000
Less: Cost	(50,000)
Untapered gain	50,000
Less: Current year capital loss	(250)
Net gain	49,750

The holding in Beta Ltd qualifies for gift relief, as it is a holding of unquoted shares in a trading company.

It is the untapered gain of £50,000 that is held over until his son disposes of the shares. In this case the taper relief relating to Paul's period of ownership will be lost.

The shares are a business asset for the purposes of taper relief. The qualifying period is two years (March 2005 to 3 April 2007 being a period of two complete years of ownership). If gift relief is not claimed, the chargeable gain would be £12,438 (49,750 × 25%).

Paul has to decide whether to claim gift relief, and pay no capital gains tax, or not to claim gift relief, in which case the chargeable gain of £12,438, less the annual exemption of £8,800 (i.e. £3,638) would be taxable.

As his taxable income for 2006/07 is £50,765, this would result in capital gains tax payable of £1,455 (3,638 × 40%).

If Paul claims gift relief, his son will suffer the capital gains tax consequences when he sells the shares in the future. Taper relief will be available in respect of the son's period of ownership only.

(iii) **Gift of Alpha plc shares (quoted shares)**

As calculated in (b) (ii) above, the current capital gains tax liability is £1,923.

In addition, there is a potential charge to inheritance tax if Paul dies within seven years of the gift on a potentially exempt transfer (PET) of £97,000.

There are various options which would reduce or eliminate the tax charge which include the following:

- 3 April 2007: Paul to gift 65% of his holding to his son. This realises a gain of £8,789 ((21,186 × 65% − 250) × 65%) which is predominantly covered by his annual exemption. This will be a PET for inheritance tax purposes of £62,000 (£65,000 − £3,000 (the 2006/07 annual exemption)).

- 6 April 2007 Paul gifts the remaining 35% of the shares. As the transaction is now in the next tax year, his gain of £4,449 (21,186 × 35% = 7,415 × 60% taper relief (one more year of ownership)) will be covered by the annual exemption for 2007/08 thus saving £1,923 capital gains tax.

For IHT purposes this will be a PET of £32,000 (£35,000 − £3,000 (2007/08 annual exemption)).

Note: Credit will be given for candidates making appropriate and valid suggestions, which do not exactly match the scenario shown above. Many answers may explore the possibility of transfers between husband and wife. Such suggestions will be given credit, but are not shown here, due to the doubt as to whether such schemes would be attacked by HMRC, in the real world.

ACCA marking scheme			
			Marks
(a)	(i)	FHA conditions (4 × ½)	2.0
	(ii)	Property B – current year	1.0
		– loss c/fwd	0.5
		Property A – current year loss	1.0
		Offset of FHA loss against other income	0.5
			3.0
(b)	(i)	Vintage car	0.5
		Race horse	0.5
		Painting	0.5
		Antique vase	1.0
		Diamond ring	1.0
		Loss c/fwd	0.5
			4.0
	(ii)	Alpha:	
		IHT: Position now	1.0
		Position on death	0.5
		CGT: Untapered gain	1.0
		Correct offset of loss	0.5
		Tapered gain	0.5
		No gift relief	0.5
		Beta:	
		IHT: Value transferred	1.0
		Annual exemption	0.5
		BPR	1.0
		CGT: Untapered gain	0.5
		Correct offset of loss	0.5

	Tapered gain	0.5
	Gift relief available re untapered gain	1.0
	Consequences of claiming/not claiming gift relief	1.5
		10.5
(iii)	Current CGT liability	1.0
	Potential IHT charge	0.5
	Mechanisms for eliminating the tax charge, via splitting/partially delaying the gift:	
	CGT effect	5.0
	IHT consequences	2.5
		9.0
	Total available (vs a maximum of 25)	28.5

26 DYLAN

(a) **Capital gain on the sale of shares in Puligny plc**

The shares qualify for business asset taper relief for the part of the period of ownership when Dylan was an employee of Puligny plc. When Dylan ceased employment on 6 April 2002, his business asset taper relief ceased, and non-business asset taper relief applied thereafter until the date of disposal (but see tutorial note):

Actual period of ownership since 6 April 1998	96 months
Qualifying business asset (6.4.98 to 5.4.02)	48 months
Non business asset (6.4.02 to 6.4.06)	48 months

The gain is apportioned and the appropriate taper relief percentage applied to each part of the gain. The business portion has 8 complete years of ownership. The non-business portion has 9 qualifying years (including the bonus year) as the shares were held on 17 March 1998.

	£
Sales proceeds (5,000 x £4.25)	21,250
Less Cost (5,000 x £2.50)	(12,500)
Unindexed gain	8,750
Indexation $\dfrac{(162.6-153.9)}{153.9}\times 12,500$	(707)
Indexed gain	8,043

The business gain is 25% chargeable.

The non-business gain is 65% chargeable

Business gain (48/96 × 8,043 × 25%)	1,005
Non business gain (48/96 × 8,043 × 65%)	2,614
Total chargeable gains	3,619

Tutorial note: The definition of business assets for taper relief purposes changed on 6 April 2000. Before 6 April 2000, the shares would not have been business assets. To qualify pre 6 April 2000, the individual had to be an employee and own >5% interest in quoted shares. However, the question says assume that the current definition of business assets applies throughout the whole period of ownership. Therefore the whole period from 6 April 1998 to 6 April 2002 is counted as business asset.

(b)   **Capital gains tax deferral relief available in corporation**

There are two CGT deferral reliefs available upon incorporation: incorporation relief and gift relief.

Incorporation relief

Incorporation relief is an automatic relief. All or part of the gains can be held over (i.e. deferred) if **all** of the following conditions are met.

- The business is transferred as a going concern
- All the assets (other than cash) are transferred
- The consideration received is wholly or partly in the form of shares.

The amount held over is derived from the following fraction:

$$\frac{\text{Value of shares received from the company}}{\text{Total value of consideration from the company}}$$

The amount of gains relating to any non-share consideration received becomes chargeable in the year of incorporation.

The held over gain is deferred by deducting the gain from the base cost of the shares received. The assets are transferred at their market value.

Incorporation relief defers the indexed gain before taper relief. Therefore any accrued is taper relief lost.

An individual can elect to disapply incorporation relief if, for example, they wish to use taper relief. The election to disapply must be made within 34 months of the end of the tax year of disposal. In this case (2006/07), the election would need to be made by 31 January 2010.

Gift relief

Where a qualifying asset is gifted or sold at an undervalue, the transferor and transferee can jointly elect that the transferor's gain is reduced to nil. Instead, the transferee is deemed to acquire the asset for its market value at the date of transfer less the deferred gain. As with incorporation relief, the deferral is before the operation of taper relief, therefore accrued taper relief is lost.

If any consideration is given in respect of a chargeable asset, any excess over allowable costs is taxed immediately and only the balance is deferred.

Qualifying assets for gift relief include business assets, or assets subject to an immediate inheritance tax charge. In this case, both the capital assets (goodwill and property) will qualify.

The election for gift relief must be made within 70 months of the end of the tax year to which the claim relates (in this case 2006/07) by 31 January 2013.

(c)   (i)   **Effect of retaining the property**

Incorporation relief requires Dylan to transfer all the assets (other than cash) to the company. Since he wishes to retain the property outside of the company, gift relief is the only option available to him.

(ii)   **Advice on the maximum cash consideration to accept**

As goodwill is a business asset, full taper relief of 75% will be available, the gain will only be 25% chargeable. Also, Dylan has £5,181 (8,800 – 3,619 (part a)) of his annual exemption remaining. The company could therefore pay Dylan £20,724 (£5,181 × 4) (see note) for part of the goodwill, either in cash or credited to his director's loan account, without incurring an immediate tax charge.

Note:

As Dylan started the business from scratch, the base cost of the goodwill will be Nil. Therefore, proceeds of £20,724 will be received by Dylan giving rise to a £5,181 chargeable gain after taper relief which is covered by the available annual exemption.

Business rates of taper relief will apply. As the gain after the operation of taper relief is 25% of the original gain, the pre-taper gain must be 100/25 (i.e. 4 times the tapered gain).

(iii) **Tax consequences of charging rent for the property**

Income tax

For income tax purposes, Dylan will receive rent, which will be charged to income tax at 40%, as Dylan is a higher rate taxpayer.

Any expenditure incurred by Dylan on the repair, maintenance or management of the property will be deductible from the taxable rents received.

The company will pay rent to Dylan. This payment will be a deductible expense against the taxable trading profits of the company. As the business is small, this deduction is likely to be worth a tax saving of 19%.

Capital gains

For capital gains tax (CGT) purposes, the property will continue to be treated as a business asset for taper relief and rollover relief purposes in Dylan's hands. Charging rent will not affect the availability of these reliefs.

Inheritance tax

For inheritance tax (IHT) purposes, the property will continue to be eligible for business property relief, although this will now be reduced to 50% as the asset is used by the company which Dylan controls. Again, charging rent will not affect the availability of this relief.

Conclusion

Thus, from a tax viewpoint, and based on current legislation, the charging of rent to the company would give rise to a current (ongoing) tax cost without any obvious long term benefit.

(d) **Capital gains tax and inheritance tax implications of land transactions**

(i) **Gift of land to wife**

Capital gains tax (CGT)

The gift of the land between Dylan and Ermintrude, in July 1996, was a chargeable disposal.

However, as the transfer was between a husband and wife, the transfer is treated as taking place at a price that gives rise to neither a gain nor a loss.

Ermintrudes's base cost is therefore Dylan's cost (probate value of £100,000) together with the indexation allowance. Dylan was entitled to indexation from May 1991 to July 1996 (£100,000 × 0.142 (152.4 - 133.5 / 133.5)) of £14,200.

The total base cost is therefore £114,200.

Inheritance tax (IHT)

Although a transfer of value has occurred, as this is between a UK domiciled husband and wife, it will be exempt for IHT purposes.

(ii) **Sale of a third of the land**

Capital gains tax (CGT)

The sale of part of the land is a chargeable disposal. As the sale took place between connected persons the sale proceeds are deemed to be equal to the market value of the asset at the date of sale, regardless of any sale proceeds received.

As the sale is also a part disposal the cost of the land must be apportioned between the third sold and the two thirds retained.

	£
Sale proceeds (market value)	250,000
Less: Cost $114,200 \times \dfrac{250,000}{250,000 + 600,000}$	(33,588)
Unindexed gain	216,412
Less: Indexation (July 1996 to April 1998) £33,588 × 0.067 (162.6 – 152.4/152.4)	(2,250)
	214,162

As a non-business asset held for six qualifying years (6 April 1998 to November 2003 = 5 years plus bonus year as land held on 17 March 1998), the gain is 80% chargeable.

Chargeable gain (214,162 × 80%)	£171,330

Inheritance tax (IHT)

As the land was sold to her sister at an under value, there was a gift of £50,000. This gift was a potentially exempt transfer (PET) at the time it was made.

As a PET no IHT was payable at the time of the gift and provided the donor survives seven years from the date of the gift, no IHT would be payable upon death either.

If the death were to occur within seven years of the date of the gift, inheritance tax would be payable, subject to a reduction for taper relief, if there were more than three years between the gift and death.

Assuming Ermintrude had made no other gifts for IHT purposes in the 2003/04 tax year, or in the previous tax year, (2002/03), there would be annual exemptions totalling £6,000 to be deducted from the value of the gift.

(iii) **Gift of remaining two-thirds of land**

Capital gains tax (CGT)

The gift of the land would be a chargeable disposal. The sale proceeds for the disposal would be deemed to be the market value of the asset at the date of the gift.

	£
Proceeds (market value)	800,000
Less: Remainder of base cost (£114,200 – 33,588)	(80,612)
Unindexed gain	719,388
Less: Indexation (July 1996 to April 1998) (80,612 × 0.067)	(5,401)
Indexed gain	713,987

As a non-business asset held for 9 qualifying years (including the bonus year), the gain is 65% chargeable.

Chargeable gain (713,987 × 65%) £464,092

Note that gift relief is not available as the land is not a qualifying business asset for gift relief purposes and there is no immediate charge to IHT.

Inheritance tax (IHT)

As the land was gifted to Zebedee there was a transfer of value of £800,000. This gift was a potentially exempt transfer (PET) at the time it was made. As a PET no IHT was payable at the time of the gift, and as explained above if the donor survives seven years from the date of the gift, no IHT would be payable. If the donor were to die within seven years of the date of the gift, inheritance tax would be payable on death, subject to a reduction for taper relief.

Assuming Ermintrude had made no other gifts for IHT purposes in the 2006/07 tax year, or in the previous tax year (2005/06), there would be annual exemptions totalling £6,000 to be deducted from the value of the gift.

ACCA marking scheme				
				Marks
(a)		Part-qualifying only for business asset taper relief		1.0
		Split of business asset/ non-business asset		0.5
		Sale proceeds /cost		0.5
		Indexation allowance		0.5
		Taper relief: business asset		0.5
		Taper relief: non-business asset		1.0
			Max	4.0
(b)		Incorporation relief		0.5
		Automatic		0.5
		Conditions (half each)		1.5
		Holdover fraction		0.5
		Holdover mechanics		0.5
		Loss of taper relief		0.5
		Election awareness		0.5
		Election time limits		0.5
		Gift Relief		0.5
		Joint election		0.5
		Holdover mechanics		0.5
		Partial deferment		0.5
		Qualifying assets		0.5
		Loss of taper relief		0.5
		Election time limit		0.5
			Max	7.0
(c)	(i)	Has to be gift relief		0.5
		Reason for selection of gift relief		0.5
			Max	1.0
	(ii)	Use balance of annual exemption		0.5
		Taper relief		1.0
		Calculation of maximum payable		0.5
			Max	2.0
	(iii)	Comparison of income tax and corporation tax rates		1.0

		Not necessary for capital gains tax reliefs		1.0
		Not necessary for IHT business property relief		0.5
		Max		2.0
(d)	(i)	Spouse transfer:		
		No capital gains tax		0.5
		Date/cost taken over by Ermintrude		0.5
		Inheritance tax exempt transfer		0.5
	(ii)	Proceeds/market value		0.5
		Apportionment of base cost on part disposal		0.5
		Indexation		0.5
		Taper relief		0.5
		IHT - gift a PET		0.5
		Annual exemption		0.5
		Chargeable if die within 7 years		0.5
		Taper relief		0.5
	(iii)	Proceeds – market value		0.5
		Use of remainder of cost		0.5
		Indexation		0.5
		Taper relief		0.5
		IHT - gift a PET		0.5
		Consequences as for (ii)		0.5
		Max		7.0
Total				23

27 GRAEME

(a) **Total chargeable gains arising on disposal of shares**

The shares acquired in Thistle Dubh Limited form part of the FA 1985 pool. The cost and indexed cost are calculated as follows:

FA85 Pool	No. of shares	Cost £	Indexed cost £
December 1986: acquisition	10,000	36,000	36,000
Indexation to March 1992: $(136.7 - 99.6)/99.6$			13,410
	10,000	36,000	49,410
March 1992: Rights issue	5,000	50,000	50,000
	15,000	86,000	99,410
Indexation to April 1998: $(162.6 - 136.7)/136.7$			18,835
Balance before reorganisation	15,000	86,000	118,245

Allocation of original cost to new holdings

As the new shares are unquoted following the reorganisation, the base costs of the existing shares are apportioned to the new holdings on the basis of their relative values at the time of the first disposal.

In this case, two 'T' and three 'D' shares are received for each one share in Thistle Dubh Limited.

The number and value of the new shares at the first disposal date is as follows:

	No. of shares	Share price £	Value £
'T' shares (2 for 1)	30,000	3.00	90,000
'D' shares (3 for 1)	45,000	6.00	270,000
	75,000		360,000

The cost of £86,000 and indexed cost of £118,245 relating to the original shares (see above) are therefore apportioned in the ratio of 1:3 (90,000:270,000) as follows:

	No. of shares	Cost £	Indexed cost £
'T' shares	30,000	21,500	29,561
'D' shares	45,000	64,500	88,684
	75,000	86,000	118,245

Disposal of 12,000 'T' shares in May 2006

	£
Sales proceeds (12,000 × 300p)	36,000
Less: Cost (12/30 × £21,500) (W2)	(8,600)
Unindexed gain	27,400
Less: Indexation (29,561 – 21,500) × 12,000/30,000	(3,224)
Indexed gain	24,176

Shares in unquoted trading companies qualify for business asset taper relief regardless of the size of holding, and as they have been held for more than 2 years the gain is 25% chargeable.

Chargeable gain (24,176 × 25%)	£6,044

Disposal of 45,000 'D' shares in October 2006

	£
Sales proceeds	85,000
Less: Cost:	(64,500)
Unindexed gain	20,500
Less: Indexation	
(88,684 – 64,500) = 24,184, restricted	(20,500)
Indexed gain	Nil

The total chargeable gains arising on the disposal of the 'T' and 'D' shares is therefore £6,044.

(b)   **Gift of the remaining 'T' Shares**

The remaining shares comprise 18,000 'T' shares.

(i)   **Gift to Catherine**

Capital gains tax

For capital gains tax (CGT) purposes, transfers between spouses are treated as being on a no gain/no loss basis so do not give rise to a chargeable disposal.

Catherine will take over the indexed cost of £17,737 (£29,561 × 18,000/30,000) and the holding history of the shares, including the length of time held for taper relief purposes by Graeme.

Inheritance tax

Transfers between UK domiciled spouses are exempt transfers for inheritance tax (IHT) purposes.

(ii)   **Gift to Barry**

Capital gains tax

The gift to Barry will constitute a chargeable disposal between connected persons for CGT purposes. The deemed disposal proceeds will be based on the current market value of the shares gifted.

	£
Deemed disposal proceeds (market value)	
(18,000 × 384p)	69,120
Less: Cost (18/30 × £21,500)	(12,900)
Unindexed gain	56,220
Indexation allowance (29,561 − 21,500) × 18,000/30,000	(4,837)
Indexed gain	51,383

As business assets held for more than two years, the gain is 25% chargeable.

Chargeable gain (£51,383 × 25%)	£12,846

However, as Thistle Dubh Limited is an unquoted trading company, Graeme can defer the indexed gain (before taper relief) of £51,383 by claiming gift relief.

The effect is that Graeme will pay no capital gains tax, but Barry's base cost will be reduced by the indexed gain deferred. However, both Graeme and Barry need to be aware that the business asset rate of taper relief he has accumulated will be lost.

Barry will have to hold the shares for a period of two years before the maximum rate of business asset taper will apply. If the gift is made in 2007/08 the relief requires a jointly written claim with Barry, and this needs to be made by 31 January 2014.

Inheritance tax

For IHT purposes, the 'T' shares gifted are a PET. The value of the PET is the market value of the shares of £69,120. However the gift is shares in an unquoted trading company, and so 100% business property relief (BRP) will apply.

Provided Barry lives for seven years, no IHT is payable. Even if Graeme dies within seven years, provided Barry continues to hold the shares from the date of gift until the date of Graeme's death 100% BPR relief will be available.

If Barry does not retain the shares, the PET will become chargeable if Graeme dies within seven years. If not already used in respect of previous gifts in the 2007/08 tax year, an annual exemption (£3,000) will be available, which will reduce the value of the PET. In addition, any unused exemption from the previous year (up to £3,000) can also be used.

The PET will remain fully chargeable on Graeme's death until a period of three years from the date of gift. Thereafter, taper relief will reduce the amount chargeable to IHT until the gift falls out of Graeme's estate entirely on the seventh anniversary of the gift.

(c) **Disposal of country cottage and purchase of foreign villa**

Disposal of the country cottage

Capital gains tax implications

The disposal of the UK property will give rise to a CGT charge.

Indexation will be available from the date of purchase up to 5 April 1998. Taper relief will be available thereafter, at the non-business rates for the period when the property was used by Graeme and Catherine, and at business rates when it was rented out as a furnished holiday let.

The period from 6 April 1998 to the date of disposal will therefore have to be time apportioned to arrive at the elements of capital gain subject to business and non-business taper relief rates.

CGT rollover relief is potentially available in respect of the proportion of the gain attributable to business use, as a furnished holiday let. However, this is dependent on the acquisition of another qualifying asset within the period of one year before and three years after the disposal of the cottage. The acquisition of the overseas villa does not qualify for this purpose as it is not a UK property and it is not furnished holiday accommodation.

Acquisition of new property

Income tax

Both Graeme and Catherine are UK resident, ordinarily resident and domiciled so will be taxed on income arising from their worldwide assets. Even if they live abroad for a significant part of the year following their retirement, they are likely to continue to be classed as UK resident.

To establish themselves as non UK resident, it will be necessary to be absent from the UK for a period which includes a complete tax year or to leave the UK to take up permanent residence abroad and to provide clear evidence to this effect, such as selling their UK home.

Any rental income arising abroad will therefore be taxed in the UK on both individuals. Any tax suffered abroad will be available for offset against the UK tax liability, but relief will be restricted to the lower of the UK tax payable and the tax suffered abroad.

The new property will not qualify for treatment as a furnished holiday letting as the conditions state that the property must be situated in the UK. Thus, the income will not qualify as earnings for personal pension relief purposes, nor will any losses be treated as available for offset against other income as if they were trading losses.

Capital gains tax

As Graeme and Catherine are resident and ordinarily resident in the UK, they will be subject to capital gains tax on disposals of assets situated anywhere in the world.

As the new villa does not qualify as a furnished holiday letting, it does not qualify as a business asset for taper relief purposes, even if it is let out 100% of the time. Thus, business asset taper relief will not be available and on disposal, taper relief will be at the non-business rates only.

			Marks
	ACCA marking scheme		
(a)	Indexation to March 1992		0.5
	Rights issue: shares, cost		0.5
	Indexation to April 1998		0.5
	Reorganisation: correct basis of apportionment		1.0
		number/value of 'T' shares	0.5
		'T' share costs	0.5
		number/value of 'D' shares	0.5
		'D' share costs	0.5
	'T' shares:	disposal cost	0.5
		indexation	0.5
	Taper relief:	business asset, rate	1.0
	'D' shares:	disposal cost	0.5
		indexation restricted	1.0
		Max	7.0
(b)	Transfers oto Catherine: no gain/no loss disposal		0.5
		spouse inherits tax history	0.5
		exempt from IHT	0.5
	Transfers to Barry:	connected persons	0.5
		proceeds (MV)	0.5
		cost	0.5
		indexation allowance	0.5
		taper relief	0.5
		availability of gift relief	0.5
		unquoted trading company	0.5
	Effect of deferring gain:	Barry's base cost reduced	0.5
		Graeme's loss of taper relief	0.5
		time to regain full taper	0.5
		jointly written claim	0.5
		time limit for claim	0.5
	Inheritance tax:	100% business property relief	0.5
		if held by Barry from gift until Graeme's death	0.5
		PET for IHT purposes	0.5
		annual exemption up to × 2	0.5
		Taper relief 3–7 years	0.5
	Max		9.0
(c)	Sale of existing property		
	Capital gains: indexation available to April 1998		0.5
		taper relief: non-business asset	0.5
		taper relief: business asset while FHL	0.5
		apportionment of gain on time basis	0.5
		qualifying asset for rollover relief	0.5
		proportion of gain while FHL	0.5
		need to acquire further qualifying	0.5

	asset within qualifying period		
	overseas villa not a qualifying asset	0.5	
Acquisition of overseas property			
Residence:	UK residents therefore taxed on worldwide income	0.5	
	significant periods of absence will not per se change residence status	0.5	
	criteria for becoming non-resident (2 × 0.5)	1.0	
Income tax:	Overseas income taxable	0.5	
	DTR: availability	0.5	
	lower of UK/foreign tax	0.5	
	villa: does not qualify as FHL	0.5	
	reason/situated outside UK	0.5	
	not relevant income for pension purposes	0.5	
	trading loss offset facility not available	0.5	
Capital gains: does not qualify as a business asset		0.5	
	Max	9.0	
Total		25.0	

RESIDENCE ISSUES

28 DANIELLA DRAKE

(a) **Status of Daniella**

An individual is normally treated as resident in the UK during the tax year if they are present in the UK for 183 days or more. However, when an individual works abroad under a full-time contract which spans a complete tax year, they are treated as if not resident and not ordinarily resident in the UK from the date of departure to the date of return.

As Daniella is leaving the UK to work full-time abroad under a contract of employment for 18 months and the period overseas includes the complete tax year (2007/08), she will be treated as not resident or ordinarily resident in the UK from the date of departure (1 December 2006) to the date of return (31 May 2008).

However Daniella will remain resident in the UK if return visits to the UK are 91 days or more per tax year on average.

(b) (i) **Daniella's income tax liability for 2006/07**

Daniella will be liable to UK income tax on her worldwide income up to the date of leaving the UK (i.e. 1 December 2006). However she will only be liable in respect of income arising in the UK during her period of non residence.

Notes

(i) Employers contributions into an employees pension scheme, premiums for permanent health insurance and personal insurance are exempt benefits.

(ii) ISA income is exempt from income tax.

(iii) Daniella received £4,500 foreign dividends before she left the UK and £2,340 after she had left. She will only be assessed on £4,500 received when she was resident in the UK, her overseas income after the date of departure is exempt.

The income tax liability will therefore be calculated as follows:

	Other income £	Dividend income £	Total £
Employment income			
– salary (£34,500 × 8/12)	23,000		
– car benefit (W)	3,680		
– fuel benefit (W)	2,208		
	28,888		28,888
Property business income			
(£1,175 × 4 months)	4,700		4,700
Overseas dividends (Note (iii))			
(£4,500 × 100/90)		5,000	5,000
STI	33,588	5,000	38,588
Less Personal allowance	(5,035)		(5,035)
Taxable income	28,553	5,000	33,553

Income tax:

£			
2,150 × 10%	(other income)		215
26,403 × 22%	(other income)		5,809
28,553			
4,747 × 10%	(dividends)		475
33,300			
253 × 32½%	(dividends)		82
33,553			
			6,581

Less Double tax relief lower of		
(i) foreign tax suffered	£500	(500)
(ii) UK tax on foreign income (475 + 82)	£557	
Income tax liability		6,081

Working: **Car and fuel benefit**

CO_2 emissions 190 g/km, available for 8 months

Appropriate % = 15% + (180 – 140) × $^1/_5$ = 23%

Car benefit = 24,000 × 23% × $^8/_{12}$ = £3,680

Fuel benefit = 14,400 × 23% × $^8/_{12}$ = £2,208

(ii) **Daniella's capital gains tax liability for 2006/07**

The shares sold on 3 April 2007 are chargeable to CGT (in the year of departure) because they were acquired before Daniella left the UK, and she is leaving for a period of less than five complete tax years.

Daniella has owned the assets for taper relief purposes since 5 April 1998 but they only qualify for the business rate from 6 April 2000 so the gain must be apportioned and the appropriate taper relief percentage applied to each part of the gain.

Actual period of ownership since April 1998	108 months
Non-business asset (6.4.98 to 5.4.00)	24 months
Qualifying business asset	84 months

The business portion has 8 complete years of ownership.

The non-business portion has 9 complete qualifying years (including the bonus year) as the shares where held on 17 March 1998.

The gain is thus calculated as follows:

	£
Proceeds	54,000
Cost (46,400 × 5,000/10,000)	(23,200)
Gain before taper relief	30,800

The non-business portion is 65% chargeable.

The business portion is 25% chargeable.

		£
Non-business gain:	(£30,800 × 24/108 × 65%)	4,449
Business gain:	(£30,800 × 84/108 × 25%)	5,989
Total chargeable gains		10,438
Less annual exemption		(8,800)
Taxable gain		1,638
CGT @ 40%		655

(iii) **Effect of delaying the sale of shares**

Unless made in the year of departure, gains made by an individual who has left the UK for a period of temporary non residence are not charged until the year that individual resumes residence in the UK.

If Daniella had delayed the disposal of the Bourbon Inc. shares until 6 April 2007, then the gain would not have been assessed until 2008/09.

In addition a further year's taper relief of 5% would have been available on the non-business portion of the gain. (Note that the business portion already qualifies for full taper relief).

(c) (i) **Employer pension contributions**

As Daniella will be non resident from 1 December 2006 she will no longer be in receipt of relevant earnings which give rise to personal pension contribution relief. However, her employer or any third party can continue to make contributions into her scheme subject to the maximum annual allowance of £215,000 for 2006/07.

(ii) **Deduction of employee costs for corporation tax**

As Daniella is no longer working for Drew Jenner Whisky, the payment of her salary and the insurance premiums paid in respect of her will no longer be allowable deductions for corporation tax purposes as they are not wholly and exclusively laid out for the purposes of the trade.

(iii)   **ISA investments**

As Daniella will no longer be UK resident she will not be permitted to make any further contributions to her ISA contracts, although her existing investments may be retained.

29   BUXUS

Notes to respond to letter from Buxus

(a)   **Basis of assessment to UK income tax in 2006/07**

Buxus has left the UK to work full time under a contract of employment for a period that includes a complete tax year. He should not therefore be regarded as UK resident nor UK ordinarily resident for the period of his overseas contract. This is providing his return visits to the UK do not exceed 90 days per tax year on average.

He will therefore only be liable to UK income tax on his worldwide income up to his departure from the UK on 31 October 2006. Between 1 November 2006 and 5 April 2007 he should only be liable on income arising in the UK.

His salary from Abies Inc will therefore not be assessable in the 2006/07 tax year and no double tax relief in respect of the Abelian taxes deducted will therefore be available.

The rental income received and the dividend received on 28 February 2007 will, however, be deemed to arise in the UK and will therefore be liable to UK income tax.

Income tax computation – 2006/07

	£
Employment income	14,625
Property business income (W)	3,375
Dividends	22,000
Statutory total income	40,000
Less: Personal allowance	(5,035)
Taxable income	34,965

Analysis of income:
Dividends £22,000, other income £12,965

Income tax:

£	
2,150 × 10% (other income)	215
10,815 × 22% (other income)	2,379
12,965	
20,335 × 10% (dividends)	2,034
33,300	
1,665 × 32.5% (dividends)	541
34,965	
Income tax liability	5,169
Less: Dividend tax credits	(2,200)
PAYE	(2,134)
Income tax payable	835

Workings: **Property business income**

Buxus gifted a 75% interest in the property to his son on 1 March 2007

His assessable rental income is therefore calculated as:

		£
6 April 2006 to 28 February 2007	(3,600 × 11/12)	3,300
1 March 2007 to 6 April 2007	(3,600 × 1/12 × 25%)	75
Property business income		3,375

(b) **Treatment of travelling expenses**

Unless Buxus could claim under general principles that the travelling expenses are wholly, exclusively and necessarily incurred in the performance of his overseas duties (which is unlikely) he will only be able to claim a deduction for the travelling expenses from the UK to Abies Inc under the overseas travelling expenses rules. However, to do so Buxus would need to be considered resident and ordinarily resident in the UK.

As Buxus he meets the conditions for qualifying as non resident and not ordinarily resident this is unlikely to be the case. As a consequence, if the reimbursements are made by Buxus Limited they are likely to be treated as taxable UK source of income. In addition because the expenses met by Buxus Limited relate to another company it is unlikely that they will be deductible against trading profits in that company's corporation tax computations.

If, however, the reimbursement is made by Abies Inc it is likely that HMRC will regard this as not being a UK source of income. As Buxus is regarded as non resident and not ordinarily resident in the UK he will therefore not be liable to UK income tax on the reimbursed expenses.

(c) **Disposal of interest in property to son on 1 March 2007**

The gift of the 75% interest in the property on 1 March 2007 is between connected parties and will therefore be valued at market value at the date of the gift.

The disposal will be treated under the CGT part disposal rules using the A/(A+B) formula to allocate base costs (which in this particular case simply amounts to 75%).

As the enhancement expenditure was incurred after April 1998, only the original acquisition costs will qualify for indexation allowance (for the period October 1996 to April 1998).

It should be noted that despite Buxus being non UK resident at the time the gift is made, disposals made in the tax year of departure from the UK remain assessable under the 'temporary non resident' rules.

The CGT position for Buxus for 2006/07 is therefore as follows:

			£
Deemed proceeds		(£250,000 × 75%)	187,500
Less:	Cost	$£77,500 \times \dfrac{187,500}{(187,500 + 62,500)}$	(58,125)
	Enhancement	(£38,000 × 75%)	(28,500)
Unindexed gain			100,875
Less:	Indexation allowance		
	£58,125 × 0.057 ((162.6 − 153.8)/153.8)		(3,313)
Indexed Gain			97,562

As Buxus Limited is Buxus's personal company (he owns greater than 5% of the ordinary shares), the proportion of the property used in the trade of Buxus Limited will qualify as a business asset for the purposes of gift relief. A joint claim may therefore be made between Buxus and Acer to defer 60% of the indexed gain.

Proportion of gain qualifying for gift relief

	£
£97,562 × 60%	58,537
Less: Gift relief	(58,537)
Chargeable gain	Nil

Proportion not qualifying for gift relief

	£
Indexed gain (£97,562 × 40%)	39,025
Less: Taper relief (working)	(29,269)
Chargeable gain (25%)	9,756
Less: Annual exemption	(8,800)
Taxable gain	956

As Buxus is a higher rate taxpayer for 2006/07 he will be required to pay capital gains tax of £382 (956 × 40%).

Deferral of disposal until after 5 April 2007

If Buxus had deferred this disposal until after 5 April 2007 the gain arising on the disposal would not have become chargeable until Buxus resumed residency in the UK, providing him with a cash flow advantage.

If, however, Buxus was not UK resident for at least some part of four of the seven tax years preceding 2006/07 (i.e. the tax year of departure) or he will be non UK resident for at least five complete tax years (perhaps following an extension to his overseas employment contract) this chargeable gain will not be caught by the temporary non-residence rules and will therefore escape UK taxation.

Working – Taper relief

Taper relief of £29,269 (39,025 × 75%) is available because the property has been held for over two complete years after 5 April 1998.

Tutorial note: the examiner's answer overlooks the fact that only part of the gain probably qualifies for the business rate of taper relief.

ACCA marking scheme		
		Marks
Letter presentation	Format	0.5
	Structure	0.5
	Communication effectiveness	1.0
(a)	Rules – full time/straddles tax year	1.0
	Conclusion – not UK resident or ordinarily resident	1.0
	Basis for UK computation	
	Splitting tax year	1.0
	Earned income	1.0
	Dividend income	1.0
	Income tax computation	
	Taxable income	1.5
	Tax calculation	2.5
	Max	7.0

(b)	Rules – general employment income expenses rule			0.5
	Overseas travelling expenses rule	–	need to be UK resident	1.0
	Payment by Buxus Limited	–	position for Buxus	1.0
		–	position for Buxus Ltd	0.5
	Payment by Abies Inc			1.0
			Max	3.0
(c)	Market value rule			1.0
	Part disposal rule			1.0
	Calculation of indexed gain			2.0
	Gift relief			1.0
	Taper relief			1.0
	Annual exemption			0.5
	Tax calculation			0.5
	Deferral until 6/4/07			
	– temporary residence rules			1.5
			Max	8.0
Total				20.0

ADMINISTRATION

30   BARRY BLOCK

(a)   **Tax liability for 2006/07**

Income tax payable – 2006/07

	£
Trading income	28,500
Property income (working)	4,100
Building society interest (360 × 100/80)	450
Dividends (9,540 × 100/90)	10,600
STI	43,650
Personal allowance	(5,035)
Taxable income	38,615

Analysis of income:
Dividends £10,600, Savings £450, Other income £27,565

Income tax

£	
2,150 × 10% (other income)	215
25,415 × 22% (other income)	5,591
27,565	
450 × 20% (savings)	90
5,285 × 10% (dividends)	529
33,300	
5,315 × 32.5% (dividends)	1,727
33,615	
Income tax liability	8,152
Tax suffered at source:	
Dividends (10,600 × 10%)	(1,060)
Building society interest (450 × 20%)	(90)
Income tax payable	7,002

Tenancy agreement

Postponing the tenancy agreement until 6 April 2007 will mean that the £4,100 assessment on the lease premium is assessed in 2007/08 rather than 2006/07.

Assuming that the bonus to the daughter has been paid, the tax saving is £1,465 (W).

In addition, the tax liability will be due on 31 January 2009 rather than on 31 January 2008. There will also be a reduction in the payments on account for 2007/08.

Sale of antique painting

Postponing the disposal of the painting until 6 April 2007 will result in taper relief being available based on a holding period of ten complete years (including a 'bonus year' as the painting was acquired before 17 March 1998).

This will reduce the taxable gain to £422 (W2) and save capital gains tax of £392 (W2) since chargeable gains are taxed at the rate applicable to savings income.

In addition, the CGT liability will be due on 31 January 2009 rather than on 31 January 2008.

Workings

(1) **Tax saving on tenancy agreement**

	£
Income re lease premium	4,100
Income assessed at effective rate of 44½% after daughter's bonus paid	
(5,315 – 2,815)	(2,500)
Income assessed at effective rate of 22%	1,600

Tax saving by reducing assessable income by a further £4,100:

£			£
2,500	× 44.5%		1,113
1,600	× 22%		352
4,100			1,465

(2) **Chargeable gain in 2007/08**

	£
Chargeable gain (18,500 – 3,130) × 60%	9,222
Annual exemption	(8,800)
Taxable gain	422
Capital gains tax at 20% (Note)	84

Note: With the other actions of paying a bonus and delaying the lease agreement, Barry will be a basic rate tax payer. His gains will therefore be taxed at 20%, not 40%.

	£
Tax saving (£476 - £84)	£392

Key answer tips

Claims to reduce payments on account require some care as they concern estimating the total tax liability and not just tax on individual sources. For example, if substantial rental income ceases due to the sale of the letting property one year but other income such as trading income then increases so that the overall tax liability does not fall, there are no grounds for reducing the payment on account.

If a trader has a year end falling early in the tax year and other sources of income are fairly predictable it might be possible to estimate the tax liability by or shortly after the payment on account is due. For example, with a 30 June 2006 year end the first payment on account falls on 31 January 2007. If a client indicates an overall decline in his income the point should be considered in good time.

31   CECILE GRAND

(a)   (i)   **Self assessment payments for 2006/07**

Cecile's payments on account will be based on her income tax and Class 4 NIC liability for 2005/06.

2005/06 tax liabilities

	£
Trading income	34,900
Property business income	800
Dividends (4,860 × 100/90)	5,400
STI	41,100
Personal allowance	(5,035)
Taxable income	36,065

Analysis of income:
Dividends £5,400, Other income £30,665

Income tax:

£	
2,150 at 10% (other income)	215
28,515 at 22% (other income)	6,273
2,635 at 10% (dividends)	264
33,300	
2,765 at 32½% (dividends)	899
36,065	

Income tax liability	7,651
Tax suffered at source – dividends (5,400 at 10%)	(540)
Income tax payable	7,111

Class 4 NIC
(33,540 – 5,035) × 8% + (34,900 – 33,540) × 1% = **2,294**

Total income tax and Class 4 NICs	9,405

Payment on account due 31.1.07 – 50% × 9,405	4,703
Payment on account due 31.7.07 – 50% × 9,405	4,702

2006/07 tax liabilities

Cecile's actual tax liability for 2006/07 is as follows:

	£
Trading income	21,750
Dividends (4,320 × 100/90)	4,800
STI	26,550
Personal allowance	(5,035)
Taxable income	21,515

Analysis of income;
Dividends of £4,800, other income £16,715

Income tax:

	£
£	
2,150 × 10%	215
14,565 × 22%	3,204
16,715	
4,800 × 10%	480
21,515	
Income tax liability	3,899
Tax suffered at source – dividends (4,800 at 10%)	(480)
Income tax payable	3,419
Class 4 NIC	
(21,750 - 5,035) × 8%	1,337
Total income tax and Class 4 NICs	4,756

	£	
Chargeable gain	20,850	
Annual exemption	(8,800)	
Taxable gain	12,050	
Capital gains tax:		
£		
11,785 (33,300 – 21,515) × 20%	2,357	
265 (12,050 – 11,785) × 40%	106	
12,050		2,463
Total tax liabilities payable under self assessment		7,219
Paid on account		(9,405)
Balancing refund due 31.1.08		(2,186)

(ii) **Maximum claim to reduce payments on account**

Cecile can ignore the CGT liability when claiming to reduce her payments on account.

She should therefore claim to reduce her payments on account by £4,649 (9,405 – 4,756) so that £2,378 (4,756 ÷ 2) will be due on 31 January 2007, £2,378 will be due on 31 July 2007, and the CGT liability of £2,463 will be due on 31 January 2008.

Key answer tips

Payments on account of CGT are never required.

(b) (i) **Tax implications if actual income exceeds estimated figures**

If Cecile's payments on account are too low, then she will be charged interest. This will run from the due dates of 31 January 2007 and 31 July 2007, up to the date of payment, which will presumably be 31 January 2008.

A penalty will be charged if a claim to reduce payments on account is made fraudulently or negligently.

(ii) **HMRC's power of enquiry**

HMRC have the right to enquire into any tax return, provided they give written notice.

Enquiries may be made by reference to information in the tax return, but they may also be made on a random basis.

The time limit for giving notice of an enquiry for 2006/07 tax returns is 31 January 2009. An enquiry after that date can normally only be made where the taxpayer has been fraudulent or negligent.

(iii) **Tax implications of understating income**

Following the completion of an enquiry, the self-assessment would normally be amended by HMRC.

The additional tax liability will be due 30 days from the date of the notice of amendment. Interest will be charged on the additional tax liability from 31 January 2008 (the due date for the tax return) up to the date of payment.

No surcharge will be due provided that the additional tax liability is paid within 28 days of the due date.

A penalty will only be charged where a tax return is filed incorrectly due to fraud or negligence.

(c) (i) **Conditions for a valid change of accounting date**

For Cecile's change of accounting date to be valid:

1   The change must be notified to HMRC by 31 January 2009.

2   There must not have been a change of accounting date within the previous five tax years prior to 2007/08. This condition will not apply if the present change is to be made for genuine commercial reasons.

3   The first accounts to the new accounting date must not exceed 18 months in length.

(ii) **Tax implications of a change in accounting date**

For 2007/08 Cecile will be assessed on trading profits for the 12 months ended 30 September 2007 of £28,875, calculated as follows:

	£
Year ended 31.3.07 (21,750 × 6/12)	10,875
Period ended 30.9.07	18,000
2007/08 trading income assessment	28,875

The profits of £10,875 for the period 1 October 2006 to 31 March 2007 are overlap profits, having already been assessed in 2006/07, and these will normally be relieved when Cecile ceases trading.

(iii) **Advantages and disadvantages of the change in accounting date**

The main advantage of Cecile changing her accounting date from 31 March to 30 September is that she should have actual trading profits available before the first payment on account is due on 31 January in the tax year.

Also, the time between earning profits and paying the related tax liability will be six months later.

The disadvantages are that the final assessment upon cessation may be for a longer period with a 30 September year end, and the fact that there is a double assessment of profits upon the actual change of accounting date.

32 MIN CHEW

(a) **Tax liabilities for 2006/07**

Income tax payable

	£
Trading profit	72,800
Capital allowances (working)	(24,395)
	48,405
STI	48,405
Personal allowance	(5,035)
Taxable income	43,370

Income tax

£	
2,150 × 10%	215
31,150 × 22%	6,853
10,070 × 40%	4,028
43,370	
Income tax liability	11,096

National insurance contributions payable

Class 4 NIC	
(33,540 − 5,035) × 8%	2,280
(48,405 − 33,540) × 1%	149
	2,429

Payment due on 31 January 2008

Total income tax and Class 4 NICs (11,096 + 2,429)	13,525
Paid on account (3,870 + 860)	(4,730)
Balancing payment due for 2006/07	8,795
Payment on account due for 2007/08 (13,525× 50%)	6,763
Due 31 January 2008	15,558

Working – **Capital allowances**

	£	Pool £	Expensive car £	Short life asset £	Allowances £
WDV b/f		26,400	16,400	2,600	
Disposals			(18,300)	Nil	
Balancing charge			(1,900) × 70%		(1,330)
Balancing allowance				2,600	2,600
Additions (no FYAs)		9,800	25,700		
		36,200			
WDA – 25%		(9,050)			9,050
WDA – restricted			(3,000) × 70%		2,100
		27,150			
Additions (with FYA)					
Equipment	16,750				
Computer	7,200				
	23,950				
FYA (50%) (Note)	(11,975)	11,975			11,975
WDV c/f		39,125	22,700		
Total allowances					24,395

Note It is reasonable to assume that Min's is a small business which qualifies for FYAs's at 50% as all purchases are between 6 April 2006 and 5 April 2007.

(b)   **Claim to reduce payments on account**

Min's liability to income tax and Class 4 NIC for 2007/08 is as follows:

	£	£
Adjusted trading profit		28,000
Capital allowances (W)		3,985
Trading income		31,985
Building society interest (2,800 × 100/80)		3,500
Dividends (4,500 × 100/90)		5,000
STI		40,485
Personal allowance		(5,035)
Taxable income		35,450

Analysis of income:
Dividends £5,000, Savings £3,500, Other income £26,950

Income tax

	£
£	
2,150 × 10%	215
24,800 × 22%	5,456
26,950	
3,500 × 20%	700
2,850 × 10%	285
33,300	
2,150 × 32.5%	699
35,450	
Income tax liability	7,355
Tax suffered at source:	
Dividends (5,000 at 10%)	(500)
Building society interest (3,500 at 20%)	(700)
Income tax payable	6,155
Class 4 NIC	
(31,985 − 5,035) at 8%	2,156
Total income tax and Class 4 NICs	8,311

Min can ignore the CGT liability for 2007/08 when claiming to reduce his payments on account.

He should therefore claim to reduce his payments on account by £5,214 (13,525 − 8,311) so that £4,156 (8,311 ÷ 2) will be due on 31 January 2008 and £4,155 will be due on 31 July 2008.

Capital gains tax liability – 2007/08

	£
Goodwill (440,000 – Nil cost)	440,000
Freehold property (265,000 − 110,000)	155,000
Total indexed gains	595,000

As business assets held for more than two years, the gains are 25% chargeable.

	£
Chargeable gains (595,000 × 25%)	148,750
Annual exemption	(8,800)
Taxable gains	139,950
Capital gains tax (139,950 × 40%)	55,980

Working: **Capital allowances**

		Pool £	Expensive car £	Allowances £
WDV b/f		39,125	22,700	
Disposal	– fixtures + fittings	(30,000)		
	– motor cars	(8,000)	(20,000)	
	– computer equipment	(7000)		
		(5,875)	2,700	
Balancing charge		5,875		(5,875)
Balancing allowance			(2,700) × 70%	1,890
Net balancing charge				(3,985)

Key answer tips

A claim to reduce payments on account for 2007/08 can be made at any time before 31 January 2009.

INHERITANCE TAX

33 DOROTHY LAKE

(a) **Gift made to Alice on 30 June 2007**

Inheritance tax implications

Gift on 30 June – lifetime tax

The gift on 30 June 2007 will be a PET as follows:

	£
Shares in Windermere Ltd	
Value of shares held before the transfer	
(based on a 50% holding) 100,000 at £4.50	450,000
Value of shares held after the transfer	
(based on a 37.5% holding) 50,000 at £3.55	(177,500)
Diminution in value of Dorothy's estate	272,500
Business property relief	
272,500 × 100% × 88% (Note)	(239,800)
	32,700
Antique painting	8,500
Holiday cottage	165,000
	206,200
Annual exemptions 2007/08	(3,000)
2006/07	(3,000)
Potentially exempt transfer	200,200

Note: As Windermere Ltd owns investments (i.e. excepted assets), BPR is only available on the 88% (100% – 12%) of the value of the shares.

No IHT liability will arise on the PET at the time of the gift.

As a result of Dorothy's death within seven years, the PET will become chargeable.

The following must then be taken into account:

(i) Business property relief will not be available in respect of the shares in Windermere Ltd if Alice disposes of the holding before 31 December 2011.

Alice should therefore consider retaining the shares until 31 December 2011, since there is no more risk in her retaining the shares than if they remain part of Dorothy's estate until that date.

(ii) At the date of Dorothy's death, the value of the holiday cottage will have fallen to £105,000, and Alice can claim 'fall in value relief' to have the IHT liability calculated on the lower value of £105,000.

IHT will be due on the PET on Dorothy's death as follows:

	£
PET (as originally calculated)	200,200
BPR no longer available	239,800
	440,000
Less Relief for fall in value (165,000 – 105,000)	(60,000)
Revised PET value	380,000
IHT liability on death	
(380,000 – 285,000) × 40%	38,000
Less Taper relief (4 – 5 years) (40%)	(15,200)
IHT payable on death	22,800

The IHT liability will be payable by Alice on 30 June 2012.

Payment by instalments

It will be possible to pay IHT of £6,300 (W1) in respect of the holiday cottage in ten equal instalments commencing on 30 June 2012.

The IHT payable by instalments could be increased if the gift of the holiday cottage was made subsequent to the other gifts, since the nil rate band of £285,000 would be allocated to the earlier gifts.

Note that it will not be possible to pay the IHT in respect of the shares in Windermere Ltd by instalments if they are immediately sold by Alice (as is suggested in the question).

Estate on death

The IHT liability due on Dorothy's estate will be as follows:

	£
Shares in Windermere Ltd (based on a 37.5% holding)	
50,000 at £4.97 (3.55 plus 40%)	248,500
Business property relief	
248,500 × 100% × 88%	(218,680)
	29,820
Other assets	350,000
Chargeable estate	379,820

There is no nil rate band remaining as it has been used against the PET in June 2007 (see key answers tips).

IHT liability on the estate (379,820 at 40%)	151,928

The IHT liability will be payable by the executors of Dorothy's estate on the earlier of 30 June 2012 or the delivery of their account.

Capital gains tax implications

Shares in Windermere Ltd

	£
Deemed consideration (based on a 12.5% holding)	
50,000 at £2.50	125,000
Less Cost (W2)	(36,000)
Unindexed gain	89,000
Indexation allowance (56,230 – 36,000) (W2)	(20,230)
Indexed gain	68,770

Tutorial note: As the shares form part of the FA85 pool, the indexation allowance is not rounded to three decimal places – see working.

The indexed gain of £68,770 in respect of the shares in Windermere Ltd can be held over if Dorothy and Alice make a joint election. However, a claim does not appear to be beneficial since Alice is to sell the shares soon after receiving them (thus crystallising the gain), and Dorothy's accrued 75% taper relief and capital loss (see below) would then be wasted.

As Windermere Ltd is an unquoted trading company the shares are business assets held for more than two years. The gain is therefore 25% chargeable. However taper relief is deducted after capital losses are considered (see below).

Antique painting	£
Deemed consideration	8,500
Cost	(1,400)
Unindexed gain	7,100
Indexation $1,400 \times \dfrac{162.6 - 106.6}{106.6} (= 0.525)$	(735)
Indexed gain	6,365

However the indexed gain can not exceed:
$(8,500 - 6,000) \times 5/3 =$ ... 4,167

As a non-business asset held for nine qualifying years (including the bonus year), the gain is 65% chargeable.

Holiday cottage	
Deemed consideration	165,000
Cost	(188,000)
Allowable capital loss	(23,000)

The capital loss will be set against the £4,167 gain on the painting first which is 65% chargeable and then against the £68,770 gain on the shares which is 25% chargeable.

Dorothy's CGT liability will therefore be:

	Indexed gain £	Allowable loss £	Net gains £	Chargeable %	Chargeable gains £
Shares	68,770	(18,833)	49,937	25%	12,484
Painting	4,167	(4,167)	Nil	65%	Nil
		(23,000)			

Total chargeable gains	12,484
Annual exemption	(8,800)
Taxable gains	3,684
CGT @ 40%	1,474

Dorothy would be advised to postpone the gift of the painting until 2008/09 so as to partly utilise that year's annual exemption and pay no tax on that gain. An extra £4,167 loss can then be deducted from the gain on the shares and reduce the CGT payable for 2007/08.

Workings

(W1) **Payment by instalments on PET**

	£
Value of holiday cottage at death	105,000
Revised value of PET @ death	380,000

Portion of IHT due on PET at death relating to the cottage

$$= \frac{105,000}{380,000} \times 22,800 = £6,300$$

(W2) **FA 1985 Pool – Coniston Ltd and Windermere Ltd shares**

	No. of shares	Cost £	Indexed cost £
March 1988 purchase	50,000	96,000	96,000
Indexation to Oct 1997 $\frac{159.5-104.1}{104.1} \times 96,000$			51,089
Balanced before takeover	50,000	96,000	147,089

Consideration received on takeover:

	£
100,000 £1 ord. in Windermere Ltd (100,000 × £1.20)	120,000
Cash (50,000 × 80p)	40,000
	160,000

Allocation of cost and indexed cost to new Windermere shares:

	No. of shares	Cost £	Indexed cost £
At takeover – Oct 1997	10,000		
$96,000 \times \dfrac{120,000}{160,000}$		72,000	
$147,089 \times \dfrac{120,000}{160,000}$			110,317
Index to April 1998 $\dfrac{162.6-159.5}{159.5} \times 110,317$			2,144
	100,000	72,000	112,461
Gift – June 2007	(50,000)	(36,000)	(56,230)
	50,000	36,000	56,231

(b) **Gift not made to Alice on 30 June 2007**

Inheritance tax implications

An IHT liability will arise in respect of Dorothy's estate, as follows:

	£
Shares in Windermere Ltd (based on a 50% holding)	
100,000 at £6.30 (4.50 plus 40%)	630,000
Business property relief	
$630,000 \times 100\% \times 88\%$	(554,400)
	75,600
Antique painting	8,500
Other assets	350,000
Holiday cottage	105,000
Chargeable estate	539,100
IHT liability on death	
$(539,100 - 285,000) \times 40\%$	101,640

Rate of IHT on estate = 101,640/539,100 = 18.854%.

The IHT liability will be payable by the executors on the earlier of 30 June 2012 or the delivery of account.

Payment by instalments

It will be possible to pay the IHT of £19,797 (105,000 × 18.854%) in respect of the holiday cottage in 10 equal instalments commencing on 30 June 2012.

As mentioned before, it will not be possible to pay the IHT in respect of the shares in Windermere Ltd by instalments if they are immediately sold by Alice.

Capital gains tax implications

No CGT liability arises in respect of transfers on death, and Alice will take over the assets with a base cost based on their market values at 31 December 2011.

Conclusion

The total tax liability if the gift of assets is made to Alice on 30 June 2007 is £176,202 (22,800 + 151,928 + 1,474), compared to a total tax liability of £101,640 if the gift of assets is not made and the assets remain in the estate.

Although it therefore appears to be beneficial for Dorothy to not make the gift to Alice, the figure of £176,202 would be substantially reduced if the tax planning advice was followed (i.e. Alice retain the shares until Dorothy's death and postpones the gift of the painting).

In addition there is always the possibility that Dorothy may live beyond 31 December 2011.

Key answer tips

The adding back of BPR on the PET where the shares gifted are no longer held by the donee at death is accumulated for the purpose of calculating IHT on subsequent transfers.

The fall in value of the lifetime gift can only reduce the IHT calculation on that gift. The chargeable value carried forward for calculating IHT on subsequent transfers is not reduced by the fall in value.

Therefore the value of the PET carried forward is £440,000 (including BPR no longer available but before fall in value relief).

---

34   JANE MACBETH

(a)   **IHT payable as a result of Jane's death**

Lifetime transfers of value – Lifetime IHT payable

		Net gift	IHT	Gross gift
	£	£	£	£
28 November 1998: CLT				
Chargeable transfers within previous 7 years		–	–	–
Value transferred	92,000			
Annual exemptions 1998/99	(3,000)			
1997/98	(3,000)			
		86,000	nil	86,000
Chargeable transfer		86,000	nil	86,000

The transfer is covered by the nil rate band of £285,000 and therefore no IHT is payable at the time of the gift.

	£
15 April 2002: PET	
Value transferred	155,000
Business property relief: (Note (i))	
155,000 × 100% × 80%	(124,000)
	31,000
Marriage exemption	(5,000)
Annual exemptions 2002/03	(3,000)
2001/02	(3,000)
Potentially exempt transfer	20,000

No lifetime IHT due on PETs

	Net gift	IHT	Gross gift
	£	£	£
10 March 2003: CLT			
Chargeable transfers within previous			
7 years (Note (ii))	86,000	–	86,000
Value transferred (Note (iii))	268,000	17,250 (below)	285,250
	354,000	17,250	371,250

Lifetime IHT liability

285,000 - 86,000 = 199,000 at nil%	Nil
268,000 - 199,000 = 69,000 × 20/80 (Note (iv))	17,250
	17,250

Notes:

(i) As Shakespeare Ltd owns quoted shares (i.e. excepted assets), BPR is only available on 80% (100% - 20%) of the value of the shares.

(ii) Ignore the PET in calculating the gross cumulative transfers brought forward in lifetime calculations as PETs are not chargeable in lifetime.

(iii) The value transferred into the discretionary trust in March 2003 is the cash amount of £268,000. There are no annual exemptions available as they have already been allocated to the PET in April 2002.

(iv) The question states the donor paid the lifetime tax.

Additional IHT due on lifetime gifts as a result of death

As a result of Jane's death on 20 November 2006 there is no additional tax to pay on the CLT on 28 November 1998 as it is more than seven years before death. The PET on 15 April 2002 becomes chargeable on Jane's death and additional tax is due on the CLT on 20 March 2003 as follows:

15 April 2002: PET

The PET becomes chargeable but is covered by the nil rate band, therefore no death IHT is payable.

10 March 2003: CLT

The revised cumulative total brought forward as a result of the PET on 15 April 2002 becoming chargeable is £106,000 (86,000 + 20,000).

	£
Gross chargeable transfer	285,250
IHT liability (285,000 – 106,000) = 179,000 at nil%	Nil
(285,250 – 179,000) = 106,250 at 40%	42,500
	42,500
Tapering relief (3 – 4 years) (20%)	(8,500)
	34,000
IHT paid in lifetime	(17,250)
Additional IHT payable on death	16,750

IHT on Estate at death – 20 November 2006

	£	£
Main residence		235,000
Mortgage		(40,000)
		195,000
Agricultural land	168,000	
Agricultural property relief (Note)	(110,000	
		58,000
Building society deposits		87,000
Ordinary shares in Banquo plc (W1)		94,800
Life assurance policy		104,000
Chargeable estate		538,800

Although the chargeable transfer on 28 November 1998 is more than seven years before the date of death and drops out of cumulation, the revised gross cumulative total of £307,750 (20,000 + 285,250) still fully utilises the nil rate band of £285,000.

The estate is therefore chargeable at 40%.

	£
IHT liability (538,800 at 40%)	215,520
Quick succession relief:	
$68,000 \times \dfrac{54,000}{360,000} \times 60\%$	(6,120)
IHT payable on estate	209,400

Note: APR is available since the property is let out for the purposes of agriculture, and has been owned for at least seven years.

Payment of IHT liability

The additional IHT of £16,750 in respect of the gift made on 10 March 2003 will be payable by the trustees of the discretionary trust by 31 May 2007.

The IHT liability of the estate will (in practice) be payable by the executors of Jane's estate on the earlier of 31 May 2007 or the delivery of their account.

It will be possible to pay IHT of £98,326 (W2) in respect of the main residence and agricultural land in ten equal instalments commencing on 31 May 2007.

Inheritance received by Jane's children

Jane's children will inherit £339,400 (W3), since specific gifts of UK property do not normally carry their own tax.

Workings:

(W1) **Value of Banquo plc shares**

Lower of   (1)   Quarter up method

$945 + (957 - 945) \times \frac{1}{4} = 948p$

(2)   Average of marked bargains

$(937 + 961) \times \frac{1}{2} = 949p$

Value of 10,000 £1 ords. = (10,000 × 948p) = £94,800

(W2) Payment by instalments

	£
Instalment property	
Main residence	195,000
Agricultural property	58,000
	253,000

$$\text{Average estate rate} = \frac{209,400}{538,800} \times 100 = 38.864\%$$

Payment by instalments = 253,000 × 38.864% = £98,326

(W3) Inheritance to children

	£
Chargeable estate	538,800
Plus APR	110,000
Value of assets in estate	648,800
Less Specific gift to brother	(100,000)
IHT payable on the estate (Note)	(209,400)
Estate value to be shared between the children	339,400

Note: The IHT payable on the whole estate comes out of the residue of the estate and is therefore borne by the residual legatees (i.e. the children). This is because specific gifts of UK property (e.g. £100,000 to the brother) do not normally carry their own tax.

(b)   Variation of the terms of Jane's will - conditions

Jane's will can be varied by a deed of variation (or deed of family arrangement) within two years of the date of her death.

The deed must be in writing, and be signed by Duncan, the children, and Jane's brother (i.e. those who benefit from the original will and the revised variations).

It must include a declaration that the will should be treated as being effective for IHT purposes.

Key answer tips

The children could not enter into the deed of variation if they were still minors.

Proposed plan

Under the revised terms of Jane's will, the entire estate is left to Duncan. This will be an exempt transfer, and so the IHT liability of £209,400 will no longer be payable (see key answer tips).

The gifts from Duncan to the children and Jane's brother will be PETs, and these will be completely exempt if Duncan lives for seven years after making the gifts.

Should the PETs become chargeable, tapering relief will be available after three years.

Duncan's annual exemptions of £3,000 for 2005/06 to 2008/09 may also be available.

As a result tax savings will be achieved. Even if Duncan dies within three years of the gift, the IHT liability should not be greater than £209,400 (subject to agricultural property relief being available), and the IHT liability will be postponed until six months after the end of the month of his death.

Key answer tips

Jane has already used her nil rate band on lifetime gifts so IHT can only be saved through making exempt transfers.

35 MING WONG

(a) **Acquiring UK domicile**

Domicile for IHT purposes

Ming will be deemed domiciled in the UK for the purposes of IHT if she is resident in the UK for 17 out of the 20 years of assessment ending with the year of assessment in which a chargeable transfer is made.

Ming has been resident in the UK since 1992/93, and will therefore be subject to UK IHT in respect of her overseas assets as well as her UK assets if she dies or makes a chargeable transfer during 2008/09 or a subsequent year.

Domicile under general law

Ming can only have one place of domicile at any given time denoting the country considered her permanent home.

She can become domiciled in the UK by acquiring a domicile of choice. This will require the severing of all ties with Yanga, and settling in the UK with the intention of staying there indefinitely.

The intention will have to be demonstrated by positive actions, such as making a will under UK law and obtaining British citizenship.

(b) **Consequences for IHT of acquiring UK domicile**

Ming will be charged to UK IHT on her worldwide assets if she becomes domiciled in the UK (whether this is under general law or is deemed for IHT purposes). However, if Ming is not domiciled in the UK she will only be charged to UK IHT in respect of her UK assets.

The following rules apply in determining the location of assets:

1   Land and buildings are situated where they are physically located. Therefore, the property in the UK is chargeable regardless of domicile, whilst the property in Yanga is not chargeable if Ming is not UK domiciled.

2   Registered shares and securities are situated where they are registered, or where they would normally be dealt with in the ordinary course of business. Therefore, the shares in Ganyan Inc. are not chargeable if Ming is not UK domiciled.

3   Chattels are situated where they are physically located at the relevant time, so the antiques are chargeable to IHT regardless of domicile.

4   Bank accounts are situated at the branch that maintains the account. Therefore, the deposit at the London branch is chargeable regardless of domicile, whilst the deposit at the Yanga branch is not chargeable if Ming is not UK domiciled.

5   A debt is situated where the debtor resides at the date of the chargeable event (i.e. gift or death). Therefore, the loan is not chargeable if Ming is not UK domiciled.

If Ming were to die owning her current portfolio of assets, the potential IHT liability on her estate can be calculated assuming she is UK domiciled and assuming she is not UK domiciled as follows:

Estate computation

	Not domiciled in UK £	Domiciled in UK £
Main residence	245,000	245,000
House in Yanga	Nil	60,000
Shares in Ganyan Inc. (40,000 at 310p)	Nil	124,000
Antiques	61,500	61,500
Bank accounts	38,000	58,000
Debtor	Nil	15,000
Chargeable estate	344,500	563,500

As Ming has made no lifetime gifts, all of the nil rate band is available.

IHT on the estate		
$(344,500 - 285,000) \times 40\%$	23,800	
$(563,500 - 285,000) \times 40\%$		111,400
Double taxation relief (W)	Nil	(36,375)
IHT liability	23,800	75,025

The potential increase in Ming's liability to UK IHT if she were to become domiciled in the UK is £51,225 (75,025 − 23,800).

Note: An endowment mortgage is repaid upon death by the related life assurance contract, and is not therefore deductible as a debt from the estate computation.

Working: **Double taxation relief**

Estate rate $= \dfrac{111,400}{563,500} \times 100 = 19.769\%$

			DTR £
Yarga house			
Lower of (1) Overseas tax suffered		£13,600	
(2) UK IHT			
($19.769\% \times £60,000$)		£11,861	11,861
Shares in Yanga			
Lower of (1) Overseas tax suffered		£34,400	
(2) UK IHT			
($19.769\% \times £124,000$)		£24,514	24,514
			36,375

(c) (i) **Income tax computation - 2006/07 (not domiciled in the UK)**

As Ming is resident and ordinarily resident in the UK but is not domiciled in the UK, she is assessed on her, overseas income only to the extent that it is remitted into the UK. As Ming has not remitted any overseas income to the UK she will be assessed on her UK income only as follows:

	£
Employment income	34,220
Bank interest (1,680 × 100/80)	2,100
STI	36,320
Personal allowance	(5,035)
Taxable income	31,285

Analysis of income:
Savings £2,100, Other income £29,185

Income tax:

£		£
2,150 × 10%		215
27,035 × 22%		5,948
29,185		
2,100 × 20%		420
31,285		
IT liability		6,583
Tax suffered at source:		
Bank interest (2,100 × 20%)		(420)
IT payable		6,163

(ii) **Income tax computation – 2006/07 (domiciled in the UK)**

If domiciled in the UK, Ming will be assessed on her worldwide income.

	£
Taxable income (as above)	31,285
Overseas income:	
Rental income	7,500
Dividends (5,950 × 100/85)	7,000
Bank interest (1,530 × 100/85)	1,800
Taxable income	47,585

Analysis of income:
Dividends £7,000, Savings £3,900, Other income £36,685

Income tax:		£	£
£			
2,150 × 10% (other income)			215
31,150 × 22% (other income)			6,853
33,300			
3,385 × 40% (other income)			1,354
36,685			
3,900 × 40% (savings)			1,560
7,000 × 32½% (dividends)			2,275
47,585			
			12,257
Double taxation relief: (see key answer tips)			
Rental income (7,500 × 35%)		2,625	
Dividends (7,000 × 15%)		1,050	
Bank interest (1,800 × 15%)		270	
			(3,945)
IT liability			8,312
Tax suffered at source: Bank interest			(420)
IT payable			7,892

Ming's additional UK income tax liability if she had been domiciled in the UK during 2006/07 is £1,729 (7,892 – 6,163).

Key answer tips

Double tax relief in the second section of part (c) is all of the overseas tax suffered. DTR is not restricted to the UK tax suffered because each category of foreign income was subject to a higher rate of UK tax.

Where there is more than one source of foreign income the UK tax suffered is found by excluding the foreign sources one by one, starting with the source suffering the highest rate of overseas tax. Thus with foreign non-savings income (e.g. rents), interest and dividends the UK tax on the rents could be determined by first excluding the rents and the tax on the foreign dividends can next be found by excluding the rents and the dividends.

However, whatever remains in the computation is still subject to the basic rule of dividends as top slice, with interest next and non-savings income as the lowest part.

36 JOAN ARK

IHT and CGT implications of gifts made in 2006/07

(a) **Ordinary shares in Orleans plc**

IHT implications

The gift of the shares into a discretionary trust in May 2006 will be a chargeable lifetime transfer.

The shares are valued at the lower of (i) quarter up method = 147p (146 + ¼ × (150 - 146)) per share or (ii) the average of the marked bargains = 147.5p ((140 + 155) ÷ 2).

The gift must be grossed up, as Joan is paying the tax.

	Net gift £	IHT £	Gross gift £
Chargeable transfers within previous 7 years	nil	nil	nil
Value transferred (250,000 × 147p)	367,500	20,625	388,125
	367,500	20,625	388,125

IHT payable: (367,500 – 285,000) × 20/80 = £20,625

The tax payable by Joan is due by 30 April 2007.

CGT implications

The disposal is initially matched with the post 5 April 1998 acquisition (i.e. the purchase on 15 August 2005), and then with the 1985 pool. The acquisition on 21 July 2006 is not within 30 days of 30 May 2006 and is therefore not relevant.

The chargeable gain is therefore:

Acquisition	Proceeds £	Indexed Cost £		Indexed Gain £
15 August 2005	110,250 (75,000 at 147p)	69,375		40,875
1985 Pool	257,250 (175,000 at 147p)	130,375	Note (ii)	126,875
Total indexed gains				167,750

The gain relating to the August 2005 disposal is 100% chargeable as the share have been held less than one year. The gain relating to the 1985 pool is 65% chargeable as the shares have been held for nine qualifying years (including the bonus year).

However, Joan can elect to have the total indexed gain of £167,750 held over with a gift relief claim as there is an immediate charge to IHT.

In this case 35% taper relief due on the 1985 pool disposal is wasted.

Notes:

(i)   there would be two annual exemptions available against this gift, however the question says to ignore the effect of annual exemptions.

(ii)   The indexed cost of the 1985 pool is calculated as (£149,000 × 175,000/200,000) = £130,375.

(b)   **Ordinary shares in Rouen Ltd**

IHT implications

Joan's gift of shares in Rouen Ltd in June 2006 to her son will be a PET for £394,000 calculated as follows:

	£
Value of shares held before the transfer	
40,000 × £17.10 (part of a 80% holding)	684,000
Value of shares held after the transfer	
20,000 × £14.50 (part of a 60% holding)	(290,000)
Value transferred	394,000

Business property relief at the rate of 100% will be available as the shares are unquoted trading company shares held for more than two years.

As a PET there is no lifetime IHT payable. An IHT liability will only arise if Joan dies before 15 June 2013 and only then if Michael disposes of the shares before that date. If Michael still owns the shares at the date of Joan's death, 100% BPR is still available.

CGT implications

Provided Joan and her son jointly elect, the indexed gain of £109,800 (W) can be held over as a gift of business assets, since Rouen Ltd is an unquoted trading company.

Again this will waste the accrued taper relief. In this case taper relief of 75% is wasted.

Working: **Indexed gain on the disposal of Rouen Ltd shares**

	£
MV of 20% holding (20,000 × £7.90)	158,000
Less Indexed cost $96,400 \times \dfrac{20,000}{40,000}$	(48,200)
Indexed gain	109,800

If gift relief is not claimed, the shares are business assets held for more than two years, therefore the gain would be 25% chargeable.

Key answer tips

For CGT purposes, the deemed proceeds is the market value of a 20% holding.

(c) **Antique vase**

IHT implications

The gift of the vase is in consideration of marriage, and will therefore qualify for an exemption of £2,500 as it is a gift from a grandparent to grandchild.

The balance of the gift of £6,000 (8,500 - 2,500) will be a PET made on 4 November 2006.

CGT implications

The gift of the vase is a disposal of a non-wasting chattel. The gain is calculated as normal at £4,350 (8,500 – 4,150), however it will be restricted by marginal relief to a maximum of £4,167 (8,500 - 6,000 = 2,500 × 5/3).

The disposal qualifies for non business asset taper relief based on nine complete years of ownership (including the bonus year), the gain is therefore 65% chargeable. The CGT liability due on 31 January 2008 is therefore £1,083 (4,167 × 65% × 40%) ignoring annual exemption.

(d) **Agricultural land**

IHT implications

The gift of the agricultural land will be a PET for £300,000 on 15 January 2007 and will not become chargeable unless Joan dies within seven years.

The increase in the value of her son Charles' property is irrelevant in valuing the PET.

If the PET becomes chargeable as a result of Joan dying before 15 January 2014, agricultural property relief at the rate of 100% based on the agricultural value of £175,000 will be available. This is because the land is let out for the purposes of agriculture and has been owned for at least seven years.

However, relief will only be available if, at the date of Joan's death, Charles still owns the land and it still qualifies as agricultural property.

CGT implications

The gift of agricultural land to Charles will be valued at its open market value on the date of the gift of £300,000.

Since the land qualifies for agricultural property relief it is also eligible for gift relief for CGT purposes. Joan and Charles can therefore jointly elect that the gain of £208,000 (300,000 - 92,000) is held over as a gift of business assets.

Taper relief accrued to the date of the gift is wasted.

(e) **Main residence**

IHT implications

The gift of the main residence is a gift with reservation because although Joan has gifted the freehold interest, she retains an interest in the property as she has continued to live rent free in the property.

The gift will be treated as a PET for £265,000 as normal on 31 March 2007, but Joan will still be treated as beneficially entitled to the property.

It will therefore be included in her estate when she dies at its market value at that date, although relief will be given should there be a double charge to IHT.

Joan could avoid these provisions by paying full consideration for the use of the property.

The pre-owned asset rules do not apply where the gift, as in this instance, is caught by the gift with reservation rules.

CGT implications

The gift of the main residence is a chargeable disposal for CGT purposes and the time of the disposal is when the ownership of the asset passes to the donee. The reservation of benefit is therefore not relevant for CGT, and a normal CGT computation is required on 31 March 2007.

The disposal qualifies for taper relief based on nine complete years of ownership (including the bonus year), therefore so the CGT liability due on 31 January 2008 is as follows:

	£
Deemed consideration	265,000
Indexed cost	(67,000)
Indexed gain before PPR relief	198,000
PPR exemption (W1)	(100,193)
Letting relief (W2)	(40,000)
Indexed gain after PPR relief	57,807

As a non-business asset held for nine qualifying years (including the bonus year), the gain is 65% chargeable.

Chargeable gain (57,807 × 65%)	37,575
Capital gains tax (37,575 × 40%)	15,030

Workings

(W1) **Principal private residence exemption**

		Notes	Months	Exempt	Chargeable
1-7-86 – 31-12-90	Owner occupied		54	54	
1-1-91 – 31-12-94	Unoccupied	(i)	48	36	12
1-1-95 – 31-12-04	Rented out	(ii)	120	9	111
1-1-05 – 31-03-07	Owner occupied	(iii)	27	27	
			249	126	123

PPR exemption = (126/249) × 198,000 = £100,193

Notes

(i)   Three years allowed for no reason provided the property is owner occupied at some time before and some time after the period of absence.

(ii)   The last 36 months are always exempt. They fall partly into the final period of owner occupation but partly in the period when the property was rented out.

(W2) **Letting relief**

			£
Lower of	(i)	PPR exemption	100,193
	(ii)	Maximum	40,000
	(iii)	Period not exempted by PPR during which the property is let	
		(111/249) × 198,000	88,265

37   JIMMY GENEROUS

(a)   **Tax relief for Gift Aid scheme donations**

To obtain tax relief on the cash gifts to charity, the donations will need to be treated as made under the Gift Aid scheme. This requires that the donor must not receive any material benefit as a result of the payment.

To benefit, Jimmy will need to make a declaration which contains:

(i)   His name and address;

(ii)   The charity's name:

(iii)   A description of the donation made

(iv)   A statement that the gift is made under the Gift Aid scheme.

It is to be noted that the statement does not need to be in writing (although in this case the charity will need to supply a written notification of the gift) nor does there need to be a separate statement for each gift to the same recipient.

Additionally, it is not necessary to make the declaration prior to the gift. It is possible, therefore, for Jimmy to make the declaration retrospectively to cover a series of payments to the same charity.

The effect of treating the payments as made under the Gift Aid scheme is as follows:

Jimmy

The cash payments made will be treated as payments net of basic rate income tax. The gross equivalent for Jimmy will therefore be £4,000 (3,120 × 100/78).

To obtain higher rate tax relief Jimmy will extend his basic rate band by this amount to £37,300 (33,300 + 4,000).

This provides relief amounting to £720

$(4,000 \times (40 - 22)\%)$.

The total net cost to Jimmy of making the payments will therefore be £2,400 (3,120 – 720 = 4,000 × (100 – 40)%).

Jimmy could elect to treat the Gift Aid donations as if they had been made in the previous tax year. This would be particularly beneficial if Jimmy was a basic rate taxpayer in 2006/07 but a higher rate taxpayer in 2005/06. The election must be made by 31 January 2008.

Charity

Charities are exempt from income tax. The charity will therefore be able to obtain a refund from HMRC of £880 (4,000 × 22%). This represents the basic rate tax deemed deducted at source by Jimmy.

(b) **Income tax and national insurance liabilities**

Income tax computation for 2006/07

	£
Salary	25,000
Less: Payroll deduction (25,000 × 10%)	(2,500)
Pension contribution	(3,750)
Employment income	18,750
Savings Income	
Interest (8,000 × 100/80)	10,000
Dividends (45,000 × 100/90)	50,000
Statutory Total Income	78,750
Less: Personal allowance	(5,035)
Taxable Income	73,715

Income tax

£	
2,150 × 10%	215
11,565 × 22%	2,544
13,715	
10,000 × 20%	2,000
13,585 × 10%	1,358
37,300 (Note 1)	
36,415 × 32·5%	11,835
73,715	
Income Tax Liability	17,952

National Insurance Contribution ('NIC') Liability for 2006/07

Class 1 employee's NIC (Note 2)

$(25,000 - 5,035) \times 11\% = £2,196$

Notes:

(1)   Jimmy's basic rate band is extended by £4,000 – see solution to part (a) above.

(2)   No relief is available for NIC purposes for the payroll deduction or the pension contributions. Jimmy's savings income is not liable to NIC.

(c)   **Inheritance Tax Implications of lifetime gifts**

June 1999 – Gift to discretionary trust

The cash gift made to the discretionary trust 4 June 1999 is a chargeable lifetime transfer. The CLT is chargeable at the time of the gift as follows:

	£	*Net gift* £	*IHT* £	*Gross gift* £
Chargeable transfers within previous 7 years		nil	nil	nil
Cash gift	291,000			
Less: 1999/00 AE	(3,000)			
1998/99 AE	(3,000)			
		285,000	nil	285,000
		285,000	nil	285,000

The transfer is covered by the nil rate band of £285,000 and accordingly no IHT will therefore be payable in relation to this gift.

March 2001 – Gift to son

The wedding gift of £10,000 to Jack, being made from one individual to another, will be a potentially exempt transfer ('PET'). There is no IHT payable during Jimmy's lift time and providing Jimmy survives until 4 March 2008 no IHT will arise in relation to this gift.

However, if Jimmy die's before 4 March 2008, the PET will become chargeable.

As the gift was made in consideration of marriage, a marriage exemption of £5,000 will be available for gifts from a parent to their child. As there is another gift on the same day (see below) Jimmy's 2000/01 annual exemption may need to be apportioned by reference to the value of the gifts made on the same day. The annual exemption is, however, only used after other exemptions and reliefs.

The gift of shares in JG limited made on the same day to Jill is likely to qualify for 100% Business Property Relief (see below). It is likely therefore that the entire annual exemption for 2000/01 will be allocated against the wedding gift to the son. The potentially exempt transfer is therefore valued at £2,000 (10,000– 5,000 – 3,000). Note that the previous years AE for 1999/00 has already been utilised.

If Jimmy dies before 4 March 2008 PET of £2,000 becomes chargeable. There will be no need to 'gross up' this gift as PET's becoming chargeable are deemed to be gross transfers. Tax is due at 40% but taper relief at a maximum rate of 80% of any IHT arising will be available, depending on the length of time between the gift and date of death.

However, as Jimmy is currently in good health and therefore unlikely to die before 4 March 2008 it seems unlikely that any IHT will arise in relation to this gift.

March 2001 – Gift to daughter

The gift of shares to Jill, being made from one individual to another, will again be a PET.

As annual exemptions are allocated in strict chronological order, and the exemption for 2000/01 and 1999/00 have already been allocated, no annual exemption will be available to reduce this transfer.

The shares will be valued applying the loss to the donor's estate principle. Before the gift Jim owned an 80% holding (see tutorial note) and after the gift Jim owned a 60% holding. The value of the transfer is therefore £150,000 (600,000 – 450,000).

As the JG Limited shares are shares in an unquoted trading company and Jimmy has owned these shares for the minimum qualifying period of two years prior to the gift, business property relief at the rate of 100% is likely to be available therefore.

No IHT is payable on this PET at the time of the gift.

In addition IHT is not payable on the death of Jimmy within seven years unless, upon Jimmy's death before 4 March 2008, Jill has ceased to own the shares gifted to her or JG Limited has ceased to be a qualifying company.

However, as stated above, Jimmy is currently in good health and it is therefore unlikely that any IHT will arise in relation to this gift.

Tutorial note: The question says Jim currently (in 2007) owns a 60% holding. At the time of the gift in March 2001, he must have had a 80% holding.

June 2005 – Gift to discretionary trust

The further cash gift of £100,000 to the discretionary trust will also be a chargeable lifetime transfer. As Jimmy has agreed to pay any IHT arising, the gift will need to be grossed up. Lifetime IHT payable on this gift will therefore be calculated as follows:

		Net £	IHT £	Gross £
Chargeable transfers within previous seven years		285,000	nil	285,000
Cash gift	100,000			
Less: 2005/06 AE	(3,000)			
2004/05 AE	(3,000)			
		94,000	23,500	117,500
		379,000	23,500 (1)	402,500

Note (1) IHT payable = (379,000 – 285,000) × 20/80 = £23,500

Jimmy will therefore have an IHT liability of £23,500 in relation to this gift. Should Jimmy die before 4 June 2012 additional IHT at death rates of 40% may become payable. Relief will, however, be available for tapering relief and also for the lifetime tax paid.

(d) **Main advantages in lifetime giving for IHT purposes**

Possible advantages of lifetime giving include:

(i) Making use of lifetime IHT exemptions in reducing a taxpayer's chargeable estate at death. In particular gifts between individuals will not become liable to IHT unless the donor dies within seven years of making the gift.

(ii) If the donor does die prematurely there may still be an IHT advantage in lifetime giving because usually:

1 The value of the asset for calculating any additional IHT arising upon death is fixed at the time the gift is made.

2 The availability of tapering relief (providing the donor survives at least three years) may help reduce the effective IHT rate.

Main factors to consider in choosing assets to gift

The main factors to consider include:

(i)   Whether or not a significant CGT liability will arise upon making the gift. Lifetime gifting therefore needs to be balanced against the fact that no CGT liability will arise upon death (which results in the 'tax free' uplift of the chargeable assets included in the deceased's estate). The availability of CGT reliefs (primarily gift relief for business assets or if there is an immediate charge to IHT) and CGT exemptions (e.g. annual exemption) is therefore relevant in selecting assets.

(ii)   Whether an asset is appreciating in value. Because any additional IHT arising as a result of death will be based on the (lower) value of the asset at the date of gift it may be advantageous to select assets that are likely to significantly appreciate in value.

(iii)   Whether the donor can afford to make the gift. Whilst lifetime gifting can result in significant IHT savings this should not be at the expense of the taxpayer's ability to live comfortably, particularly in old age.

(iv)   The availability of significant IHT reliefs, particularly BPR. There may be little point in selecting an asset that already qualifies for 100% relief.

Further gifts of JG Limited shares

If Jimmy's objective in making further gifts to JG Limited shares is to reduce his future IHT liability then the gifting for this reason would appear to be unnecessary. This is because whilst the shares in JG Limited would appear to be appreciating in value, and are likely to qualify as a business asset for CGT purposes (and will therefore attract CGT gift relief), they are also likely to qualify as relevant business property for BPR purposes. Therefore the gifts should be covered by 100% BPR if retained and held in the estate at death. There is therefore no need to transfer the shares during lifetime and the value of his estate will not be reduced as a result of the gifts. Jimmy should also consider the impact on his income if he were to gift the shares as, the income derived from these shares may be important to him in later years, particularly when he finally retires from the business.

ACCA marking scheme		Marks
(a)	Material benefit	0.5
	Declaration contents	1.0
	Oral/composite declarations/retrospective declarations	1.0
	Effect	
	Jimmy – Grossing up	0.5
	Higher rate relief	1.0
	Net cost	0.5
	Charity – Exempt/tax refund	1.0
	Available	5.0
	Maximum	4.0
(b)	Employment income	0.5
	Payroll giving	0.5
	Pension contribution	1.0
	Interest/dividends	1.0
	Personal allowance	0.5
	Income tax calculation	2.5
	Class 1 NIC calculation	1.0
	Available	7.0
	Maximum	7.0

(c)	Gift 4/6/1999	CLT/20%	1.0
		AE's	1.0
		IHT calculation	0.5
	Gift 4/3/2001	PET	1.0
		AE/Marriage exemption	1.0
		Premature death	1.0
	Gift 4/3/2001	AE	0.5
		Valuation	1.0
		BPR	1.5
	Gift 4/6/2004	Grossing up	0.5
		IHT calculation	1.0
		Premature death	1.0
		Available	11.0
		Maximum	10.0
(d)	Advantages	Lifetime exemptions/PET's	1.0
	Freezing value/tapering relief		1.0
	Factors	CGT considerations	2.0
	Appreciating value		0.5
	Affordability to taxpayer		1.0
	Availability of IHT relief		0.5
	Application		2.0
		Available	8.0
		Maximum	7.0
		Total	28.0

38 HENRY

(a) **Income tax in the year of death**

The basic rule determining the taxation of a taxpayer's income in the tax year of death is that only income due and payable up to the date of death will be included in the deceased's income tax computation.

This will include Henry's retirement pension and annuity income as well as the investment income actually received prior to his death. Apportionments of investment income are not generally required. However, the following should be noted:

- The accrued income scheme will not apply to the 10% Government stock as the transfer results from Henry's death.

Henry will therefore only be taxed on the following:

	Date received
10% Government stock	30 April 2006
Building Society	30 June 2006

- Interest received on the ISA account is exempt form income tax.

Note also that the personal allowance and MCAA are not apportioned in the tax year of death.

**Income Tax Computation for 2006/07
(date of death 5 October 2006)**

	Notes	£	Tax credits £
Dividends	(1)	10,000	1,000
Interest:			
10% government stock	(2)	1,000	
Building society	(3)	400	80
Retirement pension		4,380	
Annuity		5,100	1,020
Statutory total income		20,880	2,100
Less: Age allowance	(4)	(7,030)	
Taxable income		13,850	

Analysis of income:
Dividends £10,000, Savings £1,400, Other income £2,450

Income tax

£	£
2,150 × 10%	215
300 × 22%	218
2,450	
1,400 × 20%	280
10,000 × 10%	1,000
13,850	1,561

Less: MCAA	(6,135 × 10%)	(5)	(614)
IT liabilities			947
Less: Tax credits – dividends (restricted)		(6)	(947)
– interest and annuity			(1,100)
IT repayable			(1,100)

Notes

(1) **Dividends from Peel plc shares**

$100,000 \times 0.09 \times 100/90 = £10,000$

(2) **Interest from 10% Government Stock**

$£20,000 \times 10\% \times 6/12 = £1,000$

(3) **Building Society interest**

$£320 \times 100/80 = £400$

(4)   Personal age allowance

	£	£
PAA (age 77)		7,420
Abatement		
STI	20,880	
Limit	(20,100)	
	780 × ½	(390)
Reduced PAA		7,030

(5)   Married couple's age allowance

	£
MCAA (aged 77)	6,135

The allowance is not abated as the PAA has been abated in full for the level of Henry's STI.

(6)   Tax Credits

Tax credits relating to dividends received from UK companies are not refundable. The refund entitlement will therefore be restricted to.

(b)   Inheritance tax liabilities

Lifetime IHT on cash gifts made to Discretionary Trust

Gifts into discretionary trusts are chargeable lifetime transfers (CLTs). As Henry agreed to pay any IHT arising the gifts will be regarded as 'net' gifts and would have resulted in the following IHT liabilities:

1 January 1999

	£	*Gross* £	*IHT* £	*Net* £
Gift	168,000			
Less: Annual exemptions				
1998/99 and 1997/98	(6,000)			
		162,000	–	162,000

1 January 2002

	£	*Gross* £	*IHT* £	*Net* £
CLT's within seven years		162,000	–	162,000
Gift	137,000			
Less: Annual exemptions				
2001/02 and 2000/01	(6,000)			
		133,000	2,000	131,000
		295,000	2,000	293,000

As a consequence £2,000 IHT was payable by Henry as a result of this gift.

Notes: **IHT payable**

(1)   *Gift on 1 January 1999*

152,000 < 285,000 (nil band) – therefore no IHT payable.

(2)   *Gift on 1 January 2002*

(293,000 – 285,000) = 8,000 × 20/80 = £2,000.

IHT arising on CLT's on death of Henry on 5 October 2006

Lifetime gifts

CLT - 1 January 1999

As this gift was made more than seven years from death no additional IHT is payable.

CLT – 1 January 2002

Additional IHT is calculated as follows:

	£
$(295,000 - 285,000) \times 40\% =$	4,000
Less: Taper relief (40%) (4–5 years)	(1,600)
Lifetime tax paid	(2,000)
Additional tax payable	400

IHT on Death Estate

Henry's estate at death comprises:

	Notes	£
Shares – Peel plc	(1)	202,000
Government stock	(2)	20,100
Cash (25,000 + 18,000)		43,000
Income tax refund due		1,100
Accrued interest	(3)	332
Home		450,000
		716,532
Less: Exempt transfer to spouse		(676,532)
Chargeable estate (£20,000 × 2)		40,000
Nil rate band at death		285,000
Gross CLT's within seven years of death		(133,000)
Nil rate band available against estate		152,000

The estate is covered by the nil rate band. As a consequence, no IHT is payable on the estate at death.

Notes:

(1) **Peel plc shares**

Value for IHT purposes = the lower of:

(i) Quarter up method = $(200 + ((208-200)/4)) = 202p$

(ii) Average of recording bargains = $((201+207)/2) = 204p$

Value of 100,000 shares = $(100,000 \times 2.02) = £202,000$

BPR is not available on these shares as they are quoted shares and Henry does not have a controlling interest.

(2)   **Government stock**

The ex interest value needs to be adjusted to the cum interest value as follows:

Quarter up method = (95 + ((97 – 95)/4)) = 95.5p

	£
20,000 × 95.5	19,100
Next interest receipt due (20,000 × 10% × 6/12)	1,000
	20,100

(3)   **Accrued interest**

Accrued interest arises on the building society account and ISA deposit as follows:

(304 + 360) × 3/6 = £332

(c)   **Action to reduce or defer IHT liabilities**

Henry's will resulted in the balance of the estate above £40,000 being an exempt transfer to his wife. This is not an efficient tax planning arrangement as it has left £112,000 (152,000 – 40,000) of his nil band remained unused.

When Sally dies and passes her estate to Cecil and Ida the whole estate will be entirely chargeable to IHT at 40% to the extent her nil rate band is exceeded. As a consequence, if £112,000 of value had been transferred directly by Henry's will to his children an IHT saving of £44,800 (112,000 × 40%) will arise.

As Henry's children are already reasonably wealthy, consideration might have been given to transferring this directly to Henry's grandchildren. The idea here is to avoid a charge to IHT arising on any transfers that Cecil and Ida may make to their children.

Deed of variation

Providing various conditions are satisfied it is possible to vary a will after the testator's death and make more tax efficient provisions as outlined above by entering into a deed of variation.

The main conditions to be satisfied for a valid deed of variation are as follows:

(a)   The deed of variation must be in writing.

(b)   It must be signed by all the beneficiaries that are affected.

(c)   It must be executed within two years of the date of death.

(d)   It must not be made for a consideration.

(e)   The deed should include a statement that the variation is to be effective for IHT (and/or CGT) purposes.

The effect of making such a variation is that for IHT purposes the deceased's will is treated as rewritten. In this particular case an appropriate deed variation needs to be drafted by 5 October 2008.

Lifetime gifts by Sally

In addition to varying Henry's will, Sally could herself make lifetime gifts to her children or grandchildren (for the reason outlined above) to reduce the IHT payable on her death.

If she survives seven years, the gifts will be exempt. However, she is in a frail condition and is possibly not likely to live seven years. Nevertheless, if the survives at least three years taper relief will be available to at least partially mitigate any IHT arising on potentially exempt transfers becoming chargeable within seven years of death.

If she does not survive seven years, the PETs will become chargeable, however PETs are valued at the time of the gift and annual exemptions are available. Therefore, the chargeable amount will be less than valuing the assets in Sally's estate (assuring the assets will appreciate in value between the date of the gift and Sally's death). The IHT position would certainly be no worse than if she had not made any lifetime transfers.

Sally should also make use of her IHT exemptions available as follows: immediate gifts of £6,000 could be made in 2006/07 (to make use of her two annual exemptions) which would potentially save £2,400 (6,000 × 40%). Thereafter annual gifts of £3,000 would save £1,200 (3,000 × 40%) for each tax year that she survives.

Consideration should be given to personal circumstances. She may wish to gift her main asset (i.e. her home) to her children, but still live in it. However, this will give rise to 'gift with reservation of benefit' problems unless she pays full market rent while living in the house.

Substantial lifetime giving and paying full market rent for living in her home may not be desirable as she may wish to retain sufficient income bearing assets to maintain herself during her lifetime.

ACCA marking scheme		
		Marks
(a)	Basic rule	1.0
	Dividend	1.0
	Accrued income scheme	0.5
	ISA interest	0.5
	Statutory total income	2.0
	Age allowance/MCAA	1.5
	Tax refund	1.5
	Available	8.0
	Maximum	7.0
(b)	CLT's	
	1/1/1999	1.0
	1/1/2002	1.5
	Additional tax on CLT's	
	1/1/1999	1.0
	1/1/2002	2.0
	Death estate	
	Shares	1.0
	Government stock	1.5
	Income tax refund	1.0
	Accrued income	1.0
	Cash/house	0.5
	Exempt transfer	0.5
	7 year cumulation/IHT	1.0
	Available	12.0
	Maximum	10.0
(c)	Available Nil band	1.0
	£44,800 saving	1.0
	Generation skipping	1.0
	Deed of variation – conditions	2.0
	– effect/deadline	1.0

Sally – lifetime gifting		
PET's – beneficial if survive 3 years		1.0
Annual exemptions		1.0
– practical considerations		1.0
	Available	9.0
	Maximum	8.0
Total		25.0

39 ETHEL SMITH

(a) **Ethel – Income Tax Computation for 2006/07**

	Notes	£
Employment income		8,800
Interest		
Chaffinch plc	(1)	5,000
Cash deposits	(2)	5,250
Dividends	(3)	2,778
Statutory total income		21,828
Less: Age allowance	(5)	(6,556)
Taxable income		15,272

Analysis of income:
Dividends £2,778, Savings £10,250,
Other income £2,244

Income tax

£		£
2,150 × 10%		215
94 × 22%		21
2,244		
10,250 × 20%		2,050
2,778 × 10%		278
15,272		2,564
Less: Married couples allowance (4) £2,350 × 10%		(235)
Income tax liability		2,329

Notes:

(1) **Chaffinch plc interest**

In the absence of a declaration of beneficial entitlement the interest income on these shares will be shared equally between Ethel and George

£100,000 × 10% = 10,000/2 = £5,000.

(2) **Cash deposits**

£4,200 × 100/80 = £5,250

(3) **Dividends from Bluebird plc shares**

10,000 × 0.25 × 100/90 = £2,778

(4) **Married couples age allowance**

As Ethel and George have made a joint election the maximum married couples allowance that can be passed to Ethel in 2006/07 is £2,350 with the remainder being claimed (subject to abatement) by George.

(5)   **Personal age allowance**

	£	£
PAA (Aged 78)		7,42
Abatement		
STI	21,828	
Limit	(20,100)	
	1,728 × ½	(86
Revised PAA		6,55

(b) **Declaration of beneficial interest**

The effect of making a declaration of beneficial interest in respect of the loan stock in Chaffinch plc would be that Ethel would only be taxed upon her 25% beneficial entitlement with her husband George being taxed on the remaining 75%.

This would reduce Ethel's taxable income from this source to £2,500 and hence her statutory total income for 2006/07 would reduce to £19,328. This in turn would mean that her age allowance for this tax year would no longer be abated.

The effect for George would also need to be considered. This is because if he is a higher rate taxpayer the effect of the declaration would increase his income tax payable by 20% (i.e. 40% less 20% tax credit) of the gross income transferred.

(c) (i) **Ethel retains assets until death**

     IHT Implications

     Cash gift – September 2005

The cash gift made to Simone in September 2005 is a potentially exempt transfer which will become chargeable if Ethel dies within seven years of making the gift. There are no other lifetime gifts.

If Ethel therefore dies in four years time (i.e. June 2011) this cash gift in September 2005 will be within the seven year cumulation period.

IHT will become payable on the PET calculated as follows:

	IHT £
Gifts within $(320{,}000 - 285{,}000) \times 40\%$	14,000
Less: Taper relief (5-6 years) (60%)	(8,400)
IHT payable	5,600

Estate on death

Her estate at death will also give rise to IHT payable calculated as follows:

	Notes	£
Residence		600,000
Bluebird plc shares		200,000
Chaffinch plc loan stock	(1)	25,000
Cash deposits		160,000
Antique plates		10,000
Other chattels		20,000
		1,015,000
Less: Exempt estate	(2)	(620,000)
Chargeable estate		395,000

	£
Nil rate band on death	285,000
Gifts within previous 7 years	(320,000)
Nil rate band available against estate	Nil
IHT estate: (395,000 × 40%)	158,000

Notes:

(1)   **Chaffinch plc loan stock**

Ethel's share = £100,000 × 25% = £25,000

(2)   **Inter-spouse transfers**

Inter-spouse transfers are exempt. George is left the house and sundry chattels worth £620,000 (600,000 + 20,000).

CGT Implications

Death is not a chargeable event for the purposes of capital gains tax. Therefore there is no CGT payable if Ethel retains the assets and gifts them in her will.

The recipients of the assets will receive them at their probate value which will form their base cost for future CGT purposes.

(ii)   **Ethel gifts selected assets to Simone now**

IHT Implications

Cash gift – September 2005

The implications for the PET made in September 2005 are as above with £5,600 of IHT becoming payable as a result of Ethel's expected death in four years time.

Gifts to Simone now

The gifts of assets to Simone will be further PET's likely to become chargeable on Ethel's death, with further IHT arising as follows:

	Notes	£
Bluebird plc shares	(1)	146,200
Chaffinch plc loan stock	(2)	25,750
Antique plates	(3)	6,333
Cash deposits		145,000
		323,283
Less: Annual exemptions 2007/08		(3,000)
2006/07		(3,000)
PET		317,283

	£
As no nil rate band remains, the PET is chargeable at 40% as follows: (317,283 × 40%)	126,913
Less: Taper relief (3 – 4 years) (20%)	(25,383)
IHT payable	101,530

Notes:

(1) **Bluebird plc shares**

Quarter up method = $(1,460 + (1,468 - 1,460) \times \frac{1}{4}) + £14.62$ per share

Value of 10,000 shares = $10,000 \times £14.62 = £146,200$

There is no BPR available as the shares are quoted shares and Ethel does not have a controlling interest.

(2) **Chaffinch plc loan stock**

Quarter up method = $(102 + (106 - 102) \times \frac{1}{4}) = 103$p per share

Value of loan stock

$£100,000 \times £1.03 \times 25\%$ (Ethel's beneficial ownership entitlement) = £25,750

(3) **Value of the plates**

Valued under related party valuation rules, taking account of the fact that Ethel and George own five plates between them (the daughter Simone's plate does not count as related property) is as follows:

$$\frac{\text{Value of 3 plates}}{\text{Value of 3 + 2 plates}} = \frac{£3,800}{£3,800 + £2,200} \times £10,000 = £6,333$$

Estate on death

When Ethel dies the transfers of the house and personal chattels to George will be exempt under the inter-spouse provisions. Therefore there is no IHT payable on the estate at death.

CGT implications

Gift of cash and loan stock

The gifts of cash deposits and loan stock (a qualifying corporate bond) are exempt from CGT.

Gift of plates

Whilst the plates form a set, because Ethel has never in the past owned the plates owned by her husband and daughter there is no need to treat the gift of her plates to Simone as a part disposal nor to amalgamate the gift with any previous gifts.

The value of the consideration for CGT purposes will simply be the market value of the three plates gifted by Ethel (i.e. £3,800). As their value is less than £6,000 and they cost less than £6,000, any gain arising will also be exempt under the CGT small chattels exemption.

Gift of Bluebird plc shares

The gift of the shares in Bluebird plc will, however, give rise to a capital gain.

Assuming the gift is made on 6 July 2007, the CGT will be as follows:

	Notes	£	£
Proceeds	(1)		146,200
Less: Indexed cost	(2)		(76,569)
Indexed gain			69,631

Gift relief is not available as the shares are quoted shares and Ethel does not aim >5% interest in the company.

Under the current definition of business assets for taper relief purposes, quoted companies are only business assets if an individual is either any employee (or officer of the company) or has a 5% or more shareholding.

Whilst Ethel does not own 5% of the shares she was a director of the company until May 2006. Her shareholding therefore was a business asset for the period 6 April 1998 until May 2006 when it became a non-business asset. Taper relief is given on the shares acquired under the rights issue from the date the original shares were acquired.

Actual period of ownership since April 1998 (6 April 98 to 6 July 07)	111 months
Qualifying business asset (6 April 98 to 31 May 06)	98 months
Non-business asset (1 June 06 to 6 July 07)	13 months
Complete years of ownership since April 1998	9 years

The gain is apportioned and the appropriate taper relief percentage applied to each part of the gain based on 9 complete years of ownership for the business portion, and 10 complete years (including the bonus year) for the non business portion.

		£
Indexed gain (as above)		69,631
Chargeable gains:		
Business gain	$(98/111) \times 69,631 \times 25\%$	15,369
Non-business gain	$(13/111) \times 69,631 \times 60\%$	4,893
Total chargeable gains		20,262
Annual exemption		(8,800)
Taxable gains		11,462

The CGT payable on the taxable gains will depend on the level of Ethel's taxable income (see tutorial note).

Assuring Ethel is a basic rate tax payer in 2007/08 (as in 2006/07):

CGT $(11,462 \times 20\%)$	2,292

Notes:

(1)   Disposal proceeds

A Ethel and Simone are connected persons, the market value of the shares is used.

(2)   Indexed cost – FA 1985 pool

For CGT purposes the shares acquired under the rights issue in June 2002 are deemed to have been acquired when the original shares were acquired and are therefore pooled with the '1985 holding'.

	Number	Cost	Indexed cost
		£	£
June 1996 Purchase	5,000	25,000	25,000
April 1998 Indexation $\left(\dfrac{162.6-153.0}{153.0}\right)\times 25,000$			1,569
			26,569
June 2002 Rights issue	5,000	50,000	50,000
	10,000	75,000	76,569
Gift in 2007/08	(10,000)	(75,000)	(76,569)

Conclusion

The tax payable under both options is as follows:

	IHT	CGT	Total
	£	£	£
Retention of Assets (5,600 + 158,000)	163,600	Nil	163,600
Gifting assets now (5,600 + 101,530)	107,130	2,292	109,422

It would therefore appear that, providing the key assumptions hold (asset values in four years, Ethel survives four years), it is preferable to make the gifts to Simone now giving a tax saving of £54,178 (163,600 – 109,422).

Tutorial notes

(1) In the absence of information in respect of income arising in 2007/08, the answer assumes that any income arising will be covered by the personal allowance and that the starting rate band has been utilised so that the capital gains totally fall into the basic rate band and are taxable at 20%.

(2) Prior to 6 April 2000 shares in a trading company were only eligible as business assets if an individual owned 25% of the voting rights or they were held by a full-time employee who also owned 5% of the voting rights. This additional complexity is ignored in the answer.

ACCA marking scheme			Marks
(a)	Interest –	Employment income	0.5
		Chaffinch plc	1.0
		Deposits	0.5
		Dividends	0.5
		Age allowance	1.0
		Married couples allowance	1.0
		Income tax calculation	1.5
		Maximum	6.0
		Available	5.0

(b)	Basic rule		1.0
	Effect of declaration for Ethel		1.0
	George		1.0
			———
		Maximum	3.0
			———
		Available	3.0
			———
(c)	Ethel retains assets until death		
	IHT implications	Gift September 2005	0.5
		IHT payable	1.0
		Estate	1.5
		IHT payable	0.5
	CGT implication		1.0
	Ethel gifts assets to Simone		
	IHT implications	Additional PET becoming chargeable	0.5
		Valuation share	0.5
		loan stock	1.0
		antique plates	1.0
		annual exemptions	1.0
		IHT payable	0.5
	CGT implication	Cash/loan stock	1.0
		Antique plates	1.5
		Shares proceeds	1.0
		cost	2.0
		taper relief	3.0
		annual exemption	0.5
		CGT payable	1.0
	Conclusion		1.0
			———
		Maximum	20.0
			———
		Available	18.0
			———
Total			26.0
			———

40 AMY

(a) (i) **Basis of taxation**

Income tax

Amy will be taxed on all of her UK income as she is resident and ordinarily resident in the UK; however, she will be taxed on her overseas income only to the extent that it is remitted to the UK, as she is domiciled overseas.

Capital gains tax

Amy will be taxed on all gains on UK assets, but on overseas assets only to the extent that the gain is remitted to the UK. Losses on overseas assets are not allowable.

Inheritance tax

Amy will be taxed on the transfer of her UK assets only as she is domiciled overseas.

(ii)   **Tax liabilities for 2006/07**

Income tax computation – 2006/07

	£	£
Salary		19,200
Car benefit (W1)		3,750
Fuel benefit (W1)		3,600
Employment income		26,550
Property business income		
UK property (9 × £1,200)	10,800	
Overseas property (7 × £850 × 100/85)	7,000	
		17,800
Savings income		
NSB EASA	180	
Bank deposit interest (400 × 100/80)	500	
		680
Dividend income		
UK dividends (1,800 × 100/90)	2,000	
Overseas dividends (650 × 100/65)	1,000	
		3,000
Statutory total income		48,030
Less Personal allowance		(5,035)
Taxable income		42,995

Analysis of income:
Other income £39,315, savings income £680, dividend income £3,000

Income tax

£		£
2,090 × 10% (other income)		215
37,165 × 22% (other income)		8,176
39,315		
280 × 20% (savings)		56
39,595 (W2)		
400 × 40% (savings)		160
3,000 × 32.5% (dividends)		975
42,995		
		9,582
Less Double tax relief (W3)		(1,375)
Income tax liability		8,207
Less Tax deducted at source		
PAYE		(5,085)
Bank interest (500 × 20%)		(100)
UK dividends		(200)
Income tax payable		2,822

Capital gains tax – 2006/07

Gift of Red plc shares	£
Proceeds (market value) (50,000 × 2.22) (W4)	111,000
Less: Cost (probate value)	(20,000)
Gain before taper relief	91,000

There is no indexation allowance as the shares were acquired after April 1998.

Gift relief is not available as the shares are quoted and Amy does not have a >5% interest in the company.

As the shares are non-business assets for taper relief purposes, which have been held for less than three complete years, the gain is 100% chargeable.

Gift of the overseas property

Gains on the disposal of assets located overseas are only chargeable to capital gains tax where they are remitted to the UK. As there is no remittance to the UK, no gain is chargeable on the overseas property.

Gift of the UK property

	£
Proceeds (market value) (January 2007)	125,000
Less: Cost (June 1994)	(67,000)
Unindexed gain	58,000
Less: Indexation allowance	
(162.6 – 144.7)/144.7 = 0.124 × 67,000	(8,308)
Indexed gain	49,692

Gift relief is not available as the property is not a qualifying asset for gift relief purposes.

As the property is a non-business asset for taper relief purposes, which has been held for nine complete years (including the bonus year), the gain is 65% chargeable.

Capital gains tax liability	£
Gains on Red plc shares (91,000 × 100%)	91,000
Gain on UK property (49,692 × 65%)	32,300
Total chargeable gains	123,300
Less Annual exemption	(8,800)
Taxable gains	114,500
Capital gains tax (114,500 × 40%)	45,800

Deferral of gains

There is limited opportunity to defer the gains on the Red plc shares and the UK property. The gifts are not qualifying assets for CGT gift relief, however, gains on any assets can be deferred if Amy qualifies for Enterprise Investment Scheme (EIS) deferral relief.

If Amy subscribes for shares in companies that qualify under the Enterprise Investment Scheme, then the gains equal to the amount of EIS investment may be deferred.

The EIS investment must be made in the period one year before to three years after the date of the disposal of the shares and UK property.

Inheritance tax

The three gifts to her brother are lifetime transfers to an individual, and are therefore potentially exempt transfers (PETs). No IHT is payable at the time of the gifts. IHT only becomes payable if Amy dies within seven years of the date of the gifts.

Workings

(W1) **Car and fuel benefit**

CO_2 emissions 175 g/km, available all year

Appropriate % $= 15\% + 1/5 \times (175 - 140) + 3\%$ diesel supplement
$= 25\%$

	£
Car benefit (£15,000 × 25%)	3,750
Fuel benefit (£14,400 × 25%)	3,600

(W2) **Extended basic rate band**

	£
Basic rate band	33,300
Gross personal pension contribution (4,910 × 100/78)	6,295
Extended basic rate band	39,595

(W3) **Double taxation relief**

Where there is more than one source of foreign income, the UK tax suffered is found by excluding the foreign sources one by one, starting with the foreign income suffering overseas tax at the highest rate (i.e. dividends in this case).

			£	£
Dividend income				
Lower of	(1)	Overseas tax suffered		
		(1,000 × 35%)	350	
	(2)	UK income tax		
		(1,000 × 32.5%)	325	325
Rental income				
Lower of	(1)	Overseas tax suffered		
		(7,000 × 15%)	1,050	1,050
	(2)	UK income tax (Note)	2,070	
				1,375

Note: The UK tax suffered on the rental income is clearly more than the 15% overseas tax suffered, therefore there is no need to calculate the actual amount of UK tax on this income.

For tutorial purposes:

The UK tax on the rental income is calculated as:

	£
Excluding foreign income (7,000 × 22%)	1,540
Plus Tax savings as the interest and dividends now fall into the BR band	
(400 × 20%) (savings income)	80
(2,000 × 22½%) (UK dividends)	450
	2,070

(W4) Valuation of the Red plc shares

Lower of:

(i)	Quarter up method = 221 + ¼ (229 − 221)	223
(ii)	Average of the lowest and highest marked bargains (½ × (219 + 225))	222

Value of 50,000 shares
= 50,000 × 2.22 = £111,000

(b) (i) Inheritance tax implications of gifting the main residence

As Amy is planning to gift her main residence to her niece, but to continue to live in it, the gift will be caught by the 'gift with reservation of benefit' rules.

At the time of the gift, it is treated as a normal lifetime transfer, but it is also treated as part of Amy's estate. Relief is given for any double charges to IHT which may occur as a result of this treatment.

As Amy dies within seven years of making the gift, there is a potential for a double tax charge as the original PET becomes chargeable and the house is included in Amy's estate.

The relief operates by firstly calculating the total IHT payable ignoring the PET, then secondly calculating the total IHT payable ignoring the property in the estate on death. The calculation giving the highest overall tax charge is used.

IHT liability on Amy's death – ignoring the PET re the house

	£
1 June 2006 – Gift of Red plc shares	
Value transferred	111,000
Annual exemptions 2006/07	(3,000)
2005/06	(3,000)
PET becomes chargeable	105,000
No IHT payable as the PET is covered by the nil rate band of £285,000.	
Nil rate band remaining = (285,000 − 105,000)	180,000

6 November 2006 – Gift of overseas property

Transfer of overseas property is not chargeable to IHT as Amy is not domiciled in UK

6 January 2007 – Gift of UK property   £
PET becomes chargeable (no annual exemptions available)   125,000

No IHT payable as the PET is covered by the
nil rate band available of £180,000.
Nil rate band remaining = (180,000 – 125,000)   55,000

Estate at death – 1 September 2011
Main residence   400,000

IHT liability
(400,000 – 55,000) × 40%   138,000

IHT liability on Amy's death – treating gift of house as a PET
The IHT on other PETs remain the same   £
1 June 2007 – Gift of house
Value transferred   400,000
Annual exemption 2007/08   (3,000)

PET becomes chargeable   397,000

IHT liability
(397,000 – 55,000) × 40%   136,800
Less Taper relief (40%) (4–5 years)   (54,720)

                                                                                                    82,080

Including the house in the estate gives the higher overall charge and therefore
this basis is used.

(ii)   **Reduction of IHT liability**

The IHT liability on the gift of the house would be reduced if, after making the
gift, Amy continued to live in the house but paid her niece a market rent for
living in the property.

The rent would be taxable as property business income in the hands of her
niece, less any expenses.

The gift would no longer be a gift with reservation, but a normal PET, giving an
IHT liability of £82,080 if Amy died in September 2011.

ACCA marking scheme			
			Marks
(a)	(i)	Income tax	1.0
		Capital gains tax	1.0
		Inheritance tax	1.0
			3.0
	(ii)	Income tax:	
		Car benefit	1.0
		Fuel benefit	0.5
		UK rental income	0.5
		Overseas rental income	1.0
		NSB interest	0.5
		Bank interest	0.5
		UK dividends	0.5
		Overseas dividends	1.0
		Income tax (before DTR)	2.0

	DTR (½ + ½)		1.0
	Tax deducted at source		0.5
	CGT:		
	June gain (½ + ½)		1.0
	November – no gain		0.5
	January gain (½ + ½)		1.0
	Tapered gains (½ + ½)		1.0
	Annual exemption tax liability		0.5
	IHT		0.5
	Deferral of gains:		
	Not eligible for gift relief		0.5
	Qualifies for EIS/VCT relief		0.5
	EIS deferral relief details		0.5
			15.0
(b) (i)	Gift with reservation	– identification	0.5
		– treatment	1.0
	Potential double charge		0.5
	Calculate ignoring PET:		
	June – annual exemptions		0.5
	November – not chargeable		0.5
	Estate at death – liability		0.5
	Calculation with gift as PET:		
	Annual exemption		0.5
	Tax liability		0.5
	Taper relief		0.5
	Higher charge used		0.5
(ii)	Pay market rent		0.5
	IHT saving as not GwR		0.5
	Property income charge		0.5
			7.0
Total: available			25.0

41 DEE LIMITED

(a) **IHT Liabilities for David**

Lifetime transfers

February 2000 – Gift of cottage

The gift of the cottage is a PET and therefore no lifetime IHT is payable.

The PET is more than seven years before the date of David's death and therefore does not become chargeable on death. However, David's continued use of the cottage for 2 months a year means that this represents a gift with reservation as the property is not occupied to the exclusion of the donor (David).

As a result, the property will remain in David's estate at the time of his death, at the market value at the date of death of £150,000.

June 2001 – Gift into discretionary trust

David's gift into a discretionary trust is a chargeable lifetime transfer (CLT) and therefore lifetime IHT is payable. As David paid the tax in lifetime himself, the gift is grossed up. Two annual exemptions of £3,000 for 2001/02 and 2000/01 reduce the taxable gift to £287,000.

As there are no other chargeable lifetime transfers in the previous seven years, the lifetime IHT tax payable is:

$(287,000 - 285,000) \times 20/80$ £500

The gross gift is therefore £287,500 (287,000 + 500).

Further IHT is payable on this gift when David dies (see below).

February 2002 – Gift of shares to children

The gift of the shares to his children is a PET, therefore no lifetime IHT is due. However David dies within 7 years and therefore the PET becomes chargeable.

The value of the PET is based on the diminution in David's estate after taking account of the related property rules as follows:

	Before the transfer		After the transfer	
	Number	%	Number	%
David's holding	4,500	70%	3,000	40%
Debbie's holding (Wife)	500	30%	500	30%
	5,000	100%	3,500	70%

	£
Value of David's holding before the gift	
£900,000 × (4,500/5,000)	810,000
Value of David's holding after the gift	
£475,000 × (3,000/3,500)	(407,143)
Diminution in value of estate	402,857
BPR (100%) (Note)	(402,857)
PET	Nil

Note: As the shares are unquoted trading company shares they are relevant business property for BPR purposes and have been held for more than two years. 100% relief will therefore be available on the lifetime transfer.

Assuming both children still hold the shares on David's death, business property relief will continue to be available. Therefore no further IHT will be payable on David's death.

Additional IHT arising on death re June 2001 gift

The gross CLT of £287,500 becomes chargeable on death as follows:

	£
(287,500 – 285,000 × 40%	1,000
Less Taper relief (60%) (5 – 6 years)	(600)
	400
Less Lifetime tax paid	(500)
Additional IHT payable (Note)	nil

Note: The lifetime tax paid is never repaid.

Estate on death

	Notes	£	£
Residence			275,000
Shares in Dee Ltd	(1)	570,000	
Less: Business property relief (100%)		(570,000)	Nil
Cash deposits			60,000
Paintings			12,000
Death in service			200,000
Quoted shares			125,000
GWR: Holiday cottage			150,000
			822,000
Less: Exempt estate	(2)		(572,000)
Gross chargeable estate	(3)		250,000
IHT (250,000 × 40%)	(2)		100,000

Notes:

(1) **Shares in Dee Ltd**

Value of 60% holding on death (taking account of related property of a 10% interest)

£665,000 × (3,000/3,500) = £570,000

The shares are eligible for 100% BPR as they are unquoted trading company shares held for more than two years.

(2) **Exempt estate**

The entire estate is left to the spouse and is therefore exempt, except for the house which is a gift with reservation (GWR). This GWR remains chargeable in David's estate and the gross value of the gift needs to be established (W3).

(3) **Single grossing up on death**

As there is a chargeable gift of a UK asset and all of the residue of the estate goes to an exempt person (the spouse), to calculate the gross chargeable estate, the gift of the house needs to be grossed up as follows:

	£
Net chargeable gift	150,000
Nil rate band available =Nil	
IHT on chargeable gift	
(150,000 × 40/60)	100,000
Gross chargeable estate	250,000

(b) (i) **Debbie's death in June 2007**

Lifetime transfers

Debbie gifted the villa in June 2005. There was originally no IHT liability on this gift as it was a PET (potentially exempt transfer). However, it would be chargeable on Debbie's death in June 2007 as the transfer was within seven years.

	£
Value of transfer	192,000
Less: Annual exemption 2005/06	(3,000)
2004/05	(3,000)
PET	186,000

No IHT is payable at the time of the gift and no IHT is payable on death as the gift is covered by Debbie's nil rate band.

Debbie will still have £99,000 (£285,000 – £186,000) of her nil rate band left at death.

As Allison still owns the villa on Debbie's death, the fall in value of £82,000 (£192,000 – £110,000) is taken account of when calculating any tax payable on the PET when (if) it becomes chargeable on Debbie's death. In this case, however, this will have no effect because the gift falls entirely within Debbie's nil tax band.

The relief also has no effect on subsequent gifts and the estate computation. Therefore the £99,000 nil rate band remaining is used in the estate computation.

Estate at death

	£	£
Residence		550,000
Shares in Dee Ltd (70% holding)	665,000	
Less: Business property relief (100%)	(665,000)	Nil
Cash deposits		100,000
Paintings		18,300
Cash (Death in service)		200,000
Quoted shares		150,000
Chargeable estate		1,018,300
IHT (1,018,300 – 99,000 see above) × 40%		367,720

(ii) **Inheritance tax administration**

The tax on Debbie's estate would be paid by the personal representatives, usually an executor.

Inheritance tax is due six months from the end of the month in which death occurred (i.e. 31 December 2007) or the date on which probate is obtained (if earlier).

However, an instalment option is available for certain assets, which includes land and buildings (i.e. the residence), whereby the tax can be paid in 10 equal annual instalments starting on the normal due date.

(c) **Debbie survives until July 2011**

Debbie should consider giving away some of her assets to her children, while ensuring that she still has enough to live on. Such lifetime gifts would be PETs. The PETs will become chargeable on Debbie's death as she will not survive seven years. However, taper relief will reduce the amount chargeable to IHT provided the gifts were made prior to July 2008.

It is important to remember that Debbie's annual exemptions will reduce the value of any PET when assets are gifted. Debbie has not used her annual exemption for the last two years, and so she can gift £6,000 (2 × £3,000) in the current tax year as well as £3,000 per year in future tax years. Debbie could therefore give away £18,000 (£6,000 in 2007/08 and £3,000 in the next four years), saving tax of £7,200 (£18,000 × 40%).

Debbie can also make use of the small gifts exemption of up to £250 per donee per year.

As Andrew is shortly to be married, Debbie could give up to £5,000 in consideration of his marriage. This would save £2,000 in IHT.

Expenditure out of normal income is also exempt from IHT. This is where the transferor is left with sufficient income to maintain his/her usual standard of living. Broadly, you need to demonstrate evidence of a prior commitment, or a settled pattern of expenditure.

It does not make sense for Debbie to gift shares in Dee Limited, as these qualify for full business property relief and therefore are not subject to IHT.

Debbie should consider making gifts to Allison's children instead of Allison. This would not save any IHT now, but the gifts skip a generation and this action would ensure that the assets are not included in Allison's death should she die.

If substantial gifts are made, the donees would be advised to consider taking out insurance policies on Debbie's life to cover the potential tax liabilities that may arise on PETs in the event of her early death.

		ACCA marking scheme	Marks
(a)		Gift with reservation	1.0
		Remains in David's estate	0.5
		At market value	0.5
		Value using related property rules	0.5
		Calculation of correct values	1.5
		Relevant business property	0.5
		Unquoted company	0.5
		Held more than two years	0.5
		Business property relief	0.5
		Gift into trust being chargeable lifetime transfer	0.5
		Two annual exemptions	0.5
		Correct gross-up calculation	1.0
		40% death rate	0.5
		Taper relief	0.5
		Rate of taper relief	0.5
		Less: lifetime tax paid	0.5
		Shares in Dee ltd	0.5
		Remaining personal items (total)	0.5
		David's estate on death: holiday cottage	0.5
		Residence	0.5
		Exempt estate	0.5
		Inheritance tax on estate	0.5
		Max	12.0
(b)	(i)	Gift of villa is potentially exempt transfer	0.5
		Annual exemptions x 2 (0.5 each)	1.0
		Awareness of fall in value	0.5
		No effect on use of nil rate band	0.5
		Remaining nil rate band available	0.5
		Death estate: shares in Dee ltd	0.5
		Death estate: Remaining estate items (total)	0.5
		Tax at 40%	0.5

	Max	4.0
(ii)	Personal representatives	0.5
	6 months/31 December	0.5
	probate if earlier	0.5
	installment option re residence	0.5
	10 annual installments	0.5
	Max	2.0
(c)	Need to make lifetime gifts	0.5
	Lifetime gifts are potentially exempt transfers	0.5
	Seven year survival for PETs to disappear	0.5
	Taper relief to apply 3 – 7 years	0.5
	Gifts to grandchildren (skip generation)	1.0
	No point gifting shares as BPR is available	0.5
	Marriage gift	0.5
	Availability of two annual exemptions	0.5
	Amount of exemptions/savings	0.5
	Small exempt gifts	0.5
	Expenditure out of normal income – identify	0.5
	Detail re usual standard of living	0.5
	Use of insurance	0.5
	Max	7.0
Total (Max)		25.0

42 ALEX

(a) Income tax payable/repayable for 2006/07

	Notes	Total	Others	Savings	Dividend	Tax at source
		£	£	£	£	£
Pension		9,000	9,000			1,230
Building society interest	(2)	1,600		1,600		320
NSB EASA interest	(3)	370		370		
Dividends – other	(4)	9,000	-		9,000	900
– Nacional plc	(5)	4,000			4,000	400
Statutory total income		23,970	9,000	1,970	13,000	
Less: PAA	(6)	(5,485)	(5,485)			
Taxable income		18,485	3,515	1,970	13,000	2,850

Income tax

£		£
2,150	@ 10%	215
1,365	@ 22%	300
3,515		
1,970	@ 20%	394
13,000	@ 10%	1,300
18,485		

	£
IT Liability	2,209
Less: Tax at source	(2,850)
Income tax repayable	(641)

Notes:

(1)   Alex will be taxed on his income due and payable up to the date of death. He will have a full (non-apportioned) personal allowance for 2006/07, the tax year of death.

(2)   Building society interest = £1,280 × 100/80 = £1,600

(3)   National savings Bank Easy Access Savings Account interest is received gross.

(4)   Dividends received other than from Nacional plc = £8,100 × 100/90 = £9,000

(5)   Nacional plc dividends

The dividends are declared before Alex's death and are therefore included in Alex's last income tax computation even though they are received post death.

Gross dividends to include = 20,000 × 18p × 100/90 = £4,000

Note: The ACCA have confirmed that this is the treatment they expect for dividends declared pre-death, received post death.

(6)   Personal age allowance (PAA)

	£	£
PAA, aged 85		7,420
STI	23,970	
Abatement limit	(20,100)	
Abatement	3,870 × ½	(1,935)
Reduced PAA		5,485

(b)   Inheritance tax liability on Alex's death

The gift in July 2001 was a potentially exempt transfer (PET). No IHT is payable at the time of the gift. IHT only becomes payable when Alex dies within seven years.

The transfer into the discretionary trust in March 2002 was a chargeable lifetime transfer (CLT). Lifetime IHT is due when the gift is made and additional tax is due as Alex dies within seven years of the gift.

Lifetime inheritance tax

The value of the CLT was £293,000. No annual exemptions were available, as these are allocated in date order against the PET in only 2001.

The lifetime tax on the CLT was as follows:

(£293,000 − £285,000 nil rate band) × 20/80 = £2,000

The grossed up value of the gift was therefore £295,000 (293,000 + 2,000).

Tutorial note: The tax rate used of 20/80 (or 25%) is the rate used to calculate the lifetime tax where the donor suffers any lifetime tax due. All of the nil rate band is available against this lifetime gift; the PET is ignored as it is not chargeable during Alex's lifetime.

Additional Inheritance tax due at death

IHT on PET in July 2001

The PET becomes chargeable on death, as Alex died within seven years of making the gift. As there are no lifetime transfers in the previous seven years, all of the nil rate band is available.

	£
Value transferred	293,000
Less: Annual exemptions: 2001/02	(3,000)
2000/01	(3,000)
PET	287,000
IHT due (287,000 − 285,000) × 40%	800
Less: Taper relief (5 − 6 years) (60%)	(480)
IHT due on death	320

This additional tax is always paid by the donee, i.e. Brian in this case.

Note: The PET has used up the nil rate band, so the CLT in March 2002 is fully taxable.

IHT on CLT in March 2002

	£
Gross gift (£295,00 × 40%)	118,000
Less: Taper relief (4 − 5 years) (40%)	(47,200)
	70,800
Less: IHT paid during lifetime	(2,000)
IHT due on death	68,800

This additional tax is always paid by the donee, i.e. the trustees of the discretionary trust in this case.

Estate at death

	Notes	£	£
Residence			475,000
Touriga shares	(1)	26,950	
Less: Business property relief		(26,950)	
			Nil
Nacional shares	(2)		128,800
Building society account			15,000
NSB EASA			55,000
National Savings Certificates			180,000
Chattels			40,000
Other quoted investments			115,000
Income tax repayment (part (a))			641
Gross chargeable estate			1,009,441

The nil band has already been used against gifts made in the seven years prior to death. The full death estate is therefore taxed at 40%.

IHT on estate (1,009,441 × 40%)	403,776

The inheritance due to each of Brian and Beatrice is £316,307 (W).

Notes:

(1)   The total value of Touriga Ltd shares at death is (£11.00 x 2,450) = £26,950. As these shares are unquoted trading company shares and have been held for more than two years, 100% business property relief applies.

(2)   The Nacional plc shares are valued at the lower of:

(i)   quarter up method (624 + 0.25 × (632 – 624)) = 626p

(ii)   average of highest and lowest marked bargains (625 + 630)½ = 627.5p

Value of 20,000 shares = 626p × 20,000 = 125,200

As the shares are quoted ex-div at the date of death, to the value of the shares in the death estate, need to include the value of the next net dividend (18p x 20,000 = £3,600).

The total value of the shares is therefore £128,800 (3,600 + 125,200).

Working: Share of inheritance

	£
Value of estate	1,009,441
Value of Touriga shares	26,950
	1,036,391
IHT payable from estate	(403,776)
Estate value to share	632,615

Half share to each of Brian and Beatrice (632,615 ÷ 2) = £316,307.

(c)   (i)   **Use of a discretionary trust**

Discretionary trusts

The trustees of a discretionary trust have the discretion (hence the name) over how the funds will be used. They can thus control the assets comprising the inheritance, while allowing Colin or Charlotte access to some or all of the income.

It is likely that Brian himself would wish to be a trustee and he could therefore control how his children accessed the money.

Gifts into a discretionary trust are chargeable lifetime transfers (CLTs). They attract IHT at half the death rate to the extent that the cumulative lifetime transfers in the last seven years of the settlor (Brian) exceed the nil rate band (£285,000). The tax can be paid by the trustees out of the settled assets (i.e. borne by the trust).

Once the assets are settled in a discretionary trust, the trust will suffer a 10 year charge (the 'principal charge') based on the value of the trust at the 10 year anniversary, cumulated with the previous chargeable transfers of the settlor at the time the trust was created. The charge is 6%, based on 30% of the lifetime rate (20%).

If capital assets are removed from the trust (i.e. distributed to the beneficiaries), an exit charge is also levied at a rate based on 30% of the tax charged on the creation of the trust or the periodic charge at the last 10 year anniversary (if later), and the length of time that has elapsed since.

(c)   (ii)   **Inheritance tax planning**

If Brian creates a discretionary trust by making a lifetime gift of the inherited assets, this will give rise to a further charge to IHT.

Furthermore, as Brian will not have held the Touriga Ltd shares for the 2 year qualifying period, they will not qualify for business property relief on a lifetime transfer.

Therefore, Brian should be advised to pass his inheritance directly to his children by using a deed of variation to alter the disposition of Alex's estate.

Provided the deed includes a statement that the deed is effective for inheritance tax purposes, the transfer into the trust will be treated as a legacy under the will. There will be no alteration in the tax payable on Alex's estate but Brian will have preserved his own nil rate band for use against future lifetime gifts or the value of his own estate on death.

	ACCA marking scheme		
			Marks
(a)		Pension	0.5
		Building society interest	0.5
		National savings bank interest	0.5
		Nacional dividend	0.5
		Other dividend	0.5
		Full personal allowance for year	0.5
		Personal allowance (calculation)	1.0
		Income tax bands	1.0
		Tax credits	0.5
		Max	5.0
(b)		Lifetime gifts:	
		July 2001 a PET	0.5
		March 2002 a CLT	0.5
		No Annual exemptions (used re PET)	0.5
		CLT gross value	0.5
		Additional tax on death:	
		PET cumulated first on death	0.5
		Annual exemptions x 2	1.0
		Taper relief	1.0
		CLT all at 40%	0.5
		Taper relief	1.0
		Lifetime tax offset	0.5
		Estate:	
		Touriga 100% BPR	1.0
		Nacional	1.0
		Income tax refund	0.5
		Balance of estate	0.5
		Tax on estate at 40%	0.5
		Inherited value:	
		Net taxable estate	0.5
		Shares in Touriga	0.5
		Max	10.0
(c)	(i)	Discretionary trust (DT):	
		Basic features	1.0
		CLT on creation	1.0
		Periodic charge	1.0
		Exit charge	1.0

(ii)	Lifetime gift re Brian		0.5
	Cumulated on death within 7 years		0.5
	Loss of BPR on Touriga shares		1.0
	Deed of variation		1.0
	No change in tax on estate		0.5
		Max	3.0
Total			22

43 STUART

(a) **Taxable capital gain on sale of Plymouth House**

	£
Sales proceeds (November 2006)	422,100
Less Cost (May 1994) (probate value)	(185,000)
Unindexed gain	237,100

Indexation $\dfrac{(162.6 - 144.7)}{144.7} = 0.124 \times £185,000$ (22,940)

	£
Indexed gain before PPR relief	214,160
Less: PPR exemption (Note 1)	(127,645)
Letting exemption (Note 2)	(38,294)
Indexed gain after PPR reliefs	48,221
Less: Capital losses brought forward	(29,500)
Net indexed gain	18,721

As a non-business asset held for nine qualifying years (including the bonus year), the gain is 65% chargeable.

	£
Chargeable gain ($\times$ 65%)	12,169
Less: Annual exemption	(8,800)
Taxable gain	3,369

Notes

(1) **PPR exemption**

The periods of occupation are as follows:

Total	Months occupied	Months not occupied	
1 May 1994 – 28 February 1995	10	10 (a)	
1 March 1995 –31 December 1998	46	36 (b)	10
1 January 1999 – 31 March 2001	27		27
1 April 2001 – 30 November 2001	8	8 (a)	
1 December 2001 – 30 November 2006	60	36 (c)	24
	151	90	61

(a) Periods of a actual occupation are allowed.

(b) The first 36 months of the period from 1 March 1995 to 31 March 2001 qualifies as a deemed occupation period as Stuart and Rebecca returned to occupy the property on 1 April 2001.

The remainder of the period will be treated as a period of absence, although letting relief is available for part of the period (see below).

(c)   Note that the last 36 months count as deemed occupation, as the house was Stuart's principal private residence (PPR) at some point during his period of ownership.

The exempt element of the gain is the proportion during which the property was occupied, real or deemed. PPR exemption = $(90/151) \times$ £214,160 = £127,645.

(2)   **Letting exemption**

The chargeable gain is restricted for the period that the property was let out.

This is restricted to the lowest of the following:

(i)   the gain not exempted under PPR which is attributable to the letting period

$(27/151 \times 214,160) = $ £38,294

(ii)   £40,000 maximum

(iii)   the total exempt PPR gain = £127,645

Letting exemption is therefore £38,294

(b)   **Tax efficient alternative investments**

Tutorial note: The examiner has assumed that the shares will be held until death and therefore has ignored the capital gains tax implications. This is reasonable given Stuart's imminent death.

As both companies are listed, the only difference in taxation will be in the availability of inheritance tax relief, namely business property relief (BPR).

If Stuart and Rebecca jointly hold in excess of 50% of the share capital of a listed company, BPR will be available at the rate of 50%. Otherwise, no BPR is available.

With the proceeds from the house, Stuart can only buy 1,005,000 (£422,100/£0.42) shares in Omikron plc. This represents a shareholding of 2% (1,005,000/50,250,000). As the shares in Omikron plc are listed, a 2% holding will not qualify for BPR.

At the moment, both Stuart and Rebecca own 2,400,000 shares in Omega plc. Their shareholdings are amalgamated for IHT purposes under the related property rules. With a joint holding of 48%, BPR is not available.

A further 200,001 shares will be required to attain a holding in excess of 50% and therefore qualify for BPR. Stuart has sufficient funds from the proceeds of the house to purchase 201,000 shares (£422,100/£2.10).

Assuming Stuart and Rebecca can buy these shares, they must then hold their 50% interest in the company for the period of at least two years in order to ensure that BPR applies.

On the basis that Stuart is expected to survive for two to three years, he should therefore buy further shares in Omega plc in order to take advantage of the BPR available.

(c)   **Inheritance tax liability – Rebecca**

As Stuart's estate at death passes entirely to Rebecca, his spouse, it is an exempt transfer for inheritance tax (IHT) purposes.

Rebecca faces the following potential IHT liability on her estate:

	£	£
Residence		900,000
Shares in Omega plc (Note 1)	10,502,100	
Less: BPR (Note 2)	(5,251,050)	5,251,050
Investments		250,000
Cash		130,000
Cash from life assurance policy		200,000
Chargeable estate		6,731,050

As Rebecca has made no lifetime gifts, all of her nil rate band is available.

IHT (6,731,050 – 285,000) × 40%   2,578,420

Notes:

(1)   **Omega plc shares**

The shares in Omega plc are valued at the lower of:

(i)   quarter up method = $(208 + 0.25 \times (216 - 208))$ = 210p

(ii)   average of marked bargains = $(207 + 215)/2$ = 211p

i.e. 210p per share.

The total shareholding is therefore worth £10,502,100 ((4,800,000 + 201,000) × £2.10)

(2)   **BPR**

As Rebecca inherited the new shares on Stuart's death (her spouse) BPR is available as she is deemed to have owned the shares for the total period of ownership by the couple.

(d)   **Inheritance tax planning**

Stuart is currently not making use of his nil rate band, as all assets transferred in his will are, exempt from inheritance tax (IHT) as they go to Rebecca (his spouse) on death. He should therefore consider altering his will to transfer an amount equivalent to the nil rate band to his son, Sam.

Care should be taken in determining which assets are to be left to Sam. The Omega plc shares should not be transferred to Sam as they currently attract 50% BPR. If transferred to Sam, Rebecca's interest in the company falls below 50% and she will not be entitled to BPR on her death.

Instead, assets not subject to any reliefs (such as the insurance payout or cash deposits) should be gifted in the will. By doing this, IHT of £114,000 (£285,000 × 40%) could be saved on the ultimate death of Rebecca.

It is too late for both Stuart and Rebecca to make use of potentially exempt transfers (PETs) as no relief is obtained until three years have passed, and full relief only occurs seven years after making the gifts.

Both individuals should however make use of their annual exemptions (£3,000 per person per year). The annual exemptions not used up in the previous year can be used in this current year. This would give a saving of £2,400 each (3,000 × 2 × 40%). Exemptions for items such as small gifts (£250 per donee per year) are also available.

Gifts out of normal income should also be considered. After making such gifts, the individual should be left with sufficient income to maintain their usual standard of living. To obtain the exemption, it is usually necessary to demonstrate general evidence of a prior commitment to make the gifts, or a settled pattern of expenditure.

While there are no details of income, both Stuart and Rebecca are wealthy in their own right, and are likely to earn reasonable sums from their investments. They should therefore be able to satisfy the conditions on that basis.

If Rebecca were to make substantial lifetime gifts, the donees would be advised to consider taking out insurance policies on Rebecca's life to cover the potential tax liabilities that may arise on any PETs in the event of her early death.

		ACCA marking scheme	
			Marks
(a)		Acquisition cost	0.5
		Indexation	0.5
		Principal private residence:	
		correct treatment of each period (× 7)	3.5
		PPR exempt gain: exempt fraction	0.5
		Letting exemption:	
		awareness	0.5
		calculation of let period gain	0.5
		identification of other limits (0.5 × 2)	1.0
		lowest of three	0.5
		Offset of capital losses	0.5
		Taper relief: non-business asset	0.5
		correct number of years/rate	0.5
		Annual exemption	0.5
		Correct order of offset of exemptions and reliefs	0.5
		Max	9.0
(b)		Holding required to get BPR for listed company	0.5
		Rate of BPR that applies	0.5
		Omikron small shareholding, no BPR	1.0
		Omega: related property shareholdings	0.5
		calculation of shares required	0.5
		hold for more than two years	0.5
		Reasoned conclusion	0.5
		Max	3.0
(c)	Stuart:	exempt estate to spouse	0.5
	Rebecca:	Omega shares	
		valuation/lower of two methods	1.0
		estate: value of shares	0.5
		deduction of BPR	1.0
		other assets: investments	0.5
		cash deposits	0.5

	cash (insurance policy)	0.5
	residence	0.5
	nil rate band	0.5
	IHT at 40%	0.5
	Max	6.0
(d)	Need to use nil rate bands	0.5
	Stuart's will to transfer nil rate band assets to son	0.5
	No point gifting Omega shares as BPR is available	1.0
	Calculation of tax saved on first death	0.5
	No PETs, re Stuart or Rebecca	1.0
	Reason/reference to taper relief 3–7 years	0.5
	Make use of annual exemptions	0.5
	Availability of two annual exemptions each	0.5
	Calculation of immediate tax saving	0.5
	Small exempt gifts	0.5
	Expenditure out of normal income – identify relief	0.5
	Usual standard of living/pattern of giving (2 × 0.5)	1.0
	Use of insurance	0.5
	Max	7.0
Total		25.0

VAT

44 GEWGAW LTD

(a) (i) **VAT Return – Quarter ended 31 March 2007**

	Notes	£	£
Output VAT:			
Sales (62,500 × 97.5% × 17.5%)	(1)		10,664
Motor car scale charge (311 × 17.5/117.5)	(2)		46
			10,710
Input VAT:			
Purchases (21,000 × 17.5%)		3,675	
Bad debt (2,000 × 17.5%)	(3)	350	
Expenses (14,640 - 480 = 14,160 × 17.5%)	(4)	2,478	
			(6,503)
VAT due 30 April 2007			4,207

Notes:

(1) The calculation of output VAT on sales must take into account the discount for prompt payment, even if customers do not take it.

(2) Input VAT cannot be reclaimed in respect of either the motor car or the sunroof, as this was not fitted subsequent to the original purchase and invoiced for separately. The managing director's private use of the motor car does not affect the recovery of input VAT on the repairs.

Input VAT on the fuel provided can be recovered in full, but the scale charge on deemed supplied private fuel must be accounted for.

(3)   Relief for an irrecoverable debt is not given until six months from the time that payment is due. Therefore relief in respect of the invoice due for payment on 5 November 2006 cannot be claimed until the following VAT return.

(4)   VAT on business entertaining cannot be reclaimed.

Implications of paying VAT late – The default surcharge

Gewgaw Ltd's first VAT return due on 31 July 2006 was submitted late, so HMRC will have issued a surcharge liability notice specifying a surcharge period running to 30 June 2007.

Although the second and third returns were submitted by the due dates of 31 October 2006 and 31 January 2007 respectively, the VAT due was paid late in each case.

Surcharges of 2% and 5% will therefore have been charged, and a further late payment will result in a surcharge of £421 (4,207 × 10%). In addition, the surcharge period will be extended to 31 March 2008.

(ii)   **Conditions for joining VAT scheme**

Cash accounting scheme

Gewgaw Ltd can use the cash accounting scheme if

(i)   its expected taxable turnover for the next 12 months does not exceed £660,000, and

(ii)   it is up to date with its VAT returns and VAT payments.

The scheme will result in the tax point becoming the date that payment is received from customers. This should be advantageous since it delays the payment of output VAT, and also provides for automatic bad debt relief should a customer not pay.

In the quarter ended 31 March 2007 the company would have accounted for output VAT on sales of £9,485 (54,200 × 17.5%) instead of £10,664. However, the recovery of input VAT on purchases would have been reduced from £3,675 to £3,395 (19,400 × 17.5%).

Annual accounting scheme

Gewgaw Ltd can apply to use the annual accounting scheme if

(i)   its expected taxable turnover for the next 12 months does not exceed £1,350,000, and

(ii)   it is up to date with its VAT returns.

Under the scheme only one VAT return is submitted each year, with nine monthly payments being made on account. The balancing payment is due two months after the end of the year.

It should be beneficial for Gewgaw Ltd to join the scheme, since the reduced administration required should mean that default surcharges are avoided.

(b)   **Maintenance of company's bookkeeping**

The annual cost of using the bookkeeping agency is £6,300 (£525 × 12 months), since any VAT charged is reclaimed as input VAT.

The employee requires £5,200 pa (£100 × 52 weeks) net of income tax and employees' Class 1 NIC. Therefore an additional gross salary of £7,761 (W) will have to be paid. Employer's Class 1 NIC will increase the annual cost of employment to £8,754 (£7,761 × 112.8/100).

It is therefore beneficial, all other factors being equal, for Gewgaw Ltd to continue to use the bookkeeping agency, since this results in an overall annual saving of £2,454 (8,754 - 6,300).

Working: **Gross salary required**

	%	£
Net salary requirement		5,200
Income tax rate	22	
Class 1 NICs rate	11	
	33	
Grossed up salary (5,200 × 100/67)		7,761

45   CONFUSED LTD

(a)   **VAT return for quarter ended 31 December 2006**

Irrecoverable debt

Relief for irrecoverable debts is given six months after the time that payment was due, provided that the debt has been written off in the accounts.

No VAT bad debt relief would have been claimed in the VAT return for the quarter ended 30 September 2006 since the due date of the earliest invoice was 5 May 2006 (30 days after 5 April 2006).

Relief can be claimed in the VAT return for the quarter ended 31 December 2006 in respect of the two invoices due for payment on 5 May and 23 June 2006. The invoice dated 22 June 2006 was not due for payment until 22 July 2006 and is not six months old in this quarter. Relief will be obtained in the next quarter.

Where a discount is offered for prompt payment VAT is due on the net amount even if the discount is not taken.

The bad debt relief for the quarter ended 31 December 2006 is therefore:

	£
Invoices 5 April and 24 May	12,000
Less Prompt payment discount (5%)	(600)
	11,400
Additional input VAT claimed (11,400 × 17½%)	1,995

Refund of VAT

Claims for the refund of input VAT for the rental of the company's coffee machines are subject to a three-year time limit.

In addition to the input VAT incurred during the quarter ended 31 December 2006, Confused Ltd can therefore also claim for the input VAT incurred during the period 1 October 2003 to 30 September 2006.

The total amount of input VAT refunded on the VAT return for the quarter ended 31 December 2006 will therefore be £683 (£100 × 39 months = £3,900 at 17.5%).

Imported computers

As regards the three computers acquired from a VAT registered company in a country that is a member of the European Union, the treatment of VAT is as follows:

* The supply is zero-rated in the country of origin but chargeable at the appropriate rate in force in country of destination.

* Therefore, Confused Ltd should account for VAT of £1,260 (£2,400 × 3 computers × 17½%).

* The VAT suffered by Confused Ltd may then be treated as input VAT and reclaimed in the appropriate quarter.

As regards the two computers imported from a country that is not a member of the European Union, the treatment of VAT is as follows:

* VAT is charged on the supply at the rate applicable for the same transaction if made within the UK.

* The VAT suffered by the UK importer may be treated as input VAT and reclaimed in the appropriate quarter.

* Therefore, Confused Ltd will have paid VAT of £840 (£2,400 × 2 computers × 17.5%) at the time of importation.

In both cases, because Confused Ltd makes only taxable supplies, a corresponding input VAT deduction will be given.

On the VAT return for the quarter ended 31 December 2006 Confused Ltd will therefore have to show output VAT of £1,260 and can claim input VAT of £2,100 (1,260 + 840).

Contract

For the supply of goods the tax point is the earliest of

(1)   the date goods are removed or made available to the customer, or

(2)   the date an invoice is issued or payment received.

Where an invoice is issued within 14 days of the goods being removed or made available, this date will replace that in (1).

The payment on account of £4,000 received on 31 August 2006 should therefore have been included as a supply on the VAT return for the quarter ended 30 September 2006.

The amount of output VAT underpaid to be adjusted in the VAT return for the quarter ended 31 December 2006 is £596 (4,000 × 17.5/117.5). The balance of the output VAT of £2,029 (15,000 at 17.5% = 2,625 - 596) will be included on the VAT return for the quarter ended 31 March 2007 when the invoice is issued.

Summary

As the net errors are less than £2,000 (683 refunds + 2,100 computers - 1,260 computers – 596 contract = £927), they can therefore be corrected on the quarterly return for
31 December 2006 without informing HMRC.

(b) (i) **Hire purchase**

The aeroplane is a long-life asset since it has an expected working life of 25 years or more, and the expenditure exceeds the annual *de minimis* limit of £100,000. Therefore Confused Ltd will only be able to claim a writing down allowance of £15,000 (250,000 × 6%) for the year ended 31 March 2008.

The finance charge of £80,000 (36,500 × 20 = 730,000 - 650,000) will be a deductible expense against trading profits. The proportion relating to the year ended 31 March 2007 will be calculated using normal accounting principles.

Input VAT of £113,750 (650,000 at 17.5%) will be reclaimed on the VAT return for the quarter ended 30 June 2007.

(ii) **Leasing**

The net of VAT lease rental payments of £72,340 (85,000 at 100/117.5) for the year ended 31 March 2008 will be a deductible expense against trading profits. Capital allowances are not available.

Input VAT of £12,362 (83,000 at 17.5/117.5) included in the lease rental payment will be reclaimed on the VAT return for the quarter ended 30 June 2007.

(c) (i) **Classification as an employee**

It is necessary to consider the distinction between a contract of service (employed) and a contract for services (self-employed).

The following factors point towards a contract of service, and so the managing director is probably correct in considering the pilot to be employed:

1 The contract between Confused Ltd and the pilot is for twelve months, and such a long engagement is typical of employment.

2 The pilot must work exclusively for Confused Ltd.

3 The pilot's activities do not appear to form a profession in their own right, since he uses Confused Ltd's aeroplane and is paid a monthly fee.

4 There is no indication that the pilot has the financial risk normally associated with self-employment, or can profit from sound management.

(ii) **Net income for the pilot**

	Self-employed £	Employed £
Income (12 × 2,400/2,550)	28,800	30,600
Income tax (W1)	(4,970)	(5,151)
Class 2 NIC (52 × 2.10)	(109)	
Class 4 NIC (28,800 - 5,035) × 8%	(1,901)	
Class 1 NIC (W2)		(2,808)
Net income	21,820	22,641

It is therefore beneficial from the pilot's point of view for him to be paid as an employee, since his additional annual net spendable income is £821 (22,641 – 21,820).

Key answer tips

The pilot will also benefit from the employment rights (such as holiday etc) and a greater entitlement to state benefits.

Workings

(W1) **Income tax**

	Self-employed	*Employed*
	£	£
Income	28,800	30,600
Personal allowance	(5,035)	(5,035)
Taxable income	23,765	25,565

Income tax
£

2,150 × 10%	215	
21,615 × 22%	4,755	
23,765		
2,150 × 10%		215
23,415 × 22%		5,151
25,565		
Income tax liability	4,970	5,366

(W2) **Class 1 NICs**

Paid on a monthly basis

$(2,550 - 420) \times 11\%$ = £234 × 12 months = £2,808

46   JIMMY CHAN

(a)   **Tax adjusted trading profit – year ended 30 April 2006**

		£	£
Profit per the accounts			37,434
Add:	Depreciation	8,241	
	Entertaining non staff	155	
	Motor expenses – proprietor's own use (2,872 × 25%)	718	
	Balancing charge (W1)	1,897	11,011
			48,445
Less:	Capital allowances (W1)	7,437	
	Profit on disposal of fixed assets	4,908	(12,345)
Tax adjusted trading profit			36,100

(b)   **Partial exemption adjustment**

	£
Value of total VAT exclusive supplies	85,787
Value of VAT exempt supplies	28,596
Value of taxable supplies	57,191

Recoverable % of non directly attributable input tax
$= (57,191/85,787) \times 100 = 66.7\%$

	£
Rounded up to	67%
Input tax per question	2,940
Recoverable input tax $(2,940 \times 67\%)$	1,970
Balance apportioned to exempt supplies $(2,940 - 1,970)$	970

Monthly average = $(970 \div 12) = £81$ per month

As the monthly average is below the de minimis limit of £625 per month, and less than 50% of input tax, all of the £2,940 input VAT is recoverable.

Tutorial note: The commissions for financial services advice are exempt supplies, whilst the fees for accounting services are standard rated supplies. It is in fact clear from inspection that the *de minimis* limits are not exceeded as the total input tax is less than £625pm, and the commissions are less than 50% of the total outputs.

(c)   (i)   **Balance outstanding for year ended 30 April 2006**

Annual accounting scheme	£
Output VAT (per question)	9,728
Car fuel scale charges	
Proprietor's car (W2)	206
Employee's car (W2)	192
	10,126
Input VAT (part (b))	(2,940)
Payment due to HMRC for the year	7,186
Payment on account (per question)	
(9 months × £505)	(4,545)
Balance due to HMRC	2,641

(ii)   **Due date for payment**

The due date for payment for the final balance under the annual accounting scheme is 30 June 2006 (i.e. two months after the end of the accounting period).

(iii)   **Likely VAT POAs for year ended 30 April 2007**

Nine monthly payments on account are required, each payment being 10% of the estimated tax due for the year.

In practice, the payments are likely to be based on the previous year's liability. Therefore, monthly payments of £719 (10% × £7,186) will be due at the end of month for the period August 2006 to 30 April 2007 inclusive.

Workings

(W1) **Capital allowances**

	£	General Pool £	Expensive Car £	Car 25% Private Use £	Expensive car 25% private use £	Private use Disallowance £	Allowances Claimed £
WDV b/f		1,447	7,995	4,471			
Disposal proceeds			(7,650)	(7,000)			
			345	(2,529)			
Balancing charge				2,529		632	(1,897)
Balancing allowance			(345)				345
Additions (no FYA)		11,446			14,813		
		12,893					
Less WDA (25%)		(3,223)					3,223
– restricted					(3,000)	750	2,250
		9,670			11,813		
Additions with FYA							
31/03/06 Filing cabinets	548						
FYA (40%)	(219)	329					219
20/04/06 lap top	2,800						
FYA (50%)	(1,400)	1,400					1,400
WDV c/f		11,624	.		11,813		
Balancing charge							(1,897)
Allowances claimed							7,437
Net allowances claimed							5,540

(W2) **Car fuel scale charges**

		£
Proprietor's car	(£1,385 × 7/47)	206
Employee's car		
Spacewagon	(£1,385 × 7/47 × 8/12)	138
Polo	(£1,095 × 7/47 × 4/12)	54
		192

47   P LTD

(a)   **VAT issues facing P Ltd**

(i)   **VAT compulsory registration**

VAT registration is compulsory once taxable supplies exceed £61,000.

P Ltd's monthly taxable supplies are £10,400 (13,000 × 80%). Therefore the registration limit will be exceeded at the end of December 2006 (10,400 × 6 = £62,400).

HMRC should be notified by 30 January 2007, and registration will take effect from 1 February 2007, or an earlier agreed date.

(ii)   **Voluntary registration**

P Ltd would benefit from registering voluntarily for VAT as soon as trade commences. This is because its sales are mostly to VAT registered customers, so charging VAT will not be an additional cost to them. If registered, P Ltd's input VAT will be recoverable, subject to the partial exemption rules.

(iii)   **Partial exemption**

The company is making exempt supplies in addition to standard rated supplies. It is therefore necessary to determine the amount of input VAT recoverable using the partial exemption rules.

	£
Recoverable input VAT $(6,000 \times 17.5\% \times 80\%)$	840
Irrecoverable input VAT $(6,000 \times 17.5\% \times 20\%)$	210
	1,050

The irrecoverable VAT does not exceed £625 per month on average and does not exceed 50% of the total input tax for the prescribed accounting period, therefore all of the input VAT of £1,050 will be recoverable.

(iv)   **Tax point date**

The correct tax point date for each transaction will have to be identified.

The basic tax point date is when the goods are made available to the customer, unless an invoice is issued, or payment is received before this date, in which case the earlier date becomes the actual tax point.

The basic tax point is generally replaced with an actual tax point which is the invoice date when an invoice is issued within 14 days of the basic tax point, as in P Ltd's case.

These rules will not apply if the cash accounting scheme is used (see (vii)).

(v)   **Pre-registration input VAT**

Assets and stock have been purchased in the previous twelve months. Prior to VAT registration and trading.

As the stock was acquired for the purposes of the business in the three years prior to registration, and not consumed, any input VAT may be recovered.

Input VAT may also be recovered on fixed assets to be used for business purposes and bought within three years of registration.

If services have been purchased, for business purposes, within six months of registration, the input VAT may also be recovered.

(v)   **Bad debt relief**

Output VAT must be accounted for when a sale is invoiced not when the cash is received from the customer (unless the cash accounting scheme is adopted – see (vii) below).

If a customer does not pay and the debt becomes a bad debt, the VAT paid to HMRC can only be recovered when the debt has

–   been written off as irrecoverable in the supplier's books of account, and

–   is more than six months old (i.e. at least six months have elapsed since the due date of payment).

If bad debts are considerable, the cash accounting scheme should be adopted as automatic bad debt relief is obtained (see (vii) below).

(vii) **Cash accounting scheme**

It would be advantageous for P Ltd to use the cash accounting scheme.

Under the scheme, VAT is accounted for on a cash basis. As customers are given 30 days' credit, and some pay later than this, the scheme will give a cash flow advantage when accounting for output VAT.

However, P Ltd will be disadvantaged in the recovery of input VAT, as it is given 14 days' credit, but overall, the scheme will be beneficial.

The scheme also allows automatic relief for bad debts, as if the customer does not pay, as no output VAT is payable to HMRC until the cash is received.

P Ltd may use the cash accounting scheme, as its expected taxable turnover for the next 12 months is £124,800 (10,400 × 12) which is less than the limit of £660,000.

(viii) **Annual accounting scheme**

The annual accounting scheme has an administrative advantage, in that only one VAT return is submitted each year. The return is due within two months of the end of the year.

Nine regular monthly payments on account are made which aids the cash flow of the business thoughout the year. The balance for the year is payable with the VAT return.

P Ltd may join the scheme, as its expected taxable turnover for the next 12 months does not exceed £1,350,000 provided it is up to date with its VAT returns.

(ix) **Flat rate scheme**

The flat rate scheme simplifies administration as the VAT on individual sales and purchases does not need to be identified. The VAT accounted for is a flat rate percentage of the VAT inclusive turnover, with no credit for input VAT.

P Ltd may use the scheme as its taxable turnover for the next 12 months does not exceed £150,000, and the expected total turnover (including exempt supplies) for the next 12 months does not exceed £187,500.

A business with totally taxable supplies will benefit from the reduced administration and may benefit from lower overall VAT payments to HMRC.

However a business with exempt and taxable supplies may be worse off due to the flat rate applying to total VAT inclusive supplies, including exempt supplies.

Using the normal basis of calculating P Ltd's VAT liability, the company will have to pay £770 (W) VAT per month. Using the flat rate scheme, the company will have to pay £1,630 (W) VAT per month, which is an increase of £860 (W).

It is therefore not beneficial for P Ltd to join the scheme as there is additional VAT to pay. In addition, the company will still have to issue VAT invoices, as the majority of its customers are VAT registered and therefore the administration advantages do not outweigh the additional costs.

Working: Estimated VAT liability per month

			£
Normal accounting			
Output VAT	–	standard rated supplies (10,400 × 17½%)	1,820
Input VAT	–	all recoverable (part (a) (iii))	(1,050)
VAT liability per month			770
Flat rate scheme			
Total supplies (VAT inclusive)			
Standard rated (10,400 × 47/40)			12,220
Exempt supplies			2,600
			14,820
VAT liability per month at flat rate of 11% (14,820 × 11%)			1,630
Additional monthly VAT liability under flat rate scheme (1,630 – 770)			860

(b)   **Peter retains ownership of the car**

Implications for Peter

	£
AMAPs:	
10,000 × 40p	4,000
5,000 × 25p	1,250
Income received from company	5,250
Less Costs of running car (2,000 + 2,800)	(4,800)
Net profit	450

This profit is not taxable on Peter as the AMAPs can be paid tax free, even if it exceeds the actual costs incurred.

Implications for P Ltd

P Ltd will have tax deductible expenses of £5,250, and there will be a reduction in corporation tax of £997 (5,250 × 19%).

Peter transfers the car to P Ltd

Implications for Peter

The transfer of the car to P Ltd will not give rise to a capital gain, as motor vehicles are exempt assets for tax.

Peter will be assessed on the benefits of a company car under the employment benefit rules, as an employee of P Ltd.

	£
Car benefit (£24,000 × 29%) (W1)	6,960
Petrol benefit (£14,400 × 29%)	4,176
	11,136
Additional income tax payable (£11,136 × 22%)	2,450

Implications for P Ltd

P Ltd will have tax deductible expenses as follows:

	£
Capital allowances – maximum	3,000
Running costs	2,000
Petrol costs	2,800
Class 1A NIC (£11,136 × 12.8%)	1,425
Deductible expenses	9,225

P Ltd will have tax deductible expenses of £9,225, resulting in a reduction in corporation tax of £1,753 (£9,225 × 19%).

Summary

- Peter retains ownership of the car:

    – Tax free profit to Peter   £450

    – Net cost to P Ltd   (5,250 – 997) = £4,253

- P Ltd purchases the car:

    – Cost to Peter   £2,450

    – Cost to P Ltd   (2,000 + 2,800 + 1,425 – 1,753) = £4,472

It will be more tax efficient for Peter to retain ownership of his car and charge mileage allowances to the company (P Ltd).

ACCA marking scheme		
		Marks
(a)	Compulsory registration	2.5
	Voluntary registration	1.5
	Partial exemption	2.5
	Tax point	1.5
	Pre-registration VAT	3.0
	Bad debts	1.5
	Cash accounting	2.5
	Annual accounting	3.0
	Flat rate scheme	4.5
		22.5
(b)	Retain ownership:	
	Peter's net profit – calculation	1.0
	– not taxable	0.5
	Company's position/tax saving	1.0
	Transfer ownership:	
	Car benefit/additional tax	1.5
	Company's position/tax saving	1.5
	More efficient to retain ownership	0.5
		6.0
	Total available (vs a maximum of 25)	28.5

TAXATION OF CORPORATE BUSINESS

SINGLE COMPANIES

48   JAMES & MELVIN

Client address   Firm address

Date

Dear James and Melvin

Further to our recent meeting we are writing to set out the position regarding the queries raised.

Provision of Company Car to Melvin

Special taxation rules apply when either a benefit (such as the provision of a company car) or a loan is made to a participator (i.e. a shareholder of a close company such as JM Limited).

As Melvin is employed by JM Limited he will be assessed on the provision of the company car and fuel in 2006/07 under the 'normal assessable benefit' rules for employment income.

The following amounts will therefore form part of his assessable 2006/07 income.

	£
Company car benefit	3,240
Fuel benefit	2,592
	5,832

Appendix A sets out how these figures are derived.

As Melvin is a higher rate taxpayer, his income tax liability will be increased by £2,333 (5,832 × 40%). Tax on such benefits is usually collected by an adjustment to a taxpayer's PAYE code.

Provision of Company Car to James

James is not employed by JM Limited, nor is he a director of this company. He is, however, a participator in a close company and therefore the special close company provisions will apply.

In the case of benefits provided, the participator will be assessed on a deemed distribution (i.e. dividend) calculated in accordance with the normal benefit rules referred to above.

In 2006/07 James will therefore be assessed on a gross distribution equal to the car benefit grossed up, calculated as follows:

£5,832 × 100/90 = £6,480

As James is a higher rate taxpayer he will be assessed on this distribution via his 2006/07 self-assessment tax return at the special higher rate for dividends of 32.5%, giving a tax liability of £2,106 (6,480 × 32½%). A 10% tax credit will, however, attach to the gross dividend meaning that the net amount of additional tax payable amounts to £1,458 (6,480 × 22½%).

Settling of James' personal bills

The settling by JM Limited of James' personal bills is covered by the loans to participator rules. Under these rules the expression 'loan' is very widely defined and would include the company directly settling personal liabilities of a participator.

It is possible that HMRC will seek to assess James on a benefit calculated under the beneficial loan rules. These rules usually apply where an employee is loaned money by their employer either without being charged any interest or being charged a below market value interest rate.

If HMRC were to seek an assessment in this manner the benefit would be calculated using the normal benefit rules and once again grossed up as a deemed distribution in a similar way to that described above. However, because James is neither an employee nor a director of JM Limited and special close company rules specifically apply to such loans it is thought unlikely that a deemed distribution based on a beneficial loan benefit will arise.

It is considered more likely that James will have no personal tax implications derived from this loan until the loan is written off. When this happens it will be treated as a gross distribution of £22,222 (£20,000 × 100/90) assessable in the tax year that the loan is written off. The distribution will carry a 10% tax credit as for other dividends.

As James is a higher rate taxpayer this means that he will have to pay, via his self assessment tax return, an additional £5,000 (22,222 × 22.5%).

Position for JM Limited

Provision of car to Melvin

The cost of running the car provided to Melvin is allowable for corporation tax purposes. In addition JM Limited will obtain capital allowances of £3,000 to offset against its profits for the year ended 31 March 2007. The company will have to pay Class 1A National Insurance contributions of £746 (5,832 × 12.8%) by 19 July 2007.

Provision of car to James

As James is not an employee or director of JM Limited the company is unable to obtain any tax deductions (including capital allowances) for the car provided to him but no Class 1A NIC will arise on this car.

Settling James' personal bills

JM Limited will be required to pay 25% of the net value of any loans made to participators which have not been repaid to the company or written off by the company's normal corporation tax due date.

This means that unless the loan is written off by 1 January 2008 an amount of £5,000 (20,000 × 25%) will need to be paid to HMRC which will then only be refunded to the company when the loan is repaid by James or he is formally released from having to repay it by the company (and then usually nine months after the end of the accounting period in which the loan is repaid or released).

As it is likely that the loan is going to be written off at some future point it is therefore recommended, to assist JM Limited's cash flow position, that the write-off occurs and is formally documented prior to 1 January 2008.

Direct Sale of Shares

If James sells his shares directly to Melvin this will result in a straightforward capital gain arising with capital gains tax amounting to between £1,470 and £13,945 (depending on the number of shares actually sold).

This will be payable either on 31 January 2008 if the sale occurs on 31 March 2007 or 31 January 2009 if the sale is deferred to 31 May 2007. From a cash flow perspective a deferral to the later date therefore appears preferable if possible.

Appendix B sets out the calculation of the capital gains tax liability.

If Melvin needs to borrow to raise the funds for the share purchase then the interest on such a loan will qualify for tax relief by deduction in arriving at his taxable income (as a charge on income) for the tax year in which the interest is paid.

Company Purchase of Own Shares

If the share sale proceeds via a company purchase of its own shares, assuming the conditions for a capital gains treatment are not satisfied (see below), the basic position is that this will be treated as an income distribution (i.e. dividend) in the hands of the recipient.

The distribution is calculated on the proceeds received for the shares less the amount originally subscribed for them. If James were to sell, for example, 100 shares he would therefore be deemed to receive net dividend income of £49,900 ((100 × 500) – 100) and would have an additional tax liability of £12,475 (£49,900 × 100/90 × 22.5%) collected through his self-assessment tax return.

If the following conditions are satisfied the share purchase by JM Limited will be subject to the capital gains tax rules rather than being treated as an income distribution.

– Company is an unquoted trading company

– Vendor is UK resident and ordinarily UK resident

– Shares have been owned for five years prior to the purchase date

– The purchase is for the benefit of the purchasing company's trade (which includes the position where an outside investor wishes to either partially or fully 'cash in' his investment)

– The transaction is not part of a scheme to avoid tax

– As a result of the purchase the vendor (and his associates):

   (i) reduce their interest in the share capital to 75% or less of their percentage share immediately prior to the purchase (share reduction test); and

   (ii) must not control more than 30% of the issued share capital (or voting rights) (connection test)

This is likely to be a more favourable tax treatment because of the availability of capital gains reliefs (annual exemption, business asset taper relief) resulting in an effective tax rate of less than 10% (40% × 75% less annual exemption) compared to around 25% of the net dividend for the distribution route.

In this particular case the key conditions are the ownership period, the share reduction test and the connection test. If James sells his shares on 31 March 2007 the five year test will not have been satisfied with the result that any sale will be subject to the income distribution rules outlined above. To access the CGT reliefs it is therefore recommended, if possible, that the sale is deferred until 31 May 2007.

To satisfy the share reduction test at least 200 shares must be sold (see Appendix C).

To satisfy the connection test at least 286 shares will need to be sold giving a minimum capital gains tax charge of £10,751 (see Appendix C).

Conclusion

In conclusion, it would appear that if the purchase needs to proceeds on 31 March 2007 (in which case a company purchase will be treated as an income distribution) a direct sale to Melvin would appear preferable, primarily because of the availability of capital gains tax business asset taper relief.

If the sale could be deferred to 31 May 2007, however, providing at least 286 shares are sold either a direct sale or company purchase of shares would be dealt with under the capital gains tax rules. In this case other deciding factors may therefore become important, for example the ability of Melvin to raise the funds for the share purchase personally.

We trust that the above is helpful but should you have any queries please do not hesitate to contract me.

Yours sincerely

A N Accountant

Appendix A: Benefit calculations

Car Benefit Calculation

CO$_2$ emission level of car = 157 grams per kilometre

Base level CO$_2$ emission for 2006/07 = 140 grams per kilometre

Appropriate % = $(155 - 140) \times {}^1/_5 + 15\% = 18\%$

Benefit (£18,000 × 18%)   £3,240

Fuel Benefit Calculation

Based figure for 2006/07 = £14,400

Benefit (£14,400 × 18%)   £2,592

Appendix B: Capital Gains Tax Arising on Direct Sale of Shares to Melvin

Sale of	100 shares	350 shares
	£	£
Proceeds (@ £500 per share)	50,000	175,000
Less: Cost (May 2002)	(100)	(350)
Gain before taper relief	49,900	174,650
Less: Business asset taper relief (Note)	(37,425)	(130,988)
Chargeable gain	12,475	43,662
Less: Annual exemption	(8,800)	(8,800)
Taxable gain	3,675	34,862
CGT at 40%	1,470	13,945

Note: As the shares are unquoted and have been held for more than two years, the maximum taper relief of 75% is available. The gain is 25% chargeable.

Appendix C: Purchase of own shares

Share Reduction Test

Share % before disposal = 500/1,000		=	50%
Maximum % share permissible after buy back (50% × 75%)		=	37.5%

When shares are purchased back by the company they must be cancelled. Therefore James' holding and the total shareholding will be reduced.

(500 – n/(1,000 – n)	=	37.5% where n = number of shares purchased
500 – n	=	375 – 37.5n
500 – 375	=	62.5%n
125/62.5%	=	n
n	=	200 shares

Connection test

(500 – n)/(1,000 – n)	=	30% where n = number of shares purchased
500 – n	=	300 – 30%n
500 – 300	=	70%n
200/70%	=	n
n	=	286 shares

As a result to satisfy the requirements of CGT treatment at least 286 shares need to be sold.

Assuming 286 shares are sold the capital gains calculation will be as follows:

	£
Proceeds (286 × £500)	143,000
Less: Cost (May 2002)	(286)
Gain before taper relief	142,714
Less: Business asset taper relief	(107,036)
Chargeable gain	35,678
Less: Annual exemption	(8,800)
Taxable gain	26,878
CGT (26,878 × 40%)	10,751

ACCA marking scheme		
		Marks
Presentation		2.0
Company cars -	Melvin 'normal' rules	0.5
	Calculation	2.0
	Tax collection	0.5
	James – rule	0.5
	Calculation	1.0
	Tax collection	0.5
Personal Bills -	Settling personal bills caught	0.5
	Distribution under beneficial loan rules	1.0
	Conclusion	0.5
	Loan written off	1.0

Company Position	Melvin's car	1.5
	James's car	1.5
	Loan	1.5
Direct share sale -	Capital gains tax payable	1.5
	Dates	1.0
	Interest relief	0.5
Company purchase -	Basic rule	0.5
	Calculation	0.5
	Conditions of CGT treatment	4.0
	Ownership period test	1.0
	Share reduction test	2.0
	Connection test	1.5
	Capital gains tax payable	1.0
	Conclusions	1.5
	Available	29.0
	Maximum	25.0

49 FLOP LIMITED

(a) **Revised corporation tax payable**

Year ended 31 March 2005

There are three adjusting items:

(i) The computers are capital items, as they have an enduring benefit. These need to be added back to the trading profit for tax purposes and capital allowances claimed instead.

The company is not small or medium by Companies Act definitions and therefore no first year allowances are available. Allowances of £12,500 (50,000 × 25%) can be claimed, leaving a TWDV of £37,500.

(ii) There is insufficient information to justify the provision and it should be disallowed for tax purposes until such times as it is released or utilised.

(iii) Costs relating to trading loan relationships are allowable, as are costs relating to the trade (i.e. debt collection, trade disputes and accounting work).

However, costs relating to capital items (£5,700) are not allowable so will have to be added back to the trading profit for tax purposes.

The revised profit chargeable to corporation tax is therefore £757,500 (704,300 + 50,000 − 12,500 + 10,000 + 5,700).

There are two associated companies, and therefore the 30% tax rate applies if profit exceeds £750,000 (£1,500,000/2).

Corporation tax payable for the y/e 31 March 2005 is therefore £227,250 (30% x £757,500).

Payment date

Although the rate of tax is 30% and the company is therefore 'large', quarterly payments will not apply, as the company was not large in the previous year.

The due date for payment of tax is therefore 1 January 2006 (i.e. nine months and one day after the end of the tax accounting period.

Filing date

The filing date is the later of:

•	12 months after the end of the period of account	31 March 2006
•	3 months after the date of the notice requiring the return	1 May 2006

The filing date is therefore 1 May 2006.

Interest and penalties

The following penalties apply:

•	Failure to submit on time (1 May 2006)	£100
•	Failure to submit within 3 months (1 August 2006)	£100
•	Failure to submit within 6 months (1 November 2006) = 10% of tax unpaid at that time (£227,250)	£22,725

Interest will run from 1 January 2006 until 2 November 2006 on £227,250 and from 2 November 2006 until the date of payment on the as yet unpaid amount of £103,750 (£227,250 – £123,500)

Year ended 31 March 2006

There are two adjusting items.

(i) Capital allowances based on the capitalised addition (the computers) in 2005. The TWDV at 1 April 2005 is £37,500 so a further £9,375 (25% × £37,500) can be claimed.

(ii) The tax computation should include the irrecoverable debt. This is allowable, and will reduce the taxable profits by £50,000.

The revised profit chargeable to corporation tax is therefore £755,625 (£815,000 – 50,000 – 9,375).

Corporation tax payable for the y/e 31 March 2006 is therefore £226,687 (£755,625 × 30%).

Payment date

The company is large in the year as it pays corporation tax at the full rate. As this is the second year in succession that it is large, corporation tax is paid on quarterly instalments.

The quarterly instalments fall due on the following dates:

14 October 2005
14 January 2006
14 April 2006
14 July 2006

Filing date

This filing date is again the later of:

•	12 months after the end of the period of account	31 March 2007
•	3 months after the date of the notice requiring the return	27 October 2006

The filing date is therefore 31 March 2007.

Interest and penalties

Failure to submit on time (31 March 2007) £100

In addition, if the return is not submitted by 30 June 2007, a further £100 penalty will apply.

Interest will run from the due dates on underpaid instalments until the date of payment.

(b) **Late filing of VAT returns**

The late filing of two or more VAT returns within the period of one year will give rise to a default surcharge. This occurs when either

- The return is late, and/or

- The payment is late.

HMRC will serve a surcharge liability notice on the taxpayer when a single return is filed late and/or the VAT due is paid late. The surcharge period will run from the date of notice to the anniversary of the quarter end of the period in which the trader is in default.

Any further defaults within the surcharge period will extend the surcharge period.

If there is a late payment of VAT in the surcharge period, a surcharge will be levied at the rate of 2% on the first occasion, rising progressively to a maximum of 15% if there are several defaults. One complete year of correct compliance is necessary to escape the default surcharge regime.

For Flop Ltd, the surcharge period originally ran to 31 December 2007 but was extended to 31 March 2008 as the second return is late. This could be extended again if the June return is late.

The second default (31 March return) will give rise to a 2% surcharge, based on the tax paid late of £24,000. This gives a surcharge of £480. This exceeds the de minimus level of £400, so will be collected.

To avoid a further surcharge, the VAT return to 30 June 2007 should be submitted by 31 July at the latest. This would save 5% x £8,250 = £412.

In addition, Flop Ltd should obtain a refund of the VAT on the irrecoverable debt.

Relief is available where:

(i) the debt is more than six months old, and

(ii) the debt has been written off in the creditor's accounts.

The claim must be made within three years.

The amount of VAT repayable is £8,750 (17.5% × £50,000). If this is claimed through the VAT return to 30 June 2007, there should be a net VAT repayment of £500 (£8,250 - £8,750).

Even if this return is submitted late, the fact that no VAT is outstanding means that there will be no surcharge actually payable, but the surcharge period will nevertheless be extended.

		ACCA marking scheme	
			Marks
(a)	(i)	Computers are capital	0.5
		No first year allowances	0.5
		Calculation of allowances	0.5
		Repairs provision	1.0
		Trading loan relationship costs are allowable	0.5
		Costs relating to trade are allowable	0.5
		Costs of £5,700 capital – disallowed	0.5
		Profit chargeable to corporation tax	0.5
		Two associates	0.5
		Calculation of corporation tax payable	0.5
		Further capital allowances on computers	0.5
		Inclusion of irrecoverable debt	0.5
		Revised profit chargeable to corporation tax	0.5
		Max	7.0
	(ii)	Awareness of no quarterly payments	0.5
		Reason: company was not 'large' in 2004	0.5
		Due date nine months one day (1.1.2006)	0.5
		Filing: 12 months from period of account	0.5
		three months from date of CT203	0.5
		Take later (1 May 2006)	0.5
		First penalty (not submit on time)	0.5
		Second penalty (not submit within three months)	0.5
		Third penalty (tax geared)	0.5
		Calculation of tax geared penalty	0.5
		Interest periods: to late payment	0.5
		to balancing payment	0.5
		Payment date: large for second year	0.5
		Quarterly payments apply	0.5
		Dates of quarterly payments	1.0
		Filing date	0.5
		Penalty: late submission	0.5
		Further penalty (submission beyond 30.6.07)	0.5
		Interest from date of underpaid instalments	0.5
		Max	8.0
(b)		Default surcharge: awareness	0.5
		two or more within year	0.5
		Issue of surcharge liability notice	0.5
		Period runs from date of notice	0.5
		Runs to anniversary of quarter in which default	0.5
		Return and/or payment late	0.5
		Further defaults extend surcharge period	0.5
		Levy 2% surcharge if late payment	0.5
		Progressive rates thereafter	0.5
		Compliance for one year required	0.5
		Extension as second return late	0.5
		Extend again if June return is late	0.5
		Calculation of £480	0.5
		Exceeds de minimus level of £400	0.5
		Submission date to avoid surcharge	0.5
		Saving that would result	0.5
		Period extended though no surcharge	0.5
		Refund of VAT on irrecoverable debt	1.0
		Conditions for refund (0.5 each)	1.0
		Three year time limit for claim	0.5
		Calculation of VAT repayable	0.5
		Net VAT repayment	0.5
		Max	10.0
		Total (Max)	25.0

GROUPS AND CONSORTIA

50   PACIFIC GROUP

(a)   **Corporation tax computation for the year ended 31 March 2007**

	£
Trading profit	930,000
Interest income	14,000
Overseas dividend income (W1)	21,242
Chargeable gain (Note 1)	Nil
	965,242
Gift Aid	(3,400)
Consortium relief (76,000 × 40%) (Note 2)	(30,400)
PCTCT	931,442
Corporation tax at 30% (W4)	279,433
Double tax relief (W5)	(4,886)
Corporation tax liability	274,547

Notes

1   **Chargeable gain**

The gain on the building is £281,540 (W3). However, some of the gain can be rolled over against the base cost of the building acquired by Arctic Ltd as Pacific Ltd and Arctic Ltd are in a capital gains group.

Not all of the gain can be rolled over as £30,000 of the proceeds of sale have not been reinvested. Accordingly, £30,000 of the gain will be subject to tax.

Without any further claim, the £30,000 gain will be chargeable in Pacific Ltd's corporation tax computation. However, the two companies should elect to treat the disposal of the industrial unit as if made by Arctic Ltd. The £30,000 gain not relieved by rollover relief would then be taxed in Arctic Ltd rather than Pacific Ltd.

This is advantageous because Arctic Ltd is a small company paying tax at 19%, with PCTCT of £110,000 (£80,000 plus the additional £30,000 of profits from the gain), whereas Pacific Ltd is paying corporation tax at the full rate.

2   **Consortium relief**

Atlantic Ltd is a consortium company, as at least 75% of its shares are owned by two companies who each own at least 5%.

As a result, 40% of the losses of Atlantic Ltd can be surrendered up to Pacific Ltd with the consent of Tasman Gmbh.

(b)   **VAT on imports**

Output VAT must be paid by a UK importer on the import of goods into the UK from non-EU countries at 17½%. The VAT is due at the point of entry, but regular importers can make arrangements to defer the payment and pay monthly by direct debit if they are a taxable person for VAT purposes.

Therefore, VAT on the freezers must be paid by Arctic Ltd at the same time as any other customs and import duties. The freezers will not be released to Arctic Ltd until the VAT is paid.

The VAT can be deferred until the 15th day following the month of importation if Arctic Ltd is accepted as a member of the Duty Deferment System.

The VAT incurred by the UK importer may be treated as input VAT and reclaimed in the appropriate quarter. The VAT suffered is therefore recoverable by Arctic Ltd as input tax in the normal way.

(c) **Payments to employees travelling in Eisland**

The travel and hotel costs, paid for by Arctic Ltd, do not give rise to an employment income benefit.

The reimbursement of incidental expenses is all taxable as the amount paid exceeds the £10 per night de minimis limit.

Medical insurance in respect of employees travelling overseas is not a taxable benefit.

(d) **Acquiring Icebox Inc**

(i) **Acquisition of trade and assets**

The business in Eisland would be a branch of Arctic Ltd.

The cost of any land and buildings and fixed plant and machinery acquired would qualify as the purchase of qualifying business assets for rollover relief purposes. This would enable the remainder of the gain on the industrial unit of £30,000 to be deferred.

Plant and machinery and industrial buildings acquired will qualify for capital allowances in Arctic Ltd.

Any goodwill acquired will be dealt with under the rules for intangible fixed assets and any amounts written off would be allowed for corporation tax purposes.

The future profits of the branch would be taxed in Eisland at 26% and in the United Kingdom as part of the profits of Arctic Ltd.

Double tax relief would be available in the United Kingdom for the tax paid in Eisland.

(ii) **Acquisition of the share capital of Icebox Inc**

As Arctic Ltd will be acquiring shares rather than assets, rollover relief will not be available.

The future profits of the new subsidiary will be subject to tax in Eisland at 14%.

If Icebox Inc is not a controlled foreign company, there will be no tax in the United Kingdom unless dividends are paid. This enables profits to be accumulated in Eisland at that country's low tax rate.

If Icebox Inc is a controlled foreign company, as seems likely given the 14% tax rate in Eisland, Arctic Ltd will be liable to UK tax on the apportioned profit of Icebox Inc. The charge may be avoided if the profits are distributed to Arctic Ltd as dividends.

In any event dividends received in the UK will be taxable income in the hands of Arctic Ltd, but credit is given if any tax is paid on apportioned income under the controlled foreign company rules.

A new subsidiary would be an associate of the Pacific group therefore the limits for determining the rate of tax would be divided by three. Arctic Ltd will remain a small company if its profits do not exceed £100,000 (300,000 ÷ 3).

(e)   **Information for Finance Director**

Filing of corporation tax returns

The tax return and accounts must be submitted within 12 months of the end of the accounting period.

Penalties are levied for the late submission of self-assessment returns unless the company has a reasonable excuse.

The initial penalty is £100 which is increased to £500 if this is the third or more consecutive late return.

Where a return is submitted more than three months late the initial penalty is £200 increasing to £1,000.

Where a return is submitted more than six months late there is a further penalty of 10% of the corporation tax unpaid. This increases to 20% where the delay is more than 12 months.

Payment of tax

The due date of payment of corporation tax for Arctic Ltd is nine months and one day after the end of the accounting period.

In the year to 31 March 2007 Pacific Ltd has profits in excess of £750,000 and must make quarterly payments of corporation tax as follows:

Date	% of liability
14 October 2006	25
14 January 2007	25
14 April 2007	25
14 July 2007	25

If, however, Pacific Ltd's profits for the previous year had been less than £750,000, payment by instalments would not be necessary until the year to 31 March 2008. The corporation tax liability would instead be payable nine months and one day after the end of the accounting period.

Workings

(W1) **Overseas dividend income**

	£	Overseas tax suffered £
Dividend received	16,356	
Withholding tax (6/94)	1,044	1,044
	17,400	
Underlying tax (W2)	3,842	3,842
Gross dividend income	21,242	
Total foreign tax suffered		4,886

(W2) **Underlying tax**

$$\frac{\text{Dividend plus withholding tax}}{\text{Profits after tax}} \times \text{Tax paid} = \frac{17,400}{500,500} \times 110,500 = £3,842$$

As Pacific Ltd owns more than 10% of Caspian Inc, relief is available for underlying tax.

(W3) **Capital gain**

	£
Proceeds (July 2006)	820,000
Cost (May 1985)	(260,000)
Unindexed gain	560,000
Indexation allowance	
(260,000 × 1.71)	(278,460)
Chargeable gain	281,540

(W4) **Rate of corporation tax**

Pacific Ltd has one associate; Arctic Ltd.

The limits to determine the appropriate rate of corporation tax are therefore as follows:

		£
Small companies	– Upper limit	750,000
	– Lower limit	150,000

Pacific Ltd is therefore a large company paying tax at 30%.

Arctic Ltd is a small company paying tax at 19%.

(W5) **Double tax relief**

The consortium relief losses and charges on income are first set against UK income, and as there are sufficient UK profits to absorb the reliefs the full amount of overseas dividend is taxed in the UK at 30%.

DTR is therefore the lower of:

		£
(i)	overseas tax suffered (W1)	4,886
(ii)	UK tax on foreign income	
	(£21,242 × 30%)	6,373

51 APPLE LTD

(a) (i) **Group relationships**

Group loss relief

For group relief purposes, two companies are members of a 75% group where one of them is a 75% subsidiary of the other, or both of them are 75% subsidiaries of the holding company.

To qualify as a 75% subsidiary, the holding company must hold 75% or more of the subsidiary's ordinary share capital, and have the right to receive 75% cr more of its distributable profits and net assets (were it to be wound up). The 75% holding must be an effective interest that is held directly or indirectly.

Capital gains group

For the purposes of transferring chargeable assets between two companies without incurring a chargeable gain or an allowable loss, the definition of a 75% subsidiary is 'less rigorous' than for group relief.

The direct 75% holding rule still applies, but where there is an indirect holding the parent company must have an effective interest of over 50%.

(ii) **Surrender of trading losses**

The most important factor that should be taken into account when deciding to which group companies the trading losses should be surrendered, is the rate of corporation tax applicable to those companies.

Group relief surrender should be made initially to companies subject to corporation tax at the marginal rate of 32.75%. The amount surrendered should be sufficient to bring the claimant company's profits (PCTCT plus FII) down to the lower limit.

Surrender should then be to those companies subject to the full rate of corporation tax of 30% and finally to those subject to corporation tax at the small company rate of 19%.

The ability of companies with minority interests to compensate for group relief surrenders will be another factor.

(iii) **Chargeable assets**

Where an asset is disposed of by a group company to a third party, the group can deem (by election) that a disposal by one group company was made (wholly or partly) by another group company.

This enables capital gains to be matched with capital losses as soon as possible, and also ensures that any resulting net gains are realised in the group company paying tax at the lowest marginal tax rate.

In addition, a capital gains group is treated as a single entity for the purposes of rollover relief. Therefore gains within a group can be deferred if qualifying business assets are purchased within the qualifying period by other group companies.

(b) (i) **Profits chargeable to corporation tax**

	Apple Ltd £	Bramley Ltd £	Cox Ltd £	Delicious Ltd £
Y/e 31 March 2006				
Trading profit	620,000	Nil	83,000	
Loss relief s393A(1)			(58,000)	
PCTCT	620,000	Nil	25,000	
Year ended 31 March 2007				
Trading profit	250,000	52,000	Nil	90,000
Loss relief s393(1)		(52,000)		
Capital gain	120,000			
Loss relief s393A(1)				(15,000)
PCTCT	370,000	Nil	Nil	75,000
Year ended 31 March 2008				
Trading profit	585,000	70,000	40,000	Nil
Loss relief s393(1)		(12,000)		
Capital gain	80,000			
PCTCT	665,000	58,000	40,000	Nil

(ii)   **Corporation tax saving**

Until 31 March 2006 Apple Ltd has two associated companies, and three associated companies thereafter. The relevant lower and upper limits for the Apple Ltd group of companies are therefore:

	Y/e 31 March 2006 £	Thereafter £
Small companies		
– Upper limit (÷ 3/÷ 4)	500,000	375,000
– Lower limit (÷ 3/÷ 4)	100,000	75,000
Starting rate		
– Upper limit (÷ 3)	16,667	n/a
– Lower limit (÷ 3)	3,333	n/a

Delicious Ltd is a 75% subsidiary of Apple Ltd for the purposes of transferring chargeable assets as Apple Ltd's effective interest is > 50%, but not for group relief purposes as Apple Ltd's effective interest is < 75%. (85% × 80% = 68%).

Losses can, however, be surrendered between Delicious Ltd and Cox Ltd as they form a separate group loss relief group.

The corporation tax saving if reliefs were claimed in the most beneficial manner is as follows:

1   The leasehold factory building to be sold by Delicious Ltd on 15 February 2008, should be deemed sold by Apple Ltd. The capital loss of £44,000 can then be offset against Apple Ltd's capital gain of £80,000 for the year ended 31 March 2008. The corporation tax saving is £13,200 (44,000 at 30%).

2   A claim for rollover relief is possible because the reinvestment by Cox Ltd on 20 September 2007 took place within three years of Apple Ltd selling both of its freehold buildings.

It is beneficial (due to marginal tax rates and the capital loss setoff in the year ended 31 March 2008) to make the claim in respect of the freehold office building sold on 10 March 2007.

Only £20,000 (380,000 - 360,000) of the sale proceeds are not reinvested, and so £100,000 (120,000 - 20,000) of the gain is rolled over. The corporation tax saving is £32,750 (100,000 at 32.75%).

3   Bramley Ltd's loss of £64,000 for the year ended 31 March 2006 should be surrendered to Apple Ltd, rather than being carried forward under s393(1) ICTA 1988.

Relief will then be at the full rate of 30% rather than the small company rate of 19%. The corporation tax saving is £7,040 (64,000 × (30% - 19%)).

4   Cox Ltd's loss of £58,000 for the year ended 31 March 2007 should be surrendered to Apple Ltd, rather than being carried back under s393A(1) ICTA 1988.

Relief will then be at the marginal rate of 32.75% rather than at the small company rate of 19%. The corporation tax saving is £7,975 (58,000 × (32.75% - 19%)).

Note that Delicious Ltd's loss of £15,000 for the year ended 31 March 2008 is relieved at the marginal rate of 32.75%, and so the claim under s393A(1) ICTA 1988 should not be altered.

The total corporation tax saving is £60,965 (13,200 + 32,750 + 7,040 + 7,975).

Minority shareholders can be compensated by claimant companies paying for group relief.

Key answer tips

The advantage of a deemed transfer election lies in the opportunity to decide retrospectively where a disposal has best effect and enables a specific part of a gain or loss to be transferred as well as avoiding the legal costs of actually transferring assets within a group before selling to a third party.

Requirement (b) (ii) asks for advice on how corporation tax can be saved. Revised corporation tax computations for each company for each year are not required.

52   JUGLANS LTD AND LARIX LTD

(a)   **Most beneficial preparation of accounts**

Preparation of two sets of accounts

Under this option the two accounting reference dates will trigger the end of a chargeable accounting period for corporation tax purposes; one short accounting period to 31 March 2007 with the other of 12 months duration to 31 March 2008.

The corporation tax computations will therefore be as follows:

	CAP to 31/3/2007 £	CAP to 31/3/2008 £
Trading profits		
(3 × £25,000)	75,000	
(9 × £25,000 + 3 × £35,000)		330,000
Less: Capital allowances (W1)	(4,500)	(52,875)
Capital gain (Note)	92,000	Nil
PCTCT	162,500	277,125

Note: The capital loss of CAP to 31/3/2008 can not be set against the gain in CAP to 31/3/2007. The loss is carried forward and will be set against capital gains in the future.

Corporation tax liability (W2)		
(162,500 × 30%)	48,750	
(277,125 × 30%)		83,138
Less: Marginal relief		
(187,500 − 162,500) × $^{11}/_{400}$	(688)	
(750,000 − 277,125) × $^{11}/_{400}$		(13,004)
Corporation tax liability	48,062	70,134
Total corporation tax liability		118,196

Preparing one set of accounts for the fifteen month period to 31 March 2008

Under this option, as an accounting period cannot exceed 12 months in duration, the long period of account is divided into two accounting periods: the first to 31 December 2007, and the second to 31 March 2008.

Trading income before capital allowances is allocated on a time basis, with capital allowances and other items allocated by reference to the accounting period to which they relate.

The corporation tax computations will therefore be as follows:

	CAP to 31/12/2007 £	CAP to 31/3/2008 £
Trading profit		
12/15 × (£300,000 + £105,000)	324,000	
3/15 × (£405,000)		81,000
Less: Capital allowances (W3)	(54,000)	(6,750)
Capital gain (£92,000 – £32,000) (Note)	60,000	–
PCTCT	330,000	74,250

Note: As both the capital gain and capital loss occur in the same CAP, the loss can be set against the gain.

Corporation tax liability (W2)		
(330,000 × 30%)	99,000	
(74,250 × 30%)		22,275
Less: Marginal relief	(11,550)	
(750,000 – 330,000) × $^{11}/_{400}$		
(187,500 – 74,250) × $^{11}/_{400}$		(3,114)
Corporation tax liability	87,450	19,161
Total corporation tax liability	106,611	

Conclusion

On the basis of the information provided it would appear preferable for Juglans Limited to opt for a single 15 month long period of account.

This will result in a corporation tax saving of £11,585 (118,196 – 106,611).

Note that the saving is achieved as a result of a timing difference from using up a capital loss of £32,000, and accelerating £3,375 (104,625 – 101,250) of capital allowances.

Workings

(1)   Capital allowances

	CAP to 31/3/2007 Pool £	Allowance £		CAP to 31/3/2008 Pool £	Allowances £
TWDV b/f	72,000			67,500	
WDA (25% × 3/12)	(4,500)	4,500			
WDA (25%)				(16,875)	16,875
	67,500			50,625	
Additions (with FYA)			90,000		
FYA (40%)			(36,000)		36,000
				54,000	
Allowances claimed		4,500			52,875
Tax written down value c/f	67,500			104,625	

(2) Small Companies Rate Limits

Juglans Limited and Larix Limited are associated companies as they are both under the control of Bob.

			£
CAP to 31/3/2007	Lower limit	$(300,000 \times 3/12) \div 2$	37,500
	Upper limit	$(1,500,000 \times 3/12) \div 2$	187,500
CAP to 31/3/2008	Lower limit	$300,000 \div 2$	150,000
	Upper limit	$1,500,000 \div 2$	750,000

(3) Capital allowances

		CAP to 31/12/2007		CAP to 31/3/2008	
		Pool	Allowances	Pool	Allowances
	£	£	£	£	£
TWDV b/f		72,000		108,000	
WDA (25%)		(18,000)	18,000		
WDA (25% × 3/12)				(6,750)	6,750
		54,000		101,250	
Additions (with FYA)	90,000				
FYA (40%)	(36,000)		36,000		
		54,000			
Allowances claimed			54,000		6,750
Tax written down value c/f		108,000		101,250	

(4) Small Companies Rate Limits

			£
CAP to 31/12/2007	Lower limit	$300,000 \div 2$	150,000
	Upper limit	$1,500,000 \div 2$	750,000
CAP to 31/3/2008	Lower limit	$(300,000 \times 3/12) \div 2$	37,500
	Upper limit	$(1,500,000 \times 3/12) \div 2$	187,500

(b) (i) Reliefs available to groups

It is possible for companies within a 75% group to transfer trading losses to other companies within the group. For these purposes two companies are within a 75% group if one company is a 75% subsidiary of the other *company* or both are 75% subsidiaries of a third *company*.

As Juglans Limited and Larix Limited are entirely owned by Bob (as individual) it will unfortunately not be possible to transfer the £45,000 trading loss from Larix Limited to Juglans Limited.

Whilst capital losses can not be transferred between companies, companies which are in a capital gains group can elect that an asset which has been disposed of by one group company to a third party can be treated as if transferred to a fellow group company immediately prior to that disposal.

In this way gains and losses can be matched within a single group company and more immediate relief obtained for capital losses than might otherwise have been the case.

Companies are within a capital gains group, however, as for the group relief, if one company is a 75% subsidiary of another *company* or both are 75% subsidiaries of a third *company*.

Again, as Juglans Limited and Larix Limited are entirely owned by Bob it will not therefore be possible for the disposal of the asset giving rise to the capital loss of £30,000 made by Larix Limited to be treated as if it was a disposal made by Juglans Limited (and thereby matching with the gain made by Juglans Limited in its accounting period ended 31 December 2007).

(ii)   Group VAT registration

Companies under common control may apply for group VAT registration. For these purposes control only needs to be via a 'person' which can include individuals as well as companies in traditional parent/subsidiary relationships.

As Bob controls both Juglans Limited and Larix Limited, therefore, it is possible for these two companies to be group VAT registered.

The effect of a group registration would be that the two companies are effectively treated as a single entity for VAT purposes. As Larix Limited predominantly makes exempt sales the group will therefore become partially exempt. The issue is, therefore, whether this will lead to an overall increase or reduction of input tax recovery under the partial exemption rules.

The exempt input tax of Larix Limited is clearly above the de minimis limit of £625/month on average, and greater than 50% of its input tax relates to exempt supplies. It will therefore not be possible to treat this exempt input tax as being attributable to taxable supplies.

The current input tax recovery position is as follows:

	£
Juglans Limited (totally taxable supplies)	125,000
Larix Limted	
Relating to taxable supplies	12,000
Relating to unattributed supplies (20,000 × 10%)	2,000
	139,000

With a group VAT registration the recovery of input tax will be as follows:

	£
Relating to taxable supplies (123,000 + 12,000)	135,000
Relating to unattributed supplies (working)	10,560
	145,560

Conclusion

It would appear that, providing the information for the year ended 31 March 2008 is representative, a group VAT registration will result in an additional £6,560 (145,560 – 139,000) of input tax recovery.

With this, together with possible administrative savings that may result, it would appear that a group VAT registration is worthwhile.

Working: Partial exemption recovery of unattributed VAT

	£
Taxable supplies	
– Juglans Ltd	1,100,000
– Larix Ltd (10% × 1,550,000)	155,000
	1,255,000
Exempt supplies	
– Larix Ltd (90% × 1,550,000)	1,395,000
Total supplies	2,650,000

Recoverable portion of unattributed VAT

$$\frac{1,255,000}{2,650,000} \times 100 = 47.358\%, \text{ rounded up to } 48\%$$

Recoverable unattributed VAT

$$(20,000 + 2,000) \times 48\% = £10,560$$

ACCA marking scheme		
		Marks
(a) Two sets of accounts		
Identification of accounting periods		1.0
Trading profit		1.0
Capital allowances	AP to 31/3/07	0.5
	AP to 31/3/08	1.0
Capital gain		0.5
Associated companies		1.0
Corporation tax	AP to 31/3/07	0.5
	AP to 31/3/08	0.5
One set of accounts		
Principles		1.0
Trading profit		0.5
Capital allowances	AP to 31/12/07	1.0
	AP to 31/3/08	0.5
Capital gain		1.0
Corporation tax	AP to 31/12/07	0.5
	AP to 31/3/08	0.5
Conclusion		1.0
	Max	12.0
(b) (i) Group relief 75% groups		1.0
Conclusion		1.0
Notional asset transfers		1.0
Chargeable gains group		1.0
Conclusion		1.0
	Max	4.0
(ii) Common control		1.0
Conclusion		1.0
Partially exempt group		0.5
Consideration of *de minimis* threshold		0.5
Current recovery position		1.0
Group VAT registration recovery		1.0
Conclusion		1.0
	Max	4.0
Total		20.0

53   ROMEO LTD

(a)   **Quarterly payments for corporation tax**

Whether Romeo Ltd will need to make quarterly corporation tax payments for its CAP ending 30 June 2008 will depend on its forecast corporation tax liability for that period.

Forecast Corporation Tax Computation – CAP 30/06/2008

		£
Trading profit before capital allowances		840,000
Less: Capital allowances	(W1)	(219,570)
Trading profit		620,430
Chargeable gains	(W2)	347,000
Profits Chargeable to Corporation Tax		967,430
Corporation Tax liability (£967,430 × 30%)	(W3)	290,229

As Romeo Limited paid corporation tax at the full rate in its previous accounting period and its corporation tax for the current accounting period is expected to exceed £10,000, it will be liable to make quarterly corporation tax payments as follows:

	£
14/01/2008	72,557
14/04/2008	72,557
14/07/2008	72,557
14/10/2008	72,558

Workings

(W1)   **Capital Allowances**

	£	Plant £	Expensive Car £	Expensive Car £	Short life Asset £	Allowances £
TWDV b/f		420,000	6,000	–	15,820	
Additions (no FYA)				18,000		
Disposals (Note)		(25,000)	(8,000)		(10,000)	
		395,000	(2,000)	18,000	5,820	
WDA × 25%/ restricted		(98,750)		(3,000)		101,750
Balancing Allowance					(5,820)	5,820
Balancing charge			2,000			(2,000)
		296,250	Nil	15,000	Nil	
Additions (with FYA)						
Low emission vehicle	18,000					
Energy saving	20,000					
	38,000					
FYA (100%)	(38,000)	Nil				38,000
Commercial vehicles	50,000					
Other	40,000					
ICT	100,000					
	190,000					
FYA (40%)	(76,000)	114,000				76,000
TWDV c/f		410,250	Nil	15,000	Nil	
Total allowances						219,570

Note: for disposals, deduct the lower of the sale proceeds and original cost.

(W2) Chargeable Gains

Office building

	£	£
Proceeds (July 2007)	509,000	
Less: Cost (March 1997)	(125,000)	
Unindexed gain	384,000	
Indexation allowance		
125,000 × 0.300 [202.2 – 155·4)/155·4]	(37,500)	
		346,500

Moveable Plant (Note)

	£	£
Proceeds (July 2007)	33,000	
Less: Cost (March 1997)	(25,000)	
Unindexed gain	8,000	
Indexation allowance		
25,000 × 0.300 [(202.2 – 155·4)/155·4]	(7,500)	
		500
Chargeable gains		347,000

Note: A gain arises on the disposal of the plant and machinery. This is because wasting assets which are eligible for capital allowances (as in this case) are not covered by the wasting chattel exemption.

(W3) Corporation Tax Liability

Romeo Limited has one associated company. The upper limit for determing the rate of corporation tax is therefore £750,000 (1,500,000/2). Romeo Ltd will therefore be a large company and must pay corporation tax at the full rate of 30%.

(b) (i) Use of Leylander Limited losses

Group relief

Only current accounting period losses can be group relieved. It will not therefore be possible to relieve the brought forward losses against the profits of Romeo Limited for its accounting period ended 30 June 2008 under the group relief provisions.

As Leylander Limited will become a 100% subsidiary of Romeo Limited (which satisfies the 75% requirement for group relief purposes) it will, however, be possible to group relieve any post acquisition trading losses arising in its accounting period ended 30 June 2008.

However, its trading activities have become negligible and it would appear that any future trading losses would also be small. Use of Leylander Ltd's losses will therefore be unlikely to help with Tony's overall objective of lowering the corporation tax rate of Romeo Limited.

Placing Contracts

Specific anti-avoidance legislation exists to prevent the artificial use of brought forward losses in a company acquired into a group. The legislation covers the situation where there is a change in the company's ownership whilst its trading activities have become small or negligible and after the change there is a considerable revival in that trade (for example by the placing of profitable contracts into that company).

In such circumstances, trading losses brought forward can not be carried through the change of ownership and will therefore be lost.

For these purposes a change in ownership means that more than 50% is acquired by the new owner.

The situation with Leylander Ltd would appear to exactly mirror the circumstances described in the anti-avoidance legislation; the trade of Leylander Limited has become negligible, Romeo Limited then acquires the company and the trade is revived by the placing of profitable contracts.

It is therefore very unlikely that HMRC would allow the brought forward losses to be used in this way.

In addition, there is a general restriction of brought forward losses in so far as they can only be carried forward for use against future profits from the same trade. HMRC could argue in this case that the future profits derive from a different trade.

(ii) **Action to avoid Romeo Ltd paying by quarterly payments**

Group Rollover Relief

As Romeo Limited and Alpha Limited are in a 75% chargeable gains group they will be treated as performing a single trade for the purposes of rollover relief.

Thus providing the conditions have been satisfied, the gain on the disposal of the office building by Romeo Limited of £346,500 can be rolled into the acquisition of the factory by Alpha Limited.

The old and new assets, being land and buildings used for trading purposes, are qualifying assets and the new factory will be immediately brought into trade use. The reinvestment occurs within one year before the disposal and three years after, and therefore it would appear that the conditions for 'rollover relief' have been satisfied.

The proceeds not reinvested of £109,000 (509,000 – 400,000) will, however, be taxable in the year to 30 June 2008. The remaining £237,500 (346,500 – 109,000) gain will be deferred with a rollover relief claim.

It should be noted that the gain on the disposal of the plant can not be 'rolled over' as this was not a disposal of a qualifying asset. This is because the plant was moveable and not fixed plant & machinery.

The overall effect of a group rollover relief claim is that Romeo Limited's profits chargeable to corporation tax for its accounting period ended 30 June 2008 will be reduced to £729,930 (967,430 – 237,500).

As a consequence, it will no longer be a large company and will pay corporation tax at the small companies marginal rate.

It will therefore no longer be liable for corporation tax quarterly instalment payments for this period and also (because it will not be a full rate payer in the previous year) its accounting period ended 30 June 2009.

This decision is only true providing:

(1) its forecasts are accurate, and

(2) Leylander Limited is not acquired (in which case there will be three associated companies which will make Romeo Ltd a large company, and the Romeo Limited group may cease to be 'medium' for capital allowances purposes).

ACCA marking scheme			
			Marks
(a)	Trading profit		0.5
	Chargeable gains		0.5
	Corporation tax		1.0
	Quarterly payments/Payment dates		2.0
	Disposal proceeds		1.5
	Expensive car		0.5
	WDA		0.5
	Balancing allowance/charge		1.0
	FYA at 100%		1.5
	FYA at 40%		1.0
	Chargeable gains	Office building	1.0
		Plant	2.0
		Available and Maximum	13.0
(b)	(i) Group Relief	– current period relief	1.0
		– conclusion	0.5
		– consideration of future losses	1.5
	Placing contracts	– anti-avoidance legislation	1.0
		– control	0.5
		– effect	1.0
		– application	1.0
		– conclusion	0.5
		– same trade	1.0
		Available	8.0
		Maximum	7.0
	(ii) Group rollover relief		1.0
	Conditions		1.5
	Proceeds not reinvested		0.5
	Consideration of gain on plant disposal		1.0
	Effect – 30/6/2008		1.5
	30/6/2009		0.5
		Available	6.0
		Maximum	5.0
Total			25.0

54 ARABELLO

(a) **UK resident status for corporation tax**

A company will be regarded as UK resident for corporation tax purposes if:

(i)   it is incorporated in the UK; or

(ii) its central management and control are exercised in the UK.

For the purposes of (ii) above, control is regarded as being located where the highest level of strategic control is exercised (i.e. where the key strategic and financial decisions are made).

This is usually found to be where the company's board of directors meet.

In circumstances where this is either manipulated to achieve a certain result or where the Board is dominated by a single individual (perhaps because of a dominant personal shareholding) HMRC will try to establish where the 'real' control is actually exercised.

If the centre of management and control is found to be in the UK, the company will be regarded as UK resident.

In the case of parent/subsidiary relationships HMRC will not argue that the management and control of a subsidiary is located where the parent company is located simply by virtue of the shareholding relationship. The management and control is usually in the hands of the subsidiary.

However, in situations where the board of the subsidiary simply passively comply with the dictates of the parent company without independent consideration, it is likely that the conclusion would be that the control of the subsidiary is located where the parent's centre of management and control is exercised.

The significance of a company being UK resident is twofold:

(i)   The company will be subject to corporation tax on its worldwide profits.

(ii)   In the context of a group of companies, it may (providing the necessary shareholding relationships are in place) be part of a 'tax' group for the purposes of 'group relief' or chargeable gains. For example group relief is normally only available to, and may only be claimed from, UK resident companies.

(b)   **Arabello's understanding of using losses and shifting profits**

Use of overseas trading and capital losses

For the purposes of determining whether a 'tax' group for group relief purposes or capital gains purposes exists, non-UK resident companies are included. However, available trading and capital losses may usually only be surrendered by and claimed by group companies which are UK resident or non-UK resident companies with permanent establishments situated in the UK.

As Doimio Inc is regarded as non-UK resident, claims for the use of its expected trading losses of £300,000 in the year ending 31 March 2008 by Bastello Limited and Castillo Limited will therefore be denied.

Similarly, for the purpose of 'chargeable gains' group relief (e.g. intra-group transfers of assets on a no gain/no loss basis) will only apply providing the relevant assets remain within the charge to UK corporation tax.

As the assets that will give rise to the capital losses in Doimio Inc are outside of the charge to UK corporation tax, relief will therefore be denied.

Arabello also seems to believe that the capital losses themselves can be transferred.

There are no provisions to enable the direct transfer of capital losses between two qualifying group companies. It is possible, however, for such companies to elect that the capital loss of one company is treated for tax purposes as if made by the other company. This will enable the offset of gains and losses in the same company without the need to physically transfer assets between the two companies prior to their disposal.

Shifting Profits to Doimio Ltd

The transfer pricing legislation restricts the 'shifting' of profits in the manner Arabello suggests. These rules apply where one company 'controls' the other (as in the case of Bastello Limited and Doimio Inc) and property is transferred at a price below market value. Since Bastello Limited is a large company the rules will automatically apply.

In these circumstances HMRC would simply require an adjustment to the chargeable profits of Bastello Limited by reinstating the market value selling prices thus negating the benefit of Arabello's suggestion.

If the transactions take place at below market value, there will be a requirement to self-assess such adjustments on the corporation tax return of Bastello Limited for its accounting period ended on 31 March 2008.

Failure to do so may lead to an investigation by HMRC resulting in penalties arising for an incorrect corporation tax return and interest charges arising for any late paid corporation tax.

Bastello Limited should therefore be advised to approach HMRC under the 'advanced pricing arrangements' to negotiate mutually acceptable transfer prices prior to implementation.

(c) **Actions to allow relief for Doimio Ltd's losses**

As referred to above, to obtain the benefit of the losses expected for Doimio Inc this company would need to become UK resident for corporation tax purposes.

This could be achieved by shifting the management and control of this company to the UK with effect (at the latest) from 1 April 2007. As Doimio Inc is a 100% subsidiary of Bastello Limited there are no complications with minority interests.

As a 100% subsidiary the necessary shareholding arrangements will be satisfied for this company to become a member of a group for group relief and chargeable gains purposes.

Tutorial Note

(The following is included for tutorial purposes only and is excluded from the Paper 3.2 Syllabus)

Once Doimio Inc has returned to profitability it may be possible for its management and control to be exported once again overseas. However, there are further tax consequences in migrating a group company and the following should be noted:

(i) *A UK tax charge will arise on any unrealised chargeable gains of Doimio Inc immediately before it becomes non-UK resident. This is because the company will be deemed to have disposed of its assets at market value immediately before it migrates and to have immediately reacquired them.*

(ii) *Doimio Inc would need to inform HMRC in advance of its intention to migrate and will be required to identify any outstanding tax liabilities and how these are to be paid.*

(d) **Forecast corporation tax liabilities for Bastello Ltd and Castillo Ltd**

Assuming Doimio Inc becomes UK resident with effect from 1 April 2007 the forecast corporation tax liabilities of Bastello Limited and Castillo Limited for the accounting period ending 31 March 2008 are as follows:

	Notes	Bastello Ltd UK £	Bastello Ltd Overseas £	Castillo Ltd £
Trading profit		680,000	-	350,000
Overseas dividends	1	-	56,250	-
Net chargeable gains	2	100,000	-	75,000
Charge on income	3	(5,000)	-	-
		775,000	56,250	425,000

	Notes	Bastello Ltd		Castillo Ltd
		UK	Overseas	
		£	£	£
Less: Group relief	4			(300,000)
Profits chargeable to corporation tax		775,000	56,250	125,000
Corporation tax:				
£775,000 × 30%		232,500		
£56,250 × 30%			16,875	
£125,000 × 30%				37,500
Less: Marginal relief				
(500,000 − 125,000) × 11/400				(10,313)
Less: Double tax relief	5		(15,750)	
		232,500	1,125	
Corporation tax liability		233,625		27,187

***Notes*:**

1 **Overseas dividends**

The net dividend received from Estio Inc needs to be grossed up for both withholding tax and (because Bastello Limited owns at least 10% of the ordinary shares and hence voting rights) underlying tax.

The gross dividend is therefore:

		Overseas tax
	£	£
Cash received	40,500	
Withholding tax (40,500 × 10/90)	4,500	4,500
	45,000	
Underlying tax (see below)		
120,000 × (45,000/480,000)	11,250	11,250
Gross dividend	56,250	
Total overseas tax suffered		15,750

The underlying tax is calculated as:

$$\frac{\text{Gross dividend}}{\text{Profit after tax}} \times \text{Tax paid for the period}$$

The underlying tax is therefore based on the company's profit after tax per the financial accounts.

The only profits for Estio Inc given in the question is the tax adjusted profit of £600,000.

It is therefore assumed that these profits are also the financial accounts profits before tax. Therefore the profits after tax is taken to be £480,000 (£600,000 less the £120,000 anticipated overseas tax on these profits).

2   **Net chargeable gains for Castillo Ltd**

The portion of the capital loss arising before Doimio Inc joined the chargeable gains group (pre-entry loss) is not available to other members of the chargeable gains group.

The post acquisition available loss therefore amounts to £50,000 (75,000 – 25,000).

The post entry capital loss itself cannot be transferred within the group, however, an election can be made to treat this loss as if incurred by Castillo Limited. This will enable Castillo Limited to offset the loss against its expected gains of £125,000 and gives a net chargeable gain of £75,000.

It is better to allocate this capital loss to Castillo Limited rather than to Bastello Limited as this will ensure that the loss will attract relief at the marginal rate of 32.75% rather than 30% (see Note (4) below). As a result, an overall benefit of £1,375 (50,000 × (32.75% - 30%)) is achieved.

3   **Allocation of charges on income**

To maximise double tax relief, it is better to allocate charges on income to the UK source income first, to maximize the UK tax liability on the foreign source.

4   **Group relief**

Group relief is allocated most tax efficiently to those companies paying corporation tax at the highest marginal tax rates. This is achieved by allocating first to marginal rate tax paying companies sufficient losses to bring their profits down to the small companies rate limit.

Estio Inc is not controlled by Bastello Limited so there are three associated companies. The relevant limits therefore need to be divided by three giving an upper limit of £500,000 and lower limit of £100,000.

Castillo Limited is therefore paying corporation tax at the marginal rate of 32.7%. Group relief should therefore be allocated to Castillo Limited.

5   **Double taxation relief**

DTR is the lower of	£
(i) Overseas tax suffered (Note (1))	15,750
(ii) UK CT on foreign income	16,875

ACCA marking scheme		Marks
(a)	Incorporated in the UK	0.5
	Management and control	0.5
	Highest level of control	1.0
	Dominant shareholding – 'real' control	1.0
	Parent/subsidiary relationships	1.0
	Significance – taxed on global profits	0.5
	– part of 'tax groups'	1.0
	Available	5.5
	Maximum	5.0
(b)	Trading losses – general rule	0.5
	application of rule	1.0
	Capital losses – general rule	1.0
	application of rule	1.0
	can't directly transfer capital losses	1.0

Shifting profits	– transfer pricing recognition/general rule		1.5
	application of rule		0.5
	self-assessment issues		1.0
	advanced pricing arrangement		0.5
		Available	8.0
		Maximum	7.0
(c) Become UK resident			1.0
Do so by shifting management and control			1.0
Group relationship satisfied			1.0
		Maximum and available	3.0
Calculation of overseas dividend income			2.0
Allocation of charge on income			1.0
Calculation of double tax relief			1.0
Allocation of group relief	– general principle		1.0
	– application		1.5
Capital losses	– pre-entry portion		1.0
	– election for notional transfer		1.0
	– allocation		1.0
Corporation tax liabilities	– Bastello Limited		0.5
	– Castillo Limited		1.0
		Available	11.0
		Maximum	10.0
			25.0

55   A, B, C AND D

(a)   **Corporation tax computations**

	A Ltd y/e 31.3.07 £	B Ltd y/e 31.12.06 £	D Ltd y/e 31.3.07 £
Trading profit	205,000	Nil	Nil
Property income		50,000	
Chargeable gain (W1)	29,500	500	20,000
Overseas dividend (W2)	49,000		
	283,500	50,500	20,000
Loss relief – s393A		(50,500)	(20,000)
Consortium relief (W3)	(60,000)		
Group relief (W4)	(151,500)		
PCTCT	72,000	Nil	Nil
Corporation tax @ 19%	13,680	Nil	Nil
Less: DTR (W5)	(9,310)		
Corporation tax payable	4,370		

Beneficial reliefs

- Maximum consortium relief is taken by A Ltd from D Ltd of £60,000 (W3).

- Maximum group loss relief is claimed by A Ltd from B Ltd of £151,500 (W4).

- B Ltd has a loss left after group relief of £50,500 which can be used by B Ltd in the current year under a s393A claim against its property income of £50,000 and the balance of the gain (W1).

- D Ltd has a loss left after consortium relief of £60,000 which £20,000 is used in the current year by D Ltd under a s393A claim and the remainder is available to E Ltd, the other consortium member.

Workings:

(W1) **Chargeable gain in A Ltd**

B Ltd has a capital loss brought forward of £20,000. This can be relieved against the gain realised by A Ltd if an election is made to transfer at least 40% of the asset, disposed of by A Ltd, to B Ltd. If an election is made to transfer a further 1% (£500) this can be relieved with the remainder of B Ltd's trading loss.

As a result a gain of £20,500 (41% of £50,000) will crystallise in B Ltd of which £20,000 will be matched against the capital loss. The remaining gain of £29,500 will crystallise in A Ltd.

(W2) **Overseas dividend**

	£	£
Dividend received	29,750	
Withholding tax (£29,750 × 15/85)	5,250	5,250
	35,000	
Underlying tax (see Note)		
$\dfrac{35,000}{72,000} \times £28,800$	14,000	14,000
Gross dividends received	49,000	
Overseas tax suffered		19,250

Note: The underlying tax is calculated as:

$$\frac{\text{Gross dividend}}{\text{Profit after tax}} \times \text{Tax paid for the period}$$

The profit after tax is taken to be £72,000, calculated as the trading profit (per the question) of £100,000 less the tax provision of £28,000. The actual tax paid was £800 more than the tax provision i.e. £28,800.

(W3) **Maximum consortium relief**

Lower of

(i)   Available loss of D Ltd: (120,000 – 20,000) × 60% = £60,000

(ii)   Available PCTCT of A Ltd: £284,000

Note that the amount of loss available for surrender up to A Ltd must be reduced by any possible S393A claims against current period's profits.

(W4) **Maximum group relief**

A Ltd and B Ltd have non–coterminous year ends, therefore the maximum group relief must be calculated for the corresponding accounting period of nine months (1 April 2006 to 31 December 2006).

Maximum group relief = lower of

(i)   Available loss of B Ltd: (9/12 × £202,000) = £151,500

(ii)   Available PCTCT of A Ltd: (9/12 × £284,000) = £213,000

Note that unlike consortium relief, for group relief, the available loss that can be group relieved does not have to be reduced by any possible s393A claims.

There are four associated companies (see tutorial note below), so the limits for small company purposes are:

Small companies rate

£1,500,000 ÷ 4 =   £375,000

£300,000 ÷ 4   =   £75,000

Before loss relief, A Ltd is paying tax at 32¾% whereas B Ltd and D Ltd are paying tax at 19%. It is therefore advisable to give as much of the loss as possible to A Ltd.

Tutorial notes:

1   A Ltd, B Ltd, C Ltd and D Ltd are all associated companies (50% or more of shares owned).

2   A Ltd and B Ltd are in a group relief group (>75% of shares owned and resident in the UK).

3   A Ltd and E Ltd are eligible for consortium relief (together they own > 75% of D Ltd and neither company owns > 75%).

(b)   (1)   **Sale of shares in B Ltd to a third party**

Corporation tax (CT)

(i)   *Capital gains implications*

A Ltd is disposing of its shares in B Ltd.

No gain arises on the disposal as the disposal is of a substantial shareholding. It is therefore exempt from CT under the substantial shareholding rules provided conditions are satisfied.

The company must have at least a 10% interest in the company and must have owned the shareholding throughout a 12 month period beginning not more than two years prior to the date of disposal.

The conditions appear to be satisfied and therefore the gain will be exempt.

(ii)   *Associated company*

B Ltd is an associated company. The limits for the purpose of calculating corporation tax are divided by the number of associated companies in a group.

If B Ltd is sold in December 2007 it will continue to be associated throughout the year to 31 March 2008 (the year of disposal) but not thereafter.

This means that for the A Ltd group the small company taxation limits will decrease and will become £500,000 (£1,500,000 ÷ 3) and £100,000 (£300,000 ÷ 3) for the year to 31 March 2009 and thereafter.

Given current profit levels this may not affect the rate of tax each company pays.

(iii) *Losses – group relief*

Only profits and losses that fall into the corresponding accounting period (period during which the group relationship exists) may be set off against each other.

Group relief is denied from the date that arrangements are made whereby a company might leave a group (this date may be earlier than the actual date of sale).

(iv) *Losses – carry forward of trading losses by B Ltd*

Relief is denied when:

• there is both a change in ownership and a major change in the nature or conduct of the trade within a period of three years; or

• at any time after the scale of activities of the trade has become small or negligible, and before any considerable revival of the trade, there is a change in the ownership of the company.

Brought forward losses cannot be group relieved, but, as B Ltd has none this is not relevant.

(v) *Degrouping charge*

A degrouping charge will be assessed on B Ltd in the accounting period that it leaves the group, if it acquired assets from other group members on a no gain/no loss basis within the six years preceding the company leaving the group.

The degrouping charge may be reallocated to another group member providing both companies agree. The election must be made within two years of the end of the accounting period of the company leaving the group.

Alternatively, the degrouping charge may be rolled over if it relates to a qualifying asset, and a further qualifying asset is acquired within the normal qualifying period for rollover relief purposes.

(vi) *Degrouping charge – intangibles*

There is also a degrouping charge where a company leaves a group having acquired an intangible fixed asset from another group company within the previous six years.

Again, such a degrouping gain may be reallocated to another group company and the joint election must be made within two years of the end of the accounting period in which the company leaves the group.

Value added tax (VAT)

The sale of shares is exempt from VAT.

Stamp duty (SD)

Stamp duty at the rate of 0.5% will be charged on the consideration for the sale of the shares.

(b)   (2)   **Selling the assets of B Ltd to a third party**

Corporation tax (CT)

(i)   *Chargeable gains on disposal*

The individual chargeable assets disposed of may realise a capital gain or loss.

Rollover relief may be available if the proceeds of sale are reinvested by B Ltd, or by A Ltd, and if the sale and repurchase are of qualifying assets (such as land, fixed plant and machinery).

An election may be made (within two years of the end of accounting period of disposal) to treat any asset disposed of by B Ltd as being disposed of by A Ltd.

(ii)   *Associated company*

When the assets are sold, A Ltd retains its ownership of the shares in B Ltd. Therefore the number of associated companies remains unchanged.

However, if B Ltd becomes a dormant company, then it will cease to be an associated company, having the same effect as noted above concerning a sale of the shares.

(iii)   *Losses – group relief*

Group relief is available until the trade is sold. Thereafter, as the company is no longer trading, there will be no group relief claims allowed.

(iv)   *Losses – carry forward of trading losses within B Ltd*

Trading losses are normally carried forward within B Ltd and can only be relieved against future profits of the same trade.

As the trade is sold, and therefore, does not continue, the benefit of any losses will be lost.

(v)   *Capital allowances*

As the assets are sold, balancing adjustments will arise on the assets on which capital allowances are being claimed.

Value added tax (VAT)

The individual assets sold will be subject to output VAT, as sales by a VAT registered trader, unless the sale qualifies as a transfer of a business as a going concern.

If the conditions are satisfied so that the transfer is as a going concern, the sale will be outside the scope of VAT.

To be a transfer of a business as a going concern, the sale must be

- by a VAT registered trader to another VAT registered trader,

- of all or part of a business, which is capable of operating as a going concern.

Stamp duty and stamp duty land tax (SD/SDLT)

SD and SDLT can only be charged on the consideration for certain assets, primarily land and securities.

Thus, if the assets of B Ltd include land, then SDLT will be charged on the value of the land at a rate ranging from 0% to 4% dependent on the value transferred.

ACCA marking scheme		
		Marks
(a)	Chargeable gains	1.5
	Overseas dividends	1.5
	Loss relief (1 + 1)	2.0
	Consortium relief	1.5
	Group relief	1.5
	Small company/starting rate limits	1.0
	CT liability	0.5
	DTR	1.0
		10.5
(b)	Disposal of shares:	
	Chargeable gains on disposal	1.0
	Associated company	1.0
	Losses – group relief	1.5
	Losses – carry forward	2.5
	De-grouping charge	2.5
	De-grouping intangibles	1.0
	VAT	1.5
	Stamp duty	0.5
	Disposal of assets:	
	Chargeable gains on disposal	2.0
	Associated company	0.5
	Losses – group relief	0.5
	Losses – carry forward	1.0
	Capital allowances	0.5
	VAT	1.0
	Stamp duty/stamp duty land tax	1.0
		18.0
	Total available (vs a maximum of 25)	28.5

56   THE GOLF GROUP

(a)   (i)   **UK corporation tax payable by the subsidiary companies**

There are 5 associated companies for both the year ended 31 March 2006 and the year ended 31 March 2007. The limits for corporation tax purposes are therefore divided by 5, and the tax bands will be as follows:

Band	*Marginal Rate of CT*
0 – £60,000	19%
£60,001 – £300,000	32.75%
> £300,000	30%

Note: The question says assume that the FY2006 rates apply throughout for this part of the question. If this assumption is not made, in FY2005 a starting rate and starting rate marginal relief would need to be considered.

To maximise the tax effect of the use of any losses, losses should firstly be offset against profits falling into the highest taxed bands.

India Ltd	Notes	Year ended 31 March 2006 £	Year ended 31 March 2007 £
Trading profit		335,000	215,000
Overseas property income		15,000	Nil
Chargeable gains (25,000 – 25,000)	(1)	Nil	Nil
		350,000	215,000
Less: Charges on income		(15,000)	(10,000)
		335,000	205,000
Less: Group relief	(2)	(32,500)	(120,000)
Profits chargeable to corporation tax		302,500	85,000
Corporation tax at 30%		90,750	25,500
Less: Marginal relief			
$^{11}/_{400} \times (300,000 - 85,000)$		–	(5,913)
		90,750	19,587
Less: Double tax relief	(3)	(4,500)	–
Corporation tax liability		86,250	19,587

Juliet Ltd		£	£
Trading income		Nil	Nil
Interest income		5,000	2,000
Chargeable gains (20,000 – 20,000)	(4)	Nil	Nil
Profits chargeable to corporation tax		5,000	2,000
Corporation tax liability at 19%		950	380

Kilo Ltd		£	£
Trading profit		35,000	30,000
Interest income		2,500	2,500
Property business income		30,000	25,000
		67,500	57,500
Less: Group relief	(2)	(7,500)	Nil
Profits chargeable to corporation tax		60,000	57,500
Corporation tax liability at 19%		11,400	10,925

Notes:

(1)   **India Ltd – chargeable gains**

India Ltd has capital losses b/f of £45,000 which will be set against the £25,000 gain in y/e 31 March 2006.

Capital losses remaining of £20,000 will be carried forward.

(2)   **Optimum use of Juliet Ltd's Losses**

In the y/e 31 March 2006, before loss relief, Juliet Ltd is paying tax at 19%, India Ltd at 30% and Kilo Ltd at 32¾%.

In the y/e 31 March 2007, Juliet Ltd and Kilo Ltd are paying tax at 19%, India at 32¾%.

	Notes	Year ended 31 March 2006	Year ended 31 March 2007
		£	£
Juliet Ltd's trading loss		40,000	120,000
Used – Kilo Ltd profits	(i)	(7,500)	0
Used – India Ltd profits	(ii)	(32,500)	
– India Ltd profits	(iii)		(120,000)
Loss remaining		Nil	Nil

Notes:

(i) Bring Kilo's profits of £67,500 down to £60,000 limit threshold and save tax at 32.75%.

(ii) Relieve remaining loss against India Ltd which is paying tax at 30%.

(iii) Other companies paying tax at 19%, therefore give all loss to India Ltd and obtain relief at 32.75%.

(3) **Double tax relief**

Double tax relief is the lower of :

(i) foreign tax suffered £6,000

(ii) UK tax on foreign income (30% × £15,000 £4,500

Therefore double tax relief is restricted to £4,500.

(4) **Juliet Ltd – chargeable gains**

Juliet Ltd should transfer all or part of the asset to India Ltd in the same year as the disposal of India Ltd's asset. By doing this, the chargeable gain arising from Juliet Ltd's sale of its asset will be covered by India Ltd's capital losses.

This transfer can be done by election between the two parties.

(*Note:* In this answer the gain and loss are shown in Juliet Ltd's CT computation, strictly they should be shown in India Ltd's CT computation).

India Ltd's capital losses at 1 April 2007 are thus:

	£	£
Losses b/f at 1 April 2005		45,000
Used in year ended 31.3.06		(25,000)
Add: Losses arising in year ended 31.3.07	40,000	
Less: Used against Juliet Ltd in year	(20,000)	20,000
Losses c/f at 1 April 2007		40,000

(ii) **Tax payment dates for the year ended 31 March**

India Ltd was a large company for payment purposes in 2005 and again in 2006, so will have to make quarterly instalment payments based on its expected corporation tax liability.

Corporation tax payments for the y/e 31 March 2006 are therefore due on the following dates:

14 October 2005
14 January 2006
14 April 2006
14 July 2006

Golf Ltd, Juliet Ltd and Kilo Ltd are not large companies for payment purposes and therefore will pay corporation tax nine months and 1 day after the year end i.e. on 1 January 2007.

(b)   **Sale of Kilo Ltd in June 2007**

Gain on the sale of shares in Kilo Ltd

From the perspective of the Golf plc group, there should be no corporation tax payable on the disposal of the shares. This is because at least 10% of the shares have been held for a continuous period of at least 12 months in the last two years. As a result, the substantial shareholding exemption applies, and no corporation tax will be payable.

Degrouping charge

However, the departing company (Kilo Ltd) owns an asset which was transferred to it in the six years prior to the company leaving the group. As a result, a de-grouping charge arises.

The asset is deemed to be disposed of and immediately reacquired at its market value at the date of the original inter group transfer. This charge in assessed on the company leaving the group and is treated as occurring on the first day of the accounting period in which it leaves the group (i.e. 1 April 2007).

As the asset was transferred on a no gain / no loss basis, the original cost is indexed up to the date of transfer (from India Ltd to Kilo Ltd); this becomes the base cost to Kilo Ltd.

The potential degrouping gain is therefore calculated as follows:

		£	£
Disposal proceeds (MV at date of inter group transfer)			510,000
Less:	Cost (February 1996)	300,000	
	Indexation to date of inter group transfer £300,000 × 0.156 (174.5 - 150.9/150.9)	46,800	(346,800)
Chargeable gain			163,200

The terms of the sale are that the Golf Group assumes responsibility for the gain.

Although the gain arises in Kilo Ltd, it can be transferred to another group company as with other inter group gains as Kilo Ltd can jointly claim with an ongoing group member to make the transfer.

India Ltd can therefore take advantage of rollover relief and defer the de-grouping gain on the property against the base cost of the proposed acquisition of the new factory. Both assets are qualifying assets, and as long as the new factory building is acquired within three years of the deemed disposal, rollover relief will apply.

As the full market value of the building in Kilo Ltd (£510,000), is not being reinvested in the proposed factory building which will cost £470,000, some of the gain will be chargeable immediately.

	£
Degrouping gain	163,200
Proceeds not reinvested (£510,000 - £470,000)	40,000

Therefore a gain of £40,000 will be chargeable immediately to corporation tax.

The remaining gain of £123,200 will be deferred until the new building is sold.

However, India Ltd has £40,000 capital losses carried forward at 1 April 2007 (as calculated in (a)(i) above). These can be used to offset the gain immediately chargeable of £40,000. Therefore no tax will be payable on the sale of Kilo Ltd.

(c) **Group VAT registration – sale of Kilo Ltd**

Kilo Ltd will cease to be eligible to be a member of the VAT group as it will no longer be under common control with the other group companies following the sale.

The representative member of the VAT group should notify HMRC of the change in the group registration and the tax liabilities will be fixed and agreed.

The right of HMRC to refuse an application to change the composition of a VAT group does not apply in this case, as Kilo Ltd must leave the group, even if revenue might be lost to the Exchequer as a result.

ACCA marking scheme			
			Marks
(a) (i)	Associated companies		0.5
	Limits		1.0
	India:	Use of capital loss brought forward	0.5
		Overseas income included gross	0.5
		Offset of charges on income	0.5
		Group relief:	
		2006	1.0
		2007	1.0
		Corporation tax × 2	1.0
		Marginal relief calculation (2007)	0.5
		Double tax relief workings	1.0
	Juliet:	2007 offset of capital losses	1.0
		Corporation tax × 2	1.0
	Kilo:	Group relief: 2006	1.0
		Corporation tax × 2	1.0
		Loss memo regarding trading losses	1.0
		Calculation of capital loss carry forward in India	1.0
		Max	13.0
(ii)	Golf:	Corporation tax at 19%	0.5
	India:	Large as 2 years at 30%	0.5
		Quarterly instalment payments apply	0.5
		Dates of payment	1.0
	Juliet/Kilo:	Not large	0.5
		Date of payment	0.5
		Max	3.0
(b)	Substantial shareholding relief		1.0
	12 month rule		0.5
	10% holding rule		0.5
	Degrouping charge		1.0
	Impact of degrouping charge		0.5
	Date of tax impact		0.5
	Proceeds / cost		0.5
	Indexation allowance		0.5
	Joint claim		1.0
	Rollover relief		1.0

	Calculation		1.0
	Time limits		0.5
	Qualifying assets		0.5
		Max	7.0
(c)	Kilo no longer an eligible member		0.5
	Notify HMRC		1.0
	Agree tax liabilities		0.5
	Revenue cannot refuse application		0.5
		Max	2.0
Total			25

57 ALANTECH LTD

(a) **Chargeable gain on sale of property**

	£
Sale proceeds (May 2006)	250,000
Less: Cost (September 2000)	(150,000)
Unindexed gain	100,000
Indexation (150,000 × 0.144) ((196.4 – 171.7)/171.7)	(21,600)
Chargeable gain	78,400

Rollover relief

Boron Ltd is a 100% subsidiary of Alantech Ltd and is thus part of the same capital gains group. The gain can be deferred by the operation of rollover relief as the asset sold (the building) is a qualifying business asset that is replaced by another qualifying business asset (the fixed machinery to be purchased in the next year by Alantech Ltd) within the capital gains group.

The new asset is purchased within the time limit of three years after and one year prior to the disposal of the building. Rollover relief will therefore apply.

However, as only part of the disposal proceeds have been reinvested, part of the gain becomes chargeable immediately.

The chargeable gain arising to the lower of:

(1) the full gain of £78,400

(2) the proceeds not reinvested of £50,000 (250,000 – 200,000).

(b) **Corporation tax computations – year ending 31 December 2006**

The three companies form a group for both group relief and capital gains purposes as all shareholdings pass the 75% ownership test. There are three associated companies in the group, therefore the small companies rate limits for determing the rate of tax paid by each company are:

		£
Upper limited	1,500,000 ÷ 3 =	500,000
Lower limited	300,000 ÷ 3 =	100,000

The calculation of the corporation tax liabilities is as follows:

	Notes	Alantech £	Boron £	Bubble £
Trading profit		160,000	Nil	75,000
Less: Losses b/f	(1)	–	–	(25,000)
		160,000	Nil	50,000
Interest income		10,000	–	–
Chargeable gains	(2)	50,000	40,000	–
		220,000	40,000	50,000
Less: Current year losses		–	(10,000)	–
Group relief	(3)	(60,000)	–	(50,000)
PCTCT		160,000	30,000	Nil
CT at 30%/19%		48,000	5,700	Nil
Less: Marginal relief				
$(500,000 - 160,000) \times 11/400$		(9,350)	–	–
Corporation tax payable		38,650	5,700	Nil

Notes:

1. **Losses brought forward in Bubble**

   Losses brought forward take priority over group relieved losses. They must be set against the first available further trading profits of the same trade.

2. **Chargeable gains in Alantech**

   As shown in part (a), after a rollover relief claim only £50,000 of the £78,400 gain will be taxable on Alantech Ltd in the y/e 31 December 2006.

3. **Group relief**

   Group relief losses can only be surrendered during a period of common ownership.

   As Boron Ltd was acquired during the year ended 31 December 2006, Boron Ltd's losses must be apportioned so that only the results of the period of overlap may be set off.

   As Alantech Ltd has only owned 75% or more of the Boron shares since 1 July 2006, it can only claim group relief for losses of the last six months of the year.

   Note that Alantech Ltd's gain arose prior to the acquisition of Boron Ltd. As such, it cannot be covered by group relief from Boron Ltd.

   The maximum group relief Alantech Ltd can claim is therefore the lower of:

   (i)   Boron Ltd's available losses = $(6/12 \times £120,000) = £60,000$, and

   (ii) Alantech Ltd's corresponding available profits

   $(6/12 \times (£220,000 - 50,000)) = £85,000$.

   Bubble Ltd has no such restriction on being able to claim group relief, as Boron Ltd and Bubble Ltd were group companies throughout the accounting period.

The maximum group relief that Bubble Ltd can claim is therefore the lower of:

(i)   Boron Ltd's available losses = £120,000

(ii)   Bubble Ltd's available profits = £50,000.

Losses are used to relieve profits being taxed at the highest rates of tax. Before loss relief, Alantech Ltd is paying tax at 32.75% while Boron Ltd and Bubble Ltd are paying at the small companies rate of 19%.

Group relief to Alantech Ltd therefore takes precedence.

As Boron Ltd is expected to generate losses in 2007, any tax losses could be carried back to offset the chargeable profits remaining in 2006 (previous 12 months).

Bubble Ltd therefore takes losses in preference to Boron Ltd by way of group relief to reduce its profits down to nil.

Note that the questions says that loss reliefs are to be taken as early as possible.

Loss memorandum: Boron Ltd

	£
Trading losses	120,000
Less: Group relief to Alantech Ltd (maximum)	(60,000)
Group relief to Bubble Ltd (maximum)	(50,000)
Used against current year by Boron Ltd under s393A	(10,000)
Losses c/f	Nil

(c)   **Proposed disposal of shares in Mobile Ltd**

If Alantech Ltd and Boron Ltd sell the shares in Mobile Ltd in June 2007, the following gains will arise:

	Alantech	*Boron*
	£	£
Sale proceeds	150,000	150,000
Less: Cost	(75,000)	(55,000)
Unindexed gain	75,000	95,000
Indexation (do not round indexation factor)		
$[((201.6 - 175.9)/175.9) \times 75,000]$	(10,958)	
$[((201.6 - 173.6)/173.6) \times 55,000]$		(8,871)
Chargeable gain	64,042	86,129
Total gains (64,042 + 86,129)	£150,171	

However, an exemption from corporation tax exists for any gain arising when a trading company (or member of a trading group) sells the whole or any part of a substantial shareholding in another trading company.

A substantial shareholding is one where the investing company holds 10% of the ordinary share capital and is beneficially entitled to at least 10% of the

(i)   profits available for distribution to equity holders, and

(ii)   net assets of the company available for distribution to equity holders on a winding up.

In meeting the 10% test, shares owned by different companies in an eligible capital gains group may be amalgamated. The 10% test must have been met for a continuous 12 month period during the 2 years preceding the disposal.

The companies making the disposals must have been trading companies (or members of a trading group) throughout the 12 month period, as well as at the date of disposal. In addition, they must also be trading companies (or members of a trading group) immediately after the disposal.

The exemption against gains is given automatically, and any losses arising will not be allowable losses.

Assuming a disposal date of June 2007, Alantech Ltd has owned its holding in Mobile Ltd for more than 12 months. However, Alantech Ltd's ownership of the Boron holding has only been for 11 months since Boron Ltd was acquired on 1 July 2006. Selling the shares in June 2007 will therefore fail the 12 month test, and both of the gains will become chargeable as before July 2006 Alantech Ltd did not hold a 10% interest in its own right.

It would therefore be advisable for the companies to wait for a further month until July 2007 before selling the amalgamated shareholding. By doing so, they will both be able to take advantage of the substantial shareholdings relief, thereby saving tax of £28,532 (150,171 × 19%) assuming a corporation tax rate of 19%.

(d) **Group VAT position**

Companies under common control can apply for group registration.

The advantages of such a registration are as follows:

(i) A VAT group will appoint a representative member who will account for the group's output and input tax on behalf of the group, thereby simplifying VAT accounting.

(ii) Supplies of goods or services from one group member to another are, in general, disregarded for VAT purposes. Again, this reduces the accounting burden.

(iii) Two or more companies can be treated as a VAT group if each is established in the UK and there is a controlling relationship (one controls each of the others, one person controls all of them, or two or more persons in partnership control all of them).

(iv) An application to create, modify and/or terminate companies from a VAT group can be made at any time. Companies that fail the control test must leave the VAT group.

ACCA marking scheme		Marks
(a)	Proceeds/cost	0.5
	Indexation	0.5
	Part of same capital gains group	0.5
	Awareness of rollover relief	1
	Business asset	0.5
	Both assets qualifying	0.5
	Timing of rollover relief	0.5
	Chargeable gain: lower of	0.5
	Gain	0.5
	Proceeds not reinvested	0.5
	Calculation of chargeable gain	0.5
	Max	6.0

(b)	Group for group relief/capital gains	0.5
	Trading income	0.5
	Losses brought forward – offset	0.5
	Interest income	0.5
	Chargeable gains	0.5
	Current year losses v Boron profits	0.5
	Group relief to Alantech	0.5
	Group relief to Bubble	0.5
	Corporation tax (30% for Alantech)	0.5
	(19% for Boron)	0.5
	Marginal relief (Alantech)	0.5
	Group relief time restriction for Alantech	0.5
	Group relief: lower of	0.5
	Borons losses (× 6/12)	0.5
	Alantech profit (× 6/12)	0.5
	Losses against profits at highest rates	0.5
	Identify Alantech as suffering highest rate	0.5
	Carry back 2007 Boron losses	0.5
	Use of loss memorandum	0.5
	Losses remaining	0.5
	Max	9.0
(c)	Sale proceeds (split)	0.5
	Cost (2 × 0.5)	1.0
	Indexation calculations (2 × 0.5)	1.0
	Substantial shareholding – awareness	1.0
	10% share capital requirement	0.5
	Other 10% requirements (2 × 0.5)	1.0
	Amalgamation of shareholdings	0.5
	12 month requirement	0.5
	Trading company requirement	0.5
	Automatic exemption	0.5
	Sell shares now will fail test	0.5
	Delaying sale 1 month will pass test	0.5
	Identify tax saving	0.5
	Max	7.0
(d)	Awareness of group registration	1.0
	Appoint a representative member	0.5
	Intra group VAT supplies disregarded	0.5
	Group members established in UK	0.5
	Controlling relationship between members	0.5
	Ability to create/modify/terminate	0.5
	Max	3.0
Total (Max)		25.0

58 AQUA LIMITED

(a) (i) Corporate structure and early relief of trading losses

With the current share ownership, the two companies do not form part of a group for corporation tax group relief purposes. This means that Aria Limited cannot surrender its losses to Aqua Limited. In addition, as Aria Limited will make further anticipated losses in the years ended 31 March 2008 and 31 March 2009, the losses already incurred cannot be set against trading profits of subsequent years until at least 2010 (assuming Aria Limited makes taxable profits in that year).

To obtain early relief for Aria Ltd's losses, the solution is to ensure that the companies have a 75% common ownership by forming a group. This can be achieved in one of two ways.

1.   A new holding company could be set up. It would issue shares to Irroy and her brother in exchange for their shares in the existing companies.

This will represent a 'share for share' exchange, and can be achieved without giving rise to any capital gains tax as long as the sale is not part of a scheme whose main purpose is the avoidance of tax.

It is possible to obtain advance clearance from HMRC to confirm this treatment.

Providing the new company does not trade, it will not count as an associated company for tax purposes.

2.   As an alternative, Irroy and her brother could consider selling their shares in Aria Limited to Aqua Limited, but this may give rise to a chargeable gain on Irroy and her brother.

However, as Aria Limited is loss making, the selling price of the shares is likely to be minimal, so it is unlikely that any large chargeable gains will arise.

Business asset taper relief should also apply to reduce any potential gains, and the capital gains annual exemptions should be available to offset any remaining gains arising.

If the restructuring occurs, in both cases, the taxable trading losses can only be relieved after the date that the group is formed. Tax losses incurred prior to implementation of the amended structure can only be carried forward to be offset against taxable profits in the future if generated from the same trade.

(ii)   **Corporation tax payable – year ended 31 March 2008**

Aqua Limited is currently associated with Aria Limited by virtue of Irroy controlling both companies. The limits for the small companies rate are therefore £150,000 (£300,000/2) and £750,000 (£1,500,000/2).

The corporation tax calculations are as follows:

(1)   **Assuming no action is taken and the current structure continues**

Aqua Limited

	£
Profits chargeable to corporation tax	175,000
Corporation tax at 30%	52,500
Less: Marginal relief	
$(750,000 - 175,000) \times 11/400$	(15,813)
Corporation tax payable	36,687

Aria Limited

No corporation tax liability arises as the company is loss making.

All £60,000 loss is carried forward.

(2)   **Amended structure is implemented on 10 June 2007**

If either option is taken, the losses can be group relieved to the extent that the companies form a group.

If this takes place on 1 June 2007, 10 months worth of Aria Limited's losses can be offset. Thus, £50,000 $(60,000 \times {}^{10}/_{12})$ of the losses could be surrendered to Aqua Limited.

The resulting corporation tax payable by Aqua Limited would therefore be:

Aqua Limited	£
Trading profits	175,000
Less: Group relief	(50,000)
Profits chargeable to corporation tax	125,000
Corporation tax payable at 19%	23,750

As a result of the restructuring, the corporation tax saved is £12,937 (£36,687 – £23,750).

Aria Limited

No corporation tax liability arises as the company is loss making.

However only £10,000 (60,000 – 50,000) losses are carried forward.

(b) **Incorporating a subsidiary in the Republic of Ireland**

There are several matters that Irroy will need to be aware of in relation to value added tax and corporation tax implications of setting up an Irish subsidiary. These are set out below.

Residence status of the subsidiary

Irroy will want to ensure that the subsidiary is treated as being resident in the Republic of Ireland. It will then pay corporation tax on its profits at lower rates than in the UK.

The country of incorporation usually claims taxing rights, but this is not by itself sufficient. Irroy needs to be aware that a company can be treated as UK resident by virtue of the location of its central management and control. This is usually defined as being where the board of directors meets to make strategic decisions. As a result, Irroy needs to ensure that board meetings are conducted outside the UK.

If treated as a UK resident company

If Green Limited is treated as being UK resident, it will be taxed in the UK on its worldwide income, including that arising in the Republic of Ireland. However, as it will be conducting trading activities in the Republic of Ireland, Green Limited will also be treated as being Irish resident as its activities in that country are likely to constitute a permanent establishment. Thus it may also suffer tax in the Republic of Ireland as a consequence, although double tax relief will be available (see later).

A permanent establishment is broadly defined as a fixed place of business through which a business is wholly or partly carried on. Examples of a permanent establishment include an office, factory or workshop, although certain activities (such as storage or ancillary activities) can be excluded from the definition.

If treated as a non-UK resident company

If Green Limited is treated as being an Irish resident company, any dividends paid to Aqua Limited will be taxed as dividends from overseas companies in the UK.

Despite being non resident, Green Limited will still count as an associate of the existing UK companies, and may affect the rates of tax paid by Aqua Limited and Aria Limited in the UK. However, as a non UK resident company, Green Limited will not be able to claim losses from the UK companies by way of group relief.

Double tax relief

If treated as a UK resident company

If Green Limited is treated as UK resident, corporation tax at UK rates will be payable on all profits earned. However, income arising in the Republic of Ireland is likely to have been taxed in that country also by virtue of having a permanent establishment located there. As the same profits have been taxed twice, double tax relief is available, either by reference to the tax treaty between the UK and the Republic of Ireland, or on a unilateral basis, where the UK will give relief for the foreign tax suffered.

If treated as a non-UK resident company

If Green Limited is treated as an Irish resident company, it will pay tax in the Republic of Ireland, based on its worldwide taxable profits. However, any repatriation of profits to the UK by dividend will be taxed on a receipts basis in the UK. Again, double tax relief will be available as set out above.

Relief for double taxation

Double tax relief is available against two types of tax. For payments made by Green Limited to Aqua Limited on which withholding tax has been levied, credit will be given for the tax withheld. In addition, relief is available for the underlying tax where a dividend is received from a foreign company in which Aqua Limited owns at least 10% of the voting power. The underlying tax is the tax attributable to the relevant profits from which the dividend was paid.

Double tax relief is given at the lower rate of the UK tax and the foreign tax (withholding and underlying taxes) suffered.

Transfer pricing

Where groups have subsidiaries in other countries, they may be tempted to divert profits to subsidiaries which pay tax at lower rates. This can be achieved by artificially changing the prices charged (known as the transfer price) between the group companies.

While this is acceptable practice commercially through common control, anti avoidance legislation seeks to correct this treatment for taxation purposes by ensuring that profits on such intra-group transactions are calculated as if the transactions were carried out on an arms length basis. This legislation can also be applied to transactions between UK group companies.

If treated as a UK resident company

If Green Limited is treated as a UK resident company, the group's status as a small or medium sized enterprise means that transfer pricing issues will not apply to transactions between Green Limited and the other UK group companies.

If treated as a non-UK resident company

If Green Limited is an Irish resident company, transfer pricing issues are not likely to apply to transactions between Green Limited and the UK group companies for two reasons:

(1) The group's status as a small or medium-sized enterprise, and

(2) The existence of a double tax treaty which is based on the OECD model, between the UK and the Republic of Ireland which is likely to contain a non-discrimination clause.

When both of these are present, transfer pricing rules should not apply.

Controlled foreign companies

Tax legislation exists to prevent a UK company accumulating profits in a foreign subsidiary which is subject to a low tax rate. Such a subsidiary is referred to as a controlled foreign company (CFC), and exists where:

(1)   the company is resident outside the UK, and

(2)   is controlled by a UK resident entity or persons, and

(3)   pays a 'lower level of tax' in its country of residence.

A lower level of tax is taken to be less than 75% of the tax that would have been payable had the company been UK resident.

If Green Limited is an Irish resident company, it will be paying corporation tax at 12.5%, so it would appear to be caught by the above rules and is therefore likely to be treated as a CFC.

Where a company is treated as a CFC, its profits are apportioned to UK resident companies entitled to at least 25% of its profits.

For Aqua Limited, which would own 100% of the shares in Green Limited, any profits made by Green Limited would be apportioned to Aqua Limited as a deemed distribution. Aqua Limited would be required to self-assess this apportionment on its tax return and pay UK tax on the deemed distribution (with credit being given for the Irish tax suffered).

There are some exemptions. If these are applicable the CFC legislation does not apply and no apportionments of profits will be made. These include where chargeable profits of the CFC do not exceed £50,000 in an accounting period, or where the CFC follows an acceptable distribution policy (i.e. distributing at least 90% of its chargeable profits within 18 months of the relevant period).

Value added tax (VAT)

Green Limited will be making taxable supplies in the Republic of Ireland and thus (subject to exceeding the Irish registration limit) liable to register for VAT there.

If Green Limited is registered for VAT in the Republic of Ireland (an EU country), then supplies of goods made from the UK will be zero rated. VAT on the goods will be levied in the Republic of Ireland at a rate of 21%.

Aqua Limited will need to have proof of supply in order to apply the zero rate, and will have to issue an invoice showing Green Limited's Irish VAT registration number as well as its own. In the absence of such evidence/registration, Aqua Limited will have to treat its transactions with Green Limited as domestic sales and levy VAT at the UK standard rate of 17.5%.

In addition to making its normal VAT returns, Aqua Limited will also be required to complete an EU Sales List (ESL) statement each quarter. This provides details of the sales made to customers in the return period – in this case, Green Limited. Penalties can be applied for inaccuracies or non-compliance.

			Marks
ACCA marking scheme			
(a)	(i) Companies not part of a group		0.5
	Inability to surrender losses		0.5
	Ability to use losses in future		0.5
	Shareholding requirements to make a group		0.5
	Share for share:	possibility	0.5
		no immediate CGT consequences	0.5
		commercial requirements	0.5
		clearance procedure available	0.5
		dormant company not an associate	0.5
	Straight sale:	consideration of CGT issues	0.5
		availability of business taper relief	0.5
		availability of annual exemptions	0.5
	Existing tax losses v future trading profit only		0.5
		Max	6.0
	(ii) Awareness of associated companies		0.5
	No planning:	Corporation tax at 30%	0.5
		Marginal relief calculation	0.5
	Planning:	Restriction of group relief	0.5
		Corporation tax at 19%	0.5
	Calculation of tax saved		0.5
		Max	3.0
(b)	Residence:		
	incorporation not necessarily sufficient		0.5
	central management/control		0.5
	conduct meetings outside UK		0.5
	if resident UK:	taxed on worldwide income	0.5
		PE in ROI	1.0
		consequences	0.5
	if resident ROI:	dividends taxable	0.5
		still associated	0.5
		no group relief	0.5
	Double tax relief:	relief for withholidng tax	0.5
		relief for underlying tax	0.5
		10% plus holding	0.5
		double tax: lower of	0.5

Transfer pricing:	identify issue	0.5
	arms length	0.5
	applies in UK/exemption if SME	1.0
	situation if Irish resident	1.0
CFC issues:	identify issue	1.0
	dependent subsidiary	0.5
	material difference in tax rates	0.5
	conclusion: ROI low tax country	0.5
	deemed distribution	0.5
	requirement to self-report	0.5
	£50,000 exemption	0.5
	acceptable distribution policy	
	– identify exemption	0.5
	– 90%/details	0.5
VAT issues:	making taxable supplies in ROI	0.5
	UK zero rated	0.5
	VAT paid in ROI	0.5
	proof of supply required	0.5
	invoice to bear both VAT numbers	0.5
	alternative domestic treatment	0.5
	need for an ESL	0.5
	penalties for non-compliance	0.5
	Max	16.0
Total		25.0

TAXATION OF CORPORATE BUSINESSES – OTHER ASPECTS

59 RIMU LTD

(a) **Conditions which must be satisfied for capital treatment**

The following conditions must be satisfied for the purchase of own shares to be treated as a capital event:

1 Rimu Ltd must be unquoted.

2 Rimu Ltd must be a trading company (excluding dealing in shares and land) or the holding company of a trading group.

3 George and Clare must be resident and ordinarily resident in the United Kingdom.

4 George and Clare must have owned the shares for five years.

5 Their shareholdings must be reduced to no more than 75% of their holdings prior to the sale.

6 Their holdings must be no more than 30% after the sale.

7 The transaction must be for the benefit of the company's trade.

(b) **Number of shares to be acquired from Clare**

Clare owns 6,000 of the 40,000 shares in issue, i.e. a 15% holding. Her holding must be reduced to 75% of 15% = 11.25%.

The shares acquired by the company must be cancelled after repurchase.

George's 10,000 shares are repurchased first and the shares will be cancelled, leaving 30,000 shares in issue.

Accordingly, for Clare's interest in the company, after the purchase of her shares, to be 11.25%, the number of shares to be purchased is calculated as follows:

$$\frac{6,000 - y}{30,000 - y} \quad \text{must equal } 11.25\%$$

$$
\begin{aligned}
6,000 - y &= 11.25\% \times (30,000 - y) \\
6,000 - y &= 3,375 - 0.1125\,y \\
2,625 &= 0.8875\,y \\
y &= 2,958 \text{ shares}
\end{aligned}
$$

Clare should therefore sell at least 2,958 shares back to the company for the event to be treated as a capital event.

Clare will then own 3,042 shares out of 27,042 shares in issue, i.e. 11.25%.

(c) **Desirability of capital gains tax treatment**

Clare's base cost in the shares is £2.50, the same as her father's, due to the gift relief claim. A share price of £14.00 will result in a gain of £11.50 per share.

The gain will be reduced by 75% taper relief, as the shares are business assets for taper relief purposes and Clare has owned the shares for more than two complete years since 5 April 1998.

The gain after taper relief will be taxed at 40%. The annual exemption can be ignored due to the level of gains made by Clare each year.

The tax per share will therefore be $(11.50 \times 25\% \times 40\%) = £1.15$.

If the capital gains treatment is not available, the amount received by Clare, less the original subscription price of £1, will be treated as a net distribution. This net distribution will be grossed up and taxed at 32.5% less the 10% tax credit.

The tax per share will therefore be $(£14 - £1) \times 100/90 \times (32.5\% - 10\%) = £3.25$.

Accordingly, the capital gains tax treatment is desirable as the tax per share will be less.

Tutorial note: Prior to 5 April 2000, for unquoted shares to be business assets, an individual had to hold at least 25% of the shares, or hold at least 5% and be a full time working officer or employee for the company. If this were not satisfied, the shares would be mixed use assets and it would be necessary to apportion the gain. However the question tells you to assume Clare's shares were business assets throughout.

(d)   (i)   **Price per share**

		£
Funds available		180,000
Shares to be acquired	George	10,000
	Clare	2,958
		12,958
Price per share		£13.89

(ii)   **Net cash receivable**

	£
George	
Proceeds (10,000 × £13.89)	138,900
Cost and indexation (10,000 × (1 + 1.5))	(25,000)
Indexed gain	113,900

As business assets held for more than two years, the gain is 25% chargeable.

	£
Chargeable gain (113,900 × 25%)	28,475
Annual exemption	(8,800)
Taxable gain	19,675
Capital gains tax (19,675 × 40%)	7,870
Net cash received (138,900 – 7,870)	131,030

	£
Clare	
Proceeds (2,958 × £13.89)	41,087
Cost and indexation (2,958 × (1 + 1.5))	(7,395)
Indexed gain	33,692
Chargeable gain (33,692 × 25%)	8,423

Clare has no annual exemption remaining.

	£
Capital gains tax (8,423 × 40%)	3,369
Net cash received (41,087 – 3,369)	37,718

(e)   **Implications from ownership of Rimu Ltd and Office Design Ltd**

VAT implications

Rimu Ltd will charge output VAT on the sale of office furniture to Office Design Ltd. Unless Office Design Ltd is making any exempt supplies, which is unlikely, the VAT will be fully recoverable by Office Design Ltd.

Prior to the purchase of own shares Ben owns 37.5% (15,000/40,000) of Rimu Ltd. After the purchase of own shares however Ben's interest in Rimu Ltd is increased to 55.5% (15,000/27,042) and Ben therefore controls both Rimu Ltd and Office Design Ltd (60%).

Rimu Ltd and Office Design Ltd would therefore be eligible to apply for VAT group registration. Under a group VAT arrangement Rimu Ltd would not be required to charge VAT on the sales to Office Design Ltd.

However as Office Design Ltd can recover its input tax in full and as the companies operate quite independently of each other, the administrative arrangements of a group registration are likely to be difficult. A group VAT registration would not therefore appear to be beneficial.

Transfer pricing implications

Rimu Ltd is selling furniture to Office Design Ltd at an undervalue, thereby depressing its profits chargeable to corporation tax.

After the purchase of own shares both Rimu Ltd and Office Design Ltd will be under the control of Ben. The price being charged to Office Design Ltd is not an arms length price and the company is thereby obtaining a tax advantage from the depression of its profits. Accordingly the transfer pricing legislation will apply and Rimu Ltd will be required to increase its taxable profits by reference to an arms length price.

As Office Design Ltd is resident in the UK however it may make an equal and opposite adjustment to its taxable profits.

60   BLUETONE LTD

(a)   **Melodys' IHT liability**

Melody received a gift from her father on 10 February 2003 and was left his shares in Bluetone Ltd on his death.

She is responsible for paying the IHT in respect of both gifts. Therefore, the death tax on the gift to her on 10 February 2003 and on her father's estate needs to be calculated.

Lifetime gift to Melody

As the gift to Melody is a PET within seven years of the death of Melody's father the gift becomes chargeable on his death. The value of the PET is £39,000 (W1).

As there are no previous lifetime gifts, no IHT is payable on Melody's father's death as the PET is covered by the nil rate band of £285,000.

Gift to the discretionary trust

The gift into the discretionary trust on 4 June 2003 is valued at £176,000 (W2). There is no lifetime IHT payable and no death tax is due as the gift is covered by the nil rate band.

The remaining nil rate band available to match against the estate is £70,000 (285,000 – 39,000 – 176,000).

Estate at death – 15 February 2007

	£
Main residence	125,000
Repayment mortgage	(42,000)
	83,000
Ordinary shares in Bluetone Ltd (Note (1))	
(50,000 at £11.00)	550,000
Ordinary shares in Expanse plc (W3)	127,260
Units in World-Growth (26,000 at 80p) (Note (2))	20,800
Building society deposits	32,000
Life assurance policy	61,000
	791,060
Income tax	(6,600)
Funeral expenses	(3,460)
Chargeable estate	864,000

IHT liability (864,000 – 70,000) × 40%	317,600

The effective rate of IHT on the estate is 36.759% (317,600/864,000 × 100).

Melody is responsible for the IHT on the Bluetone Ltd shares of £202,175 (550,000 × 36.759%).

The IHT will be due on the earlier of 31 August 2007 or the delivery of the executor's account. Alternatively the tax can be paid in 10 equal annual instalments commencing on 31 August 2007.

Notes:

(1)   Business property relief is not available in respect of the shares in Bluetone Ltd because Melody's father did not own them for two years.

(2)   Units are valued at the lower bid price of 80p per unit.

Key answer tips

The gambling debts are not an allowable deduction because they are not legally enforceable (even if there may be other reasons why they are likely to be honoured by the beneficiaries!)

Specific legacies such as the gift of the shares to Melody are normally free of IHT (i.e. the specific beneficiary does not bear the tax, the residual legatee bears the tax) unless the will specifies to the contrary, as is the case in this quesion.

Workings

(1)   **Value of the PET to Melody – 10 February 2003**

		£
Value transferred		50,000
Marriage exemption		(5,000)
Annual exemption 2002/03		(3,000)
	2001/02	(3,000)
PET		39,000

(2) **Value of the CLT – 4 June 2003**

	£
Value transferred	179,000
Annual exemption 2003/04	(3,000)
CLT	176,000

(3) **Value of Expanse plc shares**

Lower of

(i) Quarter up method = $[312 + (320 - 312) \times \frac{1}{4}] = 314$p

(ii) Average of marked bargains = $(282 + 324) \times \frac{1}{2} = 303$p

Value of 42,000 shares = (42,000 × £3.03) = £127,260

(b) **Sale of shares to son**

Capital gains tax

Liam is disposing of a 15% interest (30,000/200,000) in Bluetone Ltd shares for £75,000.

As the shares are worth £9 each, the total disposal value is £270,000 (30,000 × £9).

The disposal is therefore a sale under valuation to a connected person.

Gift relief is available, but not all of the gain can be deferred. The extent to which the consideration paid by Liam's son exceeds the allowable cost is immediately chargeable to CGT i.e. £45,000 (75,000 – 30,000).

Provided that Liam and his son jointly elect, the balance of the gain can be held over as a gift of business assets since Bluetone Ltd is an unquoted trading company.

The CGT liability is calculated as follows:

	£
Deemed consideration (30,000 at £9.00)	270,000
Cost	(30,000)
Unindexed gain	240,000
Indexation $30,000 \times \dfrac{162.6 - 139.9}{139.9}$	(4,868)
Indexed gain	235,132
Gift relief (235,132 - 45,000)	(190,132)
Indexed gain after gift relief	45,000

As the shares are business assets for taper relief purposes and have been held for more than two years, the gain is 25% chargeable.

	£
Chargeable gain (45,000 × 25%)	11,250
Annual exemption	(8,800)
Taxable gain	2,450
Capital gains tax (2,450 × 40%)	980

The CGT is due on 31 January 2008.

Inheritance tax

Liam's disposal of 30,000 shares in Bluetone Ltd at an under valuation will be a PET for IHT purposes calculated taking account of the related property valuation rules as follows:

	£
Value of shares held before the transfer	
(50,000 × £15.00) (50% holding with wife)	750,000
Value of shares held after the transfer	
(20,000 × £12.50) (35% holding with wife)	(250,000)
Diminution in the value of the estate	500,000
Consideration paid	(75,000)
Value transferred	425,000

Business property relief at the rate of 100% will be available as the share are unquoted trading company shares which Liam has held for more than two years.

An IHT liability will only arise if Liam dies before 20 March 2014 and his son has disposed of the shares before that date (subject to the replacement property rules).

Key answer tips

The shares have always been a business asset for taper relief purposes as Liam is a director and holds 25% of the shares of the company. Liam's wife's shareholding is taken into account in determining the value of the shares for IHT purposes.

(c) **Purchase of own shares**

Treated as a capital gain

Noel's CGT liability for 2006/07 due on 31 January 2008 will be as follows if the event is treated as a capital gain:

	£
Sales proceeds (50,000 × £11)	550,000
Cost (50,000 × £1)	(50,000)
Unindexed gain	500,000
Indexation $50,000 \times \dfrac{162.6 - 139.9}{139.9}$	(8,113)
Indexed gain	491,887

As business assets held by Noel for more than two years, the gain is 25% chargeable.

	£
Chargeable gain (491,887 × 25%)	122,972
Annual exemption	(8,800)
Taxable gain	114,172
Capital gains tax (114,172 × 40%)	45,669

Treated as a distribution

Noel will be assessed on a grossed up distribution of £555,556 [(550,000 – 50,000) × 100/90)].

This will result in an additional income tax liability of £125,000 [555,556 × (32.5% - 10%)] for 2006/07, which will be due on 31 January 2008.

Conclusion

The special treatment as a capital gain results in a tax saving of £79,331 (125,000 – 45,669). It is therefore beneficial for the capital gains treatment to apply.

However it is important to note that there is not a choice of treatment available. If the relevant conditions are met, the capital treatment is compulsory and automatically applies.

Key answer tips

A 75% rate of taper relief results in an effective CGT rate of 10%, compared to an income tax rate of 25% on net dividends received.

61 INSECT LTD

(a) (i) **Capital treatment of a company purchasing its own shares**

Qualifying conditions

Insect Ltd's purchase of John's 50,000 £1 ordinary shares will qualify for the special treatment because the following conditions are met:

1   Insect Ltd is an unquoted trading company.

2   John is resident and ordinarily resident in the UK for the year in which the shares are purchased.

3   John has owned the shares for the five years preceding the repurchase on 31 March 2007.

4   John has disposed of all of his shares in Insect Ltd. The substantial reduction test is therefore satisfied and John is not connected with Insect Ltd immediately after the purchase of his shares.

5   The purchase of shares appears to be wholly or mainly for the benefit of the trade carried on by Insect Ltd, and not for the benefit of John.

     HMRC has indicated four circumstances that satisfy this test, one of which (the disagreement over the management of the company) would appear to be satisfied. However, the disagreement must have been having an adverse effect on the running of Insect Ltd's trade.

(ii) **Most beneficial treatment of the purchase of own shares**

Treated as a capital gain

Implications for Insect Ltd

There are no tax implications for Insect Ltd.

Implications for John

John's CGT liability for 2006/07 due on 31 January 2008 is as follows:

	£
Sale proceeds (March 2007)	680,000
Cost (October 1994)	(50,000)
Unindexed gain	630,000
Indexation to April 1998	
$50,000 \times \dfrac{162.6 - 145.2}{145.2}$	(5,992)
Indexed gain	624,008

As the shares are business assets held for more than two years, the gain is 25% chargeable.

	£
Chargeable gain (624,008 × 25%)	156,002
Annual exemption	(8,800)
Taxable gain	147,202
Capital gains tax (147,202 × 40%)	58,881

Treated as a distribution

Implications for Insect Ltd

There are no tax implications for Insect Ltd.

Implications for John

John will be assessed on a grossed up distribution of £700,000 (680,000 − 50,000 = 630,000 × 100/90).

This will result in an additional income tax liability of £157,500 (700,000 at 32.5% less the 10% tax credit) for 2006/07 which will be due on 31 January 2008.

Conclusion

The special treatment as a capital gain results in a tax saving of £98,619 (157,500 − 58,881) and is therefore beneficial for the capital gains treatment to apply.

However it is important to note that there is not a choice of treatment available. If the relevant conditions are met, the capital treatment is compulsory and automatically applies.

Key answer tips

The effective rate of CGT is only 10% (where there is 75% taper relief) compared to an income tax rate of 25% on net dividends.

(b) (i)   Provision of the three company motor cars

Implications for Insect Ltd

Insect Ltd can only claim capital allowances and expenses in respect of the motor cars provided to Paul and Richard as they are employees of the company.

As George is not an employee, but is a shareholder of a close company (i.e. a participator), the provision of a car to George is treated as a distribution (see below). As a result, the deduction of related expenses and capital allowances are not available for George's car.

The writing down allowances for the year ended 31 March 2007 on Paul and Richard's cars will be restricted to a total of £6,000 (£3,000 × 2).

Implications for Paul and Richard

For 2006/07 Paul and Richard will be assessed on employment income on benefits of £5,280 and £6,480 (W1) respectively.

Their additional income tax liabilities for 2006/07 will be £2,112 (5,280 at 40%) and £2,592 (6,480 at 40%).

Implications for George

George is neither a director nor an employee of Insect Ltd, but he is a participator. The provision of a motor car to him is therefore treated as a distribution calculated using the employment income benefit rules.

For 2006/07 the gross distribution is £7,200 (W2), so the additional income tax liability is £1,620 (7,200 × (32.5% − 10%).

Workings

(1)   **Car benefits**

	Paul	Richard	George
	£	£	£
List price of car	27,000	27,000	27,000
Less Capital contribution (maximum)	(5,000	–	–
	22,000	27,000	27,000

CO_2 emissions 187 g/km, available all year

Appropriate % = 15% + (185 − 140) × $^1/_5$ = 24%

	£
Car benefits	
Paul (22,000 × 24%)	5,280
Richard (27,000 × 24%)	6,480
George (27,000 × 24%)	6,480

(2)   **Deemed distribution to George**

The grossed up car benefit is taxed as a dividend at 32½% with a 10% tax credit.

Grossed up car benefit = (6,480 × 100/90) =   £7,200

(ii)   **Provision of the interest-free loans – Insect Ltd**

Implications for Insect Ltd

The three loans of £75,000 are all made to participators, and so Insect Ltd will be subject to a tax charge calculated at the rate of 25% on the amount of the loans.

The tax charge is due on the normal due date for corporation tax (i.e. 9 months after the end of the chargeable accounting period). If any of the loans have been repaid or written off before the due date, the tax charge applies to the amount outstanding on the due date.

The amount payable to HMRC will therefore be £50,000 (75,000 × 3 = 225,000 – 25,000 = 200,000 at 25%). The due date for this liability is 1 January 2008.

Implications for Paul and Richard

Paul and Richard will each be assessed to an employment income benefit on the beneficial loan interest rate (i.e. the difference between the interest paid on the loan and the official rate of interest).

The taxable benefit for 2006/07 will be £2,812 (75,000 × 5% × 9/12).

Their additional income tax liability for 2006/07 will be £1,125 (2,812 at 40%).

Implications for George

The loan to a participator who is not also an employee is treated as a deemed dividend distribution based on the beneficial loan rate for each year of the loan and when the loan is written off.

Therefore, when the loan is written off George will be assessed on gross dividend income of £27,778 (25,000 × 100/90) in 2006/07 which is taxed at 32.5% with a 10% tax credit.

The additional income tax liability is therefore £6,250 (27,778 × (32.5% – 10%).

A deemed distribution will also arise under the beneficial loan rules.

RESIDENCE ISSUES

62   GLOBAL PLC

(a)   **Corporation tax implications of various transactions**

Rate of corporation tax

Global plc has significant profits such that it will pay corporation tax at the full rate.

The full rate of corporation tax for the year ended 30 September 2007 is 30%.

Shareholding in Nouveau Inc

The dividend received from Nouveau Inc. will be included as overseas dividend income when calculating Global plc's corporation tax liability for the year ended 30 September 2007.

Double taxation relief will be available for the 5% withholding tax, and as Global plc owns more than 10% of the share capital of Nouveau Inc., relief will also be given for the underlying tax paid in Northia.

As Global plc owns 90% of Nouveau Inc., the dividend received before withholding tax is deducted is £270,000 (300,000 × 90%).

The gross dividend income is calculated as follows:

	£	Overseas tax suffered £
Dividend received (270,000 × 95%)	256,500	
With holding tax (270,000 × 5%)	13,500	13,500
Dividends before withholding tax deducted (£300,000 × 90%)	270,000	
Underlying tax (below)	90,000	90,000
Gross dividend income	360,000	
Overseas tax suffered		103,500

Underlying tax is calculated as follows:

Tax paid = (700,000 × 25%) = 175,000

Profit after tax = (700,000 – 175,000) = 525,000

ULT = 175,000 × (270,000/525,000) = 90,000

Alternative calculation:

(270,000 × 25/75) = 90,000

Double taxation relief is available and is calculated as the lower of:

(i)   overseas tax suffered   £103,500

(ii)   UK tax on overseas income (360,000 × 30%)   £108,000

Therefore full relief will be given for the £103,500 overseas tax suffered as a tax credit against Global plc's corporation tax liability.

Transfer pricing

Sales are going to be made to another group company, which is controlled by Global plc, at an undervalue. This will reduce UK trading profits and hence UK corporation tax. As Global plc is a large company, and the terms of the transaction would have been different if the companies were not connected then the transfer pricing rules apply and a true market price must be substituted for the transfer price.

The market price will be an 'arm's length' one that would be charged if the parties to the transaction were independent of each other. Under self assessment Global plc is required to make the adjustment in its tax return for the year to 30 September 2007.

An adjustment of £42,500 (10,000 × £12.75 × 25/75) will be required, unless the discount is justified by different trading terms.

Key answer tips

Under self-assessment the company has to decide if the transfer pricing rules apply with penalties if it transpires that they made the wrong decision. The company has to keep detailed evidence of the reasons for their decisions so that they can show they were not negligent even if with the benefit of hindsight, they got it wrong.

Branch in Eastina

The branch in Eastina is controlled from that country, and Global plc will therefore be assessed under overseas trading profits. The branch profits are subject to UK corporation tax in full regardless of the amount remitted to the UK.

The tax paid in Eastina of £70,000 (175,000 at 40%) is more than the UK corporation tax on the overseas income of £52,500 (175,000 at 30%), and so double taxation relief will be restricted to £52,500.

Sale of shareholding in Surplus ltd

Degrouping charge

The factory was transferred from Global plc to Surplus Ltd, a 75% subsidiary, within six years of the date that Surplus Ltd is to leave the group.

The transfer would originally have been at no gain/no loss, but a chargeable gain of £304,480 (630,000 − 260,000 − 65,520) will now be assessed on Surplus Ltd for the year ended 30 September 2007. The related corporation tax liability is £91,344 (304,480 × 30%).

It would be possible to elect to transfer the degrouping charge to another group member, but there do not appear to be any advantages in this instance.

There will be no tax saving resulting from the reduction in sale proceeds due to Surplus Ltd's corporation tax liability of £91,344.

Gain on the disposal of shares

No gain should arise on the disposal of the shares as they should be covered by the substantial shareholding exemption.

Assuming that Global plc is the holding company of a trading group, that Surplus Ltd is a trading company, and that the shareholding has been held for at least 12 months out of the previous two years, the gain on sale will be exempt.

Trading loss in Wanted Ltd

Wanted Ltd will be able to group relieve its trading loss to Global plc (and other 75% subsidiaries) once it has become a member of the Global plc group on 1 February 2007. It has been a member of the group for 8 months of the year ended 30 September 2007.

However, in the year ended 30 September 2007, the relief will be limited to the lower of Wanted Ltd's available loss of £160,000 (240,000 × 8/12) and 8/12 of the claimant company's PCTCT (assuming they have coterminous accounting periods).

Capital loss in Wanted Ltd

The capital loss of £170,000 is a pre-entry loss. It would not be possible for the Global plc group to utilise this loss against a degrouping charge transferred from Surplus Ltd.

The loss can be utilised by Wanted Ltd against its future gains.

(b)   **Quarterly payments for corporation tax**

Global plc is a large company for the year ended 30 September 2007 as it will pay the full rate of corporation tax. Global plc will therefore have to pay its corporation tax liability by quarterly instalments.

However, an exception would apply if profits do not exceed £10 million (reduced according to the number of associated companies at the beginning of the accounting period), and Global plc was not a large company for the year ended 30 September 2006.

The four quarterly instalments for the year ended 30 September 2007 will be due on 14 April 2007, 14 July 2007, 14 October 2007 and 14 January 2008.

Instalments will be based on the expected corporation tax liability for the year ended 30 September 2007, and so Global plc will have to produce an accurate forecast of its corporation tax liability for the year.

63 HORIZON LTD

(a) **Corporation tax computation for the year ended 31 March 2007**

	UK £	Overseas Deep Inc dividend £	Overseas Even Inc dividend £	Total £
Trading profit	44,000			44,000
Chargeable gain (W1)	32,000			32,000
Overseas dividend (W2)		230,400		230,400
Overseas dividend (W3)			21,060	21,060
	76,000	230,400	21,060	327,460
Group relief (W4)	(76,000)	–	(21,060)	(97,060)
PCTCT	–	230,400	–	230,400
FII (W5)				12,000
Profits (Note below)				242,400
Corporation tax at 30%				69,120
Marginal relief 11/400 × (375,000 - 242,400) × 230,400/242,400				(3,466)
				65,654
Double taxation relief (W6)				(65,654)
Corporation tax liability				Nil

Note:

For the year ended 31 March 2007 Horizon Ltd has three associated companies (Arc Ltd, Bend Ltd and Deep Inc). Therefore the lower and upper limits for corporation tax purposes are £75,000 (300,000/4) and £375,000 (1,500,000/4) respectively. Marginal relief is therefore applicable.

Workings

(W1) **Chargeable gain**

Horizon Ltd has a gain of £52,000.

However, a claim for rollover relief is possible because the reinvestment by Arc Ltd, a 75% subsidiary, is to take place within three years of the sale of the freehold office on 15 June 2006.

Full rollover relief is not possible as not all of the sale proceeds have been reinvested in qualifying assets. Proceeds of £32,000 (242,000 - 210,000) have not been reinvested.

Therefore £32,000 of the gain will remain chargeable in Horizon Ltd in the year ended 31 March 2007. The remaining £20,000 of the gain will be deferred.

(W2) Dividend from Deep Inc

Relief is available for the withholding tax on the dividend from Deep Inc. In addition, as Horizon Ltd owns more than 10% of the share capital of Deep Inc, relief will be given for the underlying tax paid in Slozobia as follows:

	£	*Overseas tax suffered* £
Dividend received (237,120 × 60%)	142,272	
Withholding tax (142,272 × 5/95)	7,488	7,488
	149,760	
Underlying tax (see below)	80,640	80,640
Overseas dividend income	230,400	
Overseas tax suffered		88,128

Underlying tax is calculated as follows:

Tax paid = (480,000 × 35%) = 168,000

Profit after tax (480,000 – 168,000) = 312,000

ULT = 168,000 × (149,760/312,000) = 80,640

Alternative calculation:

(149,750 × 35/65) = 80,640

(W3) Dividend from Even Inc

Horizon Ltd has a 5% interest in Even Inc. It therefore does not own 10% or more of the share capital of Even Inc, so no relief is given for the underlying tax paid in Slozobia. Relief is however available for the withholding tax suffered.

The overseas dividend income is therefore £21,060 (400,140 × 5% × 100/95).

The overseas tax is £1,053 (21,060 × 5%).

(W4) Group relief

Group relief and consortium relief can be respectively claimed in respect of the losses made by Arc Ltd (£81,000) and Bend Ltd (41,000 × 60% = £24,600).

Curve Ltd is not a consortium company because it is a 75% subsidiary of Zero Ltd.

The maximum group relief available is the lower of:

(i)   Available loss of Arc Ltd = £81,000

(ii)   Available PCTCT of Horizon Ltd = £327,460

The maximum consortium relief available is the lower of:

(i)   Available loss of Bend Ltd = (60% × £41,000) = £24,600

(ii)   Available PCTCT of Horizon Ltd = £327,460

Therefore the maximum total relief Horizon Ltd can receive is £105,600 (81,000 + 24,600).

As Horizon Ltd is paying tax at 32¾% and no other company in the group structure is entitled to receive the losses, the losses should be surrendered to Horizon Ltd.

The losses are allocated initially to Horizon Ltd's UK income and then against the overseas income.

However, the maximum amount should not be surrendered as this will result in the wastage of some double taxation relief (W6).

The maximum group/consortium relief claim should therefore be restricted to £97,060 (76,000 against UK income + 21,060 against Even Inc dividends) leaving the full £230,400 Deep Inc dividends chargeable to UK tax.

This tax will be fully covered by DTR.

The remaining loss of £8,540 (£105,600 - £97,060) can be relieved in Arc Ltd or Bend Ltd.

(W5) Franked investment income

FII is the grossed up dividends received but ignoring inter group dividends. Therefore only the dividends from Curve Ltd are included.

$(54,000 \times 20\% \times 100/90)$ £12,000
                                                        _____

(W6) Double taxation relief

Even Inc

As the overseas tax rate is 5% and the UK tax rate is between 19-30%, additional UK tax is payable on the Even Inc. dividends.

It is therefore advantageous to utilise losses against this income to save UK tax. (see key answer tips). Therefore £21,060 group loss relief is set against this income.

Deep Inc

As the overseas tax rate is 38¼% (88,128/230,400) (W2), DTR on this income will be restricted to the UK tax suffered.

To maximise DTR it is therefore not advantageous to utilise the losses against this source of income.

Therefore, the £65,654 UK tax all relates to the Deep Inc dividends and will be fully covered by DTR.

Key answer tips

Claiming full group relief against the Even Inc. income creates unrelieved foreign WHT of £1,053. The group relief claim could be restricted further to avoid creating surplus DTR in respect of Even Inc, but this would involve complicated algebra which is beyond the requirement of this question. Note however that any unrelieved ULT and WHT may be carried forward for relief in a future period.

(b) **Transfer pricing implications**

As Horizon Ltd is a large company (see note below), the transfer pricing rules will apply to both the interest free loan arrangement and the sale of electrical components.

Interest free loan

A loan has been made by Horizon Ltd to a company which it controls on terms which would have been different if the parties had been at arms-length.

The transfer pricing rules will impute notional interest on the amount of the loan, calculated using an arm's length interest rate.

For the year ended 31 March 2008 Horizon Ltd will be required to make an adjustment of £33,333 (500,000 at 8% = 40,000 × 10/12) when completing its self-assessment tax return.

Sale of electrical components

Sales have been made by Horizon Ltd to a related company at an overvalue. This will increase UK trading profits and hence UK corporation tax.

The company obtaining a tax advantage as a result of a non-arms length transaction in this situation is Deep Inc.

The transfer pricing rules only seek to increase the taxable profits of the advantaged party who is based in the UK. Therefore, no transfer pricing adjustment is required.

Note: Where the UK company is large, any transactions with companies which they control, whether UK or overseas resident, must be examined for possible transfer pricing implications.

If the UK company is not large, then only transactions with overseas controlled companies must be examined. In the latter case there is an exemption where the overseas country has an acceptable DTR agreement with a non-discrimination clause.

(c) **Earnings for duties performed in Slozobia**

The manager who is to come to the UK in order to take up employment for a period in excess of two years, will be treated as resident for the entire period in the UK, from the date of arrival to the date of departure.

The manager will not however be treated as ordinarily resident in the UK as there is no intention to stay in the UK for three years or more.

As resident but not ordinary resident in the UK, an employment income assessment will only arise on earnings for duties performed in Slozobia if those earnings are remitted to the UK.

Earnings for duties performed in the UK

The manager will be assessed on all employment income relating to earnings for duties performed in the UK regardless of his or her residence status.

Rental income arising in Slozobia

The manager is domiciled in Slozobia, and so will only be assessed to UK income tax on the rental income arising in Slozabia if he or she is resident in the UK and the income is remitted to the UK.

64   BERTIE OVERSEAS

Client Address   Firm address

Date

Dear Bertie,

Re: Overseas Expansion

Further to our recent meeting I am writing to set out the principal business tax issues regarding the setting up of Bertie Overseas in the country of Picea.

These would appear to be as follows:

–   The basis of taxation of overseas profits and relief for overseas losses.

–   Whether Bertie Overseas should take the form of an overseas branch or a limited company.

–   Whether relief can be obtained in the UK for any overseas taxes paid.

–   Whether there is any relevant anti-avoidance legislation which may apply.

Dealing with each of these in turn.

Basis of Taxation and the Branch v Limited Company Decision

Subject to the anti-avoidance measures detailed below, when Bertie Overseas starts making profits the 'usual' rules are as follows:

If Bertie Overseas takes the form of a non-UK resident limited company then dividends payable to Bertie Limited may be assessable in the UK on a remittance basis (i.e. within Bertie Limited's corporation tax computations for the accounting period in which the dividend is received).

This can be useful in two ways:

(a)   Dividends can be engineered to be received when Bertie Limited's circumstances are favourable (for example if it has offsetting losses available or in accounting periods when its corporation tax rate is below the full rate).

(b)   If the intention is to retain profits overseas in a low tax jurisdiction. With corporate taxes of only 10% Picea would appear to fall into this category.

On the other hand if Bertie Overseas is set up as an overseas branch of Bertie Limited, which is controlled from the UK, it is likely that all of the overseas profits generated (whether or not they are remitted to the UK) will be treated as part of the profits of Bertie Limited and therefore entirely taxable in the UK. In these circumstances, however, the vehicles and equipment acquired will qualify for UK capital allowances.

It should be noted that these rules could be used to your advantage. Your business plan anticipates that Bertie Overseas will make a loss in its first year of operation which will then be followed by progressively stronger profits.

If Bertie Overseas takes the form of a non-UK resident limited company in year one then it is unlikely that Bertie Limited will be able to offset the losses generated against its own profits. The use of these losses will therefore be determined by Picean tax law. It is stated that Picea has no facility to carry losses backwards or forwards and presumably therefore these losses would remain unrelieved.

If, however, Bertie Overseas takes the form of an overseas branch this is effectively regarded by UK tax law as an extension of the UK trade. Any overseas losses generated are likely therefore to be automatically offset against UK source profits generated by Bertie Limited. As Bertie Limited currently pays corporation tax at the full rate it seems probable that these will therefore all be relieved as incurred.

Clearly this would only be of benefit in year one of the overseas operations. To prevent 100% of eventual overseas profits being taxed in the UK after year one the overseas branch could then be incorporated as a non-UK resident limited company.

Some relevant points to note here are:

(a)   It may be necessary to secure the consent of the Treasury for the incorporation to proceed. It is generally illegal for a UK resident company to permit a non-UK resident company over which it has control to create or issue any shares. However, providing full market value consideration is given this transaction may be covered by published Treasury General Consents and so, in these circumstances, specific consent may not be required.

(b)   The conversion will be a disposal of the branch assets at market value.

   (i)   In the case of the equipment and vehicles this will give rise to a balancing adjustment which (if a balancing charge) may increase the profits subject to UK corporation tax. If the Picean limited company is not chargeable to UK corporation tax after the incorporation a succession election which is normally possible where such assets are passed between connected persons will not be possible.

   (ii)   In the case of the freehold premises a chargeable gain may arise. It is possible, by election, to defer this in circumstances where all the branch assets (with the exception of cash) are transferred to the Picean limited company in return for ordinary shares. If such an election is made the deferred gain will become taxable when the shares in the foreign company are sold or the foreign company disposes of any chargeable assets within six years of the incorporation.

Relief For Overseas Taxes Paid

To prevent the taxation of overseas income twice (once in the UK and once in the overseas territory) UK legislation allows for double tax relief.

In the absence of a double tax treaty this works by allowing any Picean corporation tax paid on dividends remitted from Bertie Overseas to be credited against Bertie Limited's UK corporation tax. This assumes that Bertie Overseas will be incorporated from the beginning of year two for which profits are expected and will therefore be making dividend payments.

Double tax relief is, however, restricted to the lower of the overseas corporation tax paid and the UK corporation tax on the taxable profits from the overseas source.

For these purposes the net dividends paid to the UK will need to be grossed up for the related overseas taxes. As Picean corporation tax rates are 10%, which is lower than the rate of UK corporation tax currently being paid (ie 30%), in this case all of the Picean tax should be available as a credit against Bertie Limited's corporation tax liability.

With regards to the remittance of dividends to the UK the law recognises two categories of overseas tax:

(a)   Withholding taxes – effectively tax deducted at source before paying a dividend to an overseas investor. It is noted that under Picean tax law no withholding taxes are deducted so this does not need any further consideration.

(b)   Underlying taxes – effectively the equivalent of UK corporation tax (i.e. the tax paid on the underlying profits from which any remittances are paid). To qualify for underlying tax relief the UK company must own at least 10% of the voting power of the overseas company. As Bertie Overseas will be wholly owned, Bertie Limited will therefore qualify for underlying tax relief.

Anti-Avoidance Legislation

The fact that the use of dividends allows companies to regulate their remittances to the UK and hence the incidence of UK corporation tax is of concern to HMRC. As a result a variety of anti-avoidance legislation exists to protect the UK Treasury position.

The principal pieces of such legislation are as follows:

Transfer Pricing

In circumstances where sales are made by a large UK resident company to another company which it controls, at an undervalue (thus depressing UK profits), HMRC can substitute a market value price. This is known as transfer pricing.

Assuming that Bertie Limited is classified as a large company under the transfer pricing legislation it would appear that this legislation is in point.

This is because the proposed mark up to Bertie Overseas is lower than HMRC might expect (80% compared to 85%). We are aware that Bertie Overseas will be responsible for all of its sale and distribution costs. It may be possible to explain the reduction in mark up if Bertie Overseas is required to undertake further responsibilities. This is an area that can be further explored at our next meeting.

It is likely that a transfer pricing liability may also exist relating to the differential in interest rates that will be charged of 2%.

Bertie Limited must self assess its liability under transfer pricing within its corporation tax return. Penalties can be levied if HMRC are successful in arguing that adjustments should have been made but were not. For this reason it is recommended that Bertie Limited sets out in advance its proposed transfer pricing arrangements to HMRC under a statutory procedure known as Advance Pricing Arrangements and negotiate their acceptance with them.

Residence Status of Overseas Limited Company

The remittance basis of assessment will only apply to dividends received from non-UK resident companies. If HMRC can successfully argue that Bertie Overseas is in fact UK resident then all of its profits will be subject to UK corporation tax (with double tax relief available).

A company will be UK resident if it is incorporated in the UK or it is managed and controlled from the UK. Clearly the former is not a problem but the latter may be. This is because the test is not where day to day control is exercised but rather the highest level of strategic control. If this is exercised by the UK Board of Bertie Limited it is likely that HMRC will regard control as being UK based thus making Bertie Overseas UK resident.

This is clearly something that will need to be explored in greater depth when we next meet.

Controlled Foreign Company

In certain circumstances HMRC have powers to apportion profits of controlled foreign companies ('CFC') to a UK resident company.

A CFC exists where a foreign company under UK control is resident in a low tax area (less than 75% of UK corporation tax) and is set up with a view to avoid UK tax.

On the face of it, it would appear that Bertie Overseas will be caught by this legislation but this is considered unlikely as various exemptions exist. In particular the 'exempt activities' exemption means that companies deriving all of their trading income from unconnected parties (as in this case) will not be caught. As Bertie Overseas is considered to have a genuine commercial presence in Picea this is therefore not considered further.

It is perhaps worthwhile pointing out that this anti-avoidance legislation is of no relevance if Bertie Overseas is a branch controlled from the UK as in this case all of its profits are UK taxable in any event.

I hope the above adequately summarises the position but should you have any queries please do not hesitate to contact me.

Meanwhile I look forward to hearing from you further in the near future.

Yours sincerely,

A Accountant

ACCA marking scheme	
	Marks
Presentation	2.0
Basis of taxation	
Bertie Overseas Limited Company:	
Non UK resident/remittance basis	1.0
Advantages	2.0
Bertie Overseas Branch:	
Controlled from UK/all profits taxed in UK	1.0
Availability of capital allowances	1.0
Branch v Limited Company	
Loss relief not available if limited company	1.0
Losses probably remain unrelieved	1.0
If UK controlled branch automatic loss offset	1.0
Incorporation at start of year two	1.0
Treasury Consent	1.0
Capital allowances issues	1.0
Chargeable gains issues	2.0
Double Tax Relief:	
Availability of credit relief	1.0
Restriction/conclusion	1.0
Underlying tax relief	1.0
Anti-avoidance legislation	
Transfer Pricing:	
Recognition/definition	1.0
Consideration of mark ups	1.0
Interest rates	0.5
CTSA/APA arrangements	1.0
Residence Status:	
Recognition/position	1.0
Definition/application	2.0
CFC:	
Recognition/definition	1.0
Application/exempt activities/conclusion	1.5
Available	27.0
Maximum	25.0

TAX PLANNING

65 CARL

DTF & Co

12 High Street

London

18 September 2007

C Egmort Esq
220 Main Street
London

Our ref: RF/1527

Dear Carl

Chez Egmont

It was good to meet you yesterday and to talk about your new restaurant. I set out below my advice on the initial financing of the business and the use of the start-up losses together with an explanation of the tax treatment of the renovation costs.

Initial financing costs

Of the proceeds of £88,000 generated from the sale of the oil painting, £3,825 (see Appendix 1) will be required on 31 January 2008 to pay the capital gains tax arising from the sale.

After deducting this tax liability and the costs incurred in the summer, this will leave you with a balance of £77,175 (88,000 – 7,000 – 3,825) to fund your new business.

The cost of acquiring and renovating the premises amounts to £100,000. Additional funding of £22,825 (100,000 – 77,175) is therefore required.

It is a generally accepted principle that longer-term business assets should be financed by longer-term sources of finance. An overdraft on the other hand is a short-term source of finance designed to cover short-term cash fluctuations and accordingly is not appropriate to finance the acquisition of business premises.

You therefore have the option to use your 'nest egg', remortgage your house, or take out a bank loan secured on the business premises. Both the remortgage and the business bank loan involve incurring additional bank arrangements fees as well as the cost of annual interest. Using your nest egg will cost you the loss of interest income each year, but as interest rates earned on income are lower than those paid on bank loans/mortgages the cost of using your nest egg will be lower than taking out a loan.

You have identified that you will require £6,000 of additional funds for working capital. You plan however to make a loss of £27,500 in your first year of operation and accordingly, it would appear that you may require additional short term funding considerably in excess of £6,000 to fund this first year.

I would need to look at your projected trading results and your forecast cashflow requirements to advise you further on the amount of funding that you will require. It is likely however that short-term finance in the form of either an overdraft or a short-term loan will be required for this purpose.

Use of the trading loss of the first year of trading

The budgeted loss for the year to 31 December 2008 is £27,500 plus the market research costs of £4,500. Allowable costs incurred prior to the commencement of trading are treated as incurred on the day trading commences. The costs of your visits to restaurants and hotels are classified as entertaining and are not an allowable expense.

This means that your taxable income from the business for the first two tax years, 2007/08 and 2008/09, will be nil. You will then have the following losses available for relief.

		£
2007/08	$(27,500 + 4,500) = 32,000 \times 3/12$	8,000
2008/09	$(32,000 - 8,000)$	24,000

The loss of each tax year is considered independently and can be relieved separately in different ways if required.

Your trading losses can be utilised in the following ways.

1   Offset against total income for the year of the loss and/or the previous year.

2   Following a claim under 1 above, any remaining loss can be offset against gains incurred in the same tax year.

3   As an alternative, or in addition to, the above reliefs, the losses can be offset against the total income of the three tax years prior to the loss starting with the earliest year. This relief is available because the losses have been incurred in one of the first four tax years of the business.

4   Any losses not used are carried forward against future profits of the same trade. However, profits are not expected to arise until 2009/10 and, accordingly, this method of relief is not recommended.

I set out at Appendix 2 your total income for each of the relevant years together with the rates at which you are paying tax.

In order to maximise the tax saved the loss should be used in the year in which you are paying tax at the highest rate.

In 2006/07 you will pay tax at 40% on part of the gain on the sale of the painting whereas you are paying tax at 22%/20% in all of the other years (apart from 2008/09 when you have no taxable income).

Loss of 2007/08 - £8,000

The loss can be offset against total income of 2007/08 and/or 2006/07. Alternatively it can be carried back for offset against income of 2004/05.

The loss should be offset against the total income of the previous year, 2006/07. This will save tax of £1,760 (£8,000 22%). It will also cause £5,925 of the capital gain on the painting, which would otherwise be taxed at 40%, to be taxed at 20%, thus saving a further £1,185 (5,925 × 20%).

Offsetting the loss against the total income of 2007/08 would only save £1,760. The same amount of tax would be saved if the loss were carried back to 2004/05.

Loss of 2008/09 - £24,000

The loss can be offset against total income of 2008/09 and/or 2007/08. Alternatively it can be carried back for offset against income of 2005/06.

There is no taxable income in 2008/09 so the choice is between 2007/08 and 2005/06. In 2007/08, the loss of £24,000 exceeds the STI of £21,140, and if claimed for full amount of £21,140 loss relief would need to be used. As a result, the personal allowance would be wasted, therefore wasting £5,035 of the loss unnecessarily.

The loss should therefore be offset against the income of 2005/06. This will save tax of £5,240 (Appendix 3).

Renovation costs

The wooden floor is an improvement to the building and not a repair. Accordingly the cost is not an allowable revenue expense but rather a capital cost. The lighting is also capital expenditure.

Capital expenditure on a restaurant building does not qualify for a tax deduction because a restaurant does not qualify for capital allowances. The costs will only be allowable if it can be argued that they have been incurred in respect of plant and machinery.

The distinction between a building and plant and machinery is often described as a distinction between the setting in which the business is carried on (the building) and something with which the business is carried on (plant and machinery). There have been many court cases in this area, which, whilst not always providing a clear distinction for every situation, do address the expenditure to be incurred by you.

The floor is simply a necessary part of the building and cannot qualify as plant and machinery. However, decorative lighting in hotels and restaurants has been held to be plant and accordingly the cost will qualify for capital allowances.

Please telephone me if you require any further information.

Yours sincerely

A tax senior

Appendix 1

Sale of oil painting – Capital gains tax – 2006/07

	£
Proceeds (September 2006)	88,000
Cost (Probate value, October 2004)	(66,000)
Chargeable gain (Note)	22,000
Annual exemption	(8,800)
Taxable gain	13,200

Note: There is no indexation allowance available as the painting was acquired after April 1998 and no taper relief is available as the painting is a non business asset owned for less than three complete years. The gain is therefore 100% chargeable to tax.

Rate of tax in 2006/07

	£
Employment income (£2,480 × 12)	29,760
Interest (£1,040 x 100/80)	1,300
STI	31,060
Personal Allowance	(5,035)
Taxable income	26,025

Basic rate band remaining = (33,300 – 26,025) = £7,275

Capital gains tax payable

£		£
7,275 at 20%		1,455
5,925 at 40%		2,370
13,200		3,825

Appendix 2

Rates of tax in each year

	2004/05 £	2005/06 £	2006/07 £	2007/08 £	2008/09 £
Employment income	29,760	29,760	29,760	19,840	-
Trading income	-	-	-	Nil	Nil
Interest (1,040 × 100/80)	1,300	1,300	1,300	1,300	1,300
STI	31,060	31,060	31,060	21,140	1,300
Personal allowance	(5,035)	(5,035)	(5,035)	(5,035)	(5,035)
Taxable income	26,025	26,025	26,025	16,105	Nil

The first £2,150 of income is taxed at 10%, the balance of the employment income at 22%.

The interest is taxed at 20%.

Appendix 3

Income tax liability in 2005/06 – with and without loss relief

			Without loss relief £	With loss relief £
STI			31,060	31,060
Loss offset				(24,000)
Personal allowance			(5,035)	(5,035)
Taxable income			26,025	2,025

£	£			
2,150	2,025	× 10%	215	202
22,575	–	× 22%	4,967	
1,300	–	× 20%	260	
26,025	2,025			
Income tax liability			5,442	202

Income tax saved via use of the loss = (5,442 – 202) = £5,240

66 GARDEN LTD

(a) **Taxation implications of two alternative factories**

Construction of new factory

The new factory will qualify for Industrial Buildings Allowance on £301,100 of the cost as follows:

	£
Levelling the land	10,300
Architects and legal fees	24,300
Strengthened concrete floor	16,500
Factory	187,500
General offices	62,500
	301,100

Industrial Buildings Allowance of £12,044 (301,100 × 4%) will be given, commencing in the accounting period that the factory is brought into use.

This allowance will be given for the next 25 years, except in any accounting period where the factory is used for non-industrial purposes at the end of that period.

The cost of the land does not qualify. The general offices qualify as they cost £62,500 which is less than £75,275 (being 25% of the total qualifying cost (301,100 × 25%)).

The input VAT of £70,000 will be reclaimed in full, assuming that Garden Ltd is making taxable supplies.

The cost of the ventilation and heating systems (£12,500) and the fire alarm and sprinkler system (£6,400) will not qualify for IBAs but do qualify as plant and machinery.

The cost of the strengthened floor, despite being to support machinery, is part of the factory structure. This would only qualify as plant and machinery if it consisted of expenditure on the alteration of an existing building.

As Garden Ltd is a medium sized company, first year allowances of 40% will be given in the accounting period in which the title to the factory passes to Garden Ltd. The total FYAs will be £7,560 ((12,500 + 6,400) × 40%).

A 25% WDA will then apply on a reducing balance basis for subsequent accounting periods.

Lease of factory

As the owners of the factory have exercised their option to tax the grant of the lease, Garden Ltd will be able to reclaim input tax of £70,000 $(470,000 \times \frac{7}{47})$. This again assumes that Garden Ltd is making taxable supplies.

The proportion of the premium assessed on the owners as property business income will be deductible for corporation tax purposes spread over the period of the lease, as follows:

	£
Premium paid	400,000
Less: 400,000 × 2% × (40 - 1)	(312,000)
Assessment on the owners	88,000

Relief available to the payer of the premium:

$$\frac{88,000}{40} = £2,200 \text{ pa}$$

The deduction of £2,200 will be restricted for the accounting period in which it is paid according to the length of the period from the date of payment to the end of that accounting period.

Garden Ltd will be able to reclaim input tax of £5,250 $(35,250 \times \frac{7}{47})$ in respect of each annual payment of rent. The rent paid of £30,000 (35,250 - 5,250) will be deductible for corporation tax purposes.

Debenture loan

Debenture interest is deducted from trading profits on the accruals basis as the loan is raised for a trading purpose. Whether or not it is capitalised is irrelevant.

The annual deduction will therefore amount to £24,000 (200,000 at 12%).

Garden Ltd must deduct lower rate tax from any debenture interest paid to individuals, and account for it to HMRC on a quarterly basis.

Sale of warehouse

The sale of the warehouse will result in a capital gain of £106,800 as follows:

	£
Sale proceeds	270,000
Cost	(120,000)
Unindexed gain	150,000
Indexation (120,000 × 0.360)	(43,200)
Chargeable gain	106,800

Replacement of business asset

If the new factory is constructed, the gain can be rolled over against the base cost of the factory. There is no restriction on the amount of the gain that can be rolled over, as the full proceeds of £270,000 will be reinvested. This is provided that the reinvestment of the proceeds will take place in the period beginning one year before and ending three years after the date of disposal.

If the factory is leased, the gain can only be held over for a maximum of 10 years from the date of purchase. This is because the replacement asset will be a depreciating asset with a life of less than 60 years.

The gain will crystallise in 10 years time unless the asset is sold or ceases to be used in the business within the next 10 years.

Industrial Building Allowance

The sale of the warehouse will also result in a balancing adjustment in respect of Industrial Buildings Allowance.

The allowances will have been based on the original cost of the warehouse (excluding land) and the remaining life of 25 years due to Garden Ltd, as follows:

Qualifying cost (102,000 – 42,000)	£60,000
Remaining life [25 – (10 – 7)]	22 years
Writing-down allowance per annum $\left(\frac{60,000}{22}\right)$	£2,727
Total allowances given (2,727 × 7)	£19,089

Since the sale proceeds exceed the original cost, the balancing charge will be the total allowances claimed of £19,089.

Key answer tips

Note that IBAs are calculated on the cost of the warehouse, excluding the cost of the land. However, when the warehouse is sold, the warehouse and the land is treated as a single asset, when calculating the capital gain on disposal.

(b) (i) **Subscription for new ordinary share capital**

Income tax relief under the Enterprise Investment Scheme (EIS)

Income tax relief under the EIS is available for subscriptions of new ordinary share capital. A qualifying company is one that is unquoted, trading in the UK, and carrying on a qualifying trade. The company's gross assets must be less than £7 million before the share issue.

Assuming that all of these conditions are met, the shareholders of Garden Ltd will be entitled to relief as follows:

Alex Bush

Alex Bush will not be entitled to relief under the EIS as he is connected with Garden Ltd due to his:

1   Holding more than 30% of the company's share capital.

2   Being a paid director of the company.

Carol Daisy

Carol Daisy will be entitled to relief under the EIS as she holds less than 30% of Garden Ltd's share capital $\left(^{215,000}/_{1,000,000} \times 100 = 21.5\%\right)$, and has not been a paid director of the company prior to the share issue.

In addition, she can claim deferral relief for the re-investment of the sale proceeds of her property in EIS shares (see below).

She will qualify for income tax relief on all of her investment, as the relief is available as a maximum investment of up to £400,000 per tax year. The tax relief will therefore be £43,000 (215,000 × 20%). This will be given as a credit against her tax liability for 2006/07. However, should her income tax liability for 2006/07 be less than £43,000, the relief will be restricted to that figure.

As the investment has been made between 6 April and 5 October, Carol can carry back £10,000 (£50,000 at 20%) of the relief to 2005/06 should this be beneficial.

Edward Fern

Edward Fern will be entitled to relief under the EIS as he holds less than 30% of Garden Ltd's share capital $\left(^{185,000}/_{1,000,000} \times 100 = 18.5\%\right)$, and has not been a paid director of the company prior to the share issue.

Entitlement to relief under the EIS is not affected by Edward subsequently becoming a paid director of Garden Ltd. He will qualify for relief on the full amount of his investment (i.e. £185,000).

Gary Hedge

Gary Hedge will not be entitled to relief under the EIS since he was a paid director of Garden Ltd prior to the share issue.

Deferral relief on re-investment

Carol should be entitled to deferral relief on the re-investment of her proceeds from the sale of her property, as Garden Ltd is an EIS company. This is provided that the share issue was within the period beginning one year before and ending three years after the date that the property was sold.

The relief will be limited to the amount of the share issue of £215,000, as this is less than her chargeable gain of £225,000. Her CGT liability of £90,000 (225,000 at 40%) is therefore reduced by £86,000 (215,000 × 40%) by claiming to defer the gain.

Key answer tips

Taper relief will be available when the £86,000 deferred gain becomes chargeable but only at the rate that would have been available had the gain remained chargeable in 2006/07.

(b)   (ii)   **Proposed Stock Exchange listing**

Enterprise investment scheme

Tax relief given under the EIS will be withdrawn if Garden Ltd ceases to be a qualifying company within three years of the shares being issued.

However, obtaining a Stock Exchange listing before August 2009 will not cause Garden Ltd to cease to be a qualifying company provided there were no arrangements in force to obtain a listing when the shares were issued.

Deferral relief on re-investment

The deferral relief given on re-investment will not be withdrawn as a result of Garden Ltd obtaining a Stock Exchange listing.

Business property relief (BPR)

At present, all shareholders would be entitled to BPR at the rate of 100% on a chargeable transfer of shares in Garden Ltd as they have shareholdings in an unquoted trading company.

If Garden Ltd obtains a Stock Exchange listing by issuing 500,000 new shares, the present shareholders' holdings will be diluted by one-third. All four shareholders will therefore lose their entitlement to BPR, since Garden Ltd (or plc) will be quoted, and no shareholder will have control (> 50% interest) of the company.

Alex will have a 36.6% $\left(55 \times \frac{2}{3}\right)$ shareholding. Even if the share issue was restructured so that Alex retained control of Garden Ltd, relief for BPR would only be available at the rate of 50%, not 100% as at present.

67   SCHOONER LTD

(a)   **VAT rules relating to the time of supply for goods**

The time of supply is known as the tax point date.

For the supply of goods the tax point date is the earliest of

(i)   the date goods are removed or made available to the customer, or

(ii)   the date an invoice is issued or payment received.

If an invoice is issued within 14 days of the goods being removed or made available, this date will replace that in (i). The tax point date then becomes the earliest of payment being received and an invoice being issued.

The payments on account of £50,000 and £100,000 must be included as supplies on the VAT return for the quarter in which they are received.

Output tax will be £22,340 (50,000 + 100,000 = 150,000 × 17.5/117.5).

The balance of the output tax of £38,910 (350,000 at 17.5% = 61,250 − 22,340) will be included on the VAT return for the following quarter when the invoice is issued.

(b)   (i)   **Effect of the acquisition of the new equipment on tax adjusted profit**

Outright purchase

In relation to the equipment purchased outright, Schooner Ltd will be able to claim a first year allowance of £125,000 (250,000 × 50%) as a trading expense for the year ended 31 December 2007.

Hire purchase

Schooner Ltd will be able to claim a first year allowance of £100,000 (200,000 × 50%) on the cost of the equipment as per an outright purchase.

The finance charge of £76,000 (16 × £17,250 = 276,000 – 200,000) will be deductible as a trading expense in the adjustment of profit computation. The proportion relating to the year ended 31 December 2007 will be calculated using normal accounting principles.

Leasing under a finance lease

The lease rental payment of £145,000 for the year ended 31 December 2007 will be deductible as a trading expense. The fact that the equipment is capitalised in the accounts is in theory irrelevant, although HMRC may allow the deductions (depreciation and finance charge) calculated on this basis. Capital allowances are not available.

(ii) **VAT implications of acquiring new equipment**

Outright purchase

As regards the equipment acquired from countries that are members of the European Union, VAT of £28,000 (160,000 at 17.5%) will be accounted for according to the date of acquisition.

This is the earliest of

(i)   the date an invoice is issued, or

(ii)   the 15th of the month following the removal of the goods.

As regards the equipment imported from countries that are not members of the European Union, VAT of £15,750 (250,000 - 160,000 = 90,000 at 17.5%) will be accounted for at the time of importation.

In both cases, a corresponding input tax deduction will be given. However, with an acquisition from an EU member country there is no 'VAT cost' as the input tax and VAT charge will effectively contra out on the VAT return.

With an import from countries outside the EU, VAT must actually be paid subsequent to its recovery as input tax.

Hire purchase

Input tax of £35,000 (200,000 at 17.5%) will be reclaimed on the VAT return for the period in which the equipment is purchased.

Leasing under a finance lease

Input tax of £25,375 (145,000 × 17.5%) included in each lease rental payment will be reclaimed on the VAT return for the period during which the appropriate tax point occurs.

(c) (i) **Effect of raising additional finance on tax adjusted profits**

Personal loan of managing director

There are no tax implications for Schooner Ltd since the loan is interest free.

Issue of 10% Debentures

The issue of debentures is for trading purposes. Therefore the interest, the cost of the 5% discount and the incidental expenses relating to raising loan finance will be deductible as a trading expense.

The deduction for the year ended 31 December 2007 using the accruals basis will be £34,600 calculated as follows:

	£
Debenture interest (300,000 × 10%)	30,000
Discount (300,000 × 5% = 15,000/5)	3,000
Incidental costs (8,000/5)	1,600
	34,600

Tutorial note: Under the loan relationship rules the cost of borrowing for trade purposes is allowed as a trading expense and calculated on an accruals basis. In effect the costs of borrowing should be matched to the period of the loan so the answer spreads the incidental borrowing costs and the cost of the discount evenly over the 5 years concerned. Strictly the write off should be so as to achieve a constant rate of return.

Issue of new ordinary share capital

The incidental professional fee expenses relating to the raising of share capital are not deductible as a trading expense.

(ii) **Tax relief available to Alex and Chloe**

Personal loan from Alex

The interest paid by Alex will be an allowable charge on income as it is a qualifying loan made to a close company. Alex's taxable income will effectively be reduced by the amount of gross interest paid each tax year, thus obtaining tax relief at his marginal rate.

The deduction for 2006/07 will be £2,000 (100,000 × 8% × 3/12).

Subscription for shares by Chloe

The conditions for relief under the Enterprise Investment Scheme (EIS) appear to be met since Schooner Ltd is unquoted and is carrying on a qualifying trade. The company's gross assets must be less than £7 million prior to the share issue.

Chloe Dhow will be entitled to relief under the EIS as she currently has no connection with Schooner Ltd, and will hold less than 30% of the company's share capital (100,000/[1,000,000 + (250,000/1.60)] = 8.6%).

Entitlement to relief under the EIS will not be affected by Chloe subsequently becoming a paid director of Schooner Ltd. Chloe will be entitled to a tax credit of £32,000 (160,000 at 20%) for 2006/07.

Relief will be restricted if Chloe's income tax liability for 2006/07 is less than £32,000.

Key answer tips

Interest as a charge on income relief would not have been available had Alex qualified for EIS income tax relief.

---

68   PHOENIX

(a)   **Use of losses**

Phoenix has various options regarding the use of the losses expected for the year ended 31 December 2007.

These include the facility to

(i)   offset against other income in 2007/2008 and 2006/07, or

(ii)   as the loss has been incurred in the first four tax years of his trade he could offset against other income in the tax years 2006/07, 2005/06 and 2004/05 applying the loss to the earliest tax year first.

It should be noted, however, that because these loss reliefs are given against statutory total income (STI) and that his income is so low for these years and is likely to be covered by his personal allowances, to avoid wasting these allowances it is unlikely that Phoenix will claim these particular reliefs.

In addition to reliefs available against STI, if Phoenix incorporates his business, it will be possible to claim:

(i)   terminal loss relief, carrying back the loss for the last twelve months against other current year trading income or such income of the previous three tax years, and

(ii)   special incorporation loss relief.

Terminal loss relief does not appear attractive as Phoenix's income is low in previous years and is likely to be covered by his personal allowances.

Under special incorporation loss relief, Phoenix will be permitted to carry forward the loss, augmented by any overlap profits at cessation of his sole trade, for use against his first available income from Phoenix Limited. Relief is given first against salary income and then against other income including dividends.

Relief would therefore be given against his employment income in 2007/08, however this would be covered by his personal allowance and it is therefore not an attractive option.

However, if Phoenix does not incorporate his business and does not make a claim against STI, his loss is automatically carried forward to offset against the next profits from the same trade, i.e. his profits for the year ended 31 December 2008.

Phoenix will be a higher rate taxpayer for 2008/09 if he continues as a sole trader and so this alternative will attract 40% relief. For this reason, not incorporating and carrying forward the relief is preferable in this instance.

(b)   **Capital allowances on incorporation**

If Phoenix incorporates his business he has two options regarding capital allowances:

(1)   Either balancing adjustments will be made in the sole trader capital allowance computations, calculated by reference to the market value (restricted to cost if lower) of the pool assets at cessation compared to the tax written down value at that date;

or

(2)   Because upon incorporation the trade has passed between connected persons, an election can be made for the plant to be transferred at its tax written down value to Phoenix Limited.

The election at (2) will be beneficial to Phoenix if the balancing adjustments arising under (1) are balancing charges which would have the effect of reducing or eliminating the loss.

If required the election will need to be made within two years of the date of succession (i.e. by 31 December 2009).

If the business is incorporated, in the absence of a succession election, a taxable balancing charge of £1,750 (8,000 – 6,250) will arise. For this reason it would appear that a succession election would be beneficial to Phoenix.

(c) **Sole trader vs incorporation**

On the basis of the calculations set out below Phoenix should incorporate his business on 1 January 2008. This will result in overall tax savings of £1,886 (9,777 – 7,891).

Computation of income tax and National Insurance liabilities for 2005/06 to 2008/09 inclusive

Assuming continuation on a sole trader basis

Income tax	2005/06 £	2006/07 £	2007/08 £	2008/09 £
Trading profit (W1)	1,800	3,600	–	45,828
Less: Loss relief (W2)	–	–	–	(6,563)
Job seekers allowance	1,380	–	–	–
	3,180	3,600	–	39,265
Less: Personal allowance	(5,035)	(5,035)	(5,035)	(5,035)
Taxable Income	Nil	Nil	Nil	34,230

Income tax:
	£
2,150 × 10%	215
31,150 × 22%	6,853
930 × 40%	372
34,230	

	2005/06	2006/07	2007/08	2008/09
Income tax payable	Nil	Nil	Nil	7,440
Class 4 NICs				
Class 4 NIC payable (W3)	Nil	Nil	Nil	2,337
Total income tax & Class 4 NIC				9,777

Assuming incorporation of business

Income tax	2005/06 £	2006/07 £	2007/08 £	2008/09 £
Trading profit (W4)	1,800	3,600	–	–
Employment income	–	–	4,400	7,500
Less: Loss relief (W5)	–	–	(4,400)	(1,500)
Dividend income	–	–	–	12,000
Job seekers allowance	1,380	–	–	–
	3,180	3,600	–	18,000
Less: Personal allowance	(5,035)	(5,035)	(5,035)	(5,035)
Taxable Income	Nil	Nil	Nil	12,965

	2005/06 £	2006/07 £	2007/08 £	2008/09 £
Income Tax liability £				
965 × 10% (other income)				96
12,000 × 10% (dividends)				1,200
12,965				1,296
Less Tax credit on dividend				(1,200)
Income Tax payable	Nil	Nil	Nil	96
Class 1 NICs				
Class 1 employee NICs (W6)	Nil	Nil	Nil	549
Total income tax of Class 1 NICs				645

Corporation Tax payable by Phoenix Limited for year ended 31 December 2008

	£
Trading profit (W4)	45,437
Less: Salary (W6)	(10,025)
Employer's NIC (W6)	(639)
PCTCT	34,773
Corporation tax liability (34,773 × 19%)	6,607
Total tax & NICs (645 + 6,607 + 639)	7,891

Workings

(W1) Trading profit position – Assuming continuation as a sole trader

Fiscal year	Basis period		Assessable £
2005/06	1/10/2005 to 5/4/2006	4,500 × 6/15	1,800
2006/07	12 months to 31/12/2006	4,500 × 12/15	3,600
2007/08	12 months to 31/12/2007	loss	Nil
2008/09	12 months to 31/12/2008		47,000
	Less: Capital allowances (below)		(1,172)
			45,828

Overlap profits = £900 (4,500 × 3/15) for period 1/1/2006 to 5/4/2006

Capital allowances

2007/08 – Year to 31 December 2007	£	£	
TWDV at 1 January 2007	6,250		
WDA (25%)	(1,563)	1,563	claimed
TWDV at 31 December 2007	4,687		
2008/09 – Year to 31 December 2008			
WDA (25%)	(1,172)	1,172	claimed
TWDV at 31 December 2008	3,515		

(W2) Trading Loss – Year ended 31 December 2007

	£
Trading loss before capital allowances	5,000
Capital allowances (above)	1,563
	6,563

(W3) Class 4 NIC payable – 2008/09

	£
(33,540 – 5,035) at 8%	2,280
(39,265 – 33,540) at 1%	57
	2,337

(W4) Trading profit position – Assuming Incorporation of business

Fiscal year	Basis period		Assessable £
2005/06	1/10/2005 to 5/4/2006	(4,500 × 6/15)	1,800
2006/07	12 months to 31/12/2006	(4,500 × 12/15)	3,600
2007/08	12 months to 31/12/2007	loss	Nil

Overlap profits = £900 (4,500 × 3/15) for period 1/1/2006 to 5/4/2006

Capital allowances – Claiming succession election

Sole Trader

2007/08 – Year to 31 December 2007	£	£	
TWDV at 1 January 2007	6,250		
WDA (25%) – not available in final period	Nil	Nil	claimed
TWDV at 31 December 2007 transferred to Phoenix Limited	6,250		

Phoenix Limited

CAP to 31 December 2008	£	£	
WDA (25%)	(1,563)	1,563	claimed
TWDV at 31 December 2008	4,687		

Trading profit of Phoenix Ltd – y/e 31 December 2008

	£
Trading profit before capital allowances	47,000
Capital allowances (above)	(1,563)
	45,437

(W5) Incorporation loss relief

Loss relief under s.386 ICTA 1988   = £5,000

plus unrelieved overlap profits of £900   = £5,900.

(W6) Class 1 NIC - year to 31/12/08

Phoenix's salary for y/e 31 December 2008 $= 4,400 + (7,500 \times 9/12)$

                     $= £10,025$

Employer's NIC	£
$(10,025 - 5,035) \times 12.8\%$	639
Employee's NIC	
$(10,025 - 5,035) \times 11\%$	549

ACCA marking scheme		
		Marks
Use of losses		
S380 ICTA 1988 explanation/tax years		1.5
S381 ICTA 1988 explanation/tax years		1.5
Terminal loss relief explanation/tax years		1.5
Conclusion regarding above three		1.0
Remaining sole trader	S385 ICTA 1988/explanation/40%	2.0
Incorporating	S386 ICTA 1988/explanation/income	1.5
	Max	7.0
Capital allowance options		
Balancing adjustments		1.0
Connected persons/Succession election		2.0
Benefit of election		1.0
Due date for election		1.0
Balancing charge calculation/Preference		1.0
	Max	5.0
Sole trader vs Incorporation		
Conclusion		1.0
Continuing as a sole trader		
Trading profit		2.0
Capital allowances		2.0
Loss relief (from (a))/CA's		1.0
Job seekers allowance		0.5
SPA		0.5
Income tax payable		1.0
C4 NIC payable		1.0
Incorporation		
Trading profit – sole trade		1.0
– limited company		1.0
Capital allowances		1.0
Class 1 NIC		2.0
Salary/NIC deductions		1.0
Corporation tax payable		2.0
Loss relief (from (a))/CAs/£900/use		2.0
Employment income		1.0
Other income		0.5

Income tax payable		0.5
	Max	18.0
	Total	30.0

69 ETHEL

Client Address   Firm address

Date: 4 December 2007

Dear Ethel,

Thank you for your recent letter. Dealing with the queries that you have raised in turn:

Profit Extraction

Bonus v Dividend

Appendix A provides calculations detailing the tax position of making a gross lump sum salary or dividend payment to yourself.

You will note that whilst the company will obtain a corporation tax deduction for a payment in the form of salary, the additional employee's and employer's Class 1 NIC makes this a fairly expensive option.

Taking all relevant taxes into account (including the company's corporation tax position) the dividend route provides the greater after tax cash receipt of £17,775 compared to £14,992 if the payment takes the form of salary. The dividend route is therefore recommended.

Pension Contribution

The tax treatment of making a lump sum contribution to an occupational pension scheme will depend upon whether or not the scheme is a registered scheme with HMRC.

If the scheme is a registered scheme, significant tax advantages can accrue:

– The payment made will not be a benefit taxable on yourself.

– Ethel Endeavours Limited will, however, obtain a tax deduction at its marginal corporation tax rate (currently 19%) on the contribution paid.

– You will be able to make and obtain income tax relief on additional employee contributions of up to 100% of your earned income. Such contributions will not, however, attract relief from Class 1 NIC.

– If you contribute 100% of your earnings and the company contribute £20,000, the total contributions do not exceed the annual allowance of £215,000. Therefore full relief is available for both contributions and no further tax consequences arise.

– The funds will be invested in a tax free environment.

– Upon retirement you will be able to take a tax free lump sum payment of up to 25% of the lower of the fund value and the lifetime allowance (£1,500,000 for 2006/07).

Such advantages will not accrue if the scheme is not a registered scheme with HMRC.

Loan to Ethel

Taking a lump sum payment in the form of an interest free loan may appear attractive. This is because a capital payment in this way would, in the absence of specific legislation, not be subject to income tax. However, specific tax anti-avoidance legislation exists in such circumstances and generally loans to directors are illegal from a company law perspective.

Ethel Endeavours Limited is a close company for tax purposes. When a close company makes a loan to a participator (broadly a shareholder) it will be required to make a tax payment to HMRC. This tax charge is calculated as 25% of the loan value and if the loan is made before 31 December 2007 the tax charge will be due by 1 October 2008, unless the loan is repaid before that date.

The tax charge will be repaid to the company to the extent that the loan itself is repaid by the recipient or written off.

If the loan is written off, the amount (grossed up by the fraction 100/90), will be treated as taxable income in the hands of the recipient. The loan written off will be effectively taxed as additional dividend income. As a result, income tax is payable at an additional 22·5% (32.5% – 10% tax credit) to the extent that the grossed up amount exceeds the taxpayer's higher rate tax threshold.

An employment benefit assessment will also arise on the loan as it is interest free. The normal beneficial loan benefit is calculated by applying the official rate of interest to the loan value.

Charging rent to Ethel Endeavours Limited

If you were to charge your company rent for the use of your property in the business the following taxation points need to be considered.

–   The rent which you will receive will be subject to income tax as property business income.

–   From this you will be able to make a deduction for any relevant expenditure. For expenditure that depends upon usage (e.g. electricity, heating) it is usually possible to apportion the total cost on some reasonable basis (e.g. the number of rooms used in the rental business).

    Other expenditure which does not depend entirely upon usage may be more problematic. HMRC may well resist a claim for deduction of such expenditure as council tax and home repairs (where the expenditure will be incurred irrespective of business usage). In these cases it may be easier for you to obtain a deduction if the rooms are used exclusively for business purposes and, for example, the repair relates specifically to those rooms.

    Interest relating to a loan that is used to acquire property that is let on a commercial basis can be deducted in arriving at net taxable property business income. It should therefore be possible to apportion the loan interest to that part of the property that is rented to the company and claim an appropriate deduction. To do this, however, the rented part of the property needs to be used exclusively for business purposes.

–   The rent charged should not exceed market rates, as any excess is likely to be treated as an additional dividend payment to yourself.

–   Ethel Endeavours Limited will be able to claim a corporation tax deduction for the gross rents payable.

–   As the rental income is regarded as investment rather than earned income in your hands there will be no Class 1 NIC liability either for the company or yourself.

–   To obtain relief for repairs and interest it is likely that part of the property needs to be exclusively used for the purposes of the rental business.

    This could have an impact on the future availability of the CGT principal private residence exemption. PPR may need to be restricted upon a future sale of your home as only the non-business portion will qualify.

    If the PPR exemption is not available, however, other CGT reliefs may assist, for example; rollover and business asset taper relief which may be available on an apportioned basis to the extent that the property is used exclusively for business purposes.

Gifting Shares – CGT implications

The main capital gains tax ('CGT') implications of gifting some of your shares in Ethel Endeavours Limited to your daughter are as follows.

The gifting of shares to your daughter (who is regarded as a connected person for CGT purposes) will give rise to a capital gain calculated as the difference between the market value of the shares at the date of the gift and their original cost to you.

As Ethel Endeavours Limited is an unquoted trading company, taper relief at business rates of 75% will be available to relieve this gain. You will also have an annual exemption of £8,800 to further reduce the gain chargeable.

The residual gain arising will be taxed at your marginal income tax rates for the tax year in which the gift is made with the tax due for payment by 31 January following the end of this tax year.

As you own more than 5% of the shares in Ethel Endeavours Limited which is an unquoted trading company another possibility will be to make a joint written claim with your daughter to gift relieve the gain.

The consequence will be that no capital gains tax will be payable by yourself but your daughter's base cost of the shares (i.e. market value) for future disposal purposes will be reduced by the capital gain deferred. If the shares are gifted in 2007/08 such a claim needs to be made by 31 January 2014.

You should be aware that if a gift relief claim is made you will not be able to use any accrued taper relief or your annual exemption. It may be possible, however, to make use of these if your daughter is prepared to pay an appropriate amount of consideration as any proceeds received over and above the allowable base cost is immediately taxable.

We trust that the above is of assistance to you but should you have any further queries please do not hesitate to contact me.

Yours sincerely,

A N Accountant

Appendix A: Profit extraction by bonus or dividend

Ethel's current taxable income position:

	£
Current salary	26,000
Less: PA	(5,035)
Current taxable income	20,965

Ethel's remaining basic rate band is therefore £12,335 (33,300 – 20,965)

If Ethel is paid a bonus of £20,000 (gross), the first £12,335 is taxed at 22%, the balance at 40%.

If Ethel is paid a dividend of £20,000, this represents a gross dividend of £22,222 (20,000 × 100/90).

The first £12,335 is taxed at 10% and has a tax credit of £1,233 therefore no further liability is due in respect of this portion of the dividend. The balance of £9,887 (22,222 – 12,335) is taxed at 32½% with a tax credit of 10%.

Additional Income tax

£	Additional salary £	Dividend £
12,335 × 22%	2,714	
7,665 × 40%	3,066	
20,000	5,780	
9,887 × 22.5% (32.5% – 10%)		2,225

Additional Class 1 NIC

	Additional salary £	Dividend £
Employee's		
(33,540 – 26,000) × 11%	829	Nil
(46,000 – 33,540) × 1%	125	
	6,734	2,225

Corporation Tax Savings

	Additional salary £	Dividend £
Employer's Class 1 NICs (20,000 × 12.8%)	2,560	Nil
Gross salary	20,000	Nil
Employment costs	22,560	Nil
Savings at 19%	4,286	Nil

Tax cost

	Additional salary £	Dividend £
Additional income tax and Class 1 NICs	6,734	2,225
Additional employers NIC	2,560	Nil
Corporation tax savings	(4,286)	Nil
	5,008	2,225

After tax cash received (Note)

	Additional salary £	Dividend £
Bonus/dividend received	20,000	20,000
Tax cost (above)	(5,008)	(2,225)
	14,992	17,775

Note: This after tax cash receipt takes all relevant taxes into account, including the company's corporation tax position.

ACCA marking scheme		
		Marks
Letter presentation, structure and format		2.0
(a) Additional tax – salary		1.0
– dividend		1.0
Corporation tax savings		1.0
Conclusions		1.0
	Available and max	4.0
(b) (i) Pension contribution		
Registered scheme		1.0
Tax advantages if registered		2.5
Position if not registered		1.0
Loan		
Close company recognition		1.0

	Rules		1.5
	Benefit		0.5
	Rent		
	Property business income		0.5
	Expenditure– dependent upon usage		1.0
	– other expenditure		1.0
	– interest		1.5
	Market rate		1.0
	Corporation tax deduction		0.5
	NIC implications		0.5
	CGT implications		2.0
		Max	15.5
		Available	14.0
(c)	Market value rule		0.5
	Basic gain computation		0.5
	Taper relief		1.0
	Annual exemption		0.5
	Tax rate/due date		1.0
	Gift relief		1.5
	Available and Max		5.0
Total			25.0

PERSONAL FINANCIAL PLANNING

70 ALICE AND ZARA

(a) **Income tax and CGT implications of proposed investments**

Individual savings account (ISA)

Income tax and CGT

Income and gains realised on investments held within an ISA are exempt from income tax and CGT. There is no minimum holding period so withdrawals can be made from an ISA at any time without affecting the tax relief.

Alice – maximum investment and suitability

Alice can invest £3,000 in the cash component of an ISA during 2006/07. The cash component includes those National Savings products where the income is not exempt from tax.

The balance of the subscription limit of £4,000 (7,000 – 3,000) can be invested into the stocks and shares component.

Qualifying low risk investments are

(1) fixed interest preference shares and convertible preference shares,

(2) gilts, fixed interest corporation bonds and convertible bonds with at least five years to run until maturity, and

(3) investments in unit trusts, investment trusts and open-ended investment companies.

An ISA should result in capital growth, need not be high risk, and can be easily liquidated in ten years time.

Zara – maximum investment and suitability

Zara can invest £7,000 in the stocks and shares component of an ISA during 2006/07. Ordinary shares will qualify provided they are listed on a stock exchange situated anywhere in the world.

An ISA can provide income (depending on the choice of investments), should be within the level of risk that Zara is prepared to accept, and can be easily liquidated in three years time.

Both Alice and Zara should select a maxi ISA with a single manager. Otherwise, the investment in the stocks and shares components will be restricted to £3,000.

Investment in pension schemes

Income tax and CGT

The maximum tax deductible pension contribution an individual can make is the higher of

(i)   £3,600, and

(ii)   100% of the individual's relevant earnings, chargeable to income tax in the year.

Where an individual contributes to more than one pension scheme, the annual limit applies to total contributions made by him into all schemes.

Provided the total contributions paid into a scheme by the individual member or any other party (e.g. employer, spouse) do not exceed the annual allowance of £215,000 for 2006/07, no further tax consequences apply in that year.

Assets within a registered pension fund can grow in value tax free (i.e. there is no income tax in respect of income earned from the assets and no capital gains tax in respect of any capital disposals made by the trustees of the fund).

Unless retiring through ill health, pensions will not normally be paid out until the individual is aged 50 (for members who are 50 before 5 April 2010, aged 55 thereafter).

A tax free lump sum of up to 25% of the lower of the fund value and the lifetime allowance (£1,500,000 for 2006/07) can be drawn.

The remainder of the fund must be used to pay pension income which is taxable earned income in the hands of the recipient.

Alice – maximum investment and suitability

Alice's maximum tax deductible contribution for 2006/07 is therefore £55,000.

The contribution will reduce her income tax liability by £22,000 (55,000 × 40%). The tax relief is obtained via the PAYE system.

Alice has currently paid 6% into her scheme.

She could therefore pay an additional voluntary contributions either into her employer's scheme, or pay into a separate freestanding scheme.

The pension eventually received will be taxable as earned income.

Considering Alice's objectives, the pension contribution should result in capital growth, and should not be high risk.

Alice is 50 years old and she does not want to access the fund for at least ten years. Although the pension scheme cannot be liquidated in ten years time, she will be entitled to draw a 25% lump sum and pension.

Zara – maximum investment and suitability

Zara's maximum tax deductible pension contribution for 2006/07 is £47,400.

The contribution will reduce Zara's 2006/07 income tax liability. Basic rate tax relief is given by deduction at source, higher rate relief is detained by extending the basic rate band.

The pension eventually received will be taxable as earned income.

Considering Zara's objectives, a personal pension is within the level of risk that Zara is prepared to accept. However, it will not provide income until she retires, and as she is currently aged 38 the capital lump sum will not be available in three years time.

Open-ended investment company (OEIC)

Income tax and CGT

Alice is to invest the balance of £13,000 (75,000 – 7,000 – 55,000) in an OEIC.

This will not attract any tax relief, and dividends from the OEIC will be taxable, net of 10% tax. Disposals are also subject to CGT.

This investment should result in capital growth, need not be high risk, and can easily be liquidated in ten years time.

Venture capital trust (VCT)

Income tax and CGT

Zara is to use the balance of £20,600 (75,000 – 7,000 – 47,400) to subscribe for new ordinary shares in a VCT.

She will obtain income tax relief up to a maximum of £6,180 (20,600 × 30%) for 2006/07 (the investment is below the annual limit of £200,000).

The shares must be held for three years or the tax relief will be withdrawn. Dividends received are exempt from income tax, and any disposal should be exempt from CGT.

Although high risk, a VCT would appear to be within the level of risk that Zara is prepared to accept. However, the investment is unlikely to provide a high level of income, although a disposal in three years time will not result in a withdrawal of the tax relief.

(b) (i) **Authorisation to conduct investment business**

Unless the activities do not constitute the carrying on of a business (such as providing financial advice to a friend or relative who is not otherwise a client, and who will not be charged a fee), a Chartered Certified Accountant would have to be authorised to conduct investment business under the Financial Services and Markets Act 2000 in order to give the advice to Alice and Zara.

This is because the definition of investments includes shares (the stocks and shares components of an ISA and the venture capital trust), pensions and open-ended investment companies (but not the cash component of an ISA), and the definition of investment activities includes specific advice regarding the purchase of investments.

(ii) **Carrying on of business by a non-authorised person**

Anybody who carries on investment business without being authorised to do so under the Financial Services and Markets Act 2000 commits a criminal offence, with a maximum penalty of two years imprisonment and/or an unlimited fine. Any agreement entered into by an unauthorised person is unenforceable by that person.

The client or customer may take civil action in the courts to recover any money that they have paid and to seek compensation for any losses that they have suffered.

Key answer tips

Arguably the question is only concerned with explaining the tax implications and the broad ideas of risk for the given potential investments. Until, for example, you start advising on which ISA and OEIC to invest in you are not giving specific investment advice and do not need to be authorised under FSMA 2000.

71 ABDUL, EMMA AND GEORGE

(a) **Abdul Bright – Tax saving if invested in ISAs**

Income and gains realised on investments held within an ISA are exempt from income tax and CGT. There is no minimum holding period so withdrawals can be made from an ISA at any time without affecting the tax relief.

The maximum investment in the cash component of an ISA during 2006/07 is £3,000. Abdul would therefore have saved income tax of £72 (3,000 × 6% × 40%) by investing in the cash component of an ISA rather than the building society deposit account. This assumes a similar rate of interest.

The balance of the subscription limit of £4,000 (7,000 - 3,000) could have then been invested into the stocks and shares component of an ISA.

This investment would have saved CGT of £4,000 (W1).

However, given the high level of capital gain it would have been beneficial to have invested the maximum possible into the stocks and shares component. The CGT saving would then have been £7,000 (7,000 × £2.50 (W1) × 40%).

Given an investment of £7,000 in the stocks and shares component, income tax of £187 (W2) would have been saved in respect of the dividend received from Fast-Buck plc.

Key answer tips

The £187 income tax saving comprises the reduction of tax payable by Abdul of £130 (£576 × 22.5%) and the 10% tax credit recoverable of £57 (576 × 10%) by the ISA Fund Manager.

(b) **Emma Flash – Disposal of EIS investments**

The 25,000 shares in Web-Com Ltd that Emma subscribed for on 30 November 1997 have been held for three years. The income tax relief of £5,000 (25,000 at 20%) that Emma claimed in 1997/98 will therefore not be withdrawn, and there will be no CGT in respect of the disposal.

Emma will have claimed tax relief of £30,000 (150,000 at 20%) in 2005/06 in respect of the 175,000 shares in Web-Com Ltd subscribed for on 30 January 2006. These shares will not have been held for three years, and so the income tax relief will be withdrawn.

Emma will therefore have to repay £30,000 to HMRC.

Her CGT liability for 2006/07 will be £231,428 (W3), and this will be payable on 31 January 2008.

The capital gain of £578,571 (W3) arising on the disposal of the shares in Web-Com Ltd can be deferred if Emma subscribes for shares in companies qualifying for relief under the EIS.

Deferral is available whether or not income tax relief is available, and so the whole gain can be deferred if Emma uses £578,571 of the proceeds to subscribe for qualifying shares.

The subscription must be made in the period beginning on 6 January 2006 and ending on 5 January 2010.

Key answer tips

For serial investments in EIS schemes, the combined periods of ownership can be taken into account for taper relief purposes when the gain from the first investment crystallises.

(c)   **George Hardy – Letting the house in London**

Whether the house is let unfurnished or as furnished holiday accommodation, George will be assessed on the profits of a business of letting property.

The costs of repairing the roof of £9,700 and of decorating the house of £6,900 should be deductible as pre-trading expenditure, since they were incurred within seven years of the commencement of letting on 1 January 2007. The costs would appear to be revenue expenditure, since there is no indication that the house was not usable prior to the expenditure being incurred.

If the house is let unfurnished, the premium received from the granting of a short lease will be taxed in 2006/07. The taxable proportion is £2,300 (W4).

Rent is assessed on an accruals basis, and so rent of £3,000 (12,000 × 3/12) will be assessed in 2006/07.

George will therefore have a property business loss of £11,300 (W5) for 2006/07. This will be carried forward and set against the first available property business profits.

If the house is let as furnished holiday accommodation, it should qualify as a trade under the furnished holiday letting rules. This is because 40 weeks (280 days) letting each year will mean that the house is both available as holiday accommodation for at least 140 days and so let for at least 70 days.

The furniture will qualify for a first year allowance of £6,750 (13,500 at 50%). George will therefore have a property business loss of £18,850 (W6) for 2006/07 which is treated as a trading loss.

George can claim to have the loss set off under s380 ICTA 1988 against his total income for 2006/07 and/or 2005/06, or under s381 ICTA 1988 against total income for 2003/04 to 2005/06.

Workings

(1)   **Disposal of 8,500 £1 ordinary Fast-Buck plc shares**

	£
Sales proceeds (November 2006)	29,750
Cost (April 2006)	(8,500)
Gain	21,250

There is no indexation allowance as the shares are acquired after April 1998. There is no taper relief as the shares are owned for less than a year.

Gain per share = (21,250/8,500) = £2.50

Gain on an investment of £4,000 in 4,000 £1 ordinary shares
= 4,000 × £2.50 = £10,000

As Abdul is a higher rate taxpayer and has already utilised his annual exemption, the CGT saving based on an investment in 4,000 shares
= £10,000 × 40% = £4,000.

(2)   **Dividend income**

	£
Dividend received on 8,500 shares	630
Grossed up dividend = (630 × 100/90)	700

Dividend income for 7,000 shares = (700/8,500) × 7,000

= 576

Income tax on dividend income = 576 × 32½% =	£187

(3)   **Disposal of Web-com Ltd shares**

	£
Sales proceeds (5 January 2007)	
$\left(\dfrac{850,000}{175,000}\right) \times 150,000$	728,571
Cost (30 January 2006)	(150,000)
Gain	578,571

There is no indexation allowance as the shares are acquired after April 1998. There is no taper relief as the shares are held for less than a year.

The gain is therefore 100% chargeable.

As Emma is a higher rate taxpayer and has already utilised her annual exemption all of the gain is taxed at 40%.

CGT (578,571 × 40%)	231,428

(4)   **Premium on granting a short lease**

	£
Premium received	2,500
Less 2% × (2,500) × (5 – 1)	(200)
Property income assessment	2,300

(5)   **Property business loss – unfurnished property**

	£
Premium assessment (W4)	2,300
Rental income (12,000 × 3/12)	3,000
	5,300
Roof replacement	(9,700)
Decorating costs	(6,900)
Property business loss	(11,300)

(6)   **Property business loss – furnished holiday accommodation**

	£
Rental income (3 × £1,950)	5,850
Running costs (3 × £450)	(1,350)
Roof replacement	(9,700)
Decorating costs	(6,900)
Capital allowances	(6,750)
Property business loss	(18,850)

72   CYRIL AND MABEL

(a)   **Income tax and Class 4 NICs – 2003/04 to 2006/07**

Profit Allocation

	Total	*Cyril*	*Mabel*
	£	£	£
P/e 31/01/2005	12,000	6,000	6,000
Y/e 31/01/2006	24,000	12,000	12,000
Y/e 31/01/2007	36,000	18,000	18,000

Trading income assessments

Tax Year	Basis Period	Assessment
2004/05	1/10/2004 to 5/4/2005	£
	P/e 31/01/2005	6,000
	Y/e 31/01/2006 (2/12 × 12,000)	2,000
		8,000
2005/06	Y/e 31/01/2006	12,000
2006/07	Y/e 31/01/2007	18,000

Income Tax Computations

	2004/05		*2005/06*		*2006/07*	
	Cyril	*Mabel*	*Cyril*	*Mabel*	*Cyril*	*Mabel*
	£	£	£	£	£	£
Trading income	8,000	8,000	12,000	12,000	18,000	18,000
JS allowance	2,540	–	–	–	–	–
Personal allowance	(5,035)	(5,035)	(5,035)	(5,035)	(5,035)	(5,035)
Taxable Income	5,505	2,965	6,965	6,965	12,965	12,965

	£					
10% × 2,150	215	215	215	215	215	215
22% × 3,355/815	738	179				
22% × 4,815			1,059	1,059		
22% × 10,815					2,379	2,379
Income tax	953	394	1,274	1,274	2,594	2,594

Class 4 NICs

(8,000 – 5,035) × 8%	237	237				
(12,000 – 5,035) × 8%			557	557		
(18,000 – 5,035) × 8%					1,037	1,037
Total income tax and Class 4 NICs	1,190	631	1,831	1,831	3,631	3,631

(b)   (i)   **Use of Overdraft to Purchase Fixed Assets**

From the information provided it would appear that the overdraft facility was originally used to 'set up' the business with the acquisition of various fixed assets. It is a generally accepted principle in business financial planning that longer term assets employed within a business are financed by longer term sources of capital that match the longevity of the underlying assets. It would appear that in the case of Cyril and Mabel this principle has not been followed.

Overdrafts are basically designed as short-term sources of finance to cover fluctuations in cash requirements over short periods of time. They are not designed as longer term or even permanent sources of capital. As overdraft interest rates are generally greater than those for the more traditional sources of longer term capital (e.g. bank loans, hire purchase, mortgages etc), they can be an expensive source of finance if used in this way.

It would appear therefore that the couple's cash flow problems go beyond the immediate need for funds to settle the outstanding tax liabilities and stem from a shortage of longer term capital within the business from the outset of approximately £15,000.

This is evidenced by the facts that:

- The business overdraft was originally used to purchase fixed assets needed to set the business up costing approximately £15,000.

- Whilst being exceeded on occasions, cashflows have been sufficient to stabilise the overdraft facility at around the facility level of £15,000.

(ii)   **Sources of Finance available to pay the tax settlement**

Business Overdraft/Bank Loan

It would further appear that the facility is currently being fully used and the bank manager seems reluctant to extend the facility (and hence the bank's risk) further in this situation.

The overdraft facility is currently unsecured. If security is offered (presumably in the form of a second legal charge over some of the equity within their house) the bank may consider a further extension of this facility.

It is more likely that the bank will consider offering the couple a secured bank loan. If the bank were prepared to consider this possibility it is likely that this would be offered as part of a package aimed at reducing the bank's long term overdraft exposure.

The package would possibly involve the conversion of all/part of the current overdraft facility to a longer term loan subject to monthly capital repayments (thereby reducing the couple's bank borrowings and hence the bank's risk exposure over time).

Cash/Personal Overdrafts/Credit Cards

The couple currently have savings of approximately £5,500 together with unused personal overdraft and credit card facilities of around £2,500. Thus £8,000 is potentially available from these sources.

Equity Within Home

The couple's current house value exceeds their mortgage by approximately £65,000 (250,000 − 185,000). A considerable amount of equity therefore exists within their property.

This equity could be tapped in two key ways:

- *By selling the house and trading down to a smaller property.*

    The CGT principle private residence exemption is likely to be available to fully exempt any potential gain arising. This would, however, seem to be a drastic solution for approximately £21,000 of additional funds needed to settle their tax liabilities.

    Additionally a house move is likely to involve a considerable amount of costs (legal fees, estate agents fees, stamp duty, mortgage arrangement fees etc). It is unlikely that this would therefore be considered an attractive option to the couple.

- *By using the equity as security to extend their existing mortgage.*

    This may involve some additional fees (legal and arrangement fees) but these would be much less than with a house sale.

    Given the couple's current financial position a move to a different mortgage lender to try and take advantage of more competitive mortgage products that may currently be available within the market place is considered unlikely.

Pension/Term Assurance

Term assurance has no surrender value and does not therefore represent a useable source of finance.

In addition, it will not be possible to obtain any value from the personal pension until Cyril and Mabel attain 55 years of age.

Tutorial note:

Pensions will not normally be paid out until the individual member reaches the age of 50 for members who will attain that age before 2010. The age will be 55 years old for those who do not attain the age of 50 before 2010.

(iii) **Recommendations to Cyril and Mabel**

The couple's financial problems appear to be twofold:

- There is a need to introduce approximately £15,000 of longer term funding to the business

- There is also a need to raise £21,000 of funds to settle the outstanding tax liabilities.

It would be sensible to try and resolve both of these problems simultaneously. As an ancillary there will also be a need to retain going forward (relatively small) contingency funds for both the business and themselves personally.

An examination of the sources of finance available leads to the following conclusions:

Overdraft and credit cards

Currently Cyril has a personal overdraft of £2,500 whilst Mabel has a credit card liability of £500. As these are likely to be the most expensive sources of capital available with interest rates far exceeding those being obtained on their savings the couple should seriously consider using their savings to pay off these liabilities.

The residual savings of £500 will then be available as a small personal contingency fund to meet future emergencies. This is necessary as the couple's current drawings are only sufficient to meet their living costs (i.e. they are not generating additional savings at present).

Every effort should then be made to avoid using the personal overdraft or credit cards going forward (or at least to settle the credit card bills on a monthly basis and therefore avoid incurring high charges).

This will then leave bank loans, and releasing some of the equity within their house as the most likely sources of finance to resolve their current problems.

Bank loans and equity in the house

The bank could be approached to restructure its business lending facilities. This would probably entail a mixture of a medium term loan of £15,000 and a smaller overdraft facility, of say £2,500, to meet short term fluctuations in the cash requirements of the business and represent a contingency fund going forward.

The loan would introduce the longer term capital needed by the business. The bank may require security for this restructuring, particularly if total lending is increased. This should, however, have the effect of reducing bank charges which are currently high.

The balance of £21,000 needed to settle the tax liabilities could either be sourced by an additional bank loan or by an additional mortgage advance. It seems likely that the banks would require security if they extended their current lending so the ultimate choice between these may come down to the comparative costs involved.

ACCA marking scheme		
		Marks
(a)	Profit allocation	1.0
	Trading income assessment	
	2004/05	1.0
	2005/06	0.5
	2006/07	0.5
	Tax computations	
	2004/05	2.0
	2005/06	0.5
	2006/07	0.5
	Available and Max	6.0
(b)	(i) Matching principle/conclusion	1.5
	Overdraft expensive source of long term funding	1.0
	Lack of longer term capital in business/£15,000	1.5
	Available	4.0
	Maximum	3.0
	(ii) **Business overdraft/bank loan**	
	Bank unwilling to extend	0.5
	Possibility of overdraft/loan extension if security	2.0
	offered	1.0
	Appreciation of reduction in bank's risk	1.0
	Cash/Personal Overdrafts/Credit Cards	
	£8,000	1.0
	Equity Within Home	
	£65,000	0.5
	House sale	1.0
	PPR exemption	1.0
	Drastic/Costs	1.0
	Extending existing mortgage	0.5

	Fees	0.5
	Shopping around for new mortgage	1.0
	Pension Term Assurance	
	Not usable	<u>1.0</u>
	Available	<u>12.0</u>
	Max	<u>10.0</u>
(iii)	Tackle problems together	1.0
	Need for contingency funds	1.0
	Offset savings against personal overdraft/credit cards	1.0
	Expensive sources of funds	0.5
	Restructure business bank facilities	1.0
	Additional advance for tax settlement	0.5
	Comparison of costs	1.0
	Available and Max	<u>6.0</u>
Total		<u>25.0</u>

73 FREDERICK FAIRCHILD

(a) **Income tax implications of redundancy package**

Although lump sum payments are frequently outside the scope of the general employment income charging provision (which usually applies to payments received in return for the provision of past, present or future services rendered) case law and specific provisions exist which have the effect of either fully charging or partially charging such payments.

£25,000 under the terms of his contract of employment

Case law has determined that this payment to which Frederick is contractually entitled will be fully taxable and therefore liable to income tax of £10,000 (£25,000 × 40%) in the tax year of receipt.

Statutory redundancy payment of £5,000

Statutory redundancy payments are specifically exempted from income tax. Whilst exempt, they do need to be taken into account in determining the £30,000 exemption threshold that can apply to other lump sum payments.

Payments from occupational pension scheme

The reduced pension provided by the pension scheme will be subject to income tax as employment income. Providing it is made in accordance with the rules of the scheme, however, the lump sum payment received should be tax free.

Restrictive Covenant

The payment of £10,000 to prevent Frederick from commencing a competing company is specifically subject to income tax as employment income in the tax year of receipt. Frederick will therefore be subject to an income tax liability of £4,000 (10,000 × 40%) relating to this payment.

Ex-gratia payment

Generally, providing such payments are not in return for services rendered or contractual, such payments are not caught by the general employment income charging provision.

However, they are caught by specific charging legislation to the extent that they exceed £30,000. As referred to above, in this case, this exemption threshold is reduced by the statutory redundancy payment.

The best outcome for Frederick would therefore be that an income tax liability of £14,000 arises (60,000 – (30,000 – 5,000) × 40%) in the year of receipt.

Due to Frederick's age and the possibility that he may retire following his redundancy, this treatment may prove problematic. This is because HMRC can regard such payments in these circumstances as unapproved payments made from a pension scheme.

If treated in this way such payments will be fully chargeable to income tax as employment income in the tax year of receipt which in Frederick's case will give rise to an income tax liability of £24,000.

Further, it will probably not be possible to obtain HMRC's agreement to treat the payment as exempt, because Frederick is already a member of the company's occupational pension scheme. As HMRC are unlikely to seek this treatment in cases of genuine redundancy when an individual is actively seeking new employment Frederick would therefore be advised to exercise caution in this area.

(b)   (i)   **Factors to consider in redeeming outstanding mortgage**

Factors that should be taken into account in deciding whether Frederick should use some of his lump sum to redeem his outstanding mortgage are:

–   The opportunity cost of the funds used to redeem the mortgage needs to be identified. If the rate of return that can be achieved by investing the funds is not as great as the interest rate payable on his mortgage early redemption may well be considered worthwhile by Frederick.

Unless Frederick is prepared to accept a higher level of risk (perhaps via an equity investment) with interest rates payable of 8.5% it would appear unlikely that investment returns in excess of this could be achieved in the current investment market.

This is particularly the case when it is considered that most investments will result in personal taxation being incurred at marginal tax rates (thus effectively lowering the net investment return achievable) whilst there is no mortgage interest relief available.

–   Frederick needs to establish whether an early redemption will result in penalties or charges being incurred. These may outweigh the cash-flow savings achieved by reducing net monthly outgoings.

–   Frederick also needs to consider whether he has a need for capital in the future. If so it may not be sensible to use some of his capital to redeem his mortgage now.

This is because

(1)   Frederick's current circumstances (age and income position) may make it difficult to raise capital in the future; and

(2)   the possibility of high costs being incurred in raising future replacement finance.

(ii)   **Main issues relating to an EIS investment**

It would appear that Frederick's willingness to invest in the ordinary share capital of Exciting Escapades Limited depends upon the availability of attracting tax relief under the Enterprise Investment Scheme ('EIS').

Tax advantages

Providing all conditions are satisfied the following tax advantages will be available:

(1)   Income tax relief of 20% of the amount invested (up to a maximum investment of £400,000). The relief takes the form of a tax reducing allowance which can relieve a taxpayer's income tax liability to nil but can not generate a tax refund. It is possible for taxpayers to treat up to half of an amount invested before 6 October in any tax year as having been made in the previous tax year.

(2)   Capital gains accruing on the disposal of EIS shares can be wholly exempt providing income tax relief was originally given. Capital losses on the disposal of EIS shares are given but the acquisition cost of the shares is reduced by the amount of EIS relief attributable to the shares disposed.

(3)   EIS deferral relief can also be available to defer chargeable gains arising on the disposal of other assets. This works by permitting chargeable gains to be deferred against acquisitions of eligible EIS shares until (usually) the EIS shares are themselves disposed of. It is not necessary for income tax relief to be given on the subscription for deferral relief to be claimed.

To obtain the above tax advantages Frederick will need to ensure that he is a 'qualifying individual' subscribing for 'eligible shares' in a 'qualifying company' carrying on 'qualifying activities'.

Conditions

Qualifying Individuals

To be a qualifying individual Frederick must not be connected with the EIS company. This means he should not:

–   Be an employee (but see exception below)
–   Have an interest of 30% or more in Exciting Escapades Limited.

These conditions need to be satisfied throughout the period beginning two years before the share issue and ending three years after the 'relevant date'.

The 'relevant date' is the later of

1)   the date of the share issue, and
2)   the date the company began trading.

The fact that his friend has suggested that he becomes an employee of this company could therefore be a problem. An exception to this rule is, however, made to a taxpayer who was not connected to the company before the shares were issued and becomes a director earning a reasonable level of remuneration for the services performed after this date.

Providing therefore that Frederick becomes a company director after he acquires his shareholding and HMRC agree that £35,000 represents a reasonable level of remuneration for the work he will perform this particular condition can be overcome.

In determining whether a taxpayer has an interest of 30% or more account is taken of shareholdings of certain associates, including those held by spouses.

Frederick therefore needs to exercise care here because if he acquires 25,000 new ordinary shares (i.e. a 25% stake) he and his wife will own 32.5% ((25 + 7.5)/100%) post acquisition which would mean that EIS relief would not be available.

The maximum shareholding that Frederick should subscribe for is therefore just under 22,499 new ordinary shares ((22,499 + 7,500)/100% is just less than 30%).

Eligible Shares

To qualify the new shares issued by Exciting Escapades Limited need to be new ordinary shares which:

–   Are fully paid up at the time of issue; and

–   Are not redeemable for at least 3 years from the relevant date; and

–   Do not carry any preferential rights to dividends.

Qualifying Company

To qualify Exciting Escapades Limited must be:

–   Unquoted (shares listed on the Alternative Investment Market count for this purpose); and

–   Not controlled by another company; and

–   Engaged in qualifying activities.

Qualifying Activities

To qualify the company must carry on a trading activity wholly or mainly in the UK throughout the three years following the relevant date. Certain trading activities (e.g. dealing in shares or land and banking) are excluded.

Frederick will also need to be aware that EIS relief will be partially or fully withdrawn if within 3 years of the relevant date the shares are disposed of, he receives value from the company or ceases to be a qualifying individual or the company ceases to be a qualifying company.

Providing he holds the shares for the required three year period, which should fit in with his retirement plans, relief should not be withdrawn.

(iii)   **Suitable additional investments**

Assuming Frederick uses the lump sum to redeem his mortgage and make an investment of £27,000 (30,000 × 22.5/25) in Exciting Escapades Limited he will have approximately £25,000 to invest in alternative products.

His stated aims are the possibility of tax free returns with a low to medium risk profile with capital growth more important over the medium to longer term than income generation.

Suitable investments will include:

–   *Individual Savings Accounts (ISA's)*

Investments within an ISA are exempt from both income tax and capital gains tax.

Due to of Frederick's willingness to accept medium risk a maxi-account comprising 'safer' equity investments of up to £7,000 can be invested per tax year.

Alternatively, if less risk is desirable up to £3,000 per tax year can be invested in cash deposits.

If close to a tax year end Frederick could make an investment of £7,000 at the end of one tax year and then shortly after at the beginning of the next.

–   *Investment Bonds*

The balance of funds could be used to purchase an investment bond.

The 'gains' made on the encashment of investment bonds will only become liable to income tax when the bonds are either partially or fully encashed and then only if Frederick is a higher rate taxpayer.

The rules allow for the tax free withdrawal by Frederick of up to 5% of the initial sum invested per tax year and/or encashment can be deferred until he becomes a basic rate tax payer (possibly in a few years time when he retires).

Frederick will be able to (at least partially) control the risk profile of the investment by selecting the underlying bond assets. Again due to his willingness to accept a moderate level of risk these are likely to include 'safer' equities.

Fredrick will need to be aware that if he encashes the bond in the first few years the proceeds may be less than the sum invested.

		ACCA marking scheme			
					Marks
(a)		General charging provision			0.5
		Contractual entitlement			0.5
		Statutory redundancy payment	–	exemption	0.5
			–	interaction with £30,000 limit	1.0
		Pension scheme	–	pension	0.5
			–	lump sum	1.5
		Restrictive covenant			1.0
		Ex-gratia payment	–	general rule	1.0
			–	unapproved pension payment	1.5
			–	application	1.0
				Maximum	9.0
				Available	8.0
(b)	(i)	Opportunity cost			0.5
		Interaction with risk/tax			1.5
		Early redemption penalties			0.5
		Need for future capital			1.5
				Available and maximum	4.0
	(ii)	EIS recognition			0.5
		Tax reliefs	–	income tax	1.0
			–	CGT	1.0
			–	deferral relief	1.0
		Qualifying individuals	–	definition	1.0
			–	application–employee	1.5
			–	30% rule	1.5
		Eligible shares			1.0
		Qualifying company			1.0
		Qualifying trade			0.5
		Relief withdrawal			1.0
				Maximum	11.0
				Available	9.0
	(iii)	ISA's			2.0
		Investment bonds			2.0
				Available and maximum	4.0
		Other suitable investments will be awarded equivalent marks.			
Total					25.0

74 PHILIP

(a) **Severance agreement – income tax payable**

The sums are taxable as follows:

	Notes	Taxable £	Non-taxable £	Total £
Remaining notice	(1)	10,000		10,000
Ex-gratia	(2)	10,000	30,000	40,000
Employment assistance	(3)		2,000	2,000
Use of company car	(4)	4,400		4,400
		24,400	32,000	56,400
Income tax @ 40%		£9,760		

Notes:

(1) Payment for notice periods are linked to employment and are therefore fully taxable as employment income

(2) The first £30,000 of an ex-gratia payment is exempt. The remainder is taxable.

(3) The provision of counselling and advice on outplacement following redundancy is a specifically exempt benefit of employment. It is therefore not taxable.

(4) The use of a company car is taxable in full as it is a benefit derived from his employment.

(b) **Chargeable gain on shares in Stelvin Limited**

	£
Sales proceeds (4,500 × 6.20)	27,900
Cost (4,500 × 3.50)	(15,750)
Gain	12,150

As the shares have been held for less than one year there is no taper relief available, the gain is 100% chargeable.

	£
Chargeable gain	12,150
Annual exemption	(8,800)
Taxable gain	3,350
Capital gains tax (3,350 × 40%)	1,340

(c) (i) **Tax incentives when buying shares in new and/or developing companies**

There are two key tax reliefs which might be available to Philip and at least partially compensate for the high risk nature of such an investment.

1 *Enterprise investment scheme ('EIS')*

The EIS provides tax relief on investment into unquoted trading companies which carry on a qualifying trade.

The following reliefs are available:

*   Any chargeable gains arising on any assets can be deferred against the base cost of the new shares if the shares are issued within the qualifying reinvestment period (i.e. up to one year before, or up to three years after the disposal). The deferred gain will not crystallise until the new shares are sold.

*   An income tax reducer at the rate of 20% on investments of up to £400,000 in a tax year.

*   If the investment is made in the first six months of the tax year, an election can be made for up to 50% of the shares subscribed for (and the relief) to relate to the prior year but only to a maximum carry back of £50,000.

*   Any gains arising from the sale of the EIS shares in the future are not taxable provided that the shares are held for the minimum period (i.e. three years).

*   Losses can be relieved (but are reduced by the EIS income tax relief received).

However, there are a number of conditions which need to be satisfied as follows:

*   The investor must not be an employee or director when he subscribes for the shares and, (together with his associates) must not hold more than 30% of the ordinary share capital of the company.

    If he does, he is connected, and the benefits of income tax relief and capital gains exemption will be lost. However the tax deferral relief is still available.

*   The subscription must be for new ordinary shares and be paid in cash.

*   The company must be an unquoted company which carries out a qualifying trade in the UK throughout the relevant period, or again, reliefs will be denied. Note that a future company listing will not result in the loss of relief, unless this was planned at the time of share issue.

*   The shares must be held for a minimum of three years. Failure to do so will result in the income tax relief being clawed back.

*   Any disposal not at arms length will also result in the denial of the relief.

2   *Venture capital trust ('VCT')*

Tax relief is also available for investment in a trust that itself invests in a basket of qualifying trading companies.

The reliefs and conditions are similar to those for EIS investments but with the following key differences:

*   Income tax relief is given at 30%, not 20%.

*   The deferral relief for chargeable gains against the base cost of the new shares is not available.

*   The shares must be held for a minimum of five years. Failure to do so will result in the income tax relief being clawed back.

- There is no minimum holding period for CGT exemption.

- Dividends from VCTs are exempt from tax.

From an investment perspective, a VCT investment is potentially less risky. This is because the VCT is a quoted company and the actual risk is spread in terms of a collective investment in several companies.

(ii) **Rachel low risk investments for Rachel**

Risk to capital is usually minimised by investment in deposit based investments or interest bearing securities.

The following types of saving / investment products might be considered.

- *Bank or building society deposit accounts*

  Bank and building societies offer a variable or a fixed rate of interest, but the latter will usually be linked to a restriction in (or penalty for) access to the capital.

  The monetary capital will be 100% secure but the real value may be reduced because of the effects of inflation.

  Interest is taxable, and income tax at 20% will normally be deducted at source. The exception is National Savings bank accounts, which pay interest gross.

- *Individual Savings Accounts (ISAs)*

  Up to £3,000 per year can be invested in a mini cash ISA, interest from which will be tax free. Such an account can therefore provide a useful tax free advantage over a similar taxable deposit account.

- *National Savings Certificates*

  National Savings Certificates (NSC) offer a set interest rate of a fixed amount for either a two year or a five year term or on an index linked basis for either a three year or a five year term.

  The return (interest) is tax free and in the case of the index linked certificates will also offer protection against inflation.

  The maximum cash investment in a particular issue is £15,000, but there is no limit to the number of issues that can be held.

- *Government loan stocks (gilts)*

  Gilts offer a fixed rate of interest (the coupon) and are issued for variable repayment periods. They are quoted securities and traded in the market, with the capital value varying with the relationship of the coupon rate to the market rate. Thus they are strictly low risk only if bought at issue and held to maturity or bought close to maturity at below par.

  Interest is paid gross but subject to tax.

  Similar fixed interest loan stocks are also issued by local authorities and companies. These usually offer a higher rate of interest than gilts, to reflect their higher risk compared to a government backed investment, particularly in the case of corporate bonds. Also, in such cases, interest will be paid net of tax at 20%.

Note: Candidates were only required to give three examples. Marks would also be given for other relevant savings and investment products.

(d) **Business protection (key person) insurance**

Business protection (key person) insurance is intended to cover a company (business) for the loss of earnings that will occur if one or a few key employees die or suffer a serious illness. The level of cover will need to relate to the likely level of loss that would be suffered.

The types of protection policies that are most frequently used are:

- *Term assurance*

  Term assurance to provide a lump sum in the event of the death of a key person, if occurring within the policy's fixed term. Provided that the policy is taken out for a limited period and wholly and exclusively for the purpose of the trade, then the premiums will usually be allowed as a trading expense. However, any payments received would be taxable as trading income.

- *Permanent health insurance*

  Permanent health insurance (PHI) to provide regular payments over a limited period in the event of absence from work of a key person due to sickness or accident. Premiums will usually be allowable as a trading expense provided the cover is only for the short term and the benefits are payable to the employer.

  The benefits received will be taxable, but a corresponding deduction will be received to the extent that the receipts are used to make sickness payments to the employee. Any such payments made to the employee are treated as the equivalent of a salary and will be taxed (PAYE and NIC) as such.

- *Critical illness insurance*

  Critical illness insurance (CII) to provide a lump sum in the event of a key person being diagnosed with one of a specified list of life threatening illnesses.

  The tax treatment of such policies is comparable to a term assurance policy (i.e. the premiums will usually be tax deductible and the proceeds taxable).

ACCA marking scheme		
		Marks
(a)	Notice – taxable	0.5
	Reason	0.5
	Ex gratia split	0.5
	Reason	0.5
	Employment assistance	0.5
	Reason	0.5
	Use of company car	0.5
	Reason	0.5
	Tax	0.5
	Max	4.0
(b)	Proceeds / cost	0.5
	Taper relief	0.5
	Annual exemption	0.5
	Tax @ 40%	0.5
	Max	2.0
(c)	Mention EIS	0.5
	Tax deferral	0.5
	Period of eligibility	0.5
	IT: Rate of relief	0.5
	Limits	0.5
	Carry back facility	0.5
	Details/limits	0.5
	CGT exempt	0.5
	Position re losses	0.5
	Conditions:	
	Not employee / director	0.5
	30% connection	0.5
	Cash subscription	0.5
	Trade requirement	0.5
	Time requirement	0.5
	Mention VCT	0.5
	IT relief rate	0.5
	No tax deferral	0.5
	No minimum holding period re CGT	0.5
	Dividends not taxable	0.5
	Note: additional ½ marks up to the maximum will be given for other relevant points.	
	Max	9.0
	Use deposit / interest based investments	0.5
	For each relevant specific product identified:	
	– generic product type	0.5
	– description / justification	1.0
	– tax treatment	0.5
		2.0
	Maximum number of products: 3 × 2.0	6.0
	Max	5.0
(d)	Purpose of business protection insurance	0.5
	Cover linked to lost profits	0.5
	Term assurance	2.0
	Permanent health insurance	2.0
	Critical illness insurance	1.0
	Max	5.0
Total		25

75   HAPPY HOME LTD

(a)   (i)   **Gift of 3,000 shares in Happy Home Ltd**

Shares, which are given free or sold at less than market value, are charged to income tax on the difference between the market value and the amount paid (if any) for the shares.

Henry was given 3,000 shares with a market value of £1 at the time of gift, so he was assessed to income tax on £3,000, in the tax year 2005/06.

(ii)   **Unapproved share options**

There are three events with potential tax consequences relating to unapproved share options, namely the grant and exercise of the option and sale of the shares acquired.

Grant of the option

No income tax charge arises on the grant of an option, regardless of when it can be exercised.

Exercise of the option

On the exercise of the option, the individual pays the agreed amount in return for a number of shares in the company.

The price paid (which is fixed a the time of the grant of the option) is compared with the open market value at the time of the exercise.

If less, the difference is charged to income tax. National insurance also applies, and the company has to pay Class 1 NIC.

If the company and shareholder agree, the National Insurance can be passed onto the individual, and the liability becomes a deductible expense in calculating the income tax charge.

Henry's situation

In Henry's case on exercise, the difference between market value (£14) and the price paid (£1) per share will be taxed as income.

Therefore, £130,000 (10,000 x (£14 – £1)) will be taxed as income.

In addition, National Insurance will be chargeable on the company at 12.8% (£16,640 = £130,000 × 12.8%) and on Henry at the rate of 1% (£1,300 = £130,000 × 1%).

Sale of the shares

The base cost of the shares is taken to be the market value at the time of exercise.

On the sale of the shares, any gain or loss arising falls under the capital gains tax rules, and CGT will be payable on any gain. Business asset taper relief will be available as the company is an unquoted trading company, but the relief will only run from the time that the share options are exercised (i.e. from the time when the shares were acquired).

Henry's situation

In Henry's case, the sale of the shares will immediately follow the exercise of the option (6 days later). The sale proceeds and the market value at the time of exercise are likely to be similar; thus little to no gain is likely to arise.

(b)   **Most appropriate share option scheme for Happy Home Limited**

The scheme that is best suited to Happy Home Limited is the Enterprise Management Incentive (EMI) scheme. This share option scheme is aimed at small fast growing companies, and because the potential risks are considered to be higher, the available rewards are greater.

To qualify, the company must be a trading company, carrying out a qualifying trade in the United Kingdom, with gross assets no more than £30m. The company must not be under the control of another company.

A qualifying company can grant each employee unexercised options over shares worth up to £100,000 per employee subject to a total overall limit of unexercised options of £3 million. The options must be granted for commercial reasons to recruit and retain the employee(s).

A qualifying employee is one who works on average 25 hours per week or 75% of their working time and who does not (together with his/her associates) have a material interest in the company.

Grand and exercise of options

No income tax or national insurance is charged on either the grant or the exercise of the option provided that the option is exercised not more than 10 years from the date of the grant and the amount paid is not less than the market value of the shares at the time the option was granted.

Sale of shares

On the sale of the shares, capital gains tax will apply, but business asset taper relief is available. Also in this case, the taper relief starts from the date the option is granted and not from the date of exercise, as is the case with other option schemes.

(c)   (i)   **Protection products of use to Henry**

Henry is still working and has a mortgage to support. He therefore needs to protect not only his assets but also cover any debt, or the ability to repay.

The following protection policies are relevant to Henry's situation:

Life assurance

This is a form of insurance that pays out on a chargeable event, usually death.

The main types are:

- Term Assurance which provides cover for a fixed term with the sum assured payable only on death. No investment benefits or payments arise on survival.

- Whole of Life Assurance where the policy provides life protection. The sum assured is payable on death at any time and usually some form of investment benefit will accrue in the form of a surrender value.

A qualifying policy will give a tax-free lump sum that could, for example, be used to repay the mortgage.

Permanent health insurance

Permanent health insurance (PHI) policies are designed to provide the policyholder with a benefit if s/he is unable to work through sickness or if s/he needs medical expenses or long-term care.

This would provide Henry with an income in the event of illness – again useful given his mortgage, and would avoid the need to liquidate other assets to pay the mortgage or ongoing costs.

Critical illness insurance

These policies provide a capital sum where a critical illness (from a large range listed in the policy) is diagnosed.

For the same reasons above, Henry should consider this in conjunction with permanent health insurance.

Note: Marks will also be given for other relevant protection products, e.g. specific mortgage protection insurance linked to an event other than death.

(ii) **Provision of protection: company or individual**

If any of the policies are taken out and paid for by Henry personally, then there will be no tax relief on the premiums, but neither will there normally be any tax payable on the proceeds or benefits received.

If Happy Home Ltd were to pay the premiums on a policy taken out by Henry, and of which he was the direct beneficiary, then this will constitute an employment benefit, on the grounds that the company will have satisfied a personal liability of Henry's.

Accordingly, income tax and national insurance contributions will be payable on the benefit.

If, however, Happy Home Ltd were to decide to offer protection benefits to their employees on a group basis (and not just to Henry), then it would be possible to avoid a charge under the benefits rules and/or obtain a lower rate of premium under a collective policy.

For example:

- *Death in service benefit*

  A death in service benefit of up to four times remuneration can be provided as part of a registered pension scheme. No benefit charge arises on Henry and any lump sum will be paid tax free. This could be considered a substitute for a term assurance policy.

- *Group PHI*

  If a group permanent health insurance policy were taken out, no benefit charge would arise on Henry, but any benefits payable under the policy would be paid to Happy Home Ltd in the first instance.

  When subsequently paid on to Henry, such payments would be treated as arising from his employment and subject to PAYE and national insurance as for normal salary payments.

- *Group CII*

  If a group critical illness policy were taken out, again no benefit charge would arise on Henry.

  In this case as with group PHI payments, any benefits payable under the policy received by Henry directly from Happy Home Ltd would be considered as derived from his employment and subject to income tax and national insurance.

  Such a charge to tax and national insurance would however be avoided if these payments were made in terms of a trust.

				Marks
(a)	**(i)**	Shares transferred less than market value		0.5
		Calculation of gain arising		0.5
		Application to gift of 3,000 shares		<u>0.5</u>
			Max	<u>1.0</u>
	(ii)	Share option not approved		0.5
		Grant		1.0
		Exercise: Price paid v market value		0.5
		Difference charged to income tax		0.5
		Application of national insurance		0.5
		Pass NI liability onto individual		0.5
		Transferred NI reduces income tax		0.5
		Sale: Base cost of shares		0.5
		Capital gains tax on gain		0.5
		Business asset taper relief		0.5
		Timing of taper relief		0.5
		Application to Henry		0.5
		Calculation of amount subject to income tax		0.5
		Calculation of secondary national insurance		0.5
		Calculation of primary national insurance		<u>0.5</u>
			Max	<u>8.0</u>
(b)		Identify EMI scheme as most suited		1.0
		UK trading company		0.5
		Gross assets < £30 million		0.5
		Not controlled by another company		0.5
		Grants per employee (£100,000)		0.5
		Total cap of £3m		0.5
		Reasons of recruitment/retention		0.5
		Qualifying employee: hours		0.5
		Qualifying employee: material interest		0.5
		No income tax/NIC on grant/exercise		0.5
		Meet normal conditions (10 years/MV)		0.5
		Application of CGT and taper relief		0.5
		Timing of taper relief from date of grant		<u>0.5</u>
			Max	<u>6.0</u>
(c)	**(i)**	Life assurance – awareness		1.0
		Term assurance		0.5
		Whole of life assurance		0.5
		Tax free lump sum		0.5
		Permanent health insurance – awareness		1.0
		Description of health insurance		0.5
		How income would be provided		0.5
		Critical illness policies – awareness		1.0
		Description		0.5
		Consider along with health insurance		<u>0.5</u>
			Max	<u>6.0</u>
	(ii)	Henry's personal position: premiums		0.5
		proceeds		0.5
		Benefit		0.5
		IT/NIC on benefit		0.5
		Avoid benefit though collective provision		0.5
		Death in service: benefit		0.5
		treatment		0.5
		Group PHI treatment		1.0
		Group critical illness: normal treatment		0.5
		use of trust		<u>0.5</u>
			Max	<u>4.0</u>
		Total (Max)		<u>25.0</u>

Section 3

JUNE 2006 EXAM QUESTIONS

SECTION A – BOTH QUESTIONS ARE COMPULSORY AND MUST BE ATTEMPTED

1 CHRISTOPHER

Christopher, a widower, died suddenly on 5 February 2007, aged 76. His only child, Eleanor, is 44 years old and single. Eleanor is the sole beneficiary of Christopher's estate.

Christopher had the following income in the tax year 2006/07, prior to his death:

	£
Bank interest (net)	1,600
ISA interest	600
Pension (gross)	16,500
PAYE deducted from pension	2,400

During his lifetime, Christopher had made the following gifts:

(i)   9 August 1999:   Gift of property worth £250,000 to a discretionary trust.

(ii)   10 April 2002:   Gift of £75,000 cash into the same discretionary trust.

On each occasion, Christopher paid any tax due on the gift.

The assets comprised in Christopher's estate were as follows:

	Notes	Market value 5 February 2007 £
Residence		550,000
ISA account		12,000
Cash deposits	(1)	40,000
Shares in Penfold Limited	(1)	85,000
Shares in Boise plc	(2)	see note

Notes:

(1)   In August 2005, Christopher received £30,000 in cash and 5,000 shares in Penfold Limited, with a probate value of £14 each, from his deceased uncle's estate. Inheritance tax of £75,000 was paid on a total chargeable estate of £450,000, as a consequence of the uncle's death.

Penfold Limited is an unquoted UK trading company and the 5,000 shares, which had been owned by Christopher's uncle for five years prior to his death, represent 5% of the company's share capital.

(2) Christopher held 15,000 ordinary £1 shares in Boise plc, a UK quoted company. This holding represents 2% of the company's issued share capital. At 5 February 2007, the cum dividend price per share was 700p – 708p, with marked bargains at 701p, 702p and 707p. A dividend of 18p per share had been declared on 15 January 2007. This was received on 20 February 2007.

Eleanor is wealthy in her own right, and pays income tax at the higher rate. She wishes to gift assets worth £50,000 to her friend, Sam, and has three options under consideration:

(i) Three paintings valued in total at £50,000. Eleanor paid £25,000 for a set of four paintings in June 1995. She sold one painting for £9,000 in January 2001. At that time, the remaining paintings were valued at £31,000.

(ii) Cash of £50,000 from the inheritance she is shortly to receive following the death of her father, Christopher.

(iii) 5,000 shares representing a 5% holding in Grange Limited, an unquoted UK trading company. These shares were acquired by Eleanor for £17,500 in May 1993.

Eleanor has made no previous lifetime gifts for the purposes of inheritance tax (IHT).

Required:

(a) Calculate the income tax (IT) payable/repayable on behalf of Christopher for the income tax year 2006/07. **(5 marks)**

(b) Calculate the inheritance tax (IHT) liability arising as a result of Christopher's death. **(11 marks)**

(c) Evaluate the capital gains tax (CGT) and inheritance tax (IHT) implications of each of the three options being considered by Eleanor, and recommend the most tax efficient solution.

Assume that any gift will be made in June 2007, that Eleanor will have already utilised her CGT annual exemption for the tax year 2007/08 and that gift relief will not be claimed. **(9 marks)**

You should assume that the rates and allowances for the tax year 2006/07 apply throughout this question.

Relevant retail price index figures are:

May 1993   141.1

June 1995   149.8

April 1998   162.6

(25 marks)

2   PAUL AND SHARON

Paul and Sharon are both aged 38, and are married with two children, Gisella, aged 5 and Gavin aged 2.

Paul resigned from his employment with Memphis plc, a quoted UK company, on 1 June 2007. He holds options over 5,000 company shares, granted to him on 25 June 2004. The options are part of an approved company share option plan (CSOP), and the exercise price was agreed at £3·50 per share. The current market value of the shares is £6, and this is unlikely to change in the short term. Paul has one month from the date of his resignation in which to exercise the share options and sell the shares, which are not transferable. He, therefore, intends to do so as soon as possible.

Sharon has been running a business as a sole trader for the past three years. She wishes to incorporate this business, and will hold 100% of the shares issued. Sharon would like part of the consideration for the business to be in cash, but only if no tax is payable as a result. Paul will work for the newly incorporated company. Sharon estimates that the

business is worth £120,000, comprising the following assets:

Asset	Market value £	Indexed gain £
Cash	10,000	–
Goodwill	40,000	40,000
Property	70,000	40,000
Stock	10,000	–
Creditors	(10,000)	–

Both Paul and Sharon expect to be paying income tax at the higher rate in the current tax year 2007/08. Neither Paul nor Sharon has made any capital disposals to date in the tax year 2007/08.

Paul and Sharon wish to set up a discretionary trust for Gisella and Gavin by gifting a residential property into trust. The property, which was acquired for £80,000 in August 2005, is currently worth £160,000 and generates net rental income of £4,000 per annum.

Required:

(a) (i) State the conditions that must be satisfied if the business is to be sold to a company without incurring an immediate charge to capital gains tax (CGT), and advise Sharon whether or not she will be able to take advantage of such relief.

(2 marks)

(ii) Assuming the relief in (i) is available, advise Sharon on the maximum amount of cash she could receive on incorporation, without triggering a capital gains tax (CGT) liability. **(3 marks)**

(iii) State any disadvantages to the relief in (i) that Sharon should be aware of, and identify and describe another relief that she might use. **(4 marks)**

(b) (i) State the condition that would need to be satisfied for the exercise of Paul's share options in Memphis plc to be exempt from income tax and the tax implications if this condition is not satisfied. **(2 marks)**

(ii) Calculate Paul's tax liability if he exercises the share options in Memphis plc and subsequently sells the shares in Memphis plc immediately, as proposed, and show how he may reduce this tax liability. **(4 marks)**

(c) Explain the capital gains tax (CGT) and income tax (IT) issues Paul and Sharon should be aware of in setting up a discretionary trust for Gisella and Gavin.

You are not required to consider inheritance tax (IHT) or stamp duty land tax (SDLT) issues. **(10 marks)**

You should assume that the tax rates and allowances for the tax year 2006/07 apply throughout this question. **(25 marks)**

SECTION B – TWO QUESTIONS ONLY TO BE ATTEMPTED

3   DAMIAN

Damian is the finance director of Linden Limited, a medium sized, unquoted, UK trading company, with a 31 July year end. Damian personally owns 10% of the ordinary issued share capital of Linden Limited, for which he paid £10,000 in June 1998. He estimates that the current market value of Linden Limited is £9 million and that the company will make taxable profits of £1·4 million in the forthcoming year to 31 July 2008.

(a)   Damian believes that Linden Limited should conduct its activities in a socially responsible manner and to this end has proposed that in future all cars purchased by the company should be low emission vehicles. The sales director has stated that several of his staff, who are the main recipients of company cars, other than the directors, are extremely unhappy with this proposal, perceiving it as downgrading their value and status.

The cars currently provided to the sales staff have a list price of £19,600, on which Linden Limited receives a bulk purchase discount of 6% from the dealer, and a CO_2 emission rate of 168 grams/kilometre. The company pays for up to £400 of accessories, of the salesmen's own choice to be fitted to the cars and all of the running costs, including private petrol. The cars are replaced every three years and the 'old' cars are sold at auction, because they are high mileage vehicles.

The low emission cars it is proposed to purchase will have the same list price as the current cars, but the dealer is only prepared to offer a bulk discount of 5% on these vehicles. Damian does not propose to make any other changes to Linden Limited's company car policy or practice.

Required:

(i)   Explain the tax consequences of the proposed move to low emission vehicles for both the individual salesmen and Linden Limited, illustrating your answer by means of relevant calculations of the tax and national insurance (NIC) savings arising.   **(9 marks)**

(ii)   The sales director has suggested to Damian, that to encourage the salesmen to accept the new arrangement, the company should increase the value of the accessories of their own choice that can be fitted to the low emission cars.

State, giving reasons, whether or not Damian should implement the sales director's suggestion.   **(2 marks)**

(b)   Peter, one of Linden Limited's non-executive directors, having lived and worked in the UK for most of his adult life, sold his home near London on 22 March 2007 and, together with his wife (a French citizen), moved to live in a villa which she owns in the south of France. Peter is now demanding that the tax deducted from his director's fees, for the board meetings held on 18 April and 16 May 2007, be refunded, on the grounds that, as he is no longer resident in the UK, he is no longer liable to UK income tax. All of the company's board meetings are held at its offices in Cambridge.

Despite Peter's assurance that none of the other companies of which he is a director has disputed his change of tax status, Damian is uncertain whether he should make the refunds requested. However, as Peter is a friend of the company's founder, Linden Limited's managing director is urging him to do so, stating that if the tax does have to be paid, then Linden Limited could always bear the cost.

Required:

Advise Damian whether Peter is correct in his assertion regarding his tax position and in the case that there is a UK tax liability the implications of the managing director's suggestion. You are not required to consider national insurance (NIC) issues.

(4 marks)

(c)   For commercial reasons, Damian believes that it would be sensible to place a new holding company, Bold plc, over the existing company, Linden Limited. Bold plc would also be unquoted and would acquire the existing Linden Limited shares in exchange for the issue of its own shares.

If the new structure is implemented, Bold plc will provide management services to Linden Limited, but the amount that will be charged for these services is yet to be determined.

Required:

(i)   State the capital gains tax (CGT) issues that Damian should be aware of before disposing of his shares in Linden Limited to Bold plc. Your answer should include details of any conditions that will need to be satisfied if an immediate charge to tax is to be avoided. **(4 marks)**

(ii)   Assuming the new structure is implemented with effect from 1 August 2007, calculate the level of management charge that should be made by Bold plc to Linden Limited for the year ended 31 July 2008, so as to minimise the group's overall corporation tax (CT) liability for that year. **(2 marks)**

(iii)   State the value added tax (VAT) and stamp duty (SD) issues arising as a result of inserting Bold plc as a holding company and identify any planning actions that can be taken to defer or minimise these tax costs. **(4 marks)**

You should assume that the corporation tax rates for the Financial Year 2006 and the income tax rates and allowances for the tax year 2006/07 apply throughout this question. **(25 marks)**

4   BILL AND BEN

(a)   For this part, assume today's date is 1 March 2007.

Bill and Ben each own 50% of the ordinary share capital in Flower Limited, an unquoted UK trading company that makes electronic toys. Flower Limited was incorporated on 1 August 2006 with 1,000 £1 ordinary shares, and commenced trading on the same day. The business has been successful, and the company has accumulated a large cash balance of £180,000, which is to be used to purchase a new factory. However, Bill and Ben have received an offer from a rival company, which they are considering. The offer provides Bill and Ben with two alternative methods of payment for the purchase of their shares:

(i)   £480,000 for the company, inclusive of the £180,000 cash balance.

(ii)   £300,000 for the company assuming the cash available for the factory purchase is extracted prior to sale.

Bill and Ben each currently receive a gross salary of £3,750 per month from Flower Limited. Part of the offer terms is that Bill and Ben would be retained as employees of the company on the same salary.

Neither Bill nor Ben has used any of their capital gains tax annual exemption for the tax year 2006/07.

Required:

(i) Calculate which of the following means of extracting the £180,000 from Flower Limited on 31 March 2007 will result in the highest after tax cash amount for Bill and Ben:

  (1) payment of a dividend, or

  (2) payment of a salary bonus.

  You are not required to consider the corporation tax (CT) implications for Flower Limited in your answer. **(5 marks)**

(ii) Following on from your answer to (i), evaluate the two purchase proposals, and advise Bill and Ben which course of action will result in the highest amount of after tax cash being received by the shareholders if the disposal takes place on 31 March 2007. **(4 marks)**

(iii) State how your answer in (ii) would differ if the sale were to be delayed until August 2007. **(3 marks)**

(b) For this part, assume today's date is 1 May 2011.

Bill and Ben decided not to sell their company, and instead expanded the business themselves. Ben, however, is now pursuing other interests, and is no longer involved with the day to day activities of Flower Limited. Bill believes that the company would be better off without Ben as a voting shareholder, and wishes to buy Ben's shares. However, Bill does not have sufficient funds to buy the shares himself, and so is wondering if the company could acquire the shares instead.

The proposed price for Ben's shares would be £500,000. Both Bill and Ben pay income tax at the higher rate.

Required:

Write a letter to Ben:

(1) stating the income tax (IT) and/or capital gains tax (CGT) implications for Ben if Flower Limited were to repurchase his 50% holding of ordinary shares, immediately in May 2011; and

(2) advising him of any available planning options that might improve this tax position. Clearly explain any conditions which must be satisfied and quantify the tax savings which may result. **(13 marks)**

Assume that the corporation tax rates for the Financial Year 2006 and the income tax rates and allowances for the tax year 2006/07 apply throughout this question.

(25 marks)

5 TAY LIMITED

Assume today's date is 1 May 2007.

Tay Limited is an unquoted trading company with a 31 March year end. It acquired 100% of the shares of another company, Trent Limited, on 1 September 2006. Both companies manufacture engine components.

Trent Limited has been incurring trading losses for some time, and at 1 January 2006 had tax losses of £300,000 (including £60,000 relating to the year ended 31 December 2005). Tay Limited lacks the capacity to take on more work, so intends to transfer several of its orders to Trent Limited. By doing this, it is anticipated that Trent Limited will make small profits in the year to 31 December 2007, and even greater profits in subsequent years, thereby utilising its existing corporation tax losses.

The trading results of the two companies (actual and estimated) are as follows:

Company	Year ended	Taxable profits /(losses) £
Tay Limited	31 March 2007	250,000
Trent Limited	31 December 2006	(120,000)
	31 December 2007	50,000

On 1 January 2007, Tay Limited incurred expenditure of £250,000 on intellectual property. It does not depreciate this amount and so has not claimed any writing down allowances for the expenditure.

Trent Limited owns an old building, which was purchased in September 1997. This building has always been used for the purposes of Trent Limited's trade, but because of its age was not eligible for industrial buildings allowance. The building cost Trent Limited £400,000, and was valued at £300,000 when Trent Limited was acquired by Tay Limited. The building is currently worth £250,000. Tay Limited is planning to sell a capital asset in September 2007, which will realise a capital gain of £75,000 and has recently suggested that Trent Limited sell the old building at the same time in order to take advantage of the capital loss that would arise.

Tay Limited has recently identified an opportunity to purchase either the shares or the assets of Tagus LDA, an engineering company based in Portugal. It is considered that the business of Tagus LDA will remain Portuguese resident irrespective of which acquisition route is taken. Portuguese companies and businesses pay tax on profits at the rate of 27·5%.

A recent investigation of Trent Limited's accounting records has revealed an error in its value added tax (VAT) return submitted for the quarter to 31 March 2007. Although input VAT has been correctly calculated at £40,000, the output VAT stated as £87,500, has been under declared by £55,000. The additional VAT due has not yet been paid.

Required:

(a) (i) State, giving reasons, whether or not Tay Limited is entitled to claim a tax allowance in respect of the purchased intellectual property. **(2 marks)**

(ii) Calculate the corporation tax (CT) payable by Tay Limited for the year ended 31 March 2007, taking advantage of all available reliefs. **(3 marks)**

(iii) Explain the potential corporation tax (CT) implications of Tay Limited transferring work to Trent Limited, and suggest how these can be minimised or eliminated. **(3 marks)**

(b) Advise on the capital gains implications should Trent Limited's old building be sold as proposed. Support your advice with relevant calculations. **(4 marks)**

(c) Briefly outline the corporation tax (CT) issues that Tay Limited should consider when deciding whether to acquire the shares or the assets of Tagus LDA. You are not required to discuss issues relating to transfer pricing. **(7 marks)**

(d) Advise Trent Limited of the consequences arising from the submission of the incorrect value added tax (VAT) return, assuming that the company has previously had a good compliance record with regard to accounting for VAT. **(6 marks)**

(25 marks)

6 ANDREW

Andrew is aged 38 and is single. He is employed as a consultant by Bestadvice & Co and pays income tax at the higher rate.

Andrew is considering investing in a new business, and to provide funds for this investment he has recently disposed of the following assets:

(1) A short leasehold interest in a residential property. Andrew originally paid £50,000 for a 47 year lease of the property in May 1995, and assigned the lease in May 2007 for £90,000.

(2) His holding of £10,000 7% Government Stock, on which interest is payable half-yearly on 20 April and 20 October. Andrew originally purchased this holding on 1 June 1999 for £9,980 and he sold it for £11,250 on 14 March 2006.

Andrew intends to subscribe for ordinary shares in a new company, Scalar Limited, which will be a UK based manufacturing company. Three investors (including Andrew) have been identified, but a fourth investor may also be invited to subscribe for shares. The investors are all unconnected, and would subscribe for shares in equal measure. The intention is to raise £450,000 in this manner. The company will also raise a further £50,000 from the investors in the form of loans. Andrew has been told that he can take advantage of some tax reliefs on his investment in Scalar Limited, but does not know anything about the details of these reliefs

Andrew's employer, Bestadvice & Co, is proposing to change the staff pension scheme from a defined benefit scheme to which the firm and the employees each contribute 6% of their annual salary, to a defined contribution scheme, to which the employees will continue to contribute 6%, but the firm will contribute 8% of their annual salary. The majority of Andrew's colleagues are opposed to this move, but, given the increase in the firm's contribution rate Andrew himself is less sure that the proposal is without merit.

Required:

(a) (i) Calculate the chargeable gain arising on the assignment of the residential property lease in May 2007.   **(2 marks)**

(ii) Advise Andrew of the tax implications arising from the disposal of the 7% Government Stock, clearly identifying the tax year in which any liability will arise and how it will be paid.   **(3 marks)**

(b) (i) Advise Andrew of the income tax (IT) and capital gains tax (CGT) reliefs available on his investment in the ordinary share capital of Scalar Limited, together with any conditions which need to be satisfied.

Your answer should clearly identify any steps that should be taken by Andrew and the other investors to obtain the maximum relief.   **(13 marks)**

(ii) State the taxation implications of both equity and loan finance from the point of view of a company.   **(3 marks)**

(c) State the key characteristics of a defined benefit and a defined contribution pension scheme, explaining why the employer and the employees might have differing views as to the merits of each.   **(4 marks)**

You should assume that the rates and allowances for the tax year 2006/07 apply throughout this question.   **(25 marks)**

Relevant retail price index figures are:

May 1995   149.6
April 1998   162.6

Relevant extracts from the leasehold depreciation tables are as follows:

35 years   91.981
47 years   98.902

Section 4

ANSWERS TO JUNE 2006 EXAM QUESTIONS

SECTION A

1 CHRISTOPHER

(a) **Income tax computation for 2006/07**

Christopher will be taxed on income up to the date of his death. His income tax computation for the tax year 2006/07 is as follows:

	Notes	£
Pension		16,500
Bank interest	(1)	2,000
ISA interest	(2)	–
Dividends from Boise plc	(3)	3,000
Statutory total income		21,500
Less: Age allowance	(4)	(6,720)
Taxable income		14,780

Income tax

£		
2,150 × 10% (other income)		215
7,630 × 22% (other income)		1,679
9,780		
2,000 × 20% (savings)		400
3,000 × 10% (dividends)		300
14,780		

	Notes	£
Income tax liability		2,594
Less: Tax deducted at source		
UK dividends	(5)	(300)
PAYE		(2,400)
Bank interest (2,000 × 20%)		(400)
Income tax refund due		(506)

Notes:

(1) Bank interest = £1,600 × 100/80 = £2,000

(2) Interest on ISAs is not taxable

(3)   Dividends declared prior to the date of death are taxable. The amount is 15,000 × £0·18 × (100/90) = £3,000.

(4)   Christopher is entitled to a full age allowance (£7,420) in the year of death, but reduced by £700 ((21,500 – 20,100)/2) = £6,720.

(5)   Tax credits on UK dividends are not refundable, but can be used to part satisfy any liability due.

(b)   **Inheritance tax liability as a result of Christopher's death**

Lifetime tax

The transfers into the discretionary trust are chargeable lifetime transfers (CLT). Christopher agreed to pay any IHT the gifts are net of tax and will have to be grossed up.

1.   *Gift of property on 9 August 1999*

As there are no cumulative lifetime transfers in the previous seven years, the nil rate band is available.

	£
CLT	250,000
Less: Annual Exemptions: 1999/00	(3,000)
1998/98	(3,000)
	244,000

The gift is covered fully by the nil rate band, and no lifetime tax is payable. £41,000 (£285,000 – £244,000) remains of the nil rate band.

2.   *Gift of cash on 10 April 2002*

	£
CLT	75,000
Less: Annual Exemptions: 2002/03	(3,000)
2001/02	(3,000)
	69,000

The total net cumulative lifetime transfers in the last seven years is £313,000 (244,000 + 69,000).

The lifetime tax would have been as follows:

£	£
285,000 × 0%	0
28,000 × 20/80	7,000
313,000	7,000

The grossed up cumulative lifetime transfers are £320,000 (313,000 + 7,000).

Additional tax at death

Gift of property

As the gift was both made more than seven years before the death of Christopher, and falls entirely within the nil rate band, no IHT is payable.

Gift of cash

The gift was made within seven years of Christopher's death.

Additional IHT is payable, calculated as follows:

	£	£
285,000 × 0%		0
35,000 × 40%		14,000
320,000		
Less Taper relief (4–5 years) 40%	(5,600)	
	8,400	
Less: Tax paid during lifetime	(7,000)	
Tax due	1,400	

Estate at death

	Notes	£	£
Shares in Boise plc	(1)		105,300
Shares in Penfold Limited		85,000	
Less: Business property relief (BPR)	(2)	(85,000)	–
ISA account			12,000
Income tax refund			506
Cash deposits			40,000
			157,806
Residence			550,000
Chargeable estate			707,806
Less: IHT nil band	(3)		(209,000)
Taxable amount			498,806
IHT at 40%			199,522
Less: Quick succession relief	(4)		(4,000)
IHT payable			195,522

Notes:

(1) The shares in Boise plc are valued at the lower of:

   (i) quarter up $(700 + 0.25(708 – 700)) = 702p$

   (ii) average of marked bargains $(701 + 707)/2 = 704p$

   i.e. 702p per share. The shareholding is thus worth £105,300 (15,000 × £7·02).

   No BPR applies as the shares represent a minority holding in a quoted company.

(2) BPR will apply at the rate of 100% as the shares are in an unquoted company and so are relevant business property. Although Christopher had not held the shares for a period of two years, the shares were acquired on the death of his uncle, at which time the shares did qualify for BPR, so BPR is also available on this (second) death.

(3) The total gross chargeable lifetime transfers in the last seven years is £76,000 (69,000 + 7,000). Thus, £209,000 (285,000 – 76,000) remains of the nil rate band.

(4) Christopher has already suffered IHT on the transfer to him of the cash sum from his uncle's estate, which is now included in his death estate. Quick succession relief (QSR) applies to reduce this by applying a credit.

The relief will be at 80%, as the legacy was received 1–2 years ago.

The average estate rate on his uncle's estate = 75,000/450,000 × 100 = 16.667%.

The chargeable value of the legacy received by Christopher is:

	£	£
Cash		30,000
Penfold shares (5,000 x £14)	70,000	
Less BPR (100%)	(70,000)	
	———	Nil
Value of legacy		30,000

QSR is therefore calculated as follows:

£30,000 × 16.667% × 80% = £,4000

Key answer tips

QSR was the trickiest part of this question. First you need to identify that it is available which would have earned credit. Then perform the detailed calculation which was not straightforward.

(c) **Capital gains tax and inheritance tax implications**

(i) **Gift of Paintings**

Capital gains tax

The paintings form part of a set, of which part was disposed of in 2001. The cost disposed of at that time was £5,625 (25,000 × 9,000/(9,000 + 31,000)), and so the remaining cost is £19,375 (25,000 – 5,625).

The capital gain on disposal will be as follows:

	£
Deemed proceeds	50,000
Less: Cost	(19,375)
Unindexed gain	30,625
Indexation: 162·6 – 149·8/149·8 = 0·085 × 19,375	(1,647)
Indexed gain	28,978
Gain chargeable after taper relief:	
60% (non-business asset/9 + 1 years)	17,387
Capital gains tax at 40%	£6,955

Inheritance tax

The gift counts as a potentially exempt transfer (PET) for IHT purposes. Two annual exemptions of £3,000 are available, and the remaining PET of £44,000

$(50,000 - (2 \times 3,000))$, is covered by the nil rate band, and will fall out of Eleanor's taxable estate if she survives for seven years from the date of the gift.

(ii) **Gift of cash**

Capital gains tax

A gift of cash does not constitute a chargeable disposal for CGT.

Inheritance tax

The gift will be treated as a PET with the same consequences as outlined above. However, Eleanor has the option of altering her late father's will, using a deed of variation. This will effectively rewrite Christopher's will so that the £50,000 passes directly to her friend Sam. The effect of this is that the gift never forms part of Eleanor's estate. As the £50,000 is a general (cash) legacy the IHT will be payable out of the residue of the estate and will thus be borne by Eleanor, just as it would have been if no variation of the will had taken place.

(iii) **Gift of shares in Grange Limited**

Capital gains tax

The shares acquired form part of the FA1985 pool. The cost and indexed cost are calculated as follows:

	No. of shares	Cost	Indexed cost
		£	£
December 1986: acquisition	5,000	17,500	17,500
Indexation to April 1998: $(162 \cdot 6 - 141 \cdot 1)/141 \cdot 1$			2,667
	5,000	17,500	20,167

	£
Deemed proceeds	50,000
Less: Cost	(17,500)
Unindexed gain	32,500
Indexation	(2,667)
Indexed gain	29,833
Chargeable gain after taper relief:	
25% (business asset/9 years)	7,458
Capital gains tax at 40%	2,983

Inheritance tax

A gift of shares in a trading company qualifies as a PET, but the gift will be covered by business property relief (BPR) at 100% as the shares in an unquoted trading company are relevant business property.

Eleanor should choose option (ii) by varying her father's will, as there will be no CGT or IHT implications as a result.

Key answer tips

An appreciation of the CGT and IHT implications of a particular course of action is an important skill for this examination which you need to be able to apply.

In addition, the question specifically asked you to recommend the most tax-efficient solution. As long as your conclusion s consistent with the points you have made, and figures you have calculated previously, the marks will be given.

ACCA marking scheme		Marks
(a)	ISA interest not taxable	0.5
	Bank interest (gross up)	0.5
	Dividend (gross up)	0.5
	Age allowance: correct allowance	0.5
	full allowance in year of death	0.5
	restriction due to income	0.5
	Tax liability calculated at correct rates	1.0
	Tax credits (including PAYE) offset correctly	1.0
	Max	5.0
(b)	Gifts into trust are chargeable lifetime transfers	0.5
	First gift: two annual exemptions (correct years)	0.5
	calculation of nil rate band remaining	0.5
	Second gift: two annual exemptions (correct years)	0.5
	correct gross-up calculation	1.0
	40% death rate	0.5
	Taper relief/rate (2 × 0.5)	1.0
	Less: lifetime tax paid	0.5
	Christopher's estate on death:	
	quoted shares – correct valuation	1.0
	– no BPR	0.5
	unquoted shares	0.5
	100% BPR	0.5
	tax refund	0.5
	ISA	0.5
	cash/residence	0.5
	correct restriction of nil rate band	0.5
	tax at 40%	0.5
	Quick succession relief:	
	awareness	0.5
	correct percentage	0.5
	correct calculation basis	1.0
	Max	11.0
(c)	Gift of paintings:	
	part of set/part disposal rules	0.5
	cost disposed of in 2001/cost remaining	0.5
	indexation	0.5
	taper relief/non business/rate (2 × 0·5)	1.0
	CGT at 40%	0.5
	PET for IHT	0.5
	availability of two annual exemptions	0.5
	no IHT/within nil band	0.5
	falls out of account after seven years	0.5
	Gift of cash	
	exempt for CGT purposes	0.5
	PET if made direct by Eleanor	0.5
	alter will so that gift passes directly from estate	0.5
	result is that IHT paid re estate is not affected	0.5

Gift of shares		
part of FA1985 pool		0.5
indexation – disposal cost		0.5
taper relief/business asset		0.5
CGT at 40%		0.5
PET but 100% BPR available		0.5
Recommend gift of cash by varying will		0.5
Total marks available		10.0
	Max	9.0
Total		20

2   PAUL AND SHARON

(a)   (i)   **Incorporation relief**

The following conditions must be observed for incorporation relief to be available:

1.   The transferor must be a person and not a company.

2.   The business must continue to operate as a going concern.

3.   All of the assets of the business (cash balances excepted) must be transferred.

4.   The consideration must be satisfied (wholly or partly) in the form of shares issued by the company to the transferor.

Sharon meets all of the requirements, and so incorporation relief will be available to defer the capital gains tax which would otherwise have been payable, unless she elects otherwise.

Key answer tips

This part required a textbook answer to the main incorporation relief conditions. However, the question also specifically asked you to advise Sharon as to whether or not it would be advisable to her to claim incorporation relief.

(ii)   **Maximum amount of cash to receive on incorporation**

As Sharon is entitled to the full rate of business asset taper relief, any gain will be reduced by 75%. The position is maximised where the chargeable gain equals Sharon's unused capital gains tax annual exemption of £8,800. Thus, before taper relief, the gain she requires is £35,200 (1/0·25 × £8,800).

The amount to be held over is therefore £44,800 (80,000 – 35,200). Where part of the consideration is in the form of cash, the gain eligible for incorporation relief is calculated using the formula:

Gain deferred = Gain × value of shares issued/total consideration

The formula is manipulated on the following basis:

£44,800	=	£80,000 × (shares/120,000)
Shares/120,000	=	£44,800/80,000
Shares	=	£44,800 × 120,000/80,000

i.e. £67,200.

As the total consideration is £120,000, this means that Sharon can take £52,800 (£120,000 – £67,200) in cash without any CGT consequences.

(iii) **Disadvantages of incorporation relief**

There are several disadvantages to incorporation relief as follows:

1. The requirement to transfer all business assets to the company means that it will not be possible to leave behind certain assets, such as the property. This might lead to a double tax charge (sale of the property, then extraction of sale proceeds) at a future date.

2. Taper relief is lost on the transfer of the business. This means that any disposal of chargeable business assets (the shares) within two years of the incorporation will lead to a higher chargeable gain, as the full rate of business asset taper relief will not be available.

3. The relief does not eliminate the tax charge, it merely defers the payment of tax until some future event. The deferred gain will become taxable when Sharon sells her shares in the company.

Alternative relief

Gift relief could be used instead of incorporation relief. The assets would be gifted to the company for no consideration, with the base cost of the assets to the company being reduced by the deferred gain arising. Unlike incorporation relief, gift relief applies to individual assets used in a trade and not to an entire business. This is particularly useful if the transferor wishes to retain some assets, such as property outside the company, as not all assets have to be transferred.

Note: If the business was non-trading, incorporation relief would still be available, but gift relief would not. However, this restriction should not apply to Sharon and gift relief remains an option in this case.

(b)   (i) **Approved share scheme**

Paul has options in an HMRC approved share scheme. Under such schemes, no tax liabilities arise either on the grant or exercise of the option. The excess of the proceeds over the price paid for the shares (the exercise price) is charged to capital gains tax on their disposal.

However, in order to secure this treatment, one of the conditions to be satisfied is that the options cannot be exercised within three years of the date of grant. If Paul were to exercise his options now (i.e. before the third anniversary of the grant), the exercise would instead be treated as an unapproved exercise. At that date, income tax would be charged on the difference between the market value of the shares on exercise and the price paid to exercise the option.

(ii) **Tax liabilities on the exercise of share options**

Paul's income tax liability would thus be as follows:

	£
Market value of shares on exercise date (5,000 × 6·00)	30,000
Price paid to exercise option (5,000 × 3·50)	(17,500)
Taxable income	12,500
Income tax at 40%	5,000
Class 1 employees national insurance at 1%	125
Total income tax and national insurance payable	5,125

Tax liabilities on the sale of shares

On immediate sale of the shares, no capital gains tax would be due as the shares will not have increased in value.

However, if Paul were to exercise his options after 25 June 2007, then he would be subject to capital gains tax on the subsequent sale only.

Paul's capital gains tax liability would be as follows:

	£
Proceeds	30,000
Price paid to exercise option (5,000 × 3·50)	(17,500)
Chargeable gain (see Note)	12,500
Less: Annual exemption	(8,800)
Taxable gain	3,700
Capital gains tax at 40%	1,480

Note: Taper relief only runs from the date of exercise of the options, therefore none is available.

As a result of deferring the exercise date, Paul will save tax of £3,645 (5,125 – 1,480).

(c) Setting up a discretionary trust

Key answer tips

The original question required consideration of setting up an ordinary discretionary trust compared with a specific accumulation and maintenance trust. However, for June 2007 exams, the only trusts for which the CGT implications are examinable are ordinary discretionary trusts. The question and answer for part (c) has therefore been amended accordingly.

Capital gains tax issues

As the trust is created in the settlors' (Paul and Sharon's) lifetime its creation will constitute a chargeable disposal for capital gains tax. Also, as the settlors and trustees are connected persons, the disposal will be deemed to be at market value, resulting in a chargeable gain of £80,000 (160,000 – 80,000). No taper relief will be available as the property is a non-business asset, and has been held for less than three years, but annual exemptions of £17,600 (2 × £8,800) will be available.

However, in the case of a discretionary trust, gift hold over relief will be available. This is because the gift will constitute a chargeable lifetime transfer and because there is an immediate charge to inheritance tax (even though no tax is payable due to the nil rate band).

The use of a basic discretionary trust will thus facilitate the deferral of an immediate capital gains tax charge of £24,960 (62,400 × 40%). If/when the property is disposed of, however, the trustees will pay capital gains tax on the deferred gain at the trust income tax rate of 40%, and have an annual exemption of only £4,400 (50% of the normal individual rate) available to them.

A chargeable disposal between connected persons will also arise for the purposes of capital gains tax if/when the property vests in a beneficiary, i.e. one or more of the beneficiaries becomes absolutely entitled to all or part of the income or capital of the trust. Gift hold over relief will again be available on all assets in the case of a discretionary trust.

Income tax issues

The trust will have taxable property income in the form of net rents from its creation and in future years is also likely to have other investment income, probably in the form of interest, to the extent that monies are retained in the trust.

The trustees will pay tax at the standard trust rate of 40% on income other than dividend income (32·5%), except to the extent of

(1) the first £1,000 of taxable income, which is taxed at the rate that would otherwise apply to such income (i.e. 22% for non-savings (rental) income, 20% for savings income (interest) and 10% for dividends) but, only to the extent that it is not distributed; and

(2) the legitimate trust management expenses, which are offsettable for the purposes of the higher trust tax rates against the income with the lowest rate(s) of normal tax and so bear tax only at that rate.

The higher trust tax rate always applies to income that is distributed, other than to the extent that it has been treated as the settlor's income, and taxed at that settlor's marginal tax rate.

As Paul and Sharon intend to create a trust for their unmarried minor (under 18) children, then even if the trust specifically excludes them from any benefit under the trust, the trust income will be treated as theirs for income tax purposes to the extent that it constitutes income paid for on behalf (including maintenance payments) of Gisella and Gavin; except where the total income arising does not exceed £100 gross per annum.

Key answer tips

The question only asked for the income tax and CGT issues of setting up a trust. A discussion of the inheritance tax issues was not required. You need to remember to read the specific requirements of questions carefully and confine your answer to those requirements.

ACCA marking scheme			Marks
(a)	(i)	Transfer must be by a person	0.5
		Business must be transferred as a going concern	0.5
		Transfer must comprise all assets apart from cash	0.5
		Transfer wholly or partly in exchange for shares	0.5
		Application to Sharon	0.5
		Max	2.0
	(ii)	Availability of annual exemption	0.5
		Availability of taper relief at business rates	0.5
		Taper relief rate (75%)	0.5
		Calculation of gain required/held over	0.5
		Formula for calculating gain to be rolled over	0.5
		Calculation of potential tax-free consideration	1.0
		Max	3.0

	(iii)	Must put all assets into the company	0.5
		Double tax on property: sale/extraction of proceeds	0.5
		Loss of taper relief history on incorporation	0.5
		Sale within two years gives higher tax	0.5
		Deferral, not reduction in tax	0.5
		Gift relief: awareness	0.5
		Gain deferred set against base cost of new asset	0.5
		Applies to trade, not business	0.5
		Not all assets need to be transferred	0.5
		Max	4.0
(b)	(i)	Approved options CGT treatment	0.5
		Requirement to exercise after three years	0.5
		If condition not met, exercise treated as unapproved	0.5
		Taxed as employment income on exercise if before 25 June	0.5
		Amount taxed is market value price paid on exercise	0.5
		Max	2.0
	(ii)	Calculation: amount taxable	0.5
		income tax at 40%	0.5
		national insurance at 1%	0.5
		If exercise after 25 June no tax on exercise, capital gains treatment on sale	0.5
		No taper relief/runs from date of exercise/not available	0.5
		Calculation: gain	0.5
		annual exemption	0.5
		capital gains tax at 40%	0.5
		Max	4.0
(c)		CGT: creation: chargeable disposal	0.5
		deemed market value/connected persons	0.5
		no taper relief	0.5
		two annual exemptions	0.5
		if discretionary trust gift hold over relief available	0.5
		IHT chargeable transfer/all assets	0.5
		immediate tax benefit £24,960	0.5
		deferral of liability only	0.5
		disposals by trust: CGT at 40%	0.5
		annual exemption: 50% normal rate	0.5
		vesting: charge on similar basis to creation	0.5
		gift hold over relief discretionary trust	0.5
		IT: standard trust rate 40% (32·5%)	0.5
		first £1,000: 22%/20%/10%	0.5
		only if not distributed	0.5
		trustees' management expenses:	
		allowable re higher rate	0.5
		chargeable lowest of normal rates	0.5
		parental trust for minor children	0.5
		treated as income of parents if paid for/on behalf of	0.5
		total income not >£100	0.5
		Max	10.0
TOTAL			25.0

3   DAMIAN

(a) (i)   **Tax consequences of moving to low emission vehicles**

Individual salesmen

The taxable benefit is determined by the list price of the vehicle plus the cost of the accessories (£20,000) and the CO_2 emission rate. The current vehicles have a CO_2 emission rate of 168 grams/kilometre, so the benefit will be calculated at the rate of 20% ((168 – 140)/5 + 15), resulting in a total annual car and car fuel benefit charge of £6,880 (20,000 × 20% + 14,400 × 20%).

The low emission vehicles will be chargeable at the basic percentage rate of 15% resulting in a total annual car and fuel benefit charge of £5,160 (20,000 × 15% + 14,400 × 15%).

The salesmen will thus make an annual income tax saving at their marginal rate of tax, i.e. £378 (1,720 × 22%) if they are basic rate taxpayers and £688 (1,720 × 40%) if they are higher rate taxpayers.

Linden Limited

The current vehicles will be classed as 'expensive' cars based on the discounted list price plus the cost of the accessories of £18,824 (19,600 × 94% + 400). The annual writing down allowances will thus be restricted to £3,000 throughout the period of ownership, but there will be no restriction of the balancing allowance available on disposal.

The low emission vehicles will be eligible for a 100% first year allowance of £19,020 (19,600 × 95% + 400), but there will also be a balancing charge on disposal equivalent to the sales proceeds. Therefore, the total of the allowances available over the life of the cars will be effectively the same in both cases.

As a single company with taxable profits of £1·4 million, Linden Limited will pay corporation tax at the small companies marginal rate of 32·75% in the year to 31 July 2008, giving a tax benefit in that year of £5,247 for each low emission car purchased ((19,020 – 3,000) × 32·75%).

The company will also make an annual saving in terms of the Class 1A national insurance contributions payable on the salesmen's benefits of £220 ((6,880 – 5,160) × 12·8%). But, as these Class 1A contributions are deductible for corporation tax, the net saving will only be £148 (220 × (100 – 32·75)%).

As the VAT liability payable on the provision of private fuel is based on engine capacity (not the CO2 emission rate) this will not necessarily be affected.

(ii)   **Increasing the value of the accessories**

Damian should not agree to the sales director's suggestion. The salesmen will each make a significant annual income tax saving under the proposal, whereas the company will also be offset (at least partly) by the reduction in the dealer's bulk discount.

Further, 100% first year allowance tax incentive for low emission cars is not guaranteed beyond 31 March 2008, and it is unlikely that any change in policy with regards to the provision of additional accessories will, once implemented, be easily reversible.

Key answer tips

The first part of this question requires an explanation of the move towards low emission cars. Most marks are therefore available for a narrative discussion, not for the calculations.

In the second part, the requirement needs to be red carefully to ensure that you do not consider the wrong suggestion. The sales director's suggestion concerned the provision of additional accessories, not the introduction of a low-emission vehicle which was Damian's proposal.

(b)   **Tax status of Peter**

Peter will have been resident and ordinarily resident in the UK. When such individuals leave the UK for a purpose other than to take up full time employment abroad, they normally continue to still be so regarded unless their absence spans a complete tax year.

However, where someone intends to live permanently abroad or to do so for a period of at least three tax years, they may be treated as non-resident and non-ordinarily resident from the day after the date of their departure, if they can provide evidence to HMRC of that intention.

Selling a residence in the UK and setting up home abroad will normally constitute such evidence. However to retain non-resident status the intention must actually be fulfilled, and visits to the UK must not exceed 182 days in any tax year or average more than 90 days per year over a period of four tax years.

Given that Peter would appear to have several company directorships in the UK, it is possible that he might fail to satisfy the 90 day average 'substantial visits' rule.

Even if Peter is classed as non-resident, any remuneration earned in the UK will still be liable to UK income tax, and subject to PAYE, unless it is for duties incidental to an overseas employment, which is unlikely to be the case for fees paid to a nonexecutive director for attending board meetings. Thus, income tax should still be deducted from the fees under PAYE.

Where PAYE should have been deducted from a director's emoluments and it has not been, but the tax is nevertheless accounted for by the company to HMRC, then to the extent that the tax is not reimbursed by the director, he will be treated as receiving a benefit equivalent to the amount of tax.

(c)   (i)   **Capital gains tax issues – disposal of shares**

The proposed transaction broadly falls under the 'paper for paper' rules. Where this is the case, chargeable gains do not arise. Instead, the new holding stands in the shoes (and inherits the base cost) of the original holding.

The company issuing the new shares must:

(i)   end up with more than 25% of the ordinary share capital or a majority of the voting power of the old company,

OR

(ii)   make a general offer to shareholders in the old company with a condition which would give the acquiring company control of the company if accepted.

The exchange must be for bona fide commercial reasons and not have as its main purpose (or one of its main purposes) the avoidance of capital gains tax or corporation tax.

The issue of shares by Bold plc satisfies these conditions, thus Damian, as a shareholder of Linden Limited, will not be taxed on the exchange of shares.

(ii) **Management charge to minimise group corporation tax**

For the year ended 31 July 2008, there will be two associated companies in the group. Bold plc will count as an associated company as it is not dormant throughout the period in question. As a result, the corporation tax limits will be divided by two (i.e. the number of associates) giving an upper limit of £750,000 (£1·5 million/2). As Linden Limited is anticipated to make profits of £1·4 million in the year to 31 July 2008 it will pay corporation tax at the rate of 30%.

Bold plc can earn trading profits up to £150,000 (£300,000/2) and pay tax at the rate of 19%. It will therefore minimise the group's corporation tax liability if maximum use is made of this small companies rate band, as it will save £16,500 (150,000 × (30% − 19%)) of corporation tax for the year to 31 July 2008. Bold plc should therefore make a management charge of sufficient size to give it profits for that year equal to £150,000.

While the transfer pricing legislation does not apply to small and medium sized UK enterprises, Bold plc should nevertheless ensure that there is evidence to support the actual charge made in terms of the services provided.

(iii) **VAT issues in changing group structure**

Bold plc will be making a taxable supply of services, likely to exceed the VAT threshold. It should therefore consider registering for VAT – either immediately on a voluntary basis, or when its cumulative taxable supplies in the previous twelve months exceed £61,000.

As an alternative, the new group can apply for a group VAT registration. This will simplify its VAT administration as intragroup transactions are broadly disregarded for VAT purposes, and only one VAT return is required for the group as a whole.

Stamp duty issues in changing group structure

Stamp duty normally applies at 0·5% on the consideration payable in respect of transactions in shares. However, an exemption is available in the case of a takeover, reconstruction or amalgamation where there is no real change in ownership, i.e. the new shareholdings mirror the old shareholdings, and the transaction is for commercial purposes. The insertion of a new holding company over an existing company, as proposed here, would qualify for this exemption.

There is no VAT on transactions in shares.

				Marks
		ACCA marking scheme		
(a)	(i)	Individual salesmen:		
		List price plus the cost of accessories/£20,000		0.5
		Percentage based on CO2 emission rate		0.5
		Current vehicles 20% rate		0.5
		Low emission vehicles 15% rate		0.5
		Calculation of benefit charge (incl fuel) (2 × 0·5)		1.0
		Annual income tax saving at marginal tax rate		0.5
		Linden Limited		
		Cost based on discounted list price plus the cost of the accessories (£18,824/£19,020)		0.5
		Current vehicles 'expensive' cars		0.5
		Annual WDA restricted to £3,000		0.5
		No restriction of balancing allowance on disposal		0.5
		Low emission vehicles 100% FYA		0.5
		Balancing charge on disposal		0.5
		Timing issue/deferral effect only over vehicle life		0.5
		Corporation tax at small companies marginal rate/32·75%		0.5
		Illustrate benefit in year of purchase (£5,247)		0.5
		Class 1A NIC saving because of reduction in salesmen's benefit		0.5
		Effectively only net saving because NIC deductible for corporation tax		0.5
		VAT private fuel charge based on engine capacity not emission rate		0.5
			Max	9.0
	(ii)	Should not agree		0.5
		Salesmen will get significant annual tax saving		0.5
		Benefit offset by reduction in bulk discount		0.5
		100% FYA only to 31 March 2008		0.5
			Max	2.0
(b)		Resident and ordinarily resident		0.5
		Absent for a complete tax year, if not for full time employment		0.5
		Intend to live abroad for at least three tax years/permanently		0.5
		From day after date of departure		0.5
		If can evidence intention		0.5
		182/90 day visit rules (2 × 0·5)		1.0
		Application of above to Peter		0.5
		Still subject to UK tax/PAYE even if non-resident		0.5
		Non-incidental duties performed in UK		0.5
		Benefit if accounted for by company and not reimbursed		0.5
			Max	4.0
(c)	(i)	No chargeable gains on share for share exchange		0.5
		New holding stands in shoes of old holding		0.5
		Conditions: more than 25% share capital		0.5
		majority of voting power		0.5
		general offer to shareholders		0.5
		gaining control if offer accepted		0.5
		Bona fide commercial reasons		0.5
		Not for avoidance of CGT/CT		0.5
			Max	4.0

(ii)	Two associates/limits divided by 2		0.5
	Recognition of different tax rates for Bold/Linden		0.5
	Ability to use small companies rate for first £150,000		0.5
	Quantify corporation tax saved		0.5
	Awareness of transfer pricing/SME exemption		0.5
		Max	2.0
(iii)	Supply of services is a taxable supply		0.5
	Requirement to register for VAT		0.5
	Alternative of group registration		0.5
	Administrative benefits (2 × 0·5)		1.0
	Stamp duty usually at 0·5% on shares		0.5
	Exemption where no real change in ownership		0.5
	Commercial rationale		0.5
	Would apply on insertion of holding company		0.5
		Max	4.0
	TOTAL		25.0

4   BILL AND BEN

(a)   (i)   **After tax cash from extracting £180,000 from Flower Ltd**

Income tax computation before payment of dividend/bonus:

	£
Employment income (8 × 3,750)	30,000
Personal allowance	(5,035)
Taxable income	24,965

£8,335 (33,300 – 24,965) remains of the basic rate band for both Bill and Ben.

As they each receive the same amount the calculations are the same for each of them.

Payment as dividend	£
Net payment	180,000
Gross equivalent (100/90)	200,000 (i.e. this is £100,000 each)
Income tax:	

£		£
8,335 at 10%		833
91,665 at 32·5%		29,791
100,000		30,624
Less: Tax credit		(10,000)
Income tax payable		20,624
Cash received		90,000
Income tax payable		(20,624)
Cash in hand after tax		69,376

Payment as salary   £

Gross salary payment   180,000 (i.e. this is £90,000 each)

Income tax:

£	£
8,335 at 22%	1,834
81,665 at 40%	32,666
90,000	34,500

Employees national insurance (W)	1,254
Total income tax and national insurance	35,754
Gross salary	90,000
Income tax and national insurance	(35,754)
Cash in hand after tax	54,246

Conclusion

As a result, Bill and Ben would each be better off by £15,130 (69,376 – 54,246). if the cash were extracted by way of dividend.

Tutorial note: In this answer the employers' national insurance liability on the salary has been ignored. Credit would be given to a candidate who recognised this issue.

Working: **Employees national insurance**

$(33,540 - 30,000) = 3,540 \times 2$ is payable at the 11% rate, thus:

£	£
3,540 at 11%	389
86,460 at 1%	865
90,000	1,254

Key answer tips

Calculations could be performed for Bill and Ben separately, by dividing the £180,000 equally between them, or as a single computation. However, in the latter case, you need to remember to deduct two personal allowances and two starting rate bands etc.

(ii) **After tax cash received by shareholders**

	Proposal 1 £	Proposal 2 £
Proceeds (divided equally)	240,000	150,000
Less: cost	(500)	(500)
Gain (1)	239,500	149,500
Less: annual exemption	(8,800)	(8,800)
Taxable gain	230,700	140,700
Capital gains tax:		
at 20% (£8,335/nil (2))	1,667	–
at 40% (£222,365/140,700)	88,946	56,280
	90,613	56,280
Cash remaining after capital gain	149,387	93,720
Cash remaining after dividend (above)	–	69,376
Total cash remaining	149,387	163,096

Note:

(1) As less than one year has elapsed since the shares were issued, no taper relief applies.

(2) In the case of proposal 2, Bill and Ben will have no basic rate band left because of the cash extracted as a dividend.

Bill and Ben are each £13,709 (£163,096 – 149,387) better off as a result of taking the second of the two proposals.

(iii) **If the sale is delayed**

If the sale is delayed until August 2007, then Bill and Ben will have held the shares for more than one year. Flower Limited is an unquoted trading company, and so the shares are a qualifying asset for business asset taper relief which will apply at the one year rate of 50%.

The revised position will be as follows:

	£	£
Gain (as before)	239,500	149,500
Taper relief		
(business asset/1 year)	119,750	74,750
Less: annual exemption	(8,800)	(8,800)
Taxable gain	110,950	65,950
Capital gains tax at 40% (Note)	44,380	26,380
Cash remaining after capital gain	195,620	123,620
Cash remaining after dividend (above)	–	69,376
Total cash remaining	195,620	192,996

Note: As Bill and Ben are to be retained on £3,750 per month, their annual salary of £45,000 will mean that they pay tax at the higher rate (40%) in the tax year 2007/08; thus the whole capital gain will be taxed at their highest marginal rate.

If Bill and Ben delay the sale, they should accept the first proposal (£480,000 for the company). This is £2,624 (195,620 – 192,996) better than the second proposal, and results in £32,524 (195,620 – 163,096) more cash than the better of the original proposals.

The delay in sale will also result in the gain being taxed in the tax year 2007/08 instead of 2006/07. This means that the payment of the capital gains tax liability will be deferred from 31 January 2008 to 31 January 2009.

(b) **Letter to Ben**

[Ben's address]   [Firm's address]

Dear Ben   [Date]

A company purchase of own shares can be subject to capital gains treatment if certain conditions are satisfied. However, one of these conditions is that the shares in question must have been held for a minimum period of five years. As at 1 May 2011, your shares in Flower Limited have only been held for four years and nine months. As a result, the capital gains treatment will not apply.

In the absence of capital gains treatment, the position on a company repurchase of its own shares is that the payment will be treated as an income distribution (i.e. a dividend) in the hands of the recipient. The distribution element is calculated as the proceeds received for the shares less the price paid for them. On the basis that the purchase price is £500,000, then the element of distribution will be £499,500 (500,000 – 500). This would be taxed as follows:

	£
Gross distribution (10/9 × net)	555,000
Income tax at 32·5%	180,375
Less: tax credit	(55,500)
Additional income tax payable	124,875
Cash remaining after tax	375,125

This will be collected through your self-assessment tax return for the tax year 2011/12, and the income tax will be payable by 31 January 2013.

If the company purchase of your shares was deferred until after 1 August 2011, then the five year rule as stated above would be satisfied, and capital gains treatment would be possible, as the other conditions which need to be met are satisfied in your case as follows:

–   The company is an unquoted trading company

–   The individual selling the shares in a UK resident and ordinary resident

–   The purchase of the shares is for the benefit of the company's trade which specifically includes the buying out of a dissenting shareholder

–   The transaction does not form part of a scheme to avoid tax

–   Following the purchase, the individual selling the shares (together with his associates) must:

(i)   reduce their interest in the share capital to 75% or less of the amount held before the repurchase of shares, and

(ii)   not control more than 30% of the issued share capital or voting rights in the company.

The revised tax position would be as follows:

	£
Proceeds	500,000
Less: cost	(500)
Gain	499,500
Taper relief (business asset/5 years)	124,875
Less: annual exemption	(8,800)
Taxable gain	116,075
Capital gains tax at 40%	46,430
Cash remaining after tax	453,570

Thus, if the repurchase of shares could be deferred until August 2011, then you would be £78,445 (453,570 – 375,125) better off being taxed under the capital gains tax rules. As the disposal takes place in 2011/12 the date of payment of the tax liability will be 31 January 2013.

Please note that an advance clearance application is possible, and should be sought, as this will give you clarity on the likely tax treatment. The clearance application should state that the transaction is for bona fide business purposes. HMRC have up to 30 days from receipt to respond to the application.

Please call me if you have any questions.

Yours sincerely

A N Advisor

ACCA marking scheme				Marks
(a)	(i)	Calculation of income		0.5
		Personal allowance		0.5
		Calculation of basic rate band remaining		0.5
		Gross up dividend		0.5
		Tax at 10%/32.5%		0.5
		Use of tax credit		0.5
		Income tax at 22/40%		0.5
		National insurance at 11%/1%		1.0
		Conclude that dividend is better		0.5
			Max	5.0
	(ii)	Proceeds		0.5
		Cost		0.5
		No taper relief available		0.5
		Annual exemption		0.5
		CGT (2 × 0·5)		1.0
		Total cash after tax P1 and P2 correct rates		0.5
		Conclude P2 better		0.5
			Max	0.4

(iii)	Taper relief: business asset	0.5
	correct number of years/rate	0.5
	Revised taxable gain	0.5
	Conclude P1 now better (2 × 0·5)	0.5
	Deferral of CGT now payable 31 January 2008	1.0
	Max	3.0
(b)	Shares not held for five years	0.5
	Income tax, not capital gains treatment	0.5
	Income distribution dividend	0.5
	Net distribution	0.5
	Gross distribution	0.5
	Income tax at 32·5%	0.5
	Calculation of after-tax income	0.5
	Included in self assessment tax return	0.5
	Income tax payable by 31 January 2013	0.5
	Defer repurchase to after 1 August 2011	0.5
	Further conditions	
	– unquoted trading company	0.5
	– individual is UK resident/ord resident	0.5
	– trade benefit test	0.5
	– includes buying out of dissenting shareholder	0.5
	– not part of scheme to avoid tax	0.5
	– 75% share reduction test	0.5
	– 30% connection test	0.5
	Calculation of gross capital gain	0.5
	Taper relief – business asset rate (2 × 0.5)	1.0
	Annual exemption	0.5
	Calculation of after tax cash	0.5
	Capital gains treatment better	0.5
	Payment date 31 January 2013	0.5
	Clearance application available	0.5
	Time limit to respond	0.5
	Presentation/format	2.0
	Max	13.0
	TOTAL	25.0

5 TAY LIMITED

(a) (i) Purchase of intellectual property

Writing down allowances are available on intangible assets such as intellectual property. The allowance given is normally equivalent to the allowable depreciation charge to the accounts. However, in this case, Tay Limited does not depreciate its intellectual property, so this basis is not available.

Nevertheless, Tay Limited can elect to claim allowances at the rate of 4% on a straight line basis for tax purposes. The election is irrevocable and must be made within two years of the end of the accounting period in which the expenditure was incurred.

(ii)   **Corporation tax payable – y/e 31 March 2007**

On the basis that the election in (i) is made, the trading profits for Tay Limited will be as follows:

	Notes	£
Taxable trading profit before allowances		250,000
Less: intellectual property amortisation	(1)	(10,000)
		240,000
Less: group relief	(2)	(40,000)
Profits chargeable to corporation tax		200,000
Corporation tax at 30%		60,000
Less: Marginal relief		
$(750,000 - 200,000) \times 11/400$		(15,125)
Corporation tax payable		44,875

Notes

(1)   WDA re intellectual property:

$4\% \times £250,000$

(2)   Losses of Trent Limited prior to 1 September 2006 cannot be group relieved against the profits of Tay Limited.

Group relief is available for the period 1 September 2006 to 31 December 2006, and is restricted to the lower of the following:

Profits of Tay Limited   £80,000 (4/12 × 240,000)

Available losses of Trent Limited   £40,000 (4/12 × (120,000))

i.e. £40,000

(iii)   **Corporation tax implications of transferring work to Trent Ltd**

Trading losses may not be carried forward where, within a period of three years there is both a change in the ownership of a company and a major change in the nature or conduct of its trade.

The transfer of work from Tay Limited to Trent Limited is likely to constitute a major change in the nature or conduct of the latter's trade. As a consequence, any tax losses at the date of acquisition will be forfeited.

Assuming losses were incurred uniformly in 2006, the tax losses at the date of acquisition were £380,000 (300,000 + 8/12 × 120,000)). This is worth £114,000 assuming a corporation tax rate of 30%.

Thus, Tay Limited should not consider transferring any trade to Trent Limited until after the third anniversary of the date of the change of ownership i.e. not before 1 September 2009. As the trades are similar, there should be little problem in ransferring work from that date onwards.

(b)   **Capital gains tax implications – sale of Trent Ltd's building**

The factory will be treated as a pre-entry asset for capital loss purposes. Part of the loss that would arise on sale is attributable to the period prior to the acquisition of Trent Limited by Tay Limited. The loss relief will be restricted, and only the postacquisition proportion of the loss can be used against any gains arising from assets disposed of by Tay Limited.

The pre-entry element of the loss may be calculated in two ways:

(1) by using the following formula, which applies to each element of allowable expenditure

Pre-entry loss = A × (B/C) × (D/E)

A = allowable loss, calculated in the normal manner

B = cost of allowable expenditure

C = cost of all items of allowable expenditure

D = time from when expenditure was incurred until date of joining the group

E = time from which expenditure was incurred to the date of disposal

The calculation of the allowable loss is as follows:

	£
Proceeds	250,000
Less: cost	(400,000)
Allowable loss	(150,000)

The pre-entry loss proportion (using the formula) is:

£135,000 = (150,000) × (400,000/400,000) × (108 months/120 months)

Of the total loss (£150,000), only £15,000 will be available to use against capital gains on the sale of Tay Limited's asset.

(2) Trent Limited can make an election. The result of which is that the pre-entry proportion of the loss is treated as the smaller of:

(i) the loss that would have arisen on the disposal of the asset at market value on the date of Trent Limited joining the group of £100,000 (300,000 – 400,000), and

(ii) the loss on the actual sale £150,000

i.e. £100,000.

This gives a higher post-entry loss of £50,000 (150,000 – 100,000) and so it is advisable for Trent Limited to make this election.

The £100,000 of pre-entry losses are still available, but can only be set against gains on assets which:

(i) Trent Limited sold prior to being acquired (subject to the normal carry back restrictions), or

(ii) Trent Limited already owned when it was acquired, or

(iii) Trent Limited acquired from outside the group and used in its trade after being bought by Tay Limited.

Tutorial Note:

Note that there is no evidence to suggest that at the time of the purchase of Trent Limited there was a scheme to avoid tax by utilising the capital losses of Trent limited by making a sale of the factory. Therefore the provisions of FA2006 will not apply.

If there was a scheme, all of the loss will have restricted use and can only be set against gains on assets held pre-change of ownership.

(c)   **Corporation tax issues – acquiring shares or assets**

    (1)   **Acquisition of shares**

        Status

        The acquisition of shares in Tagus LDA will add another associated company to the group. This may have an adverse effect on the rates of corporation tax paid by the two existing group companies, particularly Tay Limited.

        Taxation of profits

        Profits will be taxed in Portugal. Any profits remitted to the UK as dividends will be taxable as Schedule D Case V income, but will attract double tax relief.

        Double tax relief will be available against two types of tax suffered in Portugal. Credit will be given for any tax withheld on payments from Tagus LDA to Tay Limited and relief will also be available for the underlying tax as Tay Limited owns at least 10% of the voting power of Tagus LDA.

        The underlying tax is the tax attributable to the relevant profits from which the dividend was paid. Double tax relief is given at the lower rate of the UK tax and the foreign tax (withholding and underlying taxes) suffered.

        Losses

        As Tagus LDA is a non-UK resident company, losses arising in Tagus LDA cannot be group relieved against profits of the two UK companies. Similarly, any UK trading losses cannot be used against profits generated by Tagus LDA.

    (2)   **Acquisition of assets**

        Status

        The business of Tagus will be treated as a branch of Tay Limited i.e. an extension of the UK company's activities. The number of associated companies will be unaffected.

        Taxation of profits

        Tay Limited will be treated as having a permanent establishment in Portugal. Profits attributable to the Tagus business will thus still be taxed in Portugal. In addition, the profits will be taxed in the UK as trading income. Double tax relief will be available for the tax already suffered in Portugal at the lower of the two rates.

        Capital allowances will be available. As the assets in question will not previously have been subject to a claim for UK capital allowances, there will be no cost restriction and the consideration attributable to each asset will form the basis for the capital allowance claim.

        Losses

        The Tagus trade is part of Tay Limited's trade, so any losses incurred by the Portuguese trade will automatically be offset against the trading profits of the UK trade, and vice versa.

Key answer tips

It is important to make it clear in your answer which alternative (i.e. the purchase of shares or assets) you are addressing. Make good use of sub-headings to keep your answer focussed on the particular issues you are explaining

---

(d)   **Consequences of submitting an incorrect VAT return**

Default surcharge

Although the VAT return was submitted on time (i.e. within one month of the end of the tax period), part of the quarterly VAT liability has not yet been paid. As a result this payment will be made late and a surcharge liability notice will be issued on the company.

The surcharge period will run from the date of the notice until the anniversary of the end of the period for which the VAT was paid late (i.e. until 31 March 2008).

During this period any further default will extend the surcharge period and any further late payments of VAT will attract a surcharge penalty of 2% on the first occasion, rising to 15% for successive late payments.

Mis-declaration penalty

As the return understates the VAT payable, a potential mis-declaration penalty arises. The amount understated exceeds 30% of the sum of the true input tax and output tax, known as the gross amount of tax (GAT) ((30% of (87,500 + 55,000) + 40,000) = 54,750).

There has, thus, been a significant understatement of the true VAT return liability, resulting in a penalty rate of 15% of the VAT which would have been lost had the error not been discovered. However, where an under declaration arises out of a true error i.e. there is no intention to evade tax involved, and it is voluntarily disclosed, then a mis-declaration penalty is not normally imposed.

Although the company is still within the 'period of grace' allowed by HMRC for the correction of errors in the next following VAT return, it would be advisable for Trent Limited to notify HMRC of the error immediately, in writing, unless it has a 'reasonable excuse' for the error having occurred.

Default interest

Default interest is chargeable when an assessment to VAT arises for an amount that has been under declared in a previous period, whether as a result of voluntary disclosure or as identified by HMRC. Interest is charged on a daily basis from the date the under declaration should have been declared (i.e. 1 May 2007) to the date shown on the notice of assessment or notice of voluntary disclosure.

As given the size of the error the de minimis relief for voluntarily declared errors of less than £2,000 is not applicable, the only way for Trent Limited to minimise the interest charge is by means of early disclosure and payment of the additional VAT due.

ACCA marking scheme				
				Marks
(a)	(i)	Allowances usually equal to amortisation		0.5
		Alternative 4% allowance where no depreciation		0.5
		Time limit for election		0.5
		Election irrevocable		0.5
			Max	2.0
	(ii)	Deduction for IP allowance		0.5
		Group relieve only post-acquisition loss		0.5
		'Lower of' calculation (2×0.5)		1.0
		Corporation tax at 30%		0.5
		Marginal relief calculation		0.5
			Max	3.0

(iii)	Change of ownership and nature of trade (2×0.5)			1.0
	Three year time limit			0.5
	Losses blocked at date of acquisition			0.5
	Quantify losses/tax at risk (2×0.5)			1.0
	Advice and recommendation			0.5
			Max	3.0
(b)	Awareness of pre-entry losses			0.5
	Formula basis: Statement/explanation			1.0
	Calculation of allowable loss			0.5
	Pre-entry proportion			0.5
	Alternative election: treatment and effect			1.0
	calculation of pre-entry loss			0.5
	Recommend making the election			0.5
	Use of pre-entry loss – possibilities			1.0
			Max	4.0
(c)	Acquisition of shares:			
	associated company			0.5
	limits reduced, possibly increased tax			0.5
	profits taxed in Portugal			0.5
	remitted profits taxed as Schedule D Case V			0.5
	double tax relief for withholding tax			0.5
	double tax relief for underlying tax			0.5
	requirement for 10% plus holding			0.5
	relief is lower of UK/Portuguese tax			0.5
	losses cannot be relieved against UK profits			0.5
	Acquisition of assets			
	branch, so no extra associate			0.5
	taxed in UK as extension of trade			0.5
	permanent establishment: taxed in Portugal			0.5
	DTR available			0.5
	capital allowances can be claimed			0.5
	loss offset automatically as part of UK company			0.5
			Max	7.0
(d)	Default surcharge:	issue surcharge notice		0.5
		runs to anniversary/31 March 2008		0.5
		further defaults extend period		0.5
		further late payments will incur a penalty		0.5
		2% initially rising to 15%		0.5
	Misdeclaration penalty:			
	awareness of potential penalty			0.5
	significant understatement:	definition		0.5
		calculation		0.5
	penalty rate of 15% of VAT lost			0.5
	voluntary disclosure			0.5
	next return/period of grace			0.5
	in writing/ASAP			0.5
	Default interest:	chargeable even with voluntary disclosure		0.5
		basis period		0.5
			Max	6.0
TOTAL				25.0

6   ANDREW

(a)   (i)   **Assignment of residential property lease**

Where a lease with less than 50 years to run is assigned, the cost is restricted. A fraction, X/Y, is applied by reference to a lease table where:

X =   percentage for the years left at the date of assignment (35 years)

Y =   percentage for the years left at the date of acquisition by the seller (47 years)

The calculation is as follows:

	£
Proceeds	90,000
Less: Cost	
50,000 × X/Y (91.981/98·902)	(46,501)
Unindexed gain	43,499
Less: indexation 162·6 – 149·6/149·6 (0·087)	(4,046)
Indexed gain	39,453
Chargeable gain after taper relief:	
60% (non-business asset/9 + 1 years)	23,672

Key answer tips

Note that terminology in capital gains questions is important. The examiner has explained that a "chargeable gain" is defined as the gain after deducting taper relief but before the annual exemption.

(ii)   **Tax implications – disposal of Government stock**

Government stock is an exempt asset for the purposes of capital gains tax, however, as Andrew's holding has a nominal value in excess of £5,000, a charge to income tax will arise under the accrued income scheme. This charge to income tax will arise in 2006/07, being the tax year in which the next interest payment following disposal falls due (20 April 2006) and it will relate to the income accrued for the period 21 October 2005 to 14 March 2006 of £279 (145/182 × £350).

As interest on Government Stock is paid gross (unless the holder applies to receive it net), the tax due of £112 (£279 × 40%) will be collected via the self-assessment system.

As Andrew is an employee, it is likely that he does not need to make payments on account, therefore the tax will be due on 31 January 2008. However, as the interest was an ongoing source of income, if Andrew is required to pay half yearly payments on account, the tax will be included within his payments on account payable on 31 January and 31 July 2007.

(b)   (i)   **Income tax and capital gains tax reliefs – Investment in Scalar Ltd**

Andrew may be able to take advantage of tax reliefs under the enterprise investment scheme (EIS) provided the necessary conditions are met. The conditions that have to be satisfied before full relief is available fall into three areas, and broadly require that a 'qualifying individual' subscribes for 'eligible shares' in a 'qualifying company'.

'Qualifying Individual'

To be a qualifying individual, Andrew must not be connected with the EIS company. This means that he should not be an employee (or, at the time the shares are issued, a director) or have an interest in (i.e. control) 30% or more of the capital of the company. These conditions need to be satisfied throughout the period beginning two years before the share issue and three years after the 'relevant date' where the relevant date is defined as the later of the date the shares were issued and the date on which the company commenced trading.

Andrew does not intend to become an employee (or director) of Scalar Limited, but he needs to exercise caution as to how many shares he subscribes for. If only three investors subscribe for 100% of the shares, each will hold 33% of the share capital. This exceeds the 30% limit and will mean that EIS relief (other than deferral relief) will not be available. Therefore, Andrew and the other two investors should ensure not only that the potential fourth investor is recruited, but that s/he subscribes for sufficient shares, such that none of them will hold 30% or more of the issued share capital, as only then will they all attain qualifying individual status.

'Eligible shares'

Qualifying shares need to be new ordinary shares which are subscribed for in cash and fully paid up at the time of issue. The shares must not be redeemable for at least three years from the relevant date, and not carry any preferential rights to dividends. On the basis of the information provided, the shares of Scalar Limited would qualify as eligible shares.

'Qualifying Company'

The company must be unquoted, not controlled by another company, and engaged in qualifying business activities. The latter requires that the company engage in a trading activity, which is carried on wholly or mainly in the UK, throughout the three years following the relevant date. While certain trading activities, such as dealing in shares or trading in land, are excluded, the manufacturing trade Scalar Limited proposes to carry on will qualify.

However, it is also necessary for at least 80% of the money raised to be used for the qualifying business activity within 12 months of the relevant date and the remaining 20% to be so used within the following 12 months. Andrew and the other investors will thus have to ensure that Scalar Limited has not raised more funds than it is able to employ in the business within the appropriate time periods.

Reliefs available:

Andrew can claim income tax relief at 20% income tax relief on the amount invested up to a maximum of £400,000 in any one tax year. The relief is given in the form of a tax reducing allowance, which can reduce the investor's income tax liability to nil, but cannot be used to generate a tax refund. If the investment is made prior to 6 October in the tax year, then 50% of the amount invested (up to a maximum of £50,000) can be treated as having been made in the previous tax year.

Any capital gains arising on the sale of EIS shares will be fully exempt from capital gains tax provided that income tax relief was given on the investment when made and has not been withdrawn. If the EIS shares are disposed of at a loss, capital losses are still allowable, but reduced by the amount of any EIS relief attributable to the shares disposed of.

In addition, gains from the disposal of other assets can be deferred against the base cost of EIS shares acquired within one year before and three years after their disposal. Such gains will, thus, not normally become chargeable until the EIS shares themselves are disposed of. Further, for deferral relief to be available, it is not necessary for the investment to qualify for EIS income tax relief, i.e. deferral is available even where the investor is not a qualifying individual.

Thus, Andrew could still defer the gain arising on the disposal of the residential property lease made in order to raise part of the funds for his EIS investment, even if no fourth investor were to be found and his shareholding were to exceed 30% of the issued share capital of Scalar Limited.

Withdrawal of relief:

Any EIS relief claimed by Andrew will be withdrawn (partially or fully) if, within three years of the relevant date:

(1)   he disposes of the shares;

(2)   he receives value from the company;

(3)   he ceases to be a qualifying individual; or

(4)   Scalar Limited ceases to be a qualifying company.

With regard to receiving value from the company, the definition excludes dividends which do not exceed a normal rate of return, but does include the repayment of any loans made to the company before the shares were issued, the provision of benefits and the purchase of assets from the company at an undervalue. In this regard, Andrew and the other subscribers should ensure that the £50,000 they are to invest in Scalar Limited as loan capital is appropriately timed and structured relative to the issue of the EIS shares.

(ii)   **Taxation implications of equity and loan finance**

A company needs to be aware of the following issues:

Equity

(1)   Costs incurred in issuing share capital are not allowed as a trading deduction.

(2)   Distributions to investors are not allowed as a trading deduction.

(3)   The cost of making distributions to shareholders are disallowable.

Loan finance/debt

(1)   The incidental costs of obtaining/raising loan finance are broadly deductible as a trading expense.

(2)   Capital costs of raising loan finance (for example, loans issued at a discount) are not deductible for tax purposes.

(3)   Interest incurred on a loan to finance a business is deductible from trading income.

Key answer tips

The question only asked for the tax consequences of equity and loan finance. Avoid wasting time by discussing other commercial aspects which are not required in this particular question.

(c)   **Characteristics of pension schemes**

Defined benefit scheme

A defined benefit scheme is one in which the benefits to be received on retirement are determined by the terms of the scheme and the pension receivable is linked directly to the employee's earnings at retirement and their number of years' service.

As a consequence such schemes provide considerable certainty for the employee, but leave the employer with the financial risk if the combined contribution rate and/or the performance of the scheme's investments prove inadequate to fund the benefits promised.

Defined contribution scheme

A defined contribution scheme is one in which only the contributions to be made are determined by the terms of the scheme, so there is no guarantee as to the level of pension which will be payable at retirement, which is totally reliant on the adequacy of the contribution rate set and the performance of the scheme's investments.

As a consequence such schemes provide certainty for the employer in terms of the monetary commitment required, but transfer the financial risk to the employee, as the scheme may provide insufficient funds with which to purchase a reasonable level of pension relative to current earnings at the time of retirement.

		ACCA marking scheme	
			Marks
(a)	(i)	Restriction of cost	0.5
		Indexation	0.5
		Taper relief: non business asset rate $(2 \times 0\cdot5)$	1.0
		Max	2.0
	(ii)	Exempt from CGT	0.5
		IT under accrued income scheme	0.5
		Nominal value $>£5,000$	0.5
		Taxed when next interest payment due	0.5
		Year 2007/08	0.5
		Income accrued on a daily basis to 14 March	0.5
		Paid gross/taxed at 40% via self assessment	0.5
		Ongoing source within half-yearly payments	0.5
		Max	3.0
(b)	(i)	Identification of EIS relief	0.5
		Qualifying individual:	
		should not be an employee	0.5
		should not be a director at time of issue	0.5
		should not have an interest of 30% or more	0.5
		timing requirements	0.5
		relevant date definition	0.5
		Andrew currently connected	0.5
		investment by fourth individual advisable	0.5
		Eligible shares	
		new and fully paid up	0.5
		not redeemable for three years from relevant date	0.5
		no preferential rights to dividends	0.5
		Qualifying company	
		unquoted	0.5
		not controlled by another company	0.5
		qualifying trade, wholly/mainly in UK $(2 \times 0\cdot5)$	1.0
		time limits/% reinvestment	0.5

Income tax:			
	relief given at 20%		0.5
	£400,000 limit		0.5
	tax reducer		0.5
	up to 50% of investment before 6 October treated as made in previous tax year		0.5
Capital gains tax:			
	gains on disposal of EIS shares are exempt		0.5
	capital losses available, reduced by relief		0.5
	deferral relief for existing gains		0.5
	timing requirements		0.5
	income tax relief not essential		0.5
	application to Andrew		0.5
Relief withdrawn if:			
	shares sold within three year period		0.5
	value received from company		0.5
	individual or company ceases to qualify		0.5
	repayment of loans possible issue		0.5
		Max	13.0
(ii)	Equity:		
	Costs of issuing share capital are not tax deductible		0.5
	Cost of making distributions are not tax deductible		0.5
	Distributions themselves not tax deductible		0.5
	Loan finance/debt:		
	Interest on loan to finance business is allowable		0.5
	Capital costs not deductible as trading expense		0.5
	Incidental costs of raising loan finance are allowable		0.5
		Max	3.0
(c)	Defined benefits scheme:		1.0
	characteristics		
	balance of certainty/risk (2×0.5)		1.0
	Defined contribution scheme:		
	characteristics		1.0
	balance of certainty/risk (2×0.5)		1.0
		Max	4.0
TOTAL			25.0